MW00780237

Assessing Adult Attachment

A Norton Professional Book

ASSESSING ADULT ATTACHMENT

● ● ● ● ● ●

A Dynamic-Maturational
Approach to Discourse Analysis

Patricia M. Crittenden, PhD
Andrea Landini, MD

W. W. Norton & Company
New York • London

For information about permission to reproduce selections from this book, write to Permissions, W. W. Norton & Company, Inc., 500 Fifth Avenue, New York, NY 10110

For information about special discounts for bulk purchases, please contact W. W. Norton Special Sales at specialsales@wwnorton.com or 800-233-4830

Manufacturing by Quad Graphics, Fairfield
Production manager: Leeann Graham

Library of Congress Cataloging-in-Publication Data

Crittenden, Patricia McKinsey.
    Assessing adult attachment : a dynamic-maturational approach to discourse analysis / Patricia McKinsey Crittenden, Andrea Landini.
        p. cm. — (A Norton professional book)
    Includes bibliographical references and index.
    ISBN 978-0-393-70667-3 (hardcover)
1. Attachment behavior.   2. Adulthood—Psychological aspects.
3. Interpersonal relations.   I. Landini, Andrea.   II. Title.
    BF575.A86C75 2011
    155.6—dc22   2010044398

ISBN: 978-0-393-70667-3

W. W. Norton & Company, Inc., 500 Fifth Avenue, New York, N.Y. 10110
www.wwnorton.com
W. W. Norton & Company Ltd., Castle House, 75/76 Wells Street, London W1T 3QT

1 2 3 4 5 6 7 8 9 0

This book is dedicated to our parents.

Tell all the Truth but tell it slant—
Success in Circuit lies
Too bright for our infirm Delight
The Truth's superb surprise

As Lightning to the Children eased
With explanation kind
The Truth must dazzle gradually
Or every man be blind—

—EMILY DICKINSON

Contents

Contents

PART II: THE CLASSIFICATORY SYSTEM

x   Contents

Acknowledgments

This book is the result of the contribution of more people than can possibly be named. It is the result of reading several thousand individual AAIs, and we are grateful to each of those speakers for sharing important aspects of their lives. It also reflects the contributions of several hundred psychotherapists and researchers who attended AAI courses and who discussed both the AAIs themselves and the discourse methods. As is always the case with ideas, they evolve with dialogue, and, although it is difficult to attribute changes to specific persons, this dialogue, over two decades and in ten countries, has produced the ideas that we have written here.

We are especially grateful to Simon Wilkinson, Gordon Somerville, Steve Farnfield, Simon Howell, Peder Nørbech, Nicola Sahhar, and Sabrina Bowen for reading many of these chapters and giving us feedback that helped us to clarify the writing.

Assessing Adult Attachment

Chapter 1

Introduction

"D'you Know What I Mean?"

EVERYONE WANTS TO BE UNDERSTOOD. INDEED, THESE WORDS PEPPER THE discourse of the least clear speakers as if their best efforts were doomed to failure—and they knew it.

In this volume, we offer a way to understand the meanings behind unclear communication. More than that, we offer a theoretical model of distorted communication and dysfunctional behavior. It is a simple, intuitive model that can be understood by troubled adults. It is also a sophisticated and complex model that can guide clinicians to select effective treatments and that can help researchers to test hypotheses about the intricate and interwoven pathways to maladaptation. We combine genetic potentials, history of exposure to danger, mental processing of information about danger, and communication about danger into a functionally coherent model of psychological processes, the Dynamic-Maturational Model of attachment and adaptation (DMM; Crittenden, 1995, 2008).

The DMM addresses normal thinking and behavior with the same principles that are used to describe dysfunctional thinking and behavior. The difference is that exposure to danger increases the probability of dysfunction. In this volume, we describe a wide range of human adaptation in ways that foster understanding of maladaptation. We also recommend an assessment tool to elicit the crucial information about danger and adaptation to danger and a method for extracting information from the assessment. The tool is the Adult Attachment Interview (AAI; George, Kaplan, & Main, 1985, 1996). The method is the Dynamic-Maturational Model of discourse analysis for the AAI, as presented in this book.

Our goal is to describe maladaptation in a way that connects the experiences of threatened and threatening people with the skills of mental health professionals so that professionals can reduce distress and maladaptive behavior more successfully. We also seek to guide researchers to fine-grained, theory-based hypotheses that can refine our understanding of developmental processes in a way that multifactorial modeling alone cannot. The key, we think, is understanding. When we understand the meanings that distressed people struggle to communicate, a pathway to safety and comfort will be opened.

Our ideas build on a century of effort to understand and ameliorate psychological suffering. In both DMM theory and our method for analyzing AAIs, we have sought to retain the best ideas from all theories of psychological disorder while reframing and recombining these ideas to reflect the most current developmental and neurocognitive knowledge. The result addresses problems in assessment, diagnosis, and treatment of disorder in a fresh manner.

We chose the AAI as the assessment tool because it lets people tell their stories in their own way, thus preserving their reality. At the same time, the questions elicit crucial information without obscuring it with irrelevancies. We think these two things—the speakers' own words and pertinent questions, together with a method of discourse analysis that promotes understanding of what speakers mean—can be the bridge that connects people who dare not be clear with caring healers who understand with clarity.

THE ROOT OF THE PROBLEM

Defining Psychological Disorder

Psychological disorder has stubbornly resisted understanding and treatment for more than a century. The lack of understanding has led to fragmentation among those clinicians who cling almost religiously to a single theory of treatment (e.g., psychoanalytic, behavioral, cognitive,

cognitive-behavioral, cognitive-analytic, interpersonal, family systems). Because each theory describes the problems of suffering individuals differently and none is more effective than the others at easing psychological suffering, we think that none reflects the meaning of suffering well enough. The names of the treatments suggest what is needed: an integration of meaningful ideas, from all the theories, that goes beyond individual pathology to place people in their context of relationships and families. Add to that a focus on danger and the psychological and behavioral effects of exposure to unprotected and uncomforted danger and one has the rudiments of a new and integrative theory of the development and treatment of dysfunction.

Instead, by side-stepping differences in theory, two similar and explicitly nontheoretical systems for diagnosing disorders were developed: the *Diagnostic and Statistical Manual of Mental Disorders* (DSM, North America) and International Classifications of Disease (ICD, World Health Organization). This was a major step toward describing behavior accurately. The previous focus on theory biased observation toward theory-based expectations. The focus on describing symptoms turned attention to accurate observation of the behavior of people who suffer. But we lost the meanings that theory had! With good observation, the number of disorders increased, comorbidity increased, and diagnoses of "not otherwise specified" increased (Angold & Costello, 2009; Goldberg, 2010). It seems we know in detail what troubled people do, but we do not know how to cluster them, how their behavior functions, what it means to them, or its implications for treatment.

If we are to understand people who suffer—and whose suffering distresses and sometimes harms other people—we need both sound observations and a language of shared meanings. This language needs to express the experiences of those who suffer in ways that they can understand while, at the same time, uniting clinicians from different theoretical backgrounds in ways that lead to more effective treatment. Further, this language needs to guide researchers to discover and address the crucial inconsistencies, distortions, and omissions in theory that can clarify both developmental and rehabilitative processes.

A New Model with Familiar Roots

The Dynamic-Maturational Model (DMM) of attachment and adaptation developed out of Bowlby's integration of psychoanalytic theory with general systems theory (including emerging family systems theory), ethology, and the cognitive neurosciences (Bowlby, 1969/1982,

1973, 1980). Among theories of disorder, the DMM has the unique advantage of being prospective in that it is based on empirical evidence regarding developmental processes beginning in infancy and progressing forward to adulthood (Ainsworth, 1989; Crittenden & Ainsworth, 1989). Other models of adult psychopathology are based on the behavior and recalled history of adult patients—and this, we think, is not understood well enough because of errors in thought and communication.

The DMM assumes that all people seek to understand their experiences, but some dangerous experiences cannot be understood early in life and, sometimes, cannot be understood at all. When danger occurs early, children need protection and comfort from someone they trust. If that is absent, misunderstanding, miscommunication, and maladaptation become more likely. Tracking the process of miscommunication and misunderstanding, especially around issues of danger and comfort, is central to the DMM.

Three central points define the DMM:

1. Dysfunction is a response to intolerable threats that often occur early in development when the child is not protected and comforted (Bowlby, 1969/1982, 1973, 1980).
2. Psychological processing is transformed developmentally in a progressive attempt to understand and protect the self from that which is neither apparent nor explained (Crittenden, 1995, 2008).
3. Maladaptive behavior, that is, psychological disorder, is the individual's best attempt to apply what he or she learned about danger while growing up to the adult tasks of self-protection, reproduction, and protection of children.

Beyond that, the DMM is built on insights from all the major theories of adaptation and disorder and these will feel familiar to most professionals. It is also built on sound developmental findings and emerging cognitive, neurological, and genetic (including especially epigenetic) findings. Intrinsic and ongoing ties to empirical research will keep the DMM honest and relevant. Its unique feature is that the DMM organizes the ideas: therefore it is more than a collection of ideas. The organization is developmental and functional and, thus, suited to the needs of clinicians who must identify deviancy and select suitable treatment responses. The DMM also meets the needs of researchers who must select, from among the almost limitless number of possible variables, those hypotheses that are crucial to understanding.

What We Offer in This Volume

We offer the rudiments of DMM theory of individual differences in psychological adaptation, together with a means of extracting meaning from the interpersonal discourse of adults (Ainsworth, 1979; Bowlby, 1980; Crittenden, 2008; Crittenden & Ainsworth, 1989). The method of discourse analysis forms the bulk of this volume and expands on the work of Main and Goldwyn (M&G; 1994). It differs from the M&G method of discourse analysis in having a wider range of constructs, identifying a wider range of self- and progeny-protective organizations, and specifying more precisely how attempts to adapt can fail.

A crucial difference is in the search for meaning in communication. Main and her colleagues state explicitly that their method looks *at* the dysfluence, not behind or through it, to assess the extent of speakers' coherence, or lack of coherence, of mind (Main, Hesse, & Goldwyn, 2008). In contrast, the DMM method seeks the underlying or obscured meaning that speakers cannot articulate fully or clearly. Rather than focusing on lack of coherence, we want to understand how speakers protect themselves and, to the extent possible, how they learned that psychological and behavioral strategy. This can help us to understand how the now maladaptive behavior was once protective. This understanding can promote respect by professionals for the children who our clients and patients had once been, and self-respect by distressed people who can find in the DMM a positive way of understanding themselves.

In the sections that follow, we introduce the AAI, explore the constructs underlying the DMM, and present a model of individual differences in adaptation based on an expansion of the work of Bowlby and Ainsworth (Ainsworth, 1973; Ainsworth, Blehar, Waters, & Wall, 1978; Bowlby, 1969/1982, 1973, 1980; Crittenden, 1995, 2008; Crittenden & Ainsworth, 1989).

WHY DO WE NEED A NEW METHOD?

Problems with the Main and Goldwyn Method

Even among its advocates, there are mixed opinions about the M&G-AAI (Slade, 2007). At its best, 22% of the variance in infants' attachment can be accounted for by knowing mothers' classifications on the AAI (van IJzendoorn, 1995); this relation is stronger among middle-class and stable families than among at-risk families. This raises questions regarding the remaining 78% of variance, especially regarding less affluent and advantaged families. More recent work applying the M&G-AAI to a broader range of circumstances has found far more modest outcomes than expected (Bakermans-Kranenburg & van IJzendoorn, 2009). Specifically, analysis of 10,000 AAIs indicated that the M&G-AAI differentiated normative and at-risk samples, but with substantial overlap; security was found even in cases of maltreatment, psychiatric hospitalization, and violent criminality and the categories of very insecure attachment applied to some normative individuals. Moreover, some findings were contradictory or counter to theory. Further, little or no differentiation within at-risk groups was revealed, suggesting that the ABC+D model of attachment had little to offer that could guide differential treatment. We detail these problems in Chapters 15 and 16, but here it is worth noting that, after two decades and several hundred studies, the outcomes of the M&G-AAI, as well as ABC+D theory in general, are disappointing. Unfortunately, in spite of its wide usage, the M&G-AAI has remained under development, with neither the interview nor the manual being published for almost three decades. On the other hand, the conceptual underpinnings of the M&G method have remained unchanged since 1996 when "Cannot Classify" was introduced as a new classification (Hesse, 1996; Main et al., 2008).

We think six issues limit the current use of the M&G-AAI. First, it has been very difficult for trained coders to achieve reliability on the M&G classifications. Second, it is unclear what the M&G-AAI assesses; this problem is compounded by the unavailability of a manual for review by researchers and clinicians who have not taken the training course. Such an investment of time, prior to viewing the instrument, exceeds the resources and motivation of many potentially interested professionals. Third, the M&G classificatory method is based on work in the cognitive sciences from the late 1970s. Knowledge of mental functioning derived since Bowlby completed his 1980 volume has not been incorporated into the classificatory process. Fourth, the adult classificatory system is based on Ainsworth's infant classificatory system and does not account fully for the complexity of adult behavior. Fifth, the Ainsworth system was developed from observations of middle-income, low-risk samples of American infants and their parents. Thus, it may not adequately reflect the range of diversity found in other cultures and in risk populations. Finally, the notion of disorganization lacks empirical support and conceptual coherence (Rutter, Kreppner, &

Sonuga-Barke, 2009). With disappointing empirical findings from the M&G-AAI method, conceptual limitations to the ABC+D model, and lack of implications for treatment, we think it is time to move forward.

New Solutions

These six issues are addressed in this volume, thus, for the first time, making a classificatory method widely available for examination by the scientific and professional communities. As a consequence, both researchers and mental health professionals will be better able to evaluate this powerful, but complex, instrument. By anticipating the concerns listed above, the DMM has evolved to reflect practical solutions to the complex problems described so well by Bowlby.

First, by framing some of Main and Goldwyn's ideas in terms of functional mental processes, rather than sometimes vague or language-specific discourse markers, the coding guidelines have been made more explicit and achievement of reliability by trained coders has become more feasible. Second, by focusing on the role of danger in initiating psychological organization, the DMM clarifies the importance of assessing the adaptation of individuals to their contexts. Third, current empirical science, particularly emerging cognitive/neurological theory and research, has modified our understanding of the constructs upon which the M&G-AAI was based. The DMM-AAI incorporates new findings to generate new theory and methods that enhance and expand the scope of the AAI. As a consequence, the expanded classificatory system and DMM-AAI discourse method better fit the range of mental functioning seen in adults living in different cultures and conditions. A particular advantage of the expanded method is that it addresses how disturbed individuals *use* information, rather than simply finding that they are not integrated or cannot be classified. Fourth, the developmental array of self- and progeny-protective strategies has been expanded through the preschool (end of the second year of life to approximately 5 years of age) and school years (approximately 6 years of age to puberty) to adolescence and on to adulthood, as envisioned by Ainsworth (Ainsworth, 1989; Crittenden & Ainsworth, 1989). Fifth, the DMM-AAI fits a wider range of adult functioning than the M&G-AAI does. Specifically, questions have been added to address imaged (i.e., perceptual) memory, anger from and toward parents, dangerous experiences and abuse, adolescence, adult attachment, sexuality, and use of one's parents as models for raising one's own children. Moreover, the interview has been applied in substantial numbers to speakers who differ in either risk or culture or both. Finally, the notion of disorganization and the category of "Cannot Classify" have been eliminated.

Rather than describing what threatened people fail to do, the DMM-AAI gathers information about alternative ways of making meaning, specifically meanings tied to threat and the need to protect oneself and one's children from danger. We keep in mind that one of Bowlby's notions that excluded him from psychoanalytic theory was his belief in the reality of danger. In the DMM, the emphasis on the effects of exposure to danger, rather than the benefits of security, directs attention to those people who most need the advantage of protection, good theory, and compassionate treatment.

Problems with Psychiatric Diagnoses

Validating the new DMM classifications requires information external to the AAI. We have often used child protection and psychiatric status as defining variables. The intent, however, is not merely to accurately find differences *between* normative and maladaptive categories. Instead, with the DMM-AAI we seek to add to the information generated by child protection or diagnostic authorities. That is, we want (1) to expand the array of possibilities from the four offered in the Main and Goldwyn method and (2) to do so in a way that is informative, above and beyond assessment of child abuse or neglect or psychiatric diagnosis, to mental health personnel.

Seeking validity of our differential classifications *within* troubled populations has led to using diagnoses as a criterion. This is problematic in many ways. Many people have noted that comorbidity is the norm, rather than the exception (Angold & Costello, 2009; Goldberg, 2010). Which diagnosis shall we use for validation—or more accurately, how will we cluster adults who vary in their array of diagnoses? This is tied to the issue of a growing number of "not elsewhere classified" diagnoses and increasingly complex diagnoses (Goldberg, 2010). Where shall we cluster these adults or do we just leave them out? Similarly, the two major diagnostic systems, the *DSM* and ICD, seem unable to agree on exactly which diagnoses there are or on what the basic premises for diagnoses should be (First, 2009; Frances, 2010). How can one validate against disputed criteria?

An important observation is that most diagnoses are made on the basis of a clinical interview and most clinical interviews are poor diagnostically *because they do not account for biases in human information processing* (Angold & Costello, 2009; Dozier & Lee, 1995). That is where the DMM-AAI shines. It is *based* on current understanding of biases in information processing (i.e., transformation of information based on past experience).

Our goals in using child protection and psychiatric diagnoses as validating criteria are to demonstrate that the DMM classifications have evidence of external validity by being significantly, but not perfectly, related to diagnostic information and also to bring conceptual coherence to the diagnostic process. We think the DMM can do the latter by focusing the grouping of individuals around the basic survival issues of self-protection, reproduction, and protection of progeny and by focusing on transformations of information as the means to organizing protection strategies. By framing maladaptation in terms of danger and sexuality, we highlight the functional aspects of maladaptive behavior, thus, working from a strengths approach rather than a deficit model. We also focus on what is most crucial in human life (safety and sex) and bring coherence to a somewhat confusing array of psychiatric diagnoses. Finally, our information processing approach brings the DMM in line with current scientific understanding of the basis for behavior and positions it for continued modification as the human sciences generate new understandings.

Our hope is that with a clearer and more scientifically based conceptual framework, tied to evolutionary processes, we will be able to reduce the number of outcome categories, compared to psychiatric diagnoses, while increasing the relevance of the categories for designating appropriate treatment. The Dynamic-Maturational Model of attachment and adaptation has, we think, passed "first muster"; that is, it has shown validity in terms of adaptation in a few, small comparative studies and relevance to treatment in several published case studies (see Chapter 15). We think it is time to make the process available to the scientific and professional communities both for application and to foster the input that will promote growth of the theory and methods.

INTRODUCTION AND ORIENTATION TO THE AAI

Adult attachment is complex and fascinating. Adults have the neurological maturity, experience, and need to formulate complex plans that require integration of conflicting information. Consequently, they can exercise greater flexibility in matching strategy to context adaptively than is possible at younger ages. Complexity in response to complex conditions and change in the face of changing circumstances are the hallmarks of adult adaptation. In this book, we describe an array of adult protective strategies, consider the information processing that underlies the strategies, and outline a method for discerning the strategies in individual adults.

The Dynamic-Maturational Model of attachment and adaptation defines attachment as three entwined components: (1) relationships focused on protection and comfort, (2) patterns of mental processing of information about danger and sexual opportunity, and (3) strategies for self-protection, reproduction, and protection of progeny. Not surprisingly, however, the quality of adult relationships, the strategies, and the transformations of information underlying the strategies can be difficult to discern and correspondingly difficult to study. This is especially true because adults can dissemble, both knowingly and without awareness. As a consequence, their functioning is much less obvious and transparent to observers than is that of infants.

We present an approach to understanding and assessing adult attachment based on analysis of adults' spoken language about protection and comfort and, to a lesser extent, about sexuality and caregiving. The method of discourse analysis that we describe assumes that adults use both preconscious and explicit transformations of information and behavior to protect themselves, attract reproductive partners, and protect their children.

Attachment in Adulthood

Although infant attachment has received far more attention than adult attachment, adult attachment is more crucial to our survival as a species. A child who does not attach to his or her parents can survive through the efforts of the parents, but if adults do not attach to their infant, the infant's attachment will be useless. To promote the survival of the species, adults must protect themselves, have babies, and protect the babies to their reproductive maturity. Viewed this way, attachment refers to both oneself and one's progeny and includes sexuality. It also refers to the tie to one's reproductive partner.

ATTACHMENT AS A RELATIONSHIP

Adults live in families marked by an array of attachment relationships: reciprocal attachment to a partner including sexual behavior and motivation, changing attachment to parents, and being the attachment figure for children during the children's different stages of development. Adults must manage the integration of these different attachment relationships with other functions of the same relationships, for example, learning, working, and playing. This involves the maximum complexity of functioning in the life cycle. A hierarchically organized meta-model of relationships and functions is needed to manage the tasks successfully. When integration has not been accomplished and the context is unsupportive or threatening, behavior can become maladaptive. In that case, it is likely that self-protection, reproduction, or protection of progeny (in any combination) will be compromised and that oneself or one's family members will suffer psychological distress and, sometimes, physical harm.

ATTACHMENT AS INFORMATION PROCESSING

Information processing underlies all behavior. That is, all information is simply sensory stimulation that is given meaning by the brain; therefore, it is transformed. Adults transform incoming sensory stimulation in different ways to yield representations of the relation of self to context. These transformations enable adults to generate strategic plans of action even when information is missing, ambiguous, or false. This promotes adaptation and survival even as it makes one-to-one relations between observed behavior and psychological processes less direct. The behavior that one observes does not directly imply the underlying psychological process. Instead, the same behavior could result from different processes, and the same processes, under different contextual circumstances, could yield different behavior. Consequently, the methods employed to discern patterns of information processing must go beyond simply observing behavior.

ATTACHMENT AS A SELF-PROTECTIVE
AND CHILD-PROTECTIVE STRATEGY

Representation creates a disposition to act. When there is threat or actual danger to the self, the disposition is a self-protective strategy. When there is sexual opportunity or threat to such opportunity, the representation disposes sexually motivated behavior (but not necessarily sexual behavior). When the threat is to one's child, the representation disposes child-protective strategy. Three points are crucial.

First, individuals often have more than one dispositional representation (DR). When they tend to rely on a particular pattern of information processing to guide behavior, that pattern reflects their typical self- or child-protective strategy. Of course, all individuals vary in strategy from time to time, but as threat increases, so does uniformity of strategy.

Second, integration is needed to reconcile competing DRs. If the usual strategy involves integrating past and current information, behavior is likely to vary from occasion to occasion, reflecting variation in the context. If the strategy does not usually include psychological integration, behavior will be more similar across occasions and reflect an overreliance on information about past experience. If the current context is unlike that in the past, the resulting behavior will often be maladaptive. Because integration is a slow cortical process, endangered people usually do not take time to reflect, thus, they have less opportunity to learn to integrate and are more likely to act precipitously in the future.

Third, for adults who are parents, the situation is even more complex. In the face of some threats, the self-protective and child-protective strategy may not only be different, but may also be—or seem to be— mutually exclusive. These situations are very difficult for parents.

Assessment of attachment in adulthood should reflect the full range of adult behavior and also the salient issues of adulthood (i.e., self-regulation regarding protection and reproductive opportunities, spousal functioning, and parental functioning). Further, it should address the complexity of information processing available to adults.

The Adult Attachment Interview: Its Original Intent and Current Applications

The Adult Attachment Interview was developed in the mid-1980s by Main and her colleagues to explore the relation between infants' quality of attachment at 12 months of age and their mothers' state of mind with regard to attachment (George et al., 1985; Main, Kaplan, & Cassidy, 1985). Since that time, it has been used in many studies, some of which replicate Main's findings and others of which explore additional uses of the AAI, particularly its application to clinical populations.

It has become clear that the AAI is relevant to adults other than mothers, to relationships other than the mother-infant relationship, and to functioning outside of the normal range. Indeed, it appears that the AAI is relevant to examination of the strategies used by adults to solve problems in relationships and problems related to self-protection from danger. These issues, in turn, are central to marital relations, family functioning, individual mental health, and possibly even issues of professional or employment success. The focus on strategies for mentally processing information relevant to danger and sexual opportunity is especially pertinent to cases of psychopathology and criminal behavior. The DMM approach to the AAI goes beyond work with mothers to address the full range of adult concerns regarding danger, reproduction, and threat to one's children.

Thus, the DMM-AAI has the potential to inform researchers regarding developmental processes occurring during adulthood (i.e., from early adulthood to old age) and to identify those processes that promote adaptation, given particular life circumstances. Further, the DMM-AAI can throw light on the types of mental functioning associated with maladaptation and mental/emotional dysfunction. Although up to now, the AAI has primarily been used to yield one of four categories (i.e., secure, dismissing, preoccupied, and unresolved/Cannot Classify), it could be analyzed in terms of mental and developmental processes. For this reason, the DMM approach to the AAI may be informative regarding the process of psychological treatment both in theory and in specific cases. In particular, with the addition of a wider range of strategies, the DMM-AAI has the potential to become an efficient assessment at the beginning of psychotherapy, a part of the treatment itself, and also an evaluative tool during and at the completion of therapy. These possible uses make understanding the potential of the DMM-AAI relevant to researchers, theorists, and psychotherapists.

What Is the AAI?

The AAI is a semi-structured interview, usually lasting for 1 to 1½ hours. It consists of a specified series of questions about childhood relationships with attachment figures (usually parents), together with interviewer-generated follow-up questions. Although it is usually treated as a single entity, the AAI has four distinct components:

1. an embedded theoretical perspective;
2. a specific set of interview questions that query, in a systematic manner, about childhood experiences and adult perspectives on these;
3. a classificatory method; and

4.   a classificatory system derived from Ainsworth's system for infants. (Ainsworth, 1979)

These four components are usually referred to, as a whole, as the
Adult Attachment Interview. Nevertheless, they can be considered separately.

THEORY

Various theoretical perspectives on attachment can be applied to the
interpretation of the AAI. Main and her colleagues developed the AAI
based on a version of attachment theory that assumed that (1) by
adulthood most adults had a single representation of attachment relationships, (2) this relationship reflected one of the Ainsworth patterns
of infant attachment, (3) these patterns were transmitted from mother
to child across generations, and (4) frightening circumstances disrupted the organizational process, leading to a state of disorganization
in infancy or lack of resolution of the frightening circumstances in
adulthood (Main & Hesse, 1990; Main & Goldwyn, 1984; Main et al.,
1985).

In the Dynamic-Maturational Model of attachment and adaptation
(Crittenden, 1994, 1995, 2000a, 2000b, 2000c, 2008) none of these four
assumptions are made. To the contrary, the DMM approach to attachment theory presumes that adults have *multiple dispositional representations,* each unique to the information processing underlying it. Second,
the array of strategies is *developmentally expanded* from its roots in infancy, with endangered individuals most often using the later developing and more complex strategies (Crittenden & Ainsworth, 1989).

Third, it is understood that *each individual constructs his or her own
dispositional representation from his or her own experience.* Sometimes this
will reflect similarities to the parent's dispositional representation, but,
especially in cases of parental disturbance or inadequacy, children will
often organize the opposite strategy from the parent. Moreover, in families with several children, older children's strategies are expected to
influence the strategies of younger children. For example, if an older
child takes care of the parent in order to be protected, a younger child
may find it more adaptive to be demanding of the parent. In such a
case, the older child might use a different strategy from the mother and
the younger child might use a different strategy than either the mother
or the sibling.

Finally, *exposure to danger* is assumed to be the essential condition that elicits attachment behavior, and, across repeated experiences, leads to organized self-protective strategies. Furthermore, adapting to dangerous circumstances often takes more skill than infants have. For this reason, infants are extremely dependent upon parents for protection; a central function of their development is learning to identify danger and protect themselves from it. When dangers are unusually prevalent, difficult to discern, or hard to avoid, a threatened person will need complex psychological processes and sometimes misleading or deceptive behavior to stay safe. In the DMM, danger leads to both organization and more complex organization than does safety.

A crucial aspect of DMM theory is that it poses two basic psychological transformations of information—cognition and affect—which constitute the basic input to representation. The transformed information is combined using two basic psychological processes: association (putting together) and disassociation (keeping apart). These processes then generate dispositional representations. Together the transformations and processes generate the three basic patterns of attachment (i.e., Ainsworth's ABC patterns of attachment). Type A is a "cognitively" organized strategy that disassociates affect, Type C is "affectively" organized with association of sometimes unrelated affective information, and Type B integrates both transformations of information using both associative and disassociative processes. Within Type B, some patterns are more cognitive (B1–2) whereas others are more affective (B4–5). Thus, the model itself involves two basic transformations and two basic processes that are combined and transformed after infancy to generate more complex strategies.

The terms *classification*, *pattern*, and *strategy* each have a unique, albeit related, meaning in the DMM. *Classification* refers to the outcome of coding and is constrained with reference to reality the way data are always constrained. *Pattern* refers to the clusters of constructs used by speakers; these tend to co-occur (rather than operating independently) and are the basis for classification. *Strategy* is what the classification is meant to identify. That is, we are interested in strategies, but use a patterning of constructs to define a classification as the proxy for the strategy.

These four differences between the work of Main and colleagues and the DMM in underlying theory, together with the notions of cognition and affect, yield a new, developmentally differentiated, and complex way of thinking about the output of an AAI.

THE INTERVIEW

A different interview could be used to assess attachment or self-protective strategies; the interview could then be analyzed using the discourse analysis procedure (e.g., see Crittenden, Partridge, & Claussen, 1991 for a parenting interview analyzed with Main and Goldwyn's method). In addition, the original George, Kaplan, and Main interview could be revised or modified (George et al., 1985, 1996). Indeed, we recommend modification of this interview for clinical applications and for exploring more fully developmental pathways and a wider range of interpersonal strategies. Although transcripts using the original and revised versions of the AAI can be analyzed and classified using the DMM method described in this volume, the modified AAI (Crittenden, 2007) provides the detail needed in clinical cases.

A particular feature of the interview by George and colleagues is its replication in discourse of the process of regulating stress so as to elicit the individual's self-protective strategy that is embedded in Ainsworth's Strange Situation Procedure (SSP). That is, the questions (1) begin comfortably, (2) become a bit more challenging, but still under the control of the speaker, then (3) shift to minor forms of threat introduced by the interviewer and then to (4) fairly substantial threats, including (5) loss of attachment figures. The interview draws to a close by asking (6) a graduated series of integrative questions. In the Crittenden modification, the array of dangers is broader and the closing is (7) returned to the control of the speaker. In both versions of the AAI, it is the discourse, not the content of the answers to the questions, that is crucial.

Often, interest is expressed in selecting some of the AAI questions and delivering them to clients outside of the context of the interview. This seems to imply that the power of the AAI lies in the questions themselves. Excerpting questions from the AAI and popularizing them outside the AAI format dilutes the power of the interview to surprise the mind of the speaker and transforms the questions to ordinary questions, forcing equally ordinary, content-based interpretation.

Instead, the AAI process of regulating stress and probing different representations depends on the order of the questions and the interpersonal context in which they are delivered. The interpersonal process can be seen as a conversation with a stranger about sensitive and personal topics, addressed in surprising ways that require new, on-the-spot thinking. This unusual and special conversation with a compassionately available interviewer sets up a pathway to questions that can trigger integrative functioning, setting the mind of the speaker in motion in potentially new ways.

In this special conversation, the interviewer's role is quite precise. Its function is to create an opportunity for the speaker to be clear to himself and to the interviewer. Speakers seem intuitively aware of this. Every time they ask *"D'you know what I mean?"* or *"You know?"* or *"Am I making sense?"* speakers are asking whether the function of communication is being fulfilled. Ironically, interviewers are extremely likely to choose this moment to be reassuring as opposed to informative. It is our observation, from reading several thousand AAIs, that the less clear the speaker is, the more reassuring the interviewer is. *"Yes, I understand." "Uh huh." "Right."* And speakers learn nothing about themselves or the process of communication. It is far better for an interviewer to listen more attentively, asking herself repeatedly whether she did indeed understand the speaker and, when asked by the speaker, had answered in a way that promoted clarity. *"Yes, somewhat, but maybe you could say a bit more." "Not quite, I didn't quite understand . . .* [quoting the speaker's words]." Although there are many skills needed to give a proper AAI and these are offered in the AAI training course, this way of communicating stands out because it is so directly connected to the interpersonal process of revealing meaning.

THE CLASSIFICATORY METHOD

Main and Goldwyn (1984, 1994) constructed the original discourse analysis for the AAI. Other classificatory procedures could be applied to it, as has been done by Grossmann, Fremmer-Bombik, Rudolph, and Grossmann (1988). This volume describes a method that has been developed over almost two decades. Its roots are in the groundbreaking work of Main and Goldwyn, augmented by ideas from Bandler and Grinder (1975), Bateson (1972), Grinder and Bandler (1975), and Watzlawick, Beavin and Jackson (1967), as well as others. Many of this method's constructs have been drawn from AAIs themselves when reconciling the discourse with the history of the speaker-required tools (i.e., transformations of information and attributions of meaning) that were not in the method at that point. The process has been developmental: using existing tools to meet new challenges that produce the discrepancy of a mismatch and call for integrative thinking that yields a new construct or new organization of existing constructs. The new tool is then applied to future transcripts, sometimes yielding an unexpected mismatch and initiating the whole integrative process again.

Unlike the Main and Goldwyn method that was developed on a sample for upper middle-class American parents, the DMM method was honed from AAIs from more than 20 countries, including AAIs with normative adults, adults in outpatient treatment, adults in psychiatric hospitals, and prisoners in correctional facilities. The DMM approach was first published in 1999 but has continued to undergo refinement up to now. We expect it to continue to change as it becomes more widely applied

THE CLASSIFICATORY SYSTEM

Just as different versions of attachment theory, of the AAI, and of discourse analysis can be used, the classificatory system can vary. It could retain the Ainsworth patterns of infancy or be revised to reflect adult organizations that coalesce only after infancy (see Crittenden & Ainsworth, 1989). Describing such organizations is at the heart of the DMM method. From the three Ainsworth ABC patterns of infant attachment, an expanded DMM set of classifications is offered to address organizations of thought and behavior beyond the range described by Ainsworth. These classifications identify strategies that infants cannot yet organize. The DMM set of classifications was derived from theory (from both Bowlby's and Crittenden's theories) and observed in the transcripts of adults from many cultures and conditions in life, including, in particular, adults who were endangered in their childhood or who display various forms of psychopathology in their adulthood. The full array of Dynamic-Maturational Model patterns is displayed in Figure 1.1.

The major classifications reflect Ainsworth's ABC trichotomy and are expanded here to include patterns observed only after infancy. In Main and Goldwyn's model, Ainsworth's ABC patterns were relabeled as dismissing (Ds = A), free/autonomous (F = B), and preoccupied (E = C). In deference to Ainsworth and in order to clarify developmental relations, the original ABC terminology is retained in the Dynamic-Maturational Model.

The major ABC classifications are described below. In Chapter 2, these descriptions are extended to a brief overview of each of the classifications. In Chapter 3, the basis in information processing for the patterns is sketched. In Chapter 4, the array of constructs used in this

Figure 1.1 The Dynamic-Maturational Model of attachment strategies in adulthood.

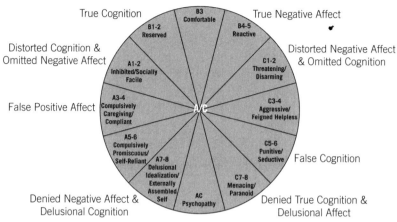

method is described, including the distinction between history and discourse. In Chapters 5 to 12, each classification is described in detail in terms of discourse and the function of the discourse, and each pattern is also described in terms of the mental strategies evident in the discourse and of the developmental history associated with the pattern. The process of this manual, in other words, is one of increasing differentiation of theory and classification through a steady accretion of concepts and detail.

THE MAJOR PATTERNS OF ATTACHMENT

Type B: Balanced Attachment

When attachment figures were both protective and comforting, adults are usually balanced with regard to processing information and managing relationships. In some cases, however, even adults who were endangered as children are able to achieve mental and emotional clarity with regard to their experiences and to function, in adulthood, in an "earned" (i.e., reorganized) balanced manner. In such cases, it is not necessary that the adult be "secure" (i.e., safe from danger or worry about danger). Indeed, security and comfort may be impossible to achieve in outer reality because of forces outside of the control of the individual (e.g., conditions of poverty or war). Nevertheless, all adults have a possibility of psychological balance.

Speakers who are classified as balanced (B) tend to describe their childhood experiences using both sources of information: (1) cognition (i.e., temporal and causal order, realistically identifying complex causal relations) and (2) affect, including both positive and negative feeling states. They also use both associative and disassociative processes in a judicious manner. In addition, balanced speakers describe their relationships with their parents in terms of varied attributes and provide evidence (in the form of recalled episodes) to support these generalizations. As adults, they are able to look back and recall their own childhood perspectives, construct an understanding of their parents' probable perspectives, and describe their current understanding of events. This current understanding contains conclusions that are complex in that they (1) acknowledge that people and relationships change over time, (2) portray the self and attachment figures as varying in behavior and being less than perfect (or unredeemingly terrible), (3) reflect the interactive effects of self and others, and (4) differentiate appearance from reality.

Type A: Dismissing of the Self

TYPES A1–2: DISMISSING ATTACHMENT IN THE CONTEXT OF PHYSICAL SAFETY (I.E., THE LOW-NUMBERED TYPE A CLASSIFICATIONS)

When attachment figures fail to protect or comfort children, defensive processes may be used. If the child is actually safe, but only partially comforted by attachment figures, only a mild distortion is expected (i.e., some mild disassociation of positive and negative characteristics). When, in addition, lack of comfort is accompanied by rejection of the child's unnecessary attachment behavior (e.g., display of anger, fear, and desire for comfort), a simple defense against negative affect is often used. In this case, the good and bad qualities of the parent are split and only the good is acknowledged and display of negative affect is inhibited (i.e., disassociated).

Consequently, in the AAI, the A1–2 speaker describes the rejecting parent in positive, idealized terms (whereas Type B speakers are accurate with regard to both desired and unpleasant qualities of their parents). In order to maintain this distortion, memories of instances in which the child was safe, but not comforted, are set aside and not recounted during the AAI, even when they are directly requested. Alternatively, episodes in which desired comfort was not given are truncated and the lack of comfort may be dismissed as trivial. Expression of affect is largely absent from interviews of speakers classified as Types A1–2. The A1 and A2 patterns are rarely associated with serious, life-threatening physical danger. To the contrary, the danger is the psychological discomfort of having attachment behavior rejected by the attachment figure (when the child was actually safe).

Types A3–8: Dismissing in the context of danger (i.e., the high-numbered, compulsive Type A classifications)

When parents are a source of danger or fail to protect children from danger and if the danger is predictable and preventable, children learn to do what is necessary to increase their safety.

In such cases, the threats are generally well remembered and recounted as episodes. Therefore, idealization is not possible; instead, in the AAI, adults who use a Type A strategy make excuses for their parents (exonerate them), take the parents' perspectives, and deny their own attachment needs and feelings, both as children and also as adults. Often there is some form of compulsion. There may be compulsive compliance if violence was the threat (A4), compulsive caregiving (role reversal) if neglect was the threat (A3), compulsive self-reliance if nothing except escape protected the child from the parents' dangerous behavior (A6), or compulsive seeking of intimacy with strangers (A5). Compulsively self-reliant children protect themselves by isolating themselves from dangerous parents, but, to do so, they give up access to parental protection and to their own feelings. Frequently, the isolation of the A6 strategy is associated with promiscuity, including sexual promiscuity, in casual relationships (i.e., A5).

The two most extreme strategies result from serious endangerment, beginning early in life and extending across developmental periods. In the case of some contact with attachment figures, adults may delusionally idealize dangerous figures, denying their negative experiences and delusionally transforming them into positive ones, thus protecting themselves in recall from danger in childhood (A7). Others who had no figure to turn to (or a series of changing figures) develop an externally constructed self (A8).

The high-numbered strategies are associated with increased rates of psychological distress and are observed in greater proportion in the transcripts of adults in psychotherapy than in the normative population (in relatively safe societies).

Type C: Preoccupied with the Self

TYPES C1–2: PREOCCUPIED WITH RELATIONSHIPS IN THE CONTEXT OF UNPREDICTABLE CARE (I.E., THE LOW-NUMBERED TYPE C CLASSIFICATIONS)

Type C speakers attempt to coerce comfort and protection from attachment figures by using exaggerated and alternating displays of anger and desire for comfort with some fear. In most cases, attachment figures were affectively available, but their unpredictable responses provided children with no confidence that they would be protected.

Such attachment figures are inconsistent, but vary regarding protection from danger. Because there is little predictability, children do not learn to attend to temporal order as a reliable source of information and are unable to draw sound causal conclusions. They also do not learn to inhibit display of negative affect. In such cases, children experience their parents as indecisively loving and are unable to explain why they continue to feel uneasy. Their response is (1) to become dependent, angry, or fearful and (2) to wonder whether, in the event of danger, the attachment figure might fail to protect them or whether they might have to rely on themselves. Their strategy is to focus on (1) feelings that signal danger and (2) threatening events and details about such events that could possibly enhance identification of threat in the future. In the AAI, mildly self-preoccupied speakers use an associative process when recalling the critical fragments of past experiences, slipping easily from past to present and back again (blurring the boundaries of time), confusing people (blurring the boundaries between people), failing to draw reasoned conclusions about their childhoods (failing to make accurate causal attributions because they have disassociated cognitive information), and showing affective arousal (e.g., giggling). In addition, they often seek confirmation that interviewers are paying attention. Temporal and causal ordering, thus, are minimized, whereas affect is exaggerated.

The C1 and C2 subpatterns are rarely associated with physical danger. To the contrary, the danger is the psychological discomfort of being uncertain when and how attachment figures would respond.

TYPES C3–8: PREOCCUPIED WITH RELATIONSHIPS IN THE CONTEXT OF DANGER (I.E., THE HIGH-NUMBERED, OBSESSIVE TYPE C CLASSIFICATIONS)

In more severe cases, dangerous events occurred and parents did not protect or comfort children. Some such children become very anxious and escalate their efforts to elicit protective responses from the parents (C3–4). Depending upon the extent to which the parent deceives the child about the danger, the child may become more (C7–8) or less (C5–6) suspicious of feeling comfortable.

In the AAI, uncertainty regarding temporal contingencies appears as the lack of logical/rational conclusions, plus irrational, magical or deceptive conclusions (i.e., disassociated cognition and transformed cognition). Distortions of affect are displayed as intense affect of one sort (e.g., anger) that is present in the interview nonverbally or in affectively intense language, while display of other incompatible affects (e.g., fear and desire for comfort) is inhibited, then the displays are reversed. For example, intense anger may be displayed without evidence of fear or desire for comfort (C5). In most cases, the speaker appears unable to tell his or her story alone and the interviewer finds himself or herself subtly pulled into the interview as an ally or opponent of the speaker and, thus, into the family conflict. Like the compulsive classifications, these high-numbered Type C classifications are associated with psychopathology (in relatively safe societies).

WHAT DOES THE AAI ASSESS?

The Adult Attachment Interview appears to be a straightforward interview about childhood experiences. The first result is a narrative that provides content on the history of the speaker and which is relevant to experience with attachment figures and with protection from danger. There is no way to know, within the interview, if what the speaker says is accurate about his or her history: It is, nevertheless, information about the speaker's perspective.

When administered and interpreted properly, the AAI addresses the question of how the speaker uses his or her perspective on past experience to predict when and where danger is likely to occur in the future and how best to prepare for it. This includes such issues as how probable danger is perceived to be, who can be trusted (and under what conditions), and what one can do to protect oneself. Put another way, the Adult Attachment Interview explores what the speaker has learned from past experience that is applied to the future and what he or she believes is specific and unique to the past (and therefore not relevant to future conditions). In particular, the AAI considers how information is transformed to give it meaning in terms of future protection of self, attachment figures, and progeny.

Framed this way, the AAI assesses more than the individual's state of mind in regard to attachment. It assesses how the mind *processes* information, in terms of how different dispositional representations are activated in response to specific stimulation, how integration draws these different representations together, and how complete and usable are the products of integrative processing.

Thus the AAI assesses the pattern of attachment of the speaker both in terms of how he or she behaves while considering dangerous topics and the underlying basis of this behavior in mental processing of information. This assessment is based on a coder's interpretation of how the behavioral evidence is patterned strategically. Like many projective tests, the AAI permits fine-grained observation of mental and interpersonal processes that often are not in the respondents' conscious awareness. The AAI can collect evidence of behaviors based on implicit, preconscious mental representations. Like more objective measures, it also permits specification of what is being assessed, why it is important, and how it contributes to the summary result. Behavior is recorded by transcribing the interview, its function is assigned to specific categories called memory systems (see Chapter 3), and these contribute in specified ways to the overall strategic pattern.

Classification of an AAI takes the form of ascribing (1) a basic attachment strategy, with the possibility of modification by (2) unresolved losses or traumas, or (3) a relatively pervasive condition, such as depression. Because each of these components of a classification is based on specified instances of behavior assigned to specific memory systems, the reasons for assignment to a classification (with its functional implications) are clear to appropriately trained coders.

FOR WHOM IS AN AAI CLASSIFICATION OF INTEREST?

Viewed as a functional description of how a person is likely to behave when threatened, an AAI classification can be used as descriptive data for research and as a diagnostic assessment in clinical settings where the main interest is planning interventions. More recently, its suitability for settings where a judgment on the adaptive qualities of an individual is needed (e.g., parenting assessment in child protection, forensic settings) is being explored.

For these reasons, the AAI has attracted the interest of researchers studying human development, theorists constructing models of human adaptation, clinicians working with adults with psychological disorders or maltreating parents, and experts testifying for courts.

PLAN FOR THE BOOK

This volume contains general guidelines for classifying normative transcripts that correspond to Main and Goldwyn's basic AAI system. In addition, it contains guidelines for an expansion of this system in the direction of wider adult variation, including both cultural variation and maladaptation, from child protection to psychopathology and criminal behavior. However, this is not a manual that can replace direct training on AAI transcripts and the feedback that accompanies training. Nevertheless, we hope that the availability of a guide will encourage others to explore the instrument, become trained and reliable on the procedure, contribute to the growing pool of findings from the AAI, and, over time, adapt the interview and discourse analysis further to varied circumstances, populations, and applications.

The book is divided into three parts. Part I addresses the theory, history, and concepts that are necessary for understanding the Adult Attachment Interview. Part II provides the details of each classification. Part III concludes the volume with a guide to the applications of the DMM method for the AAI, an overview of its possible uses, a review of the validity studies available on the DMM-AAI, and future directions for using the AAI to further our understanding of human adaptation and ways to reduce psychological suffering.

PART I

THE DYNAMIC-MATURATIONAL APPROACH TO ATTACHMENT THEORY

Chapter 2

Theoretical Background

IN THIS CHAPTER WE LAY THE THEORETICAL GROUNDWORK FOR UNDER-standing the Dynamic-Maturational Model's (DMM) approach to the AAI in two ways. First, we review briefly the accretion of ideas included in the DMM method for analyzing discourse in the AAI. In addition, we differentiate the array of patterns used in the DMM method from those used in the Main and Goldwyn method. Second, we describe the conceptual organization of the ABC strategies. That is, in Chapter 1 we described the patterns whereas here we present their underlying structures. Ainsworth offered three distinct categories (A, B, and C); in the DMM method, these are reconceptualized as reflecting two opposite psychological processes (Types A and C) and their co-occurrence (Types B and A/C).

ATTACHMENT AND PATTERNS OF ATTACHMENT

Understanding attachment in adulthood requires considerable understanding of attachment theory itself. Because much has been written about attachment theory already, only the essential rudiments are provided here in the form of a very brief discussion of the major contributions of Bowlby, Ainsworth, Crittenden, Main, and Fonagy to attachment theory, particularly as it is operationalized in the DMM approach to the Adult Attachment Interview (AAI). References to fuller discussion of these ideas are included.

Bowlby

Attachment theory, as introduced by Bowlby (1969/1982, 1973, 1980), is an organizational, systemic theory regarding the function and development of human protective behavior. Bowlby's theory integrated ethological, evolutionary, psychoanalytic, and cognitive theories. Attachment theory postulates that humans are innately predisposed to form attachment relationships to their primary caregivers, attachment relationships function to protect the attached person, and such relationships exist in an organized form by the end of the first year of life. The attachment relationship itself is defined as a tie, that endures across time and space, to a specific person to whom one turns when one feels vulnerable and in need of protection (Ainsworth, 1973). Bowlby presented considerable evidence indicating that separation from, or loss of, an attachment figure is associated with a variety of psychological and physical disorders, including anxiety, depressive disorders, and criminality (Bowlby, 1944, 1958, 1973, 1980). He believed that such disorders were relatively stable but amenable to change through treatment (Bowlby, 1979).

In his later work, Bowlby proposed the construct of internal representational models to explain how prior experience was retained over time and used to guide expectations and future behavior. He further suggested that there were multiple internal representational models tied to (a) different relationships and (b) different memory systems, such as semantic and episodic memory (Bowlby, 1980, Chapter 3). In the same chapter, Bowlby discussed mental integration of information held in different memory systems from the perspective of cognitive theory about information processing (Tulving, 1979).

Bowlby also introduced the notion of developmental pathways. Such pathways were not *trajectories*, meaning that, once the direction of the pathway was initiated, it was not necessarily maintained throughout the life-span. On the contrary, the metaphor of *pathways* was used explicitly because it contained the notion of change points and intersections where one's direction could be modified in ways that were not necessarily predictable from the original path. This aspect of mental and behavioral organization is especially important because Bowlby was dedicated to the development of theory that would be clinically relevant to initiating change. The notion of pathways is relevant to the AAI classifications that are "earned" or "reorganizing," that is, changing from a former Type A or C strategy to a Type B strategy.

Possibly the most useful of Bowlby's contributions was his example of integration of the best of empirical science and other theories into attachment theory. By doing so, he created a state-of-the-art theory and modeled the means by which its relevance could be maintained.

Ainsworth

Ainsworth's primary contribution to attachment theory was the notion of individual differences in patterns of attachment (Ainsworth et al., 1978). Patterns of attachment reflect individuals' unique expectations regarding the availability and responsivity of specific attachment figures to meet their need for protection. This notion was developed through Ainsworth's anthropological observation of infant-mother dyads in Uganda (Ainsworth, 1967), then replicated and expanded in her longitudinal research in the United States (Ainsworth et al., 1978).

Her second and crucial contribution was to tie these outcome categories to differences in maternal home behavior during the 11 months preceding the administration of the Strange Situation. Without this empirical basis, it is unlikely that attachment theory would have been taken seriously. Instead, with an elegantly designed, ecologically valid data collection and careful, detailed data analysis of a short longitudinal study, Ainsworth put attachment front and center in development psychology.

Ainsworth also introduced the idea that patterning, and not quantitative variation on multiple dimensions, was the basis of organization. Three major patterns of attachment in infancy were identified and empirically tied to their roots in maternal sensitive responsiveness:

- Infants whose mothers were consistently and sensitively responsive to infants' attachment behavior were labeled Type B (Secure).
- Infants whose mothers were predictably rejecting of attachment behavior were labeled Type A (Avoidant).
- Infants whose mothers were inconsistently or insensitively responsive to attachment behavior were labeled Type C (Ambivalent).

Early studies indicated that approximately two thirds of infants could be classified as securely attached (Type B) and almost one third as avoidantly attached (Type A) with a small percentage as ambivalently attached (Type C) (Ainsworth, 1979). Nevertheless, when the classificatory procedure was applied to infants who varied widely in socioeconomic status, culture, and quality of childrearing, the proportion of securely attached children was lower, sometimes very substantially lower. In addition, there were three expansions to the original Ainsworth system: Bell's identification of the B4 classification (Bell, 1970), Crittenden's identification of an A/C classification (1985a, 1985b), and Main and Solomon's identification of a disorganized category (Main & Solomon, 1986, 1990). The latter two expansions reduced even further the proportion of securely attached children, even in low-risk samples. Finally, the use of videotape permitted more precise and detailed observation of infant behavior. By permitting identification of fleeting behavior and subtle discrepancies among behaviors, this technological advance further reduced the proportion of children classified as Type B. Thus, a better estimate of security would be that no more than half of a nonrisk, middle-class, Anglo (specifically, American, Australian, Canadian, and English) sample would be expected to be classified as Type B (see van IJzendoorn, Goldberg, Kroonenberg, & Frenkel, 1992). The distributions for other cultures are less clear (see Crittenden, 2000b). For high-risk groups, the proportion of Type B children is substantially lower to nonexistent (cf. Pleshkova & Muhamedrahimov, 2010).

Discussion of the use of terminology is relevant here. The terms *secure* and *anxious* (including both anxious-avoidant and anxious-ambivalent) tend to be used more often than the letters A, B, and C. Nevertheless, when Ainsworth first identified the three patterns, Bowlby's advice was to give them simple letter identifiers until meanings of behaviors were understood (Ainsworth, personal communication, 1980). As work expanded to include an increasing range of cultures and subcultures, it became apparent that attachment nomenclature is sometimes perceived as offensive and pejorative. This is true of both the labels given by Ainsworth and those that Crittenden and others have applied. In addition, the terminology overlooks the contextual validity and adaptiveness of the non-B patterns. Put another way, the terminology may be prematurely evaluative. For these reasons, we use the letter notations frequently. Nevertheless, there remains a tension between the theory offered and the pattern labels. Hopefully, this discrepancy will function to instigate further research into the meaning of the patterns in varied contexts.

To summarize, Ainsworth's central contribution to attachment in adulthood is the notion of individual differences in patterns of attachment, expressed as the ABC classificatory system that she identified among infant-mother dyads and tied to the infants' developmental experience. Main applied this to the AAI in terms of both the classificatory system and the expected distributions of the classifications.[1] Ainsworth's classificatory system is applied in the DMM with modification of both the array of classifications and the distributional expectations. It should be noted that Ainsworth ultimately concluded that an expanding array of organized patterns better captured the essence of attachment than did the idea of disorganization, which she thought would only be a transitory state (Crittenden & Ainsworth, 1989).

In addition, Ainsworth exemplified a model of theory development and exploratory research that is open-ended and anthropologically descriptive and that encourages expansion and modification of earlier work. Thus, in the terminology of attachment theory, both Bowlby and Ainsworth demonstrated use of representations that were open to new information and readily modified on the basis of such information.

Crittenden

Based on several developmental theories, current work in the cognitive neurosciences, and work with risk families (particularly maltreating families), Crittenden began proposing expansions to Ainsworth's ABC model. As she prepared her thesis under Ainsworth (Crittenden, 1981), she proposed new organizations. She also proposed an A/C pattern for endangered infants while preparing her dissertation, again under Ainsworth (Crittenden, 1985b). Later, A3–4 and C3–4 patterns were added for the preschool years (Crittenden, 1992) and A5–6 and C5–6 were proposed for the school years (Crittenden, 1994). With Ainsworth, she coauthored a chapter on the self-protective strategies of maltreated children (Crittenden & Ainsworth, 1989). They argued that disorganization, if it occurred, would be transient and replaced by context-adapted strategies, including A/C, compulsive Type A (i.e., A3–6), and extremely anxious strategies.

---

1. Main retained both B4 and the disorganized category, but not A/C, in her AAI classificatory system. Hesse later included A/C equivalents under the heading of "Cannot Classify" (Hesse, 1996).

Later, the array of expansions became known as the Dynamic-Maturational Model of attachment and adaptation. The DMM describes variation and change across the life-span in the development of attachment relationships. This perspective proposes that maturation is in dynamic interaction with experience, yielding the potential for lawful change in patterns of attachment, that is, "reorganization" (Crittenden, 1994, 1995, 2008). Changes in pattern are expected to be particularly frequent near periods of rapid neurological change (i.e., near transitions in developmental "stage"). Thus, Crittenden expected the possibility of changes in pattern of attachment at several points prior to adulthood.

Further, Crittenden suggested that a very great majority of infants, *especially* those who experience dangerous circumstances, have organized strategies for relating to their attachment figures. Indeed, she argued that danger is central both to the evolution of attachment processes in our species and also to the organization of specific attachment relationships in each individual (Crittenden, 1997c, 1999b). Consequently, she considers information relevant to predicting danger and protecting oneself from it to be the basis of pattern of attachment. She uses this perspective because it focuses attention on the *function* of attachment; distortions in the way information is processed preserve the function under conditions of threat. The distortions are of considerable clinical relevance; indeed, they can be considered the means by which risk for psychopathology develops and maladaptation is maintained (Crittenden, 1996, 2002). If this perspective is accurate, understanding the organization and function of these distortions may generate new approaches to diagnosis and treatment. If the distortions can be identified in the AAI, then the AAI may become an important clinical diagnostic tool.

Because maltreated children experience both threats of danger and actual danger, they provide an exceptional opportunity to study the development of adaptation to danger. In Crittenden's studies of maltreated children, she identified one complex pattern in infancy that protected children who were both abused and neglected (i.e., A/C, Crittenden, 1985a, 1985b). Other researchers have associated this pattern with bipolar depression in mothers, that is, another source of variable danger (Radke-Yarrow, Cummings, Kuczynski, & Chapman, 1985). In addition, she hypothesized that patterns of attachment become more complex with development and has offered evidence of one new major pattern of organization, coercion (Type C), and several new patterns within Type A, including compulsive caregiving and compulsive compliance, that first develop in the preschool years (Crittenden, 1992).

This process of expanding the array of patterns, resulting from the interaction of experience with maturation, became the basis of a life-span model of the development of strategies for coping with dangerous conditions (see Figure 1.1 in Chapter 1). Because this model has been described at length in many places (Crittenden, 1995, 2000a, 2000b, 2008), it will not be described in more than a cursory manner here. It does, however, form the backbone of the DMM method for analyzing AAI transcripts.

The Dynamic-Maturational Model represents a conceptualization of self-protective strategies based on evolved aspects of information processing. Specifically, innate aspects of organic processing (somatic information), temporal order of stimulation (cognition), and intensity of stimulation (affect) are identified as the three most basic forms of information about whether, when, and where there might be danger. Reliance on cognitive information, to the relative exclusion of affect, is the basis for the Type A classifications, whereas reliance on affect, to the relative exclusion of cognition, is the basis for the Type C classifications. Type B is defined by flexible use and integration of both sources of information. Transformations of cognition and affect permit more precise identification of the most probable sources of danger as well as the organization of protective responses. Concurrently, however, the transformations distort information in ways that often lead to heightened expectation of danger and, thus, to the use of self-protective behavior under safe circumstances. Change in the array of transformations reflects change in strategy in this model. Framed in this way, the pattern of attachment becomes a dimensional construct defined by a horizontal dimension of source of information and a vertical dimension of type of transformation of information (see Figure 1.1). Type B individuals, at the top of the model, integrate true affect and cognition whereas, at the bottom of the model, falsified and sometimes delusional information is integrated by psychopathic individuals while they exclude denied information from processing (Type AC).

This model leads to at least two points of tension. First, it creates a range of functioning (as opposed to categories) within all classifications (including within Type B). Consequently, the classifications become approximations of unique individual patterns. Second, in this model every pattern carries both adaptive and maladaptive aspects.

Given this complexity, the verbal labels cannot reflect all the possibilities within a pattern or even the primary function of the pattern and primary advantages and risks associated with it. Consequently, this model offers the advantages of being theoretically comprehensive and of differentiating a wider range of functioning than the original Ainsworth system and the early expansions of it. Nevertheless, it, too, leaves a range of differentiation (ultimately individual-specific, unique differentiation) unnamed.

An important point regarding within-pattern variation is the pervasiveness of the strategy within the person's functioning. If one considers distance from the center of the model as indicative of greater penetration of the strategy into all aspects of an individual's functioning, then placement near the edges of the model should have implications for both greater risk of psychopathology and also more severe psychopathology.

An important feature of the model is the inclusion of sexuality in adolescent and adult functioning. Protection and reproduction are proposed to constitute the two major organizing functions of human behavior (Crittenden, 1997a). The emphasis on danger harkens back to the earliest work in attachment theory, for example, Bowlby's study of 44 juvenile thieves (Bowlby, 1944) and his work with children displaced during World War II (Bowlby, 1951). Because reproduction does not motivate behavior until after puberty, distortions of sexuality are reflected only in the late developing patterns. Nevertheless, the central threat of failure to reproduce successfully is presumed to interact with aspects of attachment in ways that modify mental and behavioral organization. Further, even though the AAI was not intended to address sexuality, in clinical populations speakers' responses frequently include references to sexuality. Therefore, distortions of sexuality are addressed in the coding method described here.

Finally, Crittenden emphasized the notion that patterns of attachment reflect learned patterns of mentally managing cognitive and affective information so as to predict and adapt to dangerous circumstances and opportunities for reproduction (Crittenden, 2002). In particular, she focused on the notion that the brain transforms sensory stimulation into predictive information about dangerous and safe conditions and opportunities for sex. This idea is expanded in Chapter 4 in the discussion of transformations of information, representational models, and memory systems.

With regard to the AAI, we propose that adults' discourse reflects mental processes used both to focus on the most salient and meaningful predictors of danger and reproduction and to preclude awareness of information that increases danger and feelings of anxiety. Because maturation increases the range of mental and behavioral responses, the need for and use of self-protective organizations of thought and behavior may change with development, even when circumstances themselves are unchanging. This can result in a change in pathways as well as the organization of new strategies. The outcome of the changes can be observed in AAI discourse. These changes involve a process of reorganization and that, too, can be observed in AAI discourse.

The developmental aspects of a Dynamic-Maturational approach to attachment theory suggest that new patterns that reflect increasingly sophisticated organizations of the ABC processes of managing information should be expected. One of the most exciting aspects of the AAI and its discourse analysis is its potential to enable us to identify new patterns. Thus, we think the AAI can be used for exploratory research that will extend our understanding of human development and adaptation.

Main

Main and her colleagues have made crucial contributions to the understanding and assessment of attachment in adulthood. These began with identifying unusual behavior among mildly stressed infants that were interpreted as being indicative of disorganized attachment to a caregiver who was frightened or frightening (Main & Hesse, 1990; Main & Solomon, 1986, 1990; Main & Weston, 1981). The disorganized category was hypothesized to be associated, in the AAI, with fearful preoccupation with attachment relationships (E3) and lack of resolution of loss and trauma (Main & Hesse, 1990) or Cannot Classify (Hesse, 1996).[2]

Using Bowlby's ideas regarding semantic and episodic memory, George, together with Kaplan and Main, constructed a protocol of questions for the AAI (George et al., 1985, 1996). Main and Goldwyn constructed a method of discourse analysis (Main & Goldwyn, 1984). The interview and classificatory method incorporate the notion of memory systems by asking specifically about semantic and episodic memory and the integration of these; lack of concordance between these memory systems is crucial to assigning an insecure classification.

---

2. The notion of trauma has been narrowed to abuse in childhood in more recent guides to Main and Goldwyn's method.

Based on Main's transgenerational hypothesis, mothers are thought to "transmit" their pattern of attachment to their infants. Thus, mothers of Type A infants were expected to be "Dismissing" (Ds) with regard to attachment; mothers of Type B infants would be "Free/autonomous" (F), and mothers of Type C infants would be "Preoccupied/entangled" (E). In the DMM, parents' representations are not thought to directly affect children's representations. Instead, parents act, creating a sensory context for children. From that context, children select stimuli to attend to and then transform those stimuli into representations that organize the child's behavior. That is, each person constructs his or her own representations independently of others' representations and without direct access to any other mind or representations. Thus, children's representations may (or may not) match their parents' representations (Crittenden, 2008).

A number of studies support Main's hypothesis of continuity in pattern of attachment across the life-span and across generations in middle-class, low-risk, maritally and geographically stable families (van IJzendoorn, 1995). Thus, it appears that the conditions conducive to Type B attachments are also those associated with continuity of pattern of attachment. Families in high-risk and unstable conditions and with Types A and C attachments showed considerably less stability (see, e.g., Crittenden et al., 1991). On the other hand, studies that looked at continuity *within* anxious attachment have found discontinuity in the form of A-to-C and C-to-A reversals (see Hautamäki, Hautamäki, Neuvonen, & Maliniemi-Piispanen, 2010; Shah, Fonagy, & Strathearn, 2010).

Fonagy

Peter Fonagy and his colleagues have been particularly attracted to the notion of mentalization, that is, the ability to imagine that the minds of other people might perceive things differently from one's own. Their particular contribution to the analysis of AAI discourse has been to integrate psychoanalytic perspectives and work on theory of mind with attachment theory. The outcomes were the construct of "reflective functioning" (Fonagy et al., 1995) as well as a method for identifying such processes in AAI discourse (Fonagy, Steele, Steele, & Target, 1997). Reflective thought is associated with Type B and its absence with psychopathology (Fonagy et al., 1996). In the method offered here, there is considerable overlap between the notion of reflective self-processes and what we call "reflective integration." (Because the concepts are not identical, a related term was used, rather than appropriating, and possibly distorting, Fonagy's term.) Nevertheless, Fonagy's thinking has been central to the notion of reflective integration.

There are, however, differences between Fonagy's perspective and the DMM. Like most attachment researchers, Fonagy focused on attachment as a specific dyadic relationship. In the DMM, that is one aspect of attachment, but the power of early attachment to predict later functioning is thought to lie in the influence of early relationships with attachment figures on how children learn to process information. Thus, attachment is treated here as (a) a relationship construct, (b) the pattern of mentally processing of information about danger and safety, and (c) a self-protective strategy.

In addition, Fonagy and his colleagues focused more on the positive quality of "mentalization," including how individuals monitor their own mental representations and how attachment figures' mental representations affect the mental representations of attached children. In the DMM, mental functioning is very important, but there is equal interest in how the minds of individuals who do not mentalize manage information.

Finally, according to Fonagy, reflective functioning is central to accurate prediction of others' behaviors, attachment security, differentiation of appearance from reality, and communication. Although we agree with that, we are aware that, in deceptive situations, distorted representations can predict more safely than accurate representations. Moreover, we are wary of encouraging very disturbed individuals to use mentalization for self-protective functions because this may concurrently endanger others. That is, as one approaches psychopathy, in the Dynamic-Maturational Model, the integration of false, denied, and delusional information may lead to unnervingly accurate predictions about others' behaviors, deceptively smooth communication, and uncanny distortions of appearance and reality, all couched in statements that closely resemble reflective thinking. The issue becomes differentiating these two; being able to do this might be essential for avoiding classifying criminals as "secure" (Fonagy, Target, et al., 1997). As Fonagy noted, one key to this differentiation is the ability to conceptualize concurrently and accurately both others' and one's own perspectives (Fonagy et al., 1995).

Nevertheless, most of these differences in theory are peripheral to the notion of reflective functioning itself. Fonagy's approach to reflective self-functioning is highly relevant to the method offered here and many ideas are borrowed from it.

THE DYNAMIC-MATURATIONAL CLASSIFICATORY SYSTEM

In this section, we provide a theoretical introduction to the AAI classifications in the Dynamic-Maturational Model. Ainsworth's three basic strategies form the core of the classificatory system, with the notion of cognition and affect functioning as information about when and where there might be danger constituting the explanation for the universality of the three patterns.

The central points to be made about the strategies in this chapter are that (1) Types A and C are construed as psychological opposites, with Types B and AC being their integration, and (2) the patterns are organized on several logical gradients. It should be noted that the discussion in this chapter is focused on the strategies themselves and not on the classificatory method for discerning an individual's strategy from an AAI.

Ainsworth identified three patterns of attachment descriptively. Nevertheless, to her and to many others, there appeared to be a dimensional relation among the three. In the section below, two processes and their co-occurrence are described. That is, the DMM is inherently a two-category model that includes gradations between the two processes. The two processes are drawn from information processing and refer to transformation of sensory stimulation into two basic forms of information. One is temporally ordered "cognitive" information; this is the basis for the Type A organization. The other is based on the intensity of the stimulation and yields the construct of "affect"; this is the basis of the Type C organization. Type B is their balanced integration.

Type B Patterns

The Type B pattern in adulthood is labeled "balanced" in the DMM method because it reflects a balanced integration of affect and cognition and because adults in unsafe conditions can be psychologically balanced without being secure. Within Type B, there is variation from those who emphasize cognitive information a bit (B1–2) to those who emphasize affective information a bit (B4–5), with B3 indicating (theoretically) perfect balance between the sources of information. The hallmark, however, is flexibility in the use of cognition or affect in any particular situation. Moreover, Type B individuals use true information in their own processing and, thus, do not distort, omit, or falsify information to themselves (i.e., they do not deceive themselves). Nevertheless, they can apply any of the strategies to particular problems that are best resolved with a non-B strategy. Moreover, they can both explain why they used the non-B strategy and also cease to use it when it is no longer necessary for protection. That is, individuals using a Type B strategy have access to all the information, all the transformations of information, and all the behavioral strategies. They use these in a flexible, context-specific manner, seeking always the most adaptive strategy for their own benefit and for the benefit of their partners and progeny and of their human context in general.

Type A Patterns

The Type A pattern in adulthood refers to both dismissing the perspective, intentions, and feelings of the self and also preoccupation with the perspectives, desires, and feelings of others. The source of information regarding others' perspectives is temporal consequences tied to behavior of the self. Type A individuals behave as if following the rule: *Do the right thing—from the perspective of other people and without regard to your own feelings or desires.*

The Dynamic-Maturational classifications include six patterns (A3–8) not found in Ainsworth's infant model or Main's life-span model. Some of these were described by Bowlby and some were derived from Crittenden's clinical and empirical work. The A3 (compulsive caregiving) and A6 (compulsively self-reliant) patterns have their roots in Bowlby's work (1973, 1980, respectively), and A4 (compulsive compliance) has a substantial clinical history in the child abuse literature (see Crittenden & DiLalla, 1988). The A5 (compulsively promiscuous) pattern was observed by Crittenden in AAIs of some speakers who were in therapy. It is an expected pattern, based on (a) the early work on children's indiscriminate or "promiscuous" attachment behavior during extended (or permanent) separation from parents (Robertson & Bowlby, 1952; Robertson & Robertson, 1971) and after foster placement and (b) theory (Crittenden, 1997a). The A7 (delusional idealization) pattern has been described in the clinical literature on traumatized in-

Figure 2.1. Affective structure of the Type A subpatterns.

A1–2	Inhibit negative affect regarding psychological discomfort
A3–4	Substitute false positive affect for inhibited negative affect
A5–6	Deny significance of physiological discomfort while continuing inhibition and falsification as needed
A7–8	Deny perception of pain while sometimes adding delusional positive affects, and continuing inhibition and falsification as needed

dividuals under various labels, including the "hostage syndrome" (Cassidy, 2002; Goddard & Stanley, 1994; Kuleshnyk, 1984). The A8 (externally assembled self) refers to the often masochistic strategy of individuals who have been severely mistreated from very early in life in ways that prevent the construction of a self-narrative.

These strategies all emphasize cognitive information in the organization of behavior and vary in how affect is treated. On the vertical gradient, the Type A patterns vary from omitting display of negative affect to replacing it with false positive affect to increasing negation of affective response of all kinds up to lack of response to pain (see Figure 2.1).

The gradient within cognitive information differentiates odd- and even-numbered patterns such that the odd-numbered patterns increasingly idealize the attachment figure whereas the even-numbered patterns increasingly negate the self (see Figure 2.2).

Figure 2.2. Cognitive structure of the Type A subpatterns.

Odd-numbered subpatterns Idealize Others	Even-numbered subpatterns Negate Self
A1: Idealizing others	A2: Distancing from self
A3: Compulsive Caregiving	A4: Compulsive Compliance
1. Attention	1. Performance
2. Caregiving	2. Compliance
A5: Compulsive Promiscuity	A6: Compulsive Self-Reliance
1. Social	1. Social
2. Sexual	2. Isolated
A7: Delusional Idealization	A8: Externally Assembled Self

Type C Patterns

The Type C pattern in adulthood refers to a preoccupation with the perspective of the self and justification of the self, and also dismissing of others, both as valued people and as sources of valid information. The source of information regarding the perspective of the self is one's feelings or one's arousal (i.e., affect). The strategy can be thought of as fitting the following dictum: *Stay true to your feelings and do not negotiate, compromise, or delay gratification in ways that favor the perspectives of others.*

In the Dynamic-Maturational Model, the Type C coercive strategy is organized around affect, specifically desire for comfort, anger, and fear. These feelings motivate specific sorts of behavior. Desire for comfort motivates approach with requests for affection or comfort. Anger motivates approach with verbal or physical attack. Fear motivates withdrawal/escape. Quite obviously, if all are displayed at once, one's behavior becomes incoherent, self-defeating, and nonprotective. Nevertheless, any one of these might be the best solution to a threat. Because all are activated by perceived danger, the issue becomes organizing them in a way that permits strategic use of affective arousal and motivation.

Beginning in the preschool years—and continuing throughout the life-span—this organization is managed by "splitting" the mixed feelings associated with arousal and displaying one part in an exaggerated manner that elicits a response from others while concurrently inhibiting display of the competing feelings. Once the other person has responded, the current display is maintained or reversed, contingent upon the other person's behavior. The most frequent split is between the invulnerable display of anger and the vulnerable appearance of fear and desire for comfort.

The Dynamic-Maturational classifications include increasingly extreme forms of the coercive strategy, all of which involve an even-odd alternation of displaying angry invulnerability with vulnerable fear and desire for comfort (i.e., C1–2, C5–6, etc.). C1 is a simple mildly threatening pattern in which the threat is easily and quickly disarmed by its paired strategy C2. C3 is a strategy of displaying exaggerating anger, that is, aggression, whereas C4 indicates a strategy of exaggerated fearfulness (feigned helpless). The obsessive strategies include C5 (punitively angry and obsessed with revenge) and C6 (seductive or obsessed with rescue). C5–6 also reflect the distorted integration of sexuality with the Type C strategy in which sexuality is used as a currency in interpersonal exchange to obtain other less explicitly identified advantages from the seduced person. The extreme obsessive strategies consist of C7 (menacing) and C8 (paranoid) in which anger and fear, respectively, are combined with denial of self-responsibility. As affect becomes more intense and focused, true cognition is transformed first to distorted cognition, then to falsified cognition, and, at C7–8, to denied cognition. The absence of accurate cognitive information accounts for the irrational quality of C7–8 behavior.

Viewed this way, in Figure 2.3, the odd-numbered patterns on the right side of the model all organize around feelings of anger, from very slight irritated anger (B5) to mild anger (C1), to substantial anger expressed with overt aggression (C3), to obsessive directed anger that may be covertly enacted (C5), to overwhelming, unfocused rage that is directed toward unsuspecting victims who perceive no logical connection of themselves to the aggressor (C7). On the vulnerable side, where desire for comfort and fear are used to organize behavior, the gradient is from almost complete desire for comfort to the near exclusion of anger and fear (B4) to mostly desire for comfort with some minor fear (C2), to substantial fear mixed with equal desire for comfort (C4), to dominating fear that is expressed covertly (C6), to overwhelming, unfocused fear in response to people from whom there is no logical reason to expect attack (C8).

Cognitively, Type C individuals avoid taking responsibility by using increasingly distorted transformations of information. As shown in Figure 2.4, cognitive structures include passive semantic thought, which refers to failing to reach semantic conclusions; reductionist blam-

Figure 2.3. Affective structure of the Type C subpatterns.

Anger	Desire for comfort & Fear
B5	B4
C1	C2
C3	C4
C5	C6
C7	C8

Figure 2.4. Cognitive structure of the Type C subpatterns.

C1–2	Passive semantic thought
C3–4	Reductionist blaming thought
C5–6	Rationalization of self
C7–8	Denied self-responsibility and, sometimes, delusions of power/ threat

ing thought, which refers to attributing responsibility to others by omitting information about one's own contribution; rationalization of self, which refers to creating false, but persuasive, reasons that relieve the self of responsibility (thus making the self an innocent aggressor or victim); and denied self-responsibility or delusional states in which, coupled with denial of one's own causal contribution, one perceives oneself as having overwhelming power or being completely victimized.

Other Categories

In the Dynamic-Maturational Model, any Type A or Type C strategy can be combined in an alternating A/C strategy, for example, A2/C1 or A4/C4. Strategies can also be blended, with the ultimate integration of the threatened and threatening strategies being A7–8/C7–8, psychopathy.

This is admittedly a very cursory review of the DMM classificatory method. These classifications are described more thoroughly in the remainder of this book. For a more detailed understanding of the theory underlying the new patterns, please refer to the publications in the references, particularly those by Crittenden (1995, 2000a, 2000b, 2000c, 2008).

CONCLUSION

The ideas of Bowlby, Ainsworth, Crittenden, Main, and Fonagy are all reflected in the modified AAI. However, DMM theory implies less continuity, across individual life-spans and across generations, than Main hypothesizes and this suggests the need for a broader range of adult classifications. In addition, Crittenden's thinking about the processing of cognition and affect suggests additional techniques for the analysis of AAI discourse (see Chapter 4). These additional techniques expand Main and Goldwyn's classificatory procedures by clarifying and augmenting them rather than being in conflict with them. In addition, they provide a starting point for the exploration of new classifications. Finally, a DMM approach focuses attention directly on the roles of danger and sexuality in organizing thought and behavior, particularly in disturbed individuals. This approach holds the potential to facilitate study of the meaningful function (both currently and in childhood) of apparently maladaptive behavior and, with appropriate modification of the interview, of other adult attachment relationships (e.g., with spouses, children, and aging parents). The outcome could be better understanding of

- the developmental processes that lead to dysfunction (thus, promoting prevention efforts);
- the mental processes that maintain maladaptive behavior (thus, promoting new perspectives on the nature of psychological treatment); and
- normative developmental processes.

A particular contribution of the DMM method of discourse analysis is the focus on the nature of mental processes in cases of disturbance and psychopathology. Put another way, rather than assigning most of these transcripts to a "Cannot Classify" category, an attempt has been made to understand how information is transformed and how these transformations function when speakers have been exposed to self-threatening danger.

Chapter 3

Information Processing

IN THIS CHAPTER WE FOCUS ON THE CONTRIBUTIONS OF COGNITIVE PSY-chology and the cognitive neurosciences to the discourse analysis used in the Dynamic-Maturational Model (DMM) method. In essence, we provide a guide to the relation between brain/mind and the Adult Attachment Interview (AAI), as an assessment of mental representations. That is, the brain is conceptualized as a meaning-generating organ, one that uses input to generate self-relevant meanings, particularly with regard to danger and sexual opportunity. The basic notion to be presented here is that the brain functions as a branching network of distributed parallel processing, in which each different neurological pathway transforms the input signal differently. The input to this network is initially sensory stimulation, generated from within the self and from outside the self, and, as processing continues, also from self-generated transformations that reflect attempts to bring coherence to the set of representations.

The first split in the branching network responds to two different attributes of sensory stimulation: temporal order and intensity. Thereafter, different areas of the brain receive the transformed output and transform it further before passing it forward, again in parallel branches, to other parts of the brain for further analysis and imputation of meaning. At each step, the neurological pathway constitutes a representation of the relation of self to context, with each representation being differently processed as compared to the others. When coherence among the representations is achieved, dispositions to act are clarified.

The various transformations reflect both the advantages of each pathway through particular parts of the brain and also the limitations and distortions associated with that pathway. Further, each representation reflects a disposition to respond in some manner (Damasio, 1994). Hence, the representations are called "dispositional representations." The culmination of this process occurs at the cortical level where the multiple dispositional representations can be brought together for a final analysis, integration, and construction of a best-fitting and most inclusive dispositional representation. The discussion of this process of generating self-relevant meanings is divided into five sections: (1) transformations of sensory stimuli to predictive cognitive and affective information, (2) seven transformations of cognition and affect, (3) memory systems and dispositional representational models, (4) integration and reflective integration, and (5) encoding, remembering/forgetting, and retrieval.

TRANSFORMATIONS OF SENSORY STIMULI

Based on a congruence of theory and empirical evidence regarding brain evolution and function, Crittenden proposed two basic transformations of sensory stimulation to information that is predictive of danger or sexual opportunity (Crittenden, 1995, 1997c, 2002). One is a "cognitive" transformation based on the temporal ordering of stimuli and the implicit attribution of causation to the relation between preceding and subsequent events. The word "cognitive" is being used in a very precise and limited manner to mean temporally ordered information from which attributions regarding causality can be drawn. The cognitive transformation provides information regarding *when* in the sequence of one's behavior there might be danger or opportunity for sexual activity. In the terms of attachment theory, organization of behavior and thought on the basis of cognitive information is the basis for Type A functioning.

The other transformation is an "affective" transformation based on the intensity of the stimulation, that is, the number of neurons responding to the stimulus and the rate of firing of these neurons. The variations of intensity of the stimuli are treated as an indicator of how the context has changed. The affective transformation provides information regarding *where,* relative to oneself, there might be danger or opportunity for sexual activity. Affect, negative affect in particular, is the basis of Type C functioning.

Together, cognition and affect provide information regarding when and where danger is to be expected and when and where sexual contact may be made. In attachment terms, the balanced use of both forms of information yields Type B functioning. These two basic transformations constitute the basis for further transformation.

Cognitive Information

The ability to make temporally based transformations is tied to the functioning of the brain stem and cerebellum (Green, Irvy, & Woodruff-Pak, 1999); thus, this is a relatively early evolving and primitive transformation. On the other hand, it requires relatively few synaptic connections and is, therefore, a rapid transformation. Speed can be crucial when danger is imminent.

Cognitive information is described by the principles of behavioral learning theory (Steinmetz, 1998; Thompson et al., 1997). That is, the consequences of behavior, the things that happen after one has acted, determine the meanings that can be attributed to one's behavior and, therefore, the probability that the behavior will be repeated in the future. Actions with desirable outcomes are likely to be repeated; those with undesirable outcomes are less likely to be repeated. Danger is the most undesirable outcome whereas sexual contact is one of the most pleasing outcomes.

Cognitive information can lead to inhibition of behavior that has been followed by dangerous (or unpleasant) outcomes and to more frequent display of behavior that preceded desired outcomes. Compelled behavior is particularly likely when danger was expected and failed to occur. Under this condition, an attribution of causality may be made between whatever one was doing just before the expected danger didn't occur and the absence of the danger. This behavior, in other words, will come to be defined as a protective behavior and may be displayed whenever danger is expected.

The cognitive transformation is usually the result of repeated experience with the same temporal order, but it can be made on the basis of a single trial. Single trial learning is most likely when the outcome was very dangerous (Gustavson, Garcia, Hankins, & Rusiniak, 1974). Under such conditions, individuals endeavor to see that the dangerous sequence never recurs. They do this by controlling their own initiating behavior. However, single trial learning is very vulnerable to erroneous attributions of causality when the temporal sequence was coincidental and not causal. Because single trial learning occurs most frequently under dangerous conditions, exposure to danger is very vulnerable to superstitious cognitive attributions (Tracy, Ghose, Strecher, McFall, & Steinmetz, 1999). These effects can become the basis for disorders of inhibition and compulsion.

Cognitive information is inherently linear. It requires the mind to parse sequences into initiating events and their consequences. Type A speakers tend to identify their own acts as eliciting attachment figures' responses whereas Type C speakers tend to see themselves as acted upon by others, that is, they are the victims of the consequences of others' behavior. Neither perspective is fully accurate; both distort the dynamic, multidirectional and multicausal complexity of reality.

Affective Information

The ability to make the affective transformation is tied to the evolution of the limbic system, a more recent phenomenon associated only with mammalian species. The affective transformation is based on the relative intensity of stimulation, with rapid and unexpected changes in intensity precipitating processing through the limbic structures. Thus, intensely high and low levels of stimulation (that are unexpected) initiate a cascade of neurological responses that change the physiological state of individuals in ways that prepare them to fight, flee, or freeze (Perry, 1994; Selye, 1976). Accompanying these changes is a generalized state of anxious arousal, an anticipatory state (Le Doux, 1995; MacLean, 1990). The arousing stimulation can be perceived through any of the five senses such that very loud noise or extreme silence, intense brightness or absolute darkness, strong or barely discernible tastes, overpowering or faint odors, and painful or feather-light touches evoke arousal and physiological preparation for self-defense. Moreover, although none of these sensory states is dangerous in and of themselves, all are associated with higher than usual probabilities of danger (cf. Zhong, Bohns, & Gino, 2010; Zimbardo, 1969). Among the five senses, smell and touch hold particular significance as being the best sources of information about distal and proximal danger, respectively. Taste is special as a marker of the distinction between self and nonself (Rozin &

Fallon, 1987; Schedlowski & Pacheco-López, 2010). Distasteful substances are ejected from the body. Indeed, extremely distasteful substances are treated as poisonous, that is, antithetical to the self. (For a discussion of taste, disgust, and self-identity, see Crittenden, 1994.)

Somatic arousal is the outcome of changes in physiological state that produce sensory stimulation that in turn is processed through the limbic structures. These physiological changes adapt the body to its context and include physiological changes that prepare the body to flight, flee, or freeze. Thus, it is information about the state of the self and is highly relevant to knowing what the individual is disposed to do. Consequently, somatic images are of particular importance.

It should be noted that when the sensory information signals danger and one knows procedurally how to protect the self, there will be little or no change in arousal. Instead, one does what needs to be done and is safe. This may be relevant to the "cool/cold" demeanor of some very dangerous people.

Based on experience, unfocused anxiety can be differentiated into at least three distinct feeling states: anger, fear, and desire for comfort. Whereas unfocused anxiety leads to generalized arousal and increased sensory vigilance, desire for comfort, anger, and fear are focused affective states. That is, desire for comfort motivates approach with affection, anger motivates approach with aggression, and fear motivates withdrawal. The opposite of intense stimuli are moderate stimuli that are relatively similar to preceding levels of stimulation; such stimuli elicit feelings of comfort. Comfort serves as an affective signal of lower than usual probability of danger.

Other stimuli elicit feelings of sexual desire in postpubertal humans. Sexual desire is an anticipatory state that is experienced in ways that overlap with the experience of anxiety whereas sexual arousal is a very intense state that can even override the feelings of anxiety, anger, fear, and desire for comfort. Indeed, it is such an arousing state that it can diminish feelings of pain (which itself is the most arousing nonsexual state). Sexual satisfaction, on the other hand, is similar to comfort.

Affective information can be expanded by associative learning such that the sensory aspects of experienced dangerous and safe contexts become directly associated with danger or safety. Similarly sexual success and failure become associated with experienced sensory information. As with cognitive information, the prediction of danger/safety and sexuality can be in error and exposure to danger increases the probability that learned associations will be made rapidly and erroneously. This can lead, in extreme cases, to anxiety disorders, including sexualized attempts to regulate anxiety (Crittenden, 1997a, 2002).

The capacity to make the affective transformation, being later evolved than the cognitive transformation, has three advantages. First, it has innate perceptual biases for predicting higher probabilities of danger (or sexual opportunity); cognition only generates predictions on the basis of experienced threat. Second, affect, through arousal of the autonomic nervous system, is inherently self-relevant. Third, after being experienced, display of affect produces consequences; these lead to cognitive understanding of the meaning of displays of affect.

SEVEN TRANSFORMATIONS OF COGNITION AND AFFECT

As described in the previous section, the brain transforms sensory stimulation to improve prediction. That is, the neurological activity of the brain does not function so as to produce accurate representations of the past. Instead, it is organized to predict the need to protect the self and to identify potential reproductive partners. This creates risk of error, that is, of either over- or underidentifying future danger and possibility of sex. In general, overattribution of danger and of sexual opportunity is more likely than underattribution; functionally, this reduces risk of failing to attend to danger or to find sexual partners. Seven types of transformation seem logically possible (Crittenden, 1997d); each of these can be identified in the discourse used in AAIs.

True and Erroneous Information

Both cognitive and affective transformations can be truly predictive of danger and safety or erroneously predictive. When they are truly predictive, danger or opportunity for sex is correctly identified and appropriate self-protective or sexual action can be taken. When they are erroneously predictive, an association is made on the basis of temporal order or context, but the association is spurious because there is no predictive relation between the conditions. In such cases, either cognitive beliefs are held that are irrational, but which, nevertheless, regulate behavior, or affect is mistakenly associated with contexts that are not dangerous or protective or with people who are not appropriate for sexual contact. Actions taken on the basis of erroneous information will usually be maladaptive. Thus, there can be *true* and *erroneous* transformations of cognitive and affective information.

Distorted Information

In addition, both cognition and affect can be distorted. Cognition is distorted when one aspect of a complex causal relation is emphasized to the exclusion of other aspects of the relation. In general, this means overstating a causal relation that, in fact, is only partly or sometimes true. For example, emphasizing the good qualities of a sometimes angry and hostile parent may increase a child's willingness to comply with parental demands and, thus, reduce the probability of self-endangering protest. In the DMM method for analyzing AAIs, these distortions are called idealization, exoneration, and self-responsibility (typical of speakers using a Type A strategy) and passive semantic thought, reductionist blaming thought, and rationalization (typical of speakers using a Type C strategy).

Affect is distorted when one feeling in a set of complex mixed feelings is exaggerated to the exclusion of the other feelings. For example, when an individual who feels angry, fearful, and desirous of comfort focuses only on the anger, the probability that the individual will attack and fight fearlessly is increased and the probability of flight or affection is decreased.

Splitting is the mental process that makes distortion possible, by omitting some of the information from processing. For Type A speakers, the splitting is between good and bad cognitions and tends to be static. For Type C speakers, the splitting is within negative affect (i.e., among desire for comfort, anger, and fear) and tends to be alternated, contingently upon the behavior of the other person. To conclude, there can be *distorted* transformations of cognition and affect and splitting underlies the process of distorting information.

Omitted Information

When one or the other sort of information proves not to be predictive or to be dangerous, the information may be discarded from further mental processing. This is *omitted* affect or cognition. For example, Type A individuals often discard their own feelings of anxiety, desire for comfort, anger, or fear and positive cognitions about themselves as danger-eliciting. Type C individuals often discard information about causal relations and predictable outcomes, thus, failing to discern complexly organized causal relations or their own contributions to unpleasant consequences.

False Information

Some information predicts the opposite of the apparent prediction. For example, some smiles cover anger and some statements of intention are lies. In these cases, the information is *false* and misleading. Some Type A speakers falsify negative affect, displaying, instead, false positive affect. Some Type C speakers falsify temporal predictions, thus misleading others about their future behavior.

Denied Information

Self-relevant information that speakers fear might be true (and which, if true, would require drastic reorganization of the speakers' representational process) can be *denied*. The information is perceived as threatening because it would force a reevaluation of the basic strategy, thus both undoing its strategic effectiveness and also causing emotional distress. Some Type A speakers deny all negative affect up to and including physical pain. Some Type C speakers deny their own role in causing dangerous outcomes. In both cases, denial is associated with extreme levels of endangerment (both physical and psychological and both aggressively abusive and abandoningly neglectful).

Delusional Information

The gaps left by information that is denied in high-numbered A and C strategies create discrepancies. When perceived, these either initiate corrective or *delusional* processes. Delusions are internally generated representations, the source of which is the self. However, they are not recognized as self-generated and, instead, are treated as real. The effect is to resolve the discrepancy elicited by denied information. Some Type A speakers construct delusional beliefs of being protected in the context of claiming to deserve punishment and denying responsibility of the other for harming the self. Affectively, they deny pain and delusionally claim pleasure that allows them to feel safe instead. This process is enhanced if sexual arousal accompanies the painful arousal and if they "invite" the inevitable. Some Type C speakers construct delusional affective representations that treat one set of feelings as absolute while the other is denied, for example, absolute anger and invulnerability in the context of denied fear and vulnerability. Cognitively, they deny participation of self to causality, which allows delusional plots of threat and revenge.

The seven transformations of cognition and affect lead to 14 forms of information about danger/safety and sexual possibility: true, erroneous, omitted, distorted, false, denied, and delusional affect and cognition. The DMM method of analyzing the AAI identifies all of these transformations in discourse. Further, it is proposed that compulsive Type A and obsessive Type C speakers use a greater variety of transformations and more extreme transformations than speakers using lower-numbered Ainsworth strategies. Such transformations are usually associated both with the experience of danger in early childhood and also risk for psychopathology in adulthood. In addition, it is proposed that different clinical disorders might display different patterns of transformation. Although some supporting data are offered in Chapter 15, the strength of the DMM approach lies in the specification of testable hypotheses.

MEMORY SYSTEMS AND DISPOSITIONAL REPRESENTATIONS

Recent work in cognition suggests that there are (at least) five memory systems that are crucial to how people resolve threats to safety: procedural memory, imaged (or perceptual) memory, semantic memory, episodic memory, and reflective integration memory (Tulving, 1995; see Figure 3.1). Each has both experimental and neurological support. A sixth memory system, connotative language, is proposed here.

Of these memory systems, procedural and imaged memory are similar in that they consist of implicit knowledge, do not require language, and are functional from birth on. Semantic memory and connotative language are similar in that they are verbal and have both implicit (i.e., preconscious) and explicit (i.e., consciously regulated) forms. Episodic memory is a verbal, occasion-based integration of temporal sequences, images, semantic understandings, and the language that brings the episode to life.

Working memory differs from the memory systems in not being a type of transformation, but rather the cortical process of integrating in-

Figure 3.1. Transformations of information: The organization of information and memory systems.

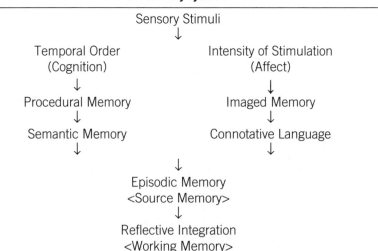

formation generated by other parts of the brain (Baddeley, 2009). Current understanding of the neurological processing that underlies memory suggests that only three to five bits of information can be held active at one time (Cowan, 2010) and that these, including representations of the self-in-context-now, determine which representation will be enacted (Klingberg, 2009). Working memory (and thus representation) is an active process in which past and present neural networks are joined to create dispositional representations (Damasio, 1994) that reflect neither past nor present experience with veridical accuracy. Such representations reflect our best predictions of the likely relation of self to context in the future. Working memory stands apart from the other systems as being entirely a process that is dependent upon the output of the other memory systems.

Procedural memory and imaged memory were not described by Bowlby. Nevertheless, because they function in the first months of life, they operate preconsciously and involve very rapid processing and are particularly relevant to cases of severe or self-threatening danger. Therefore, including them may be critical to the analysis of AAI transcripts of individuals who have experienced risk, especially risk occurring early in life. In constructing guidelines for employing these memory systems, aspects of the Main and Goldwyn (1984, 1994) method that reflect these systems have been assigned to them. For example, involving speech to the interviewer is discussed as an aspect of procedural memory. Each memory system is discussed in detail below. They are divided into two groups: implicit and explicit memory systems.

Implicit Memory Systems

The brain systems that support implicit memory are in place and functioning before those necessary for explicit memory. This is an advantage in that important aspects of experience can be learned from birth on and processing at all ages can occur far more rapidly than for explicit forms of knowledge. The drawback is that it can be very difficult to become aware of what one has learned implicitly, to predict how it will influence one's behavior, and to regulate that influence.

PROCEDURAL MEMORY

Procedural memory (Tulving, 1995) consists of preconscious, reflexive, and learned sensorimotor patterns of behavior, that is, schemata (Piaget, 1952). In Bruner's terms, it is "knowing how" (Bruner, 1972). In this method, it is described as implicit cognitive information. Procedures reflect what children and adults have learned to do to stay safe or what adults do to attract potential sexual partners. Most human behavior is procedural with only small bits becoming the focus of conscious thought and problem solving. As a consequence, procedures both reflect the predominant past experience of individuals and also their most probable future behavior. When conditions have been dangerous in predictable ways, children can develop procedural inhibitions or compulsions that function to increase safety. For example, when display of negative affect is punished, it may be inhibited; when it is rewarded, it is likely to occur more frequently. Rewarded affect may occur in three ways: (1) predictable reinforcement display of true feelings is associated with Type B classification; (2) predictable reinforcement of false positive affect is associated with the compulsive strategies (Types A4–6); and (3) intermittent, unpredictable positive reinforcement of distorted negative affect is associated with the coercive strategies (Type C).

Three sorts of procedures are of interest in discourse analysis of the AAI. Although the AAI was not constructed by George, Kaplan, and Main (1996) with the notion of eliciting procedural memory, in fact, it does so quite effectively in the form of patterns of managing discourse, spontaneous expression of affect during the AAI, and patterns of interactive behavior that are used with the interviewer (cf. the transference, Szajnberg & Crittenden, 1997).

IMAGED MEMORY

Imaged memory consists of perceptual images of past experiences (Schacter & Tulving, 1994), for example, the shrill sound of angry voices, the soothing rhythm of close holding and rocking. Recalled images often reflect contexts of safety or danger (e.g., a warm, soft bed or a dark, cold basement). Somatic images are bodily states associated with anxious arousal (e.g., lightheadedness, nausea, shortness of breath), or with comfort (e.g., a cuddly grandma). Images tend to reflect contextual information about conditions with higher than usual probability of danger/safety or sexual opportunity.

Images, particularly somatic images, function to make past events seem real, present, and immediate; thus, they create in the individual a tendency to respond to the (prior) situation associated with the image. They also have the effect of eliciting arousal, which itself feeds back into the limbic system, thus increasing arousal. Animated images (i.e., images that are acted out through dialogues or gestures) are even more effective at increasing speakers' arousal. Delusional images appear to function specifically to help speakers enter an affective state that they feel is essential to their own physical or psychological safety. That is, delusional images appear to be imagined (as opposed to recalled) images, which are presented in an arousing or animated way that activates neurological pathways in the same manner as experienced and recalled images. The difference is that, although the source of the information is the self, the image is erroneously identified as coming from outside of the self (see below for source memory). Images are particularly relevant to exposure to danger.

Explicit Memory Systems

SEMANTIC MEMORY

Both procedural memory and imaged memory are functional in infancy whereas semantic memory first develops in the second year of life. Semantic memory can be conceptualized as a generalized verbal understanding of the contingencies implied by procedural knowledge, that is, a verbal transformation of cognitive information. The prototypical form of semantic information is a when/then temporal statement transformed into an if/then causal statement where "if" refers to the preceding condition and "then" to the subsequent event, the consequence. Sometimes, however, abbreviated forms are used. For example, "You are a good boy" implies the causal relation "Because you are a good boy, you will do only good things." Such statements, of course, distort reality. The accurate conditional statement would be something like "Usually you are a good boy and I will praise and reward you, although sometimes you don't do as I expect, and you may be punished for that."

In addition, descriptive semantic statements are easily transformed into prescriptive semantic statements. In prescriptive statements, a "should," "ought to," or "must" verb form is used. For example, *"You shouldn't run into the street"*; *"You ought to clean up your room"*; or *"You must not lie."* Prescriptive statements are often used by parents, teachers, and other authority figures.

Preschool children are particularly vulnerable to distortions of semantic information because they are not yet able to comprehend more accurate and complex statements, and they cannot differentiate descriptive from prescriptive statements. Further, although older children are able to deduce their own semantic generalizations, preschool-aged children are not. Instead their generalizations are "borrowed" from their parents. When parents' statements do not reflect children's experience or when the statements are inaccurate (usually because the parent wants the child to believe something), children's emerging semantic representations of reality will be incongruent with their procedural and imaged understanding.

When children can articulate the discrepancy and when parents respond with empathy and assistance in resolving children's confusion, this maturational limitation becomes a pathway to growth. But frightened children do not ask such questions and some parents do not take children seriously or answer the questions honestly. This can result in semantic distortions that may both interfere with children's understanding and also affect the way they organize their behavior. In some cases, it results in idealization or exoneration (i.e., components of Type A functioning). A particular concern occurs when parents distort "descriptive" semantic statements about how things are into "prescriptive" semantic statements about how things ought to be, should be, or must be. When such prescriptions are applied to children as if they were descriptions, children almost always fail to meet the standard and find themselves to be bad (as opposed to recognizing that something they did was bad).

In other cases, children give up, considering semantic statements to be useless (because they are not sufficiently predictive). These children omit semantic information from further processing; in Main and Goldwyn's (1984, 1994) terms, they use "passive (semantic) thought." In some deceptively dangerous circumstances, children learn that true relations are often the opposite of what is stated verbally; they learn that semantic information can be false. Under the most threatening conditions, children cannot discern a connection between their own behavior and danger to themselves. This can lead to complete denial of cognitive information and possible substitution of the missing information with delusional information.

<h2 style="text-align:center">CONNOTATIVE LANGUAGE</h2>

Connotative language refers to the use of words to elicit affective states in listeners. Preschool-aged children are exposed to connotative language in the form of stories, songs, and rhymes, but they are not able to generate such language meaningfully until the school years and adolescence. Although connotative language has not been identified by cognitive psychologists as a memory system, it functions in parallel with semantic memory as the verbalized form of an implicit memory system, in this case imaged memory.

Connotative language typified by artificial or intellectualized discourse functions to down-regulate arousal by removing the self and feelings from the narration. This usage accentuates the denotative function of language and keeps both speaker and listener emotionally distant from the story being told. It is typical of Type A speakers.

Connotative language typified by evocative words and phrases, instead, generates feelings in listeners, through the use of onomatopoeia, juxtaposition, rhythm (particularly lulling rhythms and sharp stops), alliteration, metaphors, etc. This language lets the reader share the speaker's affective state. This usage is typical of Type C speakers.

Type B speakers combine denotative and evocative language into discourse that is able to convey both semantic meaning and emotional depth. The connotative qualities of language are used to clarify feeling without overcoming the cognitive/semantic meanings. The result is an efficient means to achieve the common goal that speaker and inter-viewer have negotiated: a clear story conveying personal meanings to an interested listener.

Episodic memory

Episodes consist of an integration of cognitive information about se-quences of events with affective information about the context and af-fective/somatic responses of the participants. Such integration requires that considerable information, generated through disparate parts of the brain (such as the sensory cortices, cerebellum, and limbic system), be held active at one moment in time with neural connections that con-verge, first, in the hippocampus where relational organization is con-structed and, finally, in the prefrontal cortex where action potentials are evaluated (see Crittenden, 1997c for a full set of citations). It should be noted that an episode is a transient construction that contains not only reactivation of neural networks that were active during the event itself, but also networks that represent the state of the self in the present. The latter influences the activation of the former, thus making episodic re-call inaccurate for the past but maximally relevant to the self in the present. The ability to construct episodes is not functional until about 3 years of age and even then it requires guidance by an attachment fig-ure. Where such guidance is not available, episodic recall may be im-paired.

Fully rendered episodes that integrate both temporal order and im-aged information are typical of Type B speakers. Sequential episodes that are "dry" of images and evocative language (i.e., that are more like scripts) are typical of A1 and A2 individuals, whereas affectively rous-ing and vivid episode fragments (perceptual images) are typical of Type C speakers.

Source memory

Source memory is a particular form of episodic memory, one that is es-sential for integration of the memory systems. It is recall of the precise source of information (Schacter, 1996). It tags all types of information with a code for the occasion when this information came to be one's own. Without this memory system, it can be difficult to evaluate the validity of information. Is this what I think now—or what I thought when I was younger? Was it your conclusion or mine? Did I read it in a scholarly book or a tabloid newspaper? Did it really happen or did I just think about doing it? Source memory permits information to be reconsidered and evaluated in terms of current conditions and implications for the self. Without source information, one basis for doubt and certainty is removed.

The implications of this are profound. Without sufficient doubt, too much is accepted as true. Without the confidence of certainty, nothing can be known to be true. Differentiating doubt and certainty is central to mental and behavioral organization. If one cannot distinguish authentically generated semantic conclusions from borrowed conclusions, that is, those learned from others, one loses one's own perspective. Knowing the source of semantic conclusions both permits assignment of information to others' perspectives (thus encouraging one to evaluate explicitly its relevance to the self) and also permits one to compare past conclusions and prior self-relevance with current understanding and desires or needs. If one cannot tell whose feelings are whose, it becomes impossible to do what is in one's own best interest and to organize one's behavior affectively. Similarly, being unable to recall time and place information in episodes prevents one from differentiating daydreams, imagined actions, wished-for or feared actions, and actual experiences. This makes delusional thought possible (Schacter, 1996).

Source memory is processed through the frontal lobes, which also manage temporal ordering. This more sophisticated form of cognitive information is not functional early in life and is applied only to explicitly known information. Its absence in preschool-aged children accounts for their susceptibility to false recall and acceptance of the statements of others as being truths for themselves. It is not until adolescence that source memory is fully functional. This makes children particularly vulnerable to distortions passed to them by trusted adults (see discussion in Schacter, 1996, pp. 123–129). As compared to the other memory systems, source memory is particularly vulnerable to distortion and error, particularly errors tied to truth and delusion (or confabulation, to use a less pejorative term) and to self-relevance. This, together with its late development, gives it the potential to be a prime contributor to severe psychopathology. That is, the inability to differentiate fantasy from reality and to establish self-awareness, self-identity, and self-relevance are key indicators of psychopathology.

Understanding the role of source memory in adults may require understanding something about their development in the school years. In school-aged children, the central concerns are (a) that adults not pass their own perspectives, biases, and experiences to children without clearly labeling their source as being outside the child and (b) that private inner sources that are not "true" in the outer world of behavior be accurately identified as dreams, daydreams, and wishes. It is noteworthy that children who talk out loud are more likely to identify themselves as the source than children who keep their thoughts in their minds (Giles, Gopnik and Heyman, 2002). Developmentally, it is important to note that preschool-aged children do not understand that their minds are private, that is, that others cannot know what they are thinking, and that this awareness is only beginning in young school-aged children. Given that troubled children are often isolated from both peers and trusted, supportive adults, that they may sleep or daydream more than other children, and that their wishes and fears are often of greater intensity and more discrepant with their experience than those of other children, there are particular risks that they will not be able to identify properly self-generated information as such. If misunderstandings are not corrected, there may be greater vulnerability to excessively rule-bound thinking or delusional thinking in adulthood.

INTEGRATION AND REFLECTIVE INTEGRATION

Making Meaning

The mind is a meaning-making organ. It seeks coherence, both internally and in relation to the context. Perception of discrepancy initiates integrative processing, with the end goal of reducing or eliminating discrepancy. Although many sorts of meaning can be generated, meanings associated with danger and sexual opportunity are critical to survival. That is, integration is not a luxury; it is a life-preserving process.

Reflective functioning is a type of integration that involves conscious thought without immediate action. It is often initiated by perception of discrepancy. In most cases, the reflective process reduces discrepancy by correcting errors in representation. Often this involves constructing a more complex and inclusive representation.

Processes versus Models

Attachment theory has tended to treat internal representational models as "things" that a person "has" and that "contain" information. Current neurophysiology conceptualizes representational models more nearly as *processes*. In Damasio's terms, each processing pathway in the brain generates information that implies a disposition for action or lack of action (Damasio, 1994). If processing were aborted before completion, the "strongest" dispositional representation active at that moment would regulate behavior. This representation could be procedural, imaged, semantic, connotative, or episodic. However, because semantic, connotative, and episodic representation require more extensive processing (and therefore more time), early termination of processing will result in a bias toward enactment of procedural and imaged dispositional representations.

Fully completed processing, on the other hand, permits conscious construction of carefully evaluated representations. These are likely to result in better adapted behavior. Sensory stimuli are repeatedly transformed in a branching network of parallel processing in which each pathway modifies the signal in a manner that clarifies some things, but at the same time generates bias or error with regard to other things (for example, the cognitive and affective transformations result in different sorts of information from the same sensory stimuli). Cortical integration refers to the process of analyzing inputs, attributing meanings, and organizing responses from the multiple transformations reaching the cortex (Schacter & Tulving, 1994).

Working integrative memory, on the other hand, is the live, on-line process of integrating information. It is real-time functioning, as opposed to recall of past integrative processes and their outcomes. In the terms of the AAI, it is metacognitive thought or active reflective functioning. The distinction between integrated conclusions and metacognitive thinking is crucial to differentiating unintegrated speakers who parrot back wise and integrated thoughts from integrated speakers who actively engaged in the lifelong process of drawing meaning from experience.

Association and Disassociation

Current thinking about cortical (integrative) processing suggests that it consists of two opposite functions. The prefrontal cortex holds information discretely, such that it can be compared and contrasted; that is, the prefrontal cortex focuses the mind. Part of the means by which this is accomplished is through inhibition of extraneous, tangential, or competing thought processes. The posterior cortex, on the other hand, performs the associative function, that is, connecting information to expand or generate meanings. The posterior cortex opens the mind to interactive interconnectivity, to an increase in the range of associated and eliciting cues and meanings. Part of the process by which this is accomplished is through disinhibition of thought. Together, these processes permit information to be classified, that is, to be clumped and separated, for efficient and productive access. Put another way, these opposing processes permit information, and the behavior derived from it, to be organized. Although both processes are essential, they must be coordinated strategically in order not to lead to chaos, to disorganization.

Together, the prefrontal and posterior cortexes promote both recognition of discrepancies in dispositional representations resulting from different processing pathways and also the generation of complex understandings and solutions based on associated and relevant information. In general, the longer the individual delays action (or the faster he or she processes information) and the more information he or she is able to keep neurologically active at once, the greater will be the extent of integration. More errors will be identified and more information will be available to correct the error and construct alternate hypotheses. The outcome will be an integrative, consciously considered, hierarchical, and conditional meta-model (Crittenden, 1990) of how to interpret and respond to current conditions. The outcome, in other words, will be a metacognition resulting from the mind's consideration of its own output. For example, making implicit procedural rules explicit in semantic memory requires the reflective "rational-emotive" process identified by Ellis (1973). Understanding the limits of this rule (and the conditions under which the limits pertain) is metacognitive.

The Effects of Exposure to Danger on Integration

Integration takes time. But, under dangerous circumstances, taking time can increase the danger. A rapid response is often needed. This creates a very basic cost/benefit problem. Rapid reflexive responses are self-protective but sometimes misguided; reflective responses are more accurate but may come too late to protect the self. This situation helps to explain the particular sorts of information-processing problems, and consequent behavior, observed in adults who have experienced danger, especially early and recurrent danger.

In some cases, however, even with sufficient time for reflection, the more accurate representation is terrorizing or beyond the intellectual capacity of the individual to accomplish. Especially for children, terror-izing representations (such as *"Your mother really hates you and wishes you were dead"*) need to be avoided to make daily life possible. In this case, the meaning-making function of the mind may "correct" the er-rors identified by discrepancy by denying accurate information and constructing delusions to cover the gap in reality.

ENCODING, REMEMBERING/FORGETTING, AND RETRIEVAL

Knowing is not as simple as having information and remembering is not as simple as accessing known information. This concluding section on information processing provides a quick overview of three proc-esses that are essential to making use of experience.

Encoding

There are two forms of encoding. The first occurs in working memory and it functions to increase the probability that the neurological path-way activated by an event will be reactivated in the future (i.e., that it will be retained for future recall). It should be stated very clearly that information is not retained as a discrete unit (a memory), like a card in a file drawer or a book in a library. To the contrary, the central nervous system retains only probabilities of the sequential firing of neurons within a distributed neural network. When these probabilities increase, information is more available for future recall. When they decrease, in-formation may be forgotten. Change in probability of future firing oc-curs at the synapse and consists of the enhanced or diminished release of neurotransmitters. This depends upon the intensity of the stimula-tion reaching the brain, that is, the emotional saliency of the event. Such long-term potentiation (LPT) constitutes a process-based form of en-coding.

The second form of encoding uses protein synthesis to generate ad-ditional synapses; this is a structurally based, more enduring form of memory consolidation. The generation of new synaptic contacts re-quires information to be elaborated. This can occur by simple repe-tition, by strategic effort, or by association. The elaborative process includes classifying the event categorically, associating it with other long-term memories, and assigning personal relevance to it. Elabora-tive encoding creates the advantages of greater efficiency of recall, greater meaning attribution (both in quantity and accuracy), and greater influence on future behavior. These, however, are also disadvantages. Greater efficiency means that new or competing approaches are less likely to be implemented. Greater meaning attribution tends to tie mental interpretations to fewer base experiences that are elicited by a wider range of cues. Greater influence on behavior means that some events will have disproportionate effects on individual functioning. When the event is recurrent and the elaboration is mature and balanced, this is an advantage. When the event is unlikely to recur or the elaboration immature, incomplete, or distorted, this may bias the individual toward maladaptive behavior. For example, "preventive" retelling of endangering experiences that are unlikely to recur may actually promote, rather than prevent, posttraumatic stress disorder (i.e., post-disaster retelling of experiences could cause iatrogenic disorder, Kenardy, 2000).

On the other hand, if information is not elaborated, it is recalled less frequently and with less detail. Further, fewer cues will elicit it. Type A speakers, in other words, may both recall information less easily than other speakers and also actually have fewer memories than other speakers.

To summarize, encoding consists of two processes. One is a relatively transient, passive, stimulus-dependent, and chemically mediated process of synapse enhancement, whereas the other is a structurally enduring, elaborative, strategic, and reflective process of synapse generation.

Remembering and Forgetting

Remembering and forgetting are complementary processes. Together, they impose order on the environment (Edelman, 1987). Forgetting irrelevant information is as necessary to thought as remembering relevant information. Forgetting is a form of mental pruning that deletes unneeded information to make space for new information, thus making mental functioning more efficient. Because failure to use synapses weakens them, forgetting occurs in direct relation to experienced need to know. This is obviously advantageous—except when important information is not activated through an inhibitory process. Under these conditions, information may be lost altogether as infrequently used synapses wither away and dendritic structures are adapted to other pathways. Without periodic firing, the probability of future firing (i.e., future recall), the range of cues that can elicit recall, and the wealth of recalled associations will be reduced or eliminated. In other words, not everything is remembered and not everything that is remembered is infinitely recoverable. Memories are reconstructed from their elaborations (Schacter, 1996). Without these, there is no recall. With a paucity of these, memory will be limited.

Retrieval

Retrieval is a temporary constellation of activity in different parts of the brain that join to create a representation, one that will never be precisely duplicated again. It is an emergent entity; that is, the past is not recalled. On the contrary, recall is a process of activating disparate neural networks. Some represent current states of activation (the state of self in the present); others are activated by a retrieval cue. The retrieval cue, however, is tied to encoding cues (Tulving, 1995). Retrieval cues activate pathways that have been activated in the past, that is, aspects of the remembered event, connecting them with presently active pathways to create the memory, as it is recalled on this specific occasion. This incomplete mixture of past and present is what the network "remembers." Thus, all recall is currently self-relevant. This process also implies that the manner of encoding determines what sorts of cues can elicit recall.

There are two types of retrieval: associative retrieval (automatic, state-dependent retrieval) and strategic retrieval (in which one deliberately searches through categories and logical associations). The retrieval environment, including interviewer or therapist, greatly affects which cues are presented, whether they tend to be strategic or associative, and whether they are matched, in terms of generality versus specificity, to the prior encoding and elaborative process that generated the potential to recall. This fluid, emergent quality of memory is both adaptive and distorting.

A potentially misleading aspect of the experience of remembering is the individual's certainty of recall. Confidence in one's memory is totally unrelated to actual veracity.

CONCLUSION

The AAI uses five aspects of information processing (cognitive and affective aspects of sensory stimuli, seven types of transformation, memory systems, integration, and encoding and retrieval) to guide both interviewing and the analysis of the interview. In the AAI, the speaker's history is co-constructed with an interviewer. The interviewer systematically probes each of the memory systems, using very general cues, cues of moderate specificity, and unique person-specific follow-up questions to maximize the possibility that the speaker will have access to relevant information. The coder of the interview examines the transcribed discourse, seeking (a) evidence of preferential reliance on cognitive or affective information, (b) distortions of information, (c) conflict in the content of representations drawn from different memory systems, and (d) evidence of the ability and willingness of the speaker to use the "on-line" relationship with the interviewer to examine self-relevant information. In the chapters to follow, these ideas are expanded to create a method of discourse analysis for the AAI.

Chapter 4

Constructs Used in the Discourse Analysis of the Adult Attachment Interview

CODING AND CLASSIFYING ADULT ATTACHMENT INTERVIEWS DEPENDS ON three sources of information: (1) childhood history of life events; (2) procedural, imaged, semantic, connotative and episodic dispositional representations and their integration; and (3) discourse markers that identify instances of transformation of information or discrepancy between memory systems.

HISTORY OF LIFE EVENTS/EXPERIENCE

Life events are important for understanding the psychological support and challenges faced by the speaker (a list of constructs is shown in Figure 4.1). It is in light of these that the speaker's behavioral adaptation and mental coherency can be evaluated. The following events, which are important, themselves do *not* determine classification, even when the events were experienced as traumatic.

Comfort

It is presumed that all parents "love" their children in some way; this construct refers to a specific affective way in which the love is experienced. Comforting parents are those who are described semantically

Figure 4.1. Constructs about history of life events/experience.

Comfort	Role reversal
Protection	Neglect
Danger	Performance
Rejection	Deception
Involvement	Sexuality

with at least some positive adjectives and for whom there are believable episodes of comforting behavior. In evaluating the comforting quality of the episodes, it is more important that the parent served a comforting function when the speaker was in distress or danger than that the parent provided basic caretaking (i.e., dressing, feeding) or that they were available for play or giving the children material objects. Consequently, the responses to the questions about illness, injury, and distress are important for evaluating this construct (in addition to any relevant adjectives). Speakers with comforting parents typically are classified as balanced (B).

Protection

Protective parents were protective and caring when their children were in danger. However, they may not have shared many positive times with their children, have been perceived as loving by the children, or supported their children emotionally. Nevertheless, when their children were physically endangered, they protected them. In addition, the parents were not a source of threat to the children (i.e., they did not attack, abandon, taunt, or fail to respond to their children, nor did they threaten these things). They may, however, have failed to attend to children's feelings when children were safe but uncomfortable, or they may have been so self-preoccupied or unpredictable that the children did not feel safe. Speakers with protective parents who were not perceived by their children as displaying comfort are often assigned to the low-numbered Type A (A1–2) and Type C (C1–2) patterns.

Danger

Danger is, of course, crucial. Whenever a child's physical or emotional health or safety is threatened, there is danger. This includes natural disasters, severe medical illnesses, parental unavailability for protection (for any reason), war, and so forth. It also includes parentally caused dangers such as spousal violence, divorce, child abuse, and so forth, and threats that are intentionally inflicted or that are not actively assuaged.

Not all danger results in distortions of thought, however. It is often critical to understand how the parent handled the event and whether any other person was available to support the child. Danger is associated with all classifications, but, in general, greater exposure to danger leads to greater probability of the high-numbered categories in the Dynamic-Maturational Model (DMM). Several common sorts of physically or psychologically dangerous conditions are listed below.

Rejection[1]

Rejection refers to parents who reject, or threaten to reject, children's attachment behavior. Although this includes rejection of the child, such an extreme response is not necessary for rejection. Indeed, most rejection is simply rejection of the child's display of *unnecessary* attachment behavior, for example, a child displaying fear when he or she is actually safe (such as during separations in the Strange Situation), crying when one's injury is being cared for, or seeking comfort when there is no danger. In more serious cases, all negative affect is rejected and, in the most threatening cases, the child is rejected physically (e.g., sending the child to live with relatives) or psychologically (e.g., telling a biological child that he or she was adopted or unwanted). Rejection is usually associated with the Type A classification, but may occur in an "earned" B.

Involvement[2]

Involving refers to parents who seek excessive closeness with their children. This can take various forms, each with different consequences for the children. In the simplest cases, the parent joins the child as though the parent were a member of the sibling subsystem. Such involvement often reflects a process of "affect contagion" in which the parent "catches" the child's distressed affect, thus, becoming distressed

1. This construct was introduced by Ainsworth (Ainsworth et al., 1978) and applied to the AAI by Main and Goldwyn (1984); it is applied without substantial change here.
2. This construct was introduced by Main and Goldwyn (1984, 1994), but is modified somewhat in the DMM method. Specifically, they treat involving and role reversal as the moderate and high ends of one dimension (involving/role reversal) in which the low end is the absence of both involvement and role reversal.

him- or herself and unable to provide appropriate care to the child. Involving parents often compete with their children for the role of child (i.e., the recipient of attention, caregiving, and comfort). Alternatively, one parent may draw the child into a triangulated parental subsystem and use the child in some form of negotiation between the parents. Usually, this is done in ways that are inexplicit to the child such that he or she finds it difficult to discern the causal conditions preceding parental behavior directed to the child. A third possibility is that the child is brought into the spousal subsystem as though the child were an adult romantic partner for the parent (i.e., spousification). In all cases, the boundaries between adult and child roles are violated.

When children are overly involved with their parents, they often feel anxious and uncomforted, experience mixed feeling states, have diffuse or blurred boundaries between self and attachment figures (as though unsure whose feeling is whose), and attempt to maintain excessive physical contact with the involving parent. When children find themselves in triangulated parental relationships, they often also experience causal confusion (i.e., lack of semantic accuracy and clarity). Children in sexualized parental relationships experience a wider range of confusion among affective states as well as misunderstandings regarding responsibility for the effects of their and their parents' behavior.

On the other hand, the child may experience role reversal; instead of competing with his or her parents, the child yields the child role and functions as a caregiver to the parent; in the DMM method, this pattern is associated with Type A speakers and is discussed below. Speakers with involving parents are typically classified as Type C, although, in some cases, the speakers are Type A and role reversing (see A3 below) or are "earned" Bs.

Role Reversal[3]

Role reversal refers to situations in which the speaker, as a child, had cared for the parent as though the parent were the child and the speaker were the parent. This is most crucial when the speaker was endangered or needed comfort and protection, but instead provided these to the parent. Role reversal is differentiated from both involving (in which parent and child share and compete for the child role) and also from

---

3. This construct was introduced by Main and Goldwyn (1984, 1994), but is modified somewhat in the DMM method. Specifically, they treat involving and role reversal as the moderate and high ends of one dimension (involving/role reversal) in which the low end is the absence of both involvement and role reversal.

parentification (in which the child acts like a parent to younger siblings, but not to the parent, who retains the adult role.) Systemically, role reversal involves rigidity of hierarchical role boundaries, that is, there is a boundary between the parent and child roles but a reversal of who functions in each role. Psychologically, role-reversing children inhibit their own feelings, display the (false) nurturant affect that their parents desire, and obtain the benefit of some parental attention by doing this. This pattern is often associated with either incompetent, childlike parents (i.e., feigned helpless [C4] parents) or parental neglect or depression (i.e., Type A parents). In either case, the childhood history is usually consistent with the child having displayed the preschool pattern of compulsive caregiving (A3).[4] Providing physical care for incapacitated parents who, nevertheless, retain the adult role psychologically, that is, they remain in authority and provide comfort to the child, is not role reversal. "Earned" Bs may have been role-reversing children.

Neglect[5]

Neglecting parents are psychologically distant from their children and, thus, unaware of, and inattentive to, their children's needs. Parents who retreat from the family into excessive work are often neglecting, as are parents who are depressed. Physical neglect, especially under conditions of poverty, is much less critical to the construct of neglect than cases in which the child seems not to have been identified by the parents as needing protection. Most speakers with neglectful parents are classified as Type A on the AAI, although, again, reorganization can lead to classification as a B.

Performance[6]

Pressure to perform is important when parents demand excessively high performance (of any sort, including scholarly achievement, athletic success, creative accomplishment, compliance, caregiving, atten-

4. According to Main and Goldwyn (1984, 1994), role reversal is usually associated with the Type C pattern; in DMM-AAIs, however, a history of role reversal is usually associated with Type A discourse and procedural evidence of ongoing role reversal (i.e., A3).
5. This construct was introduced by Ainsworth (Ainsworth et al., 1978) and applied to the AAI by Main and Goldwyn (1984); it is applied without substantial change here.
6. This construct was introduced by Main and Goldwyn (1984, 1994), but is modified somewhat in the DMM method.

tion, dress or appearance, cleanliness, or independence) in order to accept and love the child or in order not to harm the child.[7] In other samples, however, children feel compelled to satisfy parents in other ways. Compulsive overachievement can be differentiated from (desirable and adaptive) high achievement when performance is tied to parental demands, threats, or earning love; little personal satisfaction is gained from achievement; other aspects of development are limited in order to permit the focusing of effort on achievement; and the individual always has future goals that must be met while successful achievement of current goals is disparaged. Compulsive behaviors can be identified by their association with danger and with discourse that is spoken (procedurally) from the parent's perspective. Pressure to perform is usually associated with the Type A classification, specifically the compulsive performance classification, A4-. Again, reorganization can lead to a less extreme classification or to a B.

Deception

Deception or trickery, especially when combined with danger, is a critical childhood event that is often associated with later psychopathology. In mild cases, it involves misleading children regarding temporal contingencies. An example is when parents tell children that they will be rewarded or punished in order to elicit desired behavior, but parents repeatedly fail to fulfill the bribe or threat. In more dangerous cases, it involves leading a child to feel comfortable and then attacking, physically or psychologically. Deception and trickery are associated with the Type C classifications, specifically the C3–8 classifications. Bs, of course, can have any history.

Sexuality

Sexuality is important when it is intruded unnecessarily into discussions of other topics (especially when this occurs early in the interview) and when it becomes thematic across responses. It is also critical to note whether sexuality is frequently associated with anxiety or comfort. Speakers who dwell on sexuality or who sexualize nonsexual top-

7. In Main and Goldwyn's method (1984, 1994), this is "pressure to achieve." Their narrower construction probably reflects the middle-class sample used to develop the AAI.

ics are often assigned to the high-numbered patterns, particularly A5 and C6.

Although this list covers many important aspects of physical and psychological danger, it should not be presumed to be complete. Danger and protection are the key constructs that are central to human relationships.

DISCOURSE AND ASSOCIATED MEMORY SYSTEMS

The Modified Adult Attachment Interview (Crittenden, 2007) can assess procedural, imaged, semantic, connotative, episodic, and integrative memory. It collects evidence from procedural memory in the discourse construction, in the nonverbal expression of affect, and in the dialectic process with the interviewer. Also, the modified interview often elicits imaged memories in response to probes of other memory systems. Each memory system is addressed systematically in the interview, so that coders can make comparisons among them. Each memory system can be evaluated independently, with discrepancies among memory systems providing the clearest guide to the speaker's mental functioning.

Procedural Memory

Procedurally, a *balanced speaker's* discourse has ordinary, *nontransforming dysfluence* and is relatively clear and easy to follow. Expressed nonverbal affect is generally positive and changes according to the topic discussed. Type B speakers engage with the interviewer in a *cooperative* manner. This includes taking the listener's perspective and providing the information necessary to make the story comprehensible while, nevertheless, telling the story from one's own perspective.

Type A speakers use *distancing* discourse, which focuses on temporal clarity and distances the self from their negative feelings. They inhibit the display of negative feelings, substitute *false positive affect, or deny feeling negative affect.* They tend to attribute too much power to the interviewer; as a consequence, they may withhold parts of the story that they do not want to discuss, thus cutting the interviewer off by being too concise (or even silent). Alternatively, they may anticipate and comply with the needs, demands, and judgments of the interviewer. In this case, they may try to soothe and comfort the interviewer (or apologize too much for their story); comply excessively with precise, minute, or unarticulated demands (five descriptive words or even six!); or provide negative self-evaluations before the interviewer could do so.

Type C speakers use *involving* discourse, which focuses on their negative feelings and confuses temporal order, people, and places. They express their negative feelings emphatically. They also tend to seek the support of interviewers by involving them in the telling of the story. Sometimes this includes presuming that the speaker and interviewer know the same things (i.e., share a mind) whereas, in other cases, it involves seeking the agreement of the interviewer or even the interviewer's guidance. In the more extreme cases, it involves seeking complicity with the interviewer in long-standing disputes with family members; complicity may be sought overtly or covertly, that is, the interviewer may be seduced into allying with the speaker against the speaker's family. In the most extreme cases, the speaker behaves as though presuming that the interviewer were in complicity with others (for example, the authorities or the speaker's parents).

Imaged Memory

In terms of images, *balanced speakers* integrate lively, fresh images into their episodes.

Type A speakers either eliminate them (A1) or provide them but as unconnected to the self and unique to the context, such that the image appears to represent the speaker's unacknowledged (and unintegrated) affect (all other Type A speakers). Images of comforting places are often substituted for discussions of attachment figures and comfort from attachment figures; images of discomfort are displaced or disembodied, that is, not associated with the self.

Type C speakers tend to use many images and to use them to clarify one of their mixed feelings. The images are associated with the self but decontextualized, that is, they seem to "live" independently of their source in time and space. These images frequently dominate other memory systems such that few complete episodes are given (i.e., temporal order, particularly causal events and their outcomes, is often missing) and semantic statements are decomposed into images of specific occasions.

Semantic Memory[8]

Semantically, *balanced speakers* give qualified evaluations that sometimes contain

- if/then (or if/when) contingencies (e.g., "If he was sober, he was generous, but sometimes when he was drunk, he was violent");
- multiple causal factors;
- differentiation of temporal order from causation from responsibility.

For example, with regard to the last of these, the speaker's action as an infant may have caused (temporally preceded in a causal manner) a bad event, but the infant is not responsible for others' wrong actions. Individuals using a Type B strategy recognize this. Thus, responsibility is distributed with regard to maturity (children are not responsible for adults' actions), power/hierarchy (truly powerless people are not responsible for the actions of powerful people), and knowledge (what was known by the individual when action was taken). However, because maturity is a changing variable across childhood (i.e., infants are not responsible at all, children bear some responsibility, and adolescents more), balance must be interpreted in age-appropriate ways.

Type A speakers tend to offer unqualified semantic statements that reference the good/bad qualities of individuals (including the self) in relatively stark and uncompromising ways (see Figure 4.2). In particular, they confuse causation with responsibility and in the very high-numbered As, they confuse temporal order with both causation and responsibility. Thus, in the As, there is a gradation of assignment of responsibility to self and others.

Type C speakers use the inverse of the Type A process of splitting responsibility and find *others* more responsible than themselves (see Figure 4.3). Put another way, Type C speakers account for the child's lack of responsibility as a function of immaturity, powerlessness, and lack of knowledge, but they carry this forward unchanged into later life, including the present. Low-numbered, that is, almost balanced, Type C speakers generally fail to make semantic statements, do so with only

---

8. This construct was introduced by Bowlby and applied to the AAI by Main and Goldwyn (1984, 1994); it is used without substantial change here.

Figure 4.2. Self-responsibility among Type A speakers.

A1–2   There is no problem, so I don't have to decide about responsibility (i.e., idealization).

A3–4   There is a problem and my attachment figure caused it, but, for these (stated) reasons, he or she is not responsible (i.e., exoneration). Furthermore, my own behavior can prevent it; therefore, there is no reason to blame my attachment figure and I must accept responsibility for the outcomes of my behavior.

A5–6   There is a problem and, because my act preceded it or I knew it would happen, I am either responsible for failing to prevent it (i.e., self-responsibility) or I sought this (bad) thing (i.e., masochism). Furthermore, because my acts precipitated my attachment figure's response, I bear responsibility for his or her behavior as well.

A7–8   There is a problem and it is myself; it is what and how I am. Any relief from this must be provided by others because I cannot understand what or how I am.

Figure 4.3. Lack of self-responsibility in Type C.

C1–2   These events aren't ordered meaningfully and, therefore, don't lead to any conclusion, so I don't have to assign responsibility (i.e., passive semantic thought).

C3–6   Bad things happened and, because I was young, powerless, or unknowing, my attachment figures are responsible (i.e., reductionist blaming thought).

C3/C5 I'm strong, they can't hurt me; I'll get back at them.

C4/C6 I'm weak. Someone must rescue me. (Both perspectives are usually implied, that is, false strength/anger hides weakness and vice versa.)

C7–8   Bad things happened and, because I was hurt by them, I am a victim and anyone else might be responsible, except me (i.e., denial of cognition).

great hesitation, often nullify previously made semantic statements (or make them vague to the point of meaninglessness), or provide conflicting and unintegrated semantic statements (oscillations in judgment). Some high-numbered speakers so exaggerate small aspects of the truth or deny critical information about the self's contributions as to generate misleading conclusions.

Thus, in the Cs, there is the reverse gradation.

Connotative Language

Although connotative language has not been identified by cognitive psychologists as a memory system, it is a logical extension of a memory systems approach to transformations of sensory stimulation to create increasingly sophisticated and precise forms of representation. Connotative language, as used here, reflects a verbalized form of imaged memory. It is the logical contrast to semantic memory being the verbalized extension of procedural memory and consists of nonverbal qualities of speech and word choice and combination. The components of connotative language include rhythm, rhyme, alliteration, onomatopoeia, hyperbole, parallel structure, simile, metaphor, symbolism, irony, sarcasm, and so forth. Metaphor and symbolism provide particular issues in interpretation. In the Dynamic-Maturational Model, the meanings of these must be defined by the speaker (i.e., use of universally understood metaphors cannot be attributed to speakers in the AAI). The use of connotative language can both illuminate and obscure meaning.

Artificial or intellectualized discourse removes the self and feelings from the discourse. It also removes all arousing elements from linguistic constructions, leaving a neutrality of presentation that focuses all attention on the content. To do this, it uses many of the distancing features of Type A discourse but does so without (necessarily) committing errors of syntax or thought. Artificial discourse excludes listeners from knowledge of the speaker's affective state, preferences, or personal perspectives and biases and elicits no feelings in them. Most scientific communication uses this form of linguistic discourse.

Evocative language is the opposite of artificial discourse. It includes strongly evocative words (e.g. *"whisked," "strangled," "horrific," "tucked in"*) as well as numerous literary devices, such as alliteration, onomatopoetic words, repetitions that reflect the activity itself (e.g., *"moving and moving and moving"*), rhyming, metaphor, and simile, among others, to generate feeling in listeners. Put another way, evocative language creates an image in the mind of listeners and may, in addition, elicit feelings in the listener. This enables the listener to experience the speaker's perspective. Evocative language is typically used by Type C speakers.

Type B speakers combine both sorts of language into discourse that is both clear and lively. The moderate use of both analytical language and evocative language permits listeners to both focus on the content of what the speaker has said and also share an empathic understanding of the speaker's affective state. If in addition, the speaker can articulate explicitly his or her own biases and self-relevant meanings, listeners are best able to understand the speaker's perspective, differentiate it from his or her own, and negotiate a compromise between these. This, of course, requires high levels of reflective, integrative thought on the part of the speaker. Such thought is fostered by the moderate use of both forms of linguistic communication.

In general, low-numbered A and C speakers use connotative language sparingly and it functions specifically to add meaning to the communicative process. High-numbered pattern speakers, on the other hand, depend heavily on connotative language to replace denotative meanings and, in the highest numbered patterns, to obscure meaning.

Episodic Memory[9]

Episodically, *balanced speakers* provide episodes that have both cognitive information (temporal order, initial events and their outcomes, and causal clarity) and affective information (statements about feeling, lively images).

Type A speakers vary from claiming that they are unable to remember episodes and so can provide none (A1), to constructing episodes through semantic reasoning (A1–2), cutting episodes off before unpleasant outcomes occur (A2), recalling negative episodes but telling them from the attachment figure's perspective (A3–6), and distorting episodes to omit information that would permit assignment of some responsibility to attachment figures.

Type C speakers freely speak of affectively rousing episodes, including negative episodes, but they seem more concerned with how they felt than with what happened; in addition, they ramble through par-

---

9. This construct was introduced by Bowlby and applied to the AAI by Main and Goldwyn (1984, 1994); it is used without substantial change here.

tially told episodes without apparent order. Underlying their wandering speech, however, is a pattern of cutting directly to the affective climax (the portion most likely to elicit cut-offs from Type A speakers) without attention to temporal or causal sequence. In very high-numbered pattern Type C speakers, the temporal order is accurate, but with such flagrant omissions of information that the causal relations are falsified, that is, the self appears to be an innocent victim when the self is actually responsible for threat to others.

Reflective Integration[10]

Integratively, *balanced speakers* use working memory to consider together all of the transformations of information. They focus on discrepancies and use these to identify and correct transformed information, thus generating new and more judicious understandings. A particularly important cortical function is to apply new integrative possibilities and new information to the interpretation of past experience, so as to construct more accurate expectations regarding future events. Such integration can enable balanced speakers to understand and forgive parental behavior that was hurtful in the past. It is important, however, that speakers both recognize the validity of the new perspective and also not deny the truth of their childhood experience.

Type A speakers more often use optimistic platitudes or lack of interest to avoid integrative thinking. Moreover, they fail to note when the information that they provided semantically fails to match that which they provided in episodes or images. When new abilities or information enable them to explain parental behavior, they tend to deny their childhood perspective or to blame themselves for "selfish" feelings.

Type C speakers, on the other hand, give the appearance of understanding by using psychological jargon and conclusions that are "borrowed" from books, television, and other people but fail to note that they have not really addressed the questions asked, that they have violated the boundaries of time, place, or person, or that they have mixed feelings about a complex reality. Psychological jargon, in particular, is used to "explain" what it only "describes." Thus, only balanced speakers show congruence (or the ability to achieve congruence) between

---

10. This construct was introduced by Main and Goldwyn (1984, 1994), but is modified somewhat in the DMM method.

information processed in different ways, that is, in different memory systems.

DISCOURSE CHARACTERISTICS AND PATTERNS OF ATTACHMENT

Dysfluency of speech marks points where speakers have integrative problems. Often these reflect competing thoughts or feelings. Rather than proposing that dysfluencies have specific meaning, it is proposed here that they simply indicate points of mental discrepancy. The discrepancy may be between what the speaker is willing to think, feel, or remember and what he or she actually thinks, feels, and remembers or between what was always thought and what seems true now. The former is likely to result in a defensive process, whereas the latter is more likely to result in a fresh answer, possibly even a new insight, a metacognition. Thus, dysfluencies mark points at which the mind is struggling between (a) differing sources of information, (b) previous perspectives and current ones, (c) incompatible transformations of information, and (d) implementing a defense and discovering a truth.

Dysfluencies occur more often in the AAI than in other interviews because the questions are unexpected, challenging, and affectively arousing. The coder must evaluate each dysfluency in terms of whether it hides information or, ultimately, makes important information available. This evaluation involves considering the morphology of the dysfluency (e.g., an omitted word, a stutter, a tense change in the verb); the context of the dysfluency (especially whether it is associated with danger); the content and nature of any omitted information (e.g., imaged, semantic, episodic); and the speaker's pattern of using this and other dysfluencies throughout the interview. The final decision regarding how to interpret a given dysfluency is determined by the patterning of discourse behavior, with priority given to psychological clarity of thought around danger. The major types of dysfluency described by Main and Goldwyn (1984, 1994) are retained in the method offered here. The interpretation of any given dysfluency is, however, determined by its function and not by its morphology. Consequently, in the DMM method, dysfluencies are not rated (i.e., measured); rather, they are evaluated (i.e., assessed qualitatively) with regard to frequency, function, circumstance, and consistency of use.

Several discourse markers are described below. They are organized by strategy and, within strategy, by memory system (also see Figure 4.4). Further, mild transformations are described prior to severe ones. In all cases, it should be remembered that the presence of a single instance of dysfluence does not determine the overall pattern, that use of transformations around danger is more important than at other times, that there will necessarily be disagreements of category at the border between categories, and that there is variability (sometimes important variability) within patterns.

Discourse Characteristics Typical of the Type B Strategy

PROCEDURAL MEMORY

1. Discourse. *Nontransforming dysfluency* occurs in the speech of all speakers and consists of such things as stutters, restarts, hesitations, and mistaken words that do not reflect underlying transformations of meaning. Put another way, these dysfluencies do not distort or hide information. Indeed, they often result in a clearer presentation of information as though, while speaking, the speaker found a better way to convey the meaning.

2. Display of affect. *Appropriate nonverbal affect* is affect of all sorts (such as positive, negative, humorous) that is consistent with the content of the speaker's words. Balanced speakers are often aware of the expressive and communicative functions of their affect.

3. Relationship with the interviewer. A *cooperative relationship with the interviewer*[11] is one in which the speaker attends to and addresses the questions posed by the interviewer while concurrently fitting these questions into an awareness of important issues in his or her history and guiding the interviewer toward discussion of these.

IMAGED MEMORY

Fresh and integrated images[12] are used to illustrate the context of events and convey their personal meaning to the speaker. Although they may

11. This construct was introduced by Bowlby and applied in a limited form to the AAI by Main and Goldwyn (1984, 1994); it is applied with considerable expansion here.
12. This construct was introduced by Main and Goldwyn (1984, 1994), but is modified somewhat in the DMM method.

Figure 4.4. DMM-AAI discourse constructs.

	Type B	Type A	Type C
Procedural memory (discourse)	Nontransforming dysfluency	Distancing discourse	Involving discourse Involving anger Involving fear
Procedural memory (expression of affect)	Appropriate nonverbal affect	Disparaging humor Omitted true negative affect False positive affect Denied negative affect and physical pain	Disarming affect Mocking/gotcha! humor Arousing nonverbal affect Distorted positive affect Cold or sadistically cruel affect
Procedural memory (relationship with the interviewer)	Cooperative	Neutral Analytical Deference to others	Involving Confronting/collusive Appealing/submissive Parrying Seductive Intimidating/spooky
Imaged memory	Fresh and integrated images	Omitted images Displaced images Unconnected images Obliquely connected images Delusionally protective images Delusionally punitive images	Intense images Animated images (of anger, fear or desire for comfort) Generalized images Delusionally threatening images

(continued)

Figure 4.4. Continued.

	Type B	Type A	Type C
Semantic memory	Differentiated general-izations	Idealization Exoneration Self-responsibility Misattribution of intent Non-agency	Passive semantic thought Idealized expectations about the future Reductionist blaming thought Derogation Person-defined negative meaning Misattribution of causality False cognition Denial of responsibility
Connotative language	Spontaneous, lively discourse	Artificial language	Evocative language
Episodic memory	Complete episodes Credible evidence	Cut-off or opposite episodes Lack of recall of positive episodic experience Displaced episodes (including displaced negative affect) Parental perspective Distorted guilt Delusional idealization External reference	Blurred or circular episodes Lack of a negative episode Fragmented episodes Negative episode but without harmful effects on the self Triangulated episodes False innocence/blame Delusional revenge
Reflective integration	Reflective functioning Metacognition	Omitted integration Platitudes Failed metacognitions Inconclusive metacognitions	Omitted integration Pseudoreflections Rationalization Skillful misleading

have been used before, they are not simply familiar clichés. Further, their meaning is clear to the speaker (i.e., they are not dissociated from the event or the speaker). Balanced speakers associated the image with both the self and with the context and use this information to select when to apply the meaning for the self to future experiences of the self.

SEMANTIC MEMORY

Differentiated generalizations refer to complex semantic conclusions that account for variation in person, context, and time (i.e., they are conditional); for interactive effects; and for relationship-relevant distinctions. That is, they are semantic statements that are qualified in psychologically sound ways. These range from the relatively crisp, somewhat overgeneralized accounts that distance the speaker from the details of difficult experiences (without distorting the nature of the experience), which are typical of B1–2 speakers, to the somewhat more wordy, undergeneralized narratives that are more occasion-specific (but without losing the focus of how this sort of event recurred), which are typical of B4–5 speakers.

CONNOTATIVE LANGUAGE

Spontaneous, lively discourse is a balanced mix of analytical (i.e., a reality-based form of artificial language) and evocative language that engages listeners without capturing them. It enables listeners (and speakers) to both participate in recall of experience and think about the experience.

EPISODIC MEMORY

Complete episodes[13] address the questions asked and have initiating, developing, and concluding conditions, together with the speaker's affective response to the experience, that is, they contain an integration of affect and cognition. Often, in addition, there is overt awareness that the different participants probably saw the same events differently or that the speaker's perspective has changed over time.

---

13. This construct was introduced by Main and Goldwyn (1984, 1994); it is applied without substantial change here.

Credible evidence refers to evidence offered by the speaker that may not be a full episode but that provides credible evidence that the event in question is recalled personally by the speaker. Credible evidence provides evidence of an occurrence at a specific time and/or place; is unique to the speaker, that is, it is not a common experience for most children or would not be told precisely this way by other people; contains events with a temporal order (even if the order is distorted or confused) or contains images or evocative language that are specific to the situation (phrases that are common in the culture are not to be treated as personal images or evocative language); and is offered spontaneously, that is, details that must be dragged out of the speaker are treated with greater skepticism than details that are offered spontaneously. In addition, credible evidence is self-relevant and, when it is about an attachment figure, it is also other-relevant.

REFLECTIVE INTEGRATION

Reflective functioning refers both to spontaneous statements and to the answers to the integrative questions that describe the motivations, organization, and the consequences of behavior. This concept was introduced by Fonagy et al. (1996). Reflective statements include making astute psychological distinctions. To be reflective, they must account for both cognitive and affective information, although the speaker may emphasize one or the other. B1–2 speakers tend to emphasize cognition whereas B4–5 speakers emphasize affect. Further, they must account for both the perspectives of others and the speaker's perspective, including acknowledging differences in these.

Metacognition[14] is a form of cortical functioning that involves conscious examination of the process and products of mental functioning. The outcome—thought about thinking or self-reflective thought—is metacognition. Metacognitive thought is often elicited by discrepancy, which itself is often indicated by dysfluency. Thus, dysfluency provides the alert mind with the opportunity to identify, examine, and possibly resolve dilemmas. Metacognitions, at their best, approach wisdom by enabling the individual to place his or her unique experience in the whole of human possibility. Thus, metacognitions indicate an understanding of the complexity of life processes that serves as a balanced

---

14. This construct was introduced by Main and Goldwyn (1984, 1994); it is applied without substantial change here.

guide to behavior. (The alternatives are simplification or incomprehensible complexity.) Metacognition is associated with the balanced pattern, especially the "earned" form of the pattern.

Discourse Constructs Typical of the Type A Strategy

PROCEDURAL MEMORY

1. Discourse. *Distancing*[15] refers to linguistic constructions that remove the self from dangerous circumstances and from feelings of anger, fear, and desire for comfort when these are directed toward attachment figures. Put another way, distancing creates artificially rigid boundaries in time (between past and present), between persons, and between dangerous and safe places. Distancing is frequently indicated by removal of first-person pronouns (for example, deleting "I" from sentences about the self, using instead third-person indefinite constructions) or by substituting impersonal pronouns for personal ones (for example, saying "the" parents rather than "my" parents). Often, there is excessive use of the past tense, as though childhood attachments were not ongoing relationships. Distancing of the self and the self's negative affects is associated with the Type A classification. Type C speakers often use distancing speech with regard to the split-off and denied affect. They may also dismiss others' affect. These characteristics are most noticeable in the high-numbered Type C patterns (C5–8).

2. Expression of affect. *Disparaging humor* reduces the value of the self or the meaning of harm to the self without attempting to elicit sympathy or rescue from the listener (e.g., small nervous or bitter laughs).

Omitted true negative affect is usually signaled by silence or by a pattern of unintelligible words spoken too softly to be discerned. Such silence and low-volume speech tend to occur when the self is being discussed, particularly when the self was endangered or uncomfortable. The critical feature to interpretation is identification of a pattern in the dysfluence.

False positive affect refers to the speaker's use of inappropriate positive affect at times when negative affect would be more appropriate, particularly when danger is discussed. In AAI transcriptions, false affect is usually noted in parenthetical statements, for example, notes

15. This construct was introduced by Main and Goldwyn (1984, 1994); it is applied without substantial change here.

that the speaker laughed. A pattern of inappropriate laughter, combined with omission of anger, fear, and desire for comfort, is indicative of false affect and associated with the Type A classification, particularly the compulsive classifications.

Denial of negative affect and physical pain refers to the absence of arousal and expression of affect when the event being described necessarily involves intense distress or pain. This can be coupled with *delusional comfort*.

3. Relationship with the interviewer. A *neutral relationship with the interviewer* is one in which the speaker avoids lengthy or thoughtful exchanges with the interviewer by giving excessively brief and noncooperative answers that close the discussion and preclude follow-up questions.

An *analytical relationship with the interviewer* is one in which the speaker remains distant from the self and speaks from the perspective of others, including both the parents (i.e., a parental perspective) and also therapist/interviewers (i.e., an implied "professional" association with the interviewer). The self, especially the childhood self, is treated as an object of inquiry that is viewed from a great distance (as opposed to being treated as a precious and integral part of one's adult self).

Deference to others refers to speakers who are largely without a personal perspective of any kind. That is, they do not have their own perspective, and they do not take on others' perspectives as their own (i.e., they are not analytical with regard to using a parental or therapist's perspective).

IMAGED MEMORY

Omitted images are implicit in dry descriptions, that is, the speaker provides image-free descriptions of affect-inducing events.

Displaced images are images of comfort or threat that are attributed to the context, that is, they are usually images of place or location.

Unconnected images, on the other hand, tend to occur in the discourse of compulsive Type A speakers who (a) experienced affect-arousing events (usually dangerous events), (b) say little or nothing about their own feelings in the interview, and (c) describe aspects of the context in startlingly vivid, intrusive, and recurrent images. The images are not associated with the self and overassociated with context and, therefore, they cannot be interpreted or used to predict other dangerous or safe circumstances. They are often intruded into the discourse and frequently substitute for discussion of the attachment figure (e.g., the speaker describes his house rather than his mother). On the other hand, unconnected images are precisely tied to the event or context in which they were experienced. Their function is to retain information about context and the speaker's feelings without focusing the speaker's mind upon the meaning for the self of the experience; their drawback is that, by being so precisely tied to particular circumstances, they are not easily used to generate predictions relevant to the self in other circumstances. The effect is to under-identify dangerous circumstances.

Obliquely connected images contain specific words or fragments of images that are repeated in other parts of the transcript (without a full image being carried forward and without the speaker's awareness of the connection), providing a thread of connecting language that gives alternate meanings (usually self-threatening meanings) to the obliquely tied-together sections. The connection is often marked by the unusualness of the connecting word or phrase in the nonimaged context. Comfort, pain, and sexuality are very often the topics of these images. If the speaker could associate the image with the self and free it a bit from context, the protective and predictive meanings of feelings could become useful information to the speaker.

Delusionally protective images are explanations for dangerous events that involve inaccurate presumptions of a protective figure who supports the self (often a harmful attachment figure, i.e., the "hostage syndrome," or a personal God, or spirits of some sort). That is, they are images of a positive sort that represent a form of comfort or protection that not only was not available to the speaker, but also could not have been available (i.e., it is impossible and, therefore, delusional). They are functionally coupled with the denial of negative affective information. Such images tend to be associated with the A7 pattern.

Delusionally punitive images are imaged versions of the punitive contingencies that the person anticipates (but that did not and could not occur). As such, they motivate obedience in the absence of obedience cues and are protective because the punishment administered by the self motivates safe behavior without incurring the risk of real punishment. Delusionally punitive images are person-specific and refer to an attachment figure (or an attachment figure substitute such as God) who accuses and punishes the speaker for acts of which the actual attachment figure would not approve. These images fill the gap left by the denied negative affective information about the impact of negative events on the self. This is the irrational extension of the compulsive compliant pattern.

<h2 style="text-align:center">SEMANTIC MEMORY</h2>

Idealization[16] is defined as describing *past* relationships in very positive terms when (a) the evidence better supports a negative description or (b) no supportive evidence is offered. Casting an ordinary past in a somewhat more favorable light is not idealization. Often idealization is marked by words such as "very, very" or "really"; in other cases, clichés are used (e.g., *"He walked on water"*). Because of the split nature of good and bad among idealizing speakers, when parents are idealized the self is generally derogated, that is, seen as negative, responsible for relationship problems, or shameful. Idealization uses distancing discourse and is associated with the low-numbered Type A patterns (A1–2).

Exoneration involves acknowledging and excusing parents' inadequacies by taking their perspectives and relinquishing one's own. It is the latter, the overlooking of the child's pain and the adult's sorrow, that differentiates exoneration from forgiveness and resolution. Often this is accomplished by blaming the self for difficulties in the relationship. That is, the joint contribution from parent and child to the relationship is distorted such that the child (i.e., the speaker) bears all responsibility for shortcomings. Exoneration uses distancing discourse and is associated with the compulsive Type A patterns A3–6.

Self-responsibility refers to an overattribution of responsibility to the self. These are errors of thought in which the speaker presumes that temporal order is identical to causation, which, in turn, results in the self being responsible for outcome, without regard to the contributions of others or the condition of the self at the time the action was taken. From the more integrated perspective of an observer, the individual has failed to distribute responsibility for outcomes properly. Specifically, unforeseen and unforeseeable outcomes may be treated as intentional. Alternatively, causal relations occurring in childhood or when the self was not in a position of power are treated as being the responsibility of the self, rather than of older or more powerful people.

16. This construct was introduced by Main and Goldwyn (1984, 1994); it is applied without substantial change here.

Misattribution of intent refers to distorting the intent of harmful caregivers so as to reframe hostile or dangerous treatment, in a delusional way, as loving. This is functionally coupled with denial of negative affect.

Nonagency is the expressed semantic belief that the self is not an active agent in one's life, that the self is, instead, acted upon as the recipient of others' actions. It refers to recognition that the self is not active in causal ways in what happens to the self but nevertheless is the recipient of the actions of others. It is, in other words, in a state of passive accommodation to others and the logical outcome of too extensive overattribution of responsibility of the self. Nonagency is facilitated by the denial of all affective dispositional representations. Nonagency is typical of A8 speakers. Moreover, although it is not necessarily indicative of depression, it often is associated with the Dp modifier in the DMM method.

CONNOTATIVE LANGUAGE

Artificial language is language that consists of dry distanced language, usually formulated in complex syntactical structures, using polysyllabic vocabulary that refers to constructs. It is more than merely the denotative use of language. Indeed, it is the use of artificial language that prevents the connection between language and life experience. Type A speakers often use connotative language to represent affect states in ways that keep them separate from the self, including self-mockery and irony.

EPISODIC MEMORY

Cut-off or opposite episodes[17] are episodes that are recounted to support positive semantic adjectives but that are cut off just before the expected loving, comforting, or protective conclusion should occur or that provide evidence in opposition to the semantic word. They reflect the mental problem of a speaker who remembers, discerns the conflict of fact with semantic information, and escapes having to consider the negative information about attachment figures by distracting the self

---

17. This construct was introduced by Main and Goldwyn (1984, 1994); it is applied without substantial change here.

(and interviewer) with digressions, changing the topic (cut-off), or providing a positive semantic conclusion (positive wrap-up) without providing evidence.

Lack of recall of positive episodic experience[18] is the stated inability to recall episodic information that supports (i.e., provides evidence for) the positive semantic generalizations made by the speaker. Although lack of recall is often marked by words such as "I can't remember," such words do not always imply lack of access to episodic memory. For example, when speakers say that they cannot remember five adjectives, they claim lack of semantic memory; this is passive semantic thought (see the Type C strategy discussed in this chapter). Similarly, Type C speakers sometimes use silence obstructively or seductively; this is usually in response to negative semantic probes. Type A speakers usually try to cover their lack of episodic detail with a semantic description; this meets the social obligation to respond while failing to provide episodic validation of the positive semantic words. It should be noted that the pattern of being unable to recall certain things and showing dysfluence around the missing information is itself evidence that the speaker is vigilant regarding this information. Lack of recall of episodes is typical of the low-numbered Type A patterns (A1–2).

Displaced episodes occur when the speaker begins a negative episode about the self and attachment figure and then either (a) changes the attachment figure's negative behavior to another adult who then harms the speaker or (b) attributes the speaker's behavior to another child who then receives the attachment figure's attack. In either case, the self is not harmed by the attachment figure. Displaced episodes can include *displaced negative affect*: This refers to the speaker's attribution of his or her own negative affect to a self-substitute (i.e., a sibling). This permits the speaker to retain the feeling, albeit in a distanced manner. It does not refer to "projection" of the affect onto an oppositional figure because this process rids the self of the feeling and assigns it to a nonself figure (this would be a coercive, Type C process).

Episodes told from a *parental perspective* are episodic events that include negative events and outcomes but which are described as the parents would have perceived them, without the speaker's stipulation of this. Thus, speakers deny their own perspectives, substitute the parents' perspectives for it, and exonerate the parents of culpability. Often

---

18. This construct was introduced by Main and Goldwyn (1984, 1994); it is applied without substantial change here.

speakers claim responsibility through their own failings for eliciting the parents' negative behavior. Recounting episodes from the parents' perspectives is associated with the A3–6 patterns.

Distorted guilt episodes omit information about the actions of others that would lead to others being at least partially responsible for the (negative) outcomes that the speaker experienced and takes full responsibility for.

Delusional idealization refers to episodes in which the unprotected (and unprotectable) self is protected or comforted by imaginary persons or by real persons behaving in imaginary ways. The delusional comfort is possible when negative affective information is denied.

External reference refers to episodes that others tell about the self, particularly those told to, and kept in records by, professionals. These episodes are not simply references to what the parents have told the speaker about their earliest years or about events recalled primarily from family photographs (these are common events and exist for almost everyone). Externally referenced episodes are those that substitute for a self-generated self-narrative.

REFLECTIVE INTEGRATION

Omitted integration is displayed as refusal to consider the integrative questions thoughtfully and implying they are not worthy of consideration: *"I don't know"*; *"I can't remember"' "You'd have to ask her."* A1–2 speakers are the most likely to omit integrative thought altogether.

Platitudes are trite, superficial, and thoughtless, but also irrefutable, ideas that ignore the feelings of the self and dismiss important issues from further thought (e.g., *"Why did your parents behave as they did?"* *"Because of the way they were raised"* or *"Because they loved us"*). They include appeals to moral or ethical systems such as religious principles or educational/scientific precepts. They tend to be impersonal, generalized judgments that preclude the need for unique and personal consideration of alternatives or adapted applications to particular situations and circumstances.

Failed metacognitions result from discrepancies that are noticed by the speaker and given psychological importance. That is, they are moments of recognition on the part of the speaker that something he or she had said did not make sense: There is a mental dysfluency of thought (rather than merely of speech). This recognition creates the opportunity for reflective or metacognitive thought, but, in actuality, having noticed the problem, the speaker moves on and does not address the discrepancy productively. In avoiding reflection, the speaker may draw a conclusion, sometimes even a thoughtful and compassionate conclusion, that does not reflect his or her own experience. Instead, this conclusion denies the speaker's own perspective and feelings in favor of taking the parents' perspective. At other times, speakers simply move on with no further acknowledgment of the discrepancy. Failed metacognitions are associated with the compulsive Type A patterns (A3–6).

Inconclusive metacognitions take the form of reflective thought but do not lead to a conclusion. However, they are not dismissed (as are failed metacognitions). Instead, the speaker acknowledges the discrepancy and the importance of resolving the discrepancy. At the same time, resolution is impossible due to denial of crucial affective information. The speaker must then rely on others (usually professional others) to resolve the discrepancy. This is consistent with delusional idealization and an externally assembled self (A7–8).

Discourse Characteristics Typical of the Type C Strategy

PROCEDURAL MEMORY

1. Discourse. *Involving discourse*[19] can be of several types but is most likely to emphasize feelings (of anger, fear, or desire for comfort). All forms of involving discourse have in common that the boundaries to time, person, or place are violated in ways that make separate things seem more connected than they really are. Involving discourse is the opposite of distancing discourse and is associated with the Type C pattern. Involving anger and involving fear are specific sorts of involving discourse.

*Involving anger** is not simply the mention of anger. Rather, it is limited to those situations in which the speaker seems actually to become angry (during the interview) as prior experience is related. Functionally, the boundary between past and present has become blurred. Morphologically, this is often indicated in the transcript by (a) long run-on sentences that are complaining in content, (b) efforts to obtain the interviewer's support against the parent with whom the speaker is angry, (c)

---

19. This construct was introduced by Main and Goldwyn (1984, 1994); it is applied without substantial change here.

speech that slips into the present tense when complaining about the past, (d) loss of awareness of the context of being interviewed, and (e) the use of speech to an absent person with loss of awareness that the person is not present. Put another way, in mild cases, the speaker becomes caught up with trying to resolve (in the present) past problems; in more severe cases, the speaker forgets that a story about the past is being told to the interviewer and acts as if the incident were actually unfolding in the present. Involving anger requires loss of the present context (an interview) in which the boundary between past and present becomes blurred (cf. discussion of biases in mental processing of information in Crittenden, 1997d. It is associated with the odd-numbered Type C patterns, specifically, C1, C3, C5, and C7.

Involving fear[20] is very much like involving anger except that the affect is fear and not anger. Thus, run-on-sentences with fearful content, use of fear-defining words, and fearful speech to people present only in the past are indicative of preoccupying fear. Involving fear is indicative of some of the obsessive Type C patterns, specifically, C4, C6, and C8.

2. Expression of affect. *Disarming affect* consists of embarrassed laughs, giggles, and so forth, that accompany mildly threatening or angry statements. These function to soften the effect of the words or deflect an angry response away from the speaker.

Mocking/gotcha! humor can be used derisively to mock others (C3) or self-deprecatingly to mock the self (C4). It functions to create a hierarchy of power between the speaker and someone else, but also to take the edge off the power structure with humor.

Arousing nonverbal affect consists of intense outbursts of affect that (a) are overly intense for the topic of discourse, (b) elicit caregiving from the interviewer, or (c) distract attention from the speaker's words. Often the affect makes the speech unintelligible; a pattern of arousal and unintelligible speech that recurs whenever thoughtful responses are called for is indicative of the arousingly preoccupying pattern. Arousing nonverbal affect is associated with all the Type C patterns, but especially the mid-range patterns.

Distorted positive affect falls just short of sadistically cruel affect in that it isn't tied to the speaker's actively inflicting the harm (to another person) that brings pleasure. Its meaning is well covered by the Ger-

---

20. This construct was introduced by Main and Goldwyn (1984, 1994), but is modified somewhat in the DMM method.

man word *Schadenfreude,* meaning "malicious joy." (It literally means pleasure derived from another person's being harmed.) Psychologically, it results from the integration of feelings of anger and fear with designation of the source of threat (i.e., the cognitive information) into the emotions of "hate" and "dread." The individual's own instrumental use of exaggerated negative affect creates the possibility of dismissing the validity of others' expressed feelings (by presuming their display to be falsified for instrumental purposes).

Cold or sadistically cruel affect is sometimes used by obsessive speakers, especially those with C7–8 classifications. It consists of a cold, calculating appearance in the face of others' distress or suffering, especially when the self has deliberately inflicted this suffering. Often it has a ghoulish quality. Cold, sadistic affect is associated with the very high-numbered obsessive Type C patterns.

3. Relationship with the interviewer. *Involving relationships with the interviewer*[21] occur when a speaker seeks excessive evidence that the interviewer understands and accepts (confirms) what is being said, often with the implication that the interviewer understands all that the speaker experienced even without it being said or that the interviewer will supply meanings that the speaker does not have. This is typical of the low-numbered Type C patterns (C1–2).

Confronting/collusive relationships with interviewers establish power hierarchies either by the speaker confronting the interviewer or by creating triangulating coalitions. In these coalitions, speakers try to engage interviewers against the speakers' attachment figures, as though, with the interviewers' involvement, the outcome of historic family struggles could be changed. In a confronting speaker, the interviewer is treated as the parents' proxy and is attacked, disparaged, embarrassed, or defied by the speaker; in a collusive relationship, the interviewer is treated as a potential ally against the parents. Triangulation is typical of mid-range Type C patterns, (i.e., C3, C5).

Appealing/submissive relationships with interviewers establish reverse power hierarchies in which the speaker appears needy or appeasing with reference to the interviewer. Often deference to the interviewer's professional status is used manipulatively to generate a coalition of the speaker/interviewer against the speaker's family. This is typical of mid-range Type C even-numbered patterns (C4, C6).

21. This construct was introduced by Main and Goldwyn (1984, 1994); it is applied with considerable expansion here.

Parrying relationships avoid the direct confrontation of openly oppo-sitional speakers and instead create an invisible battle of words. Ac-cording to the *New Shorter Oxford Dictionary*, the function is to "stop, avert, or ward off; counter; or avert a threat to oneself; deal skillfully with an awkward question or demand" (Brown, 1993).

There is an implication of deception to the term "parry" that is ap-parent only in its gamelike, teasing quality. Thus, there is necessarily an indirectness to verbal parrying such that, from the perspective of dis-course analysis, parrying is more sophisticated than silence, refusal to answer, or saying you can't recall. It implies an engagement in the bat-tle, a "catch me if you can" or "cat and mouse" quality.

Seductive relationships with interviewers involve using deceptive means of engaging the interviewer in the goals of the speaker. Specifically, it involves tempting others by offering what you believe they want and misleading them with regard to what you want. Functionally, it in-volves displaying intense affect that elicits comfort (e.g., repeated weeping or dangling tantalizingly irresistible bits of information before the interviewer without explaining them). It is particularly powerful when sex is implied (but not overtly stated). Opposite, but extreme, means are used to achieve this effect: Silence can mutely, but power-fully, intrude a threat (to the interviewer or to the apparently exposed self) into the interview, whereas tossing out bits of information just as a topic, or the interview itself, is being closed can lure an interviewer into prolonged exploration of the topic. A more subtle form of seduction involves the speaker appearing to espouse a flawed argument, which the interviewer then corrects—in the distorted manner desired by the speaker. The interviewer, in other words, is duped by the speaker and, as a consequence, consummates the deception for the speaker. Intimi-dation and seduction are typical of the high-numbered Type C catego-ries (C5–8).

Intimidating/spooky relationships with interviewers involve the intru-sion into the interview of danger and violence that is unexpected and whose source is not certain. The means for generating the unfocused sense of threat can range from silence to sudden "in-the-face" assaul-tive discussion of extremely violent acts in the speaker's history. Al-though usually the acts are set in the past or attributed to others, the speaker's failure to prepare the listener for them or to set them in an appropriate affective context creates an aura of unspecifiable danger. The implied threat often causes interviewers to feel so uncomfortable that they are hesitant to ask appropriate questions.

IMAGED MEMORY

Intense images are affect-arousing images of places, somatic responses, or dangerous/safe agents. They are of particular importance when they are used frequently and take precedence over event sequences or generalizations in conveying the speaker's meaning in response to semantic or episodic probes. They consist of auditory images (including speech), tactile images, olfactory images, gustatory images, and (of course) visual images. Frequent use of intense images is typical of low-numbered Type C speakers (C1–2, C3–4). Images with a frightening quality are indicative of C3–4 (or higher) speakers.

Animated images (of anger, fear, or desire for comfort) are images that "act" as though they are alive. They range from simple involving speech in which current context and time are temporarily suspended to motivating images in which recall elicits behavioral responses. Often the image becomes more real than the current context. Animated images are typical of C3–6 speakers.

Generalized images are images that are both decontextualized and applied without restriction to other contexts and overly associated with the self. The effect is to carry representations of threatening circumstances to as many similar circumstances as possible. This increases both the probability of identifying all actual danger and also of misidentifying nonthreatening circumstances as dangerous.

Delusionally threatening images are images of the omnipotence of the speaker or of the vengefulness of others toward the self. These images not only reflect experiences for which there is no credible evidence, but these experiences also could not occur, that is, they are delusional. They are functionally coupled with the denial of the role of self in causality, replacing the denied cognitive information.

SEMANTIC MEMORY

Passive semantic thought[22] is the failure to reach semantic conclusions, especially semantic conclusions in which the self shares responsibility with attachment figures for negative outcomes. In most cases, the evidence for the conclusions has already been presented. Passive thought often occurs in response to the five descriptive words question. For ex-

---

22. This construct was introduced by Main and Goldwyn (1984, 1994), but is modified somewhat in the DMM method.

ample, the speaker may say that he or she *"can't remember,"* give episodes or scripts (particularly those with active verbs) rather than offering descriptive words, wander without identifying specific characteristics, or complain that the task is very hard. In addition, passive semantic thought often occurs after long episodes (or episode fragments) in which speakers fail to come to obvious conclusions for which they themselves have provided substantiating information. C2 speakers often blur semantic distinctions with vague statements, confusing word usage, and wandering discourse. The indicative discourse marker is long, run-on sentences with joining conjunctions (e.g., *and, then, that is*). In addition, making a clear word vague by adding *"sort of"* and *"kind of"* diminishes the meaning of semantic conclusions; this, too, is passive thought. Vacillating between opposite semantic conclusions (for example, *"He was mean, well, not really mean; he was sort of nice"*) without coming to a resolution is also indicative of passive thought and is used commonly by C1 speakers. Often the indicative words are causal conjunctions (e.g., *so, therefore, because*) and contradicting conjunctions (e.g., *but, although, nevertheless*) when these are not followed by an appropriate semantic conclusion.

Idealized expectations about the future refers to recognition of negative information about the past combined with expectation of ideal circumstances in the future. When the future is idealized, the speaker both fails to articulate clearly the nature of the problems to be overcome and also claims a future solution to them, without articulating a process that could yield resolution. It is as though Type C speakers believed that suffering long enough and refusing to give up on a problem gives one rights to a solution. It is typical of Type C speakers. (B4–5 speakers are idealistic about the future but recognize that they must make their own solutions, that they cannot force others to fit their plans, and that "deserving" is not a causal condition.)

Reductionist blaming thought involves arriving at extreme semantic distinctions that have been simplified by exclusion of contradictory information. Slights and injustices from the (often very distant) past are retained as proximal causes of current feelings and behavior. This permits speakers to clarify their perspectives and, thus, to act more effectively. There is often a strong theme of justice, with others behaving in unfair ways (and, therefore, deserving retribution) and the self having "rights" that others have violated. C3 speakers tend to have self-righteous perspectives that blame others for problems and to claim, with false bravado, invulnerability and powerfulness to others' aggressive behavior. C4 speakers are similarly self-righteous and blaming of others, but they present themselves with feigned helplessness, emphasizing their innocence and powerlessness in the face of others' attacks.

Derogation[23] is defined as describing parents or relationships in extremely negative terms. Derogation involves the same mental process as idealization with the opposite outcome; that is, both dichotomize reality into unmixed good and bad components of which only one is acknowledged verbally. In the case of derogation, the self is usually viewed as good or protected, and parents or relationships with parents are viewed as bad or dangerous. Derogation uses distancing discourse but is associated with the Type C obsessive patterns, specifically the C5 pattern.

Person-defined negative meaning refers to words that seem, on the surface, to be positive or neutral, but, when defined episodically, they turn out to be negative in the mind of the speaker. This is different from a positive word with a negative episode, that is, idealization with an opposite episode. In this case, the speaker thinks of the positive word in negative ways, for example, the word "protective" is used when the speaker means "intrusively over-protective, not possible to shake off." The error is that speakers cannot foresee the interviewers' understanding of the word and, therefore, do not alert them to their self-defined negative meaning.

Misattribution of causality refers to inaccurate attributions of causality that minimize the contribution of the self and fail to recognize the complicitous involvement of the self, often in obscuring triangulated relationships. That is, the underlying reality is of complex multiperson relationships in which the former child could not discern accurately what was happening between the parents and how this affected the child's life. It is, therefore, a transformation in which incomplete or ambiguous information is treated as boding ill for oneself and in which even clear information may be twisted to carry self-endangering meanings that are probably inaccurate.

False cognition involves a reversal of causal relations, that is, misleading others regarding the temporal order of events and one's own contribution to the false expectation. More specifically, it consists of (a)

23. This construct was introduced by Main and Goldwyn (1984, 1994); it is applied with considerable change here.

suspicion regarding others' apparent motives and intentions, (b) expectation that things will turn out differently than is apparent, and (c) the construction of false appearances to mislead others. The third of these can take either implicit or explicit forms. When deception is implicit, it is usually out of the awareness of the individual. In this case, what they lead us to believe and what is actual are in opposition. It is deemed deceptive because it recurs in a patterned, predictable, and self-protective manner. The underlying mechanism in memory is probably excessive reliance for the organization of behavior on dispositional representational models drawn from implicit (preconscious) memory systems (i.e., procedural, imaged, and implicit semantic memory). Implicit deception is typical of C5–6 speakers. In the AAI, the clearest evidence of false cognition is misleading the interviewer regarding the temporal order of events or causal relations. False cognition is subtle, highly deceptive, and manipulative. It should not be confused with a history of having parents who used false cognition against the speaker in childhood. Neither is it false cognition when the speaker openly states that he or she deceived others in the past (although, in both cases, increased skepticism regarding the current veracity of the speaker is warranted). It should be noted that in the actual history most false cognitive victims were complicitous victims and most false cognitive perpetrators were themselves victims of deceptive parental relationships. It is the complex reality of holding both roles that creates problems in understanding causation for the adult and, correspondingly in the reverse, for the treatment and judicial systems.

Denial of responsibility focuses the speaker on self-protection, leaving the motivating feelings of unfocused hate/dread free from semantic interference. This involves the intent to deceive by careful regulation of what others know and feel, which is framed as essential to self-protection, given the power and treachery of others. Concurrently the harmful potential for others of one's own behavior is denied. This denial of the role of the self in danger-related causality is associated with C7–8 and AC speakers.

CONNOTATIVE LANGUAGE

Evocative language functions in the opposite manner from artificial language. It uses words and syntactical constructions that evoke feeling and facilitate the connection between language and experience. Evocative language also evokes the expressed state in listeners. Examples include all the usual conventions of poetry (e.g., onomatopoeia, juxta-position, alliteration, rhyme and rhythm), as well as more elaborated forms (including simile, metaphor, and irony). It can be used effectively to persuade listeners, often by Type C3–6 speakers, or to induce affective resonance in listeners, often by C5–8 speakers.

EPISODIC MEMORY

Blurred or circular episodes[24] are of two types: those in which there is slippage from one episode to another similar one and those in which the meaning of the word, as used by the speaker, is unclear. The blending of several events involves violation of the boundaries between persons, places, and time. The effect is that of generalizing many experiences and obscuring individuals' causal input and ultimate responsibility for events. Put another way, blurred episodes reflect the use of semantic generalizing functions within episodic memory. Unlike true semantic thought, everything remains particular and occasion-specific but, unlike true episodic functioning, the episodes are blended without the speaker's awareness. Blurring of meanings refers to episodes that are associated with the word but which neither support nor refute the word. Often the word appears to have a "personal" meaning rather than a public, generally agreed-upon meaning. Blurred episodes are typical of C1–2 speakers.

Lack of a negative episode is the failure to provide a negative episode to support a negative, blaming word.

Fragmented episodes[25] refer to the failure of the speaker to order events accurately in episodes. Instead, time is disordered as the speaker moves back and forth through events, critical initiating and concluding events are omitted such that outcomes appear unpredictable and unrelated to the sequence of events (i.e., magical thinking), or the episodes consist only of fragments that have imaged, sensory/affective information but are without temporal form. Particularly likely omissions include redeeming aspects of others' behavior or contributing aspects of the speaker's behavior. Usually there is an emphasis on the present such that episodes about the past are quickly associated with something in

24. This construct was introduced by Main and Goldwyn (1984, 1994); it is applied without substantial change here.
25. This construct was introduced by Main and Goldwyn (1984, 1994), but is modified somewhat in the DMM method.

the present that then dominates the discourse. Fragmented episodes are associated with the Type C classification.

Negative episode but without harmful effects on the self refers to the speaker's attitude of being invulnerable: *"Yeah, they were terrible, horrible, but it didn't hurt me. Nothing and nobody hurts me!"* The distortion is in the false bravado.

Triangulated episodes result from a twisting of information and infusion of actors in events in incoherent ways, such that things appear to happen differently than they actually happened. Nevertheless, there remains a kernel of truth to what the speaker says. Usually, in childhood, the speaker was caught up in the functioning of the spousal or parental dyad in ways that were not apparent or could not be understood by the child. In adulthood, the episode is told in ways that simplify the complex reality but distort its meaning in ways that protect or vindicate the speaker. This is most frequent among speakers classified as C5–6 or C5–6+.

False innocence/blame refers to episodes in which the stated role of the speaker is the opposite of that which is most likely the actual role. For example, a murderer may state that he or she is actually the victim of other persons' misunderstanding or malevolence. This is usually associated with dangerous events in which the speaker directly states that the parents were "innocent" and then provides evidence that leads the listener to conclude that the parents were a source of threat, (i.e., "guilty") or the speaker was a source of threat but presents himself or herself as an innocent victim. Indicative features include episodes containing unexplained danger or danger in which the temporal and causal links are omitted, without the speaker's attention to the omission. Episodes are distorted in this way by speakers classified as C5–6+.

Delusional revenge occurs when the delusional figure is an enemy and the delusion is of revenge or escape. The episode is organized almost exclusively around affective information that is integrated with delusional (irrational) cognitive information substituting for the denied true cognitive information about the role of self in causality. Instead, the self appears as a righteous avenger or glorified victim. This is indicative of a C7–8 pattern.

REFLECTIVE INTEGRATION

Omitted integration is a simple mechanism to avoid acknowledging what could easily be known. Low-numbered Type C speakers simply decline to integrate information in order to avoid achieving a balanced and informative perspective on their past experiences. Instead, when asked why people behaved as they did or what effects their experiences have had on their functioning, they say they don't know, can't remember, or speak of irrelevancies. Omitted integration is common among C1–2 speakers.

Pseudoreflections are reflective statements that speakers have borrowed from others (including religious leaders, books, and therapists) but have been unable to relate fully to their own experiences. Such statements tend not to be associated with speakers' awareness of discrepancy; rather, they are offered almost gratuitously in response to integrative questions by self-satisfied speakers, that is, speakers who are satisfied with their own functioning and see no need for further reflection and change. Pseudoreflections function to justify the self as it now exists.[26] Low-numbered Type C speakers use such "psychobabble."

Rationalization consists of an idealized form of self-serving, reductionist justice that is integrated with the speaker's split and exaggerated feelings to lead to rationalized exoneration of the self. To the careful reader these facile integrative statements are found ultimately to be irrational. Rationalization tends to be used most frequently by obsessive speakers (C3–8).

Skillful misleading refers to a series of psychological processes. First is the speaker's ability to know what information already exists in the listener's mind, so as not to contradict it. Based on that knowledge, the speaker often offers it, in an apparently confessional manner, thus establishing the speaker's validity as a source of information. Finally, the speaker offers a series of details, feelings, and ideas such that the listener derives a false conclusion that is never actually stated by the speaker. Having the listener derive and articulate to himself or herself the conclusion reduces the likelihood that the listener will critically evaluate the conclusion, as compared to conclusions that are stated explicitly by the speaker. The function is to engage the listener in the creation of a false conclusion that parallels the efforts of the speaker to minimize his or her own role in causal sequences that involve danger. Speakers using the C5–6 patterns have some awareness of their role, and their effort is focused on misleading listeners. By the C7–8 patterns, the misleading is primarily to protect the self from the awareness of the role of the self in causality, that is, denial of self-responsibility.

---

26. Main and Goldwyn refer to pseudoreflections as "jargon."

CHANGE PROCESSES: MODIFIERS OF STRATEGIES

Although change is a natural life process, not all mental processes are equally responsive to change. Following Bowlby's (1973) notion of developmental pathways, the perspective used here emphasizes the possibility of both historical change in mental organization and pattern of behavior and also current change. Such change occurs continually in balanced speakers as they use self-reflective and integrative processes on an ongoing basis. In others, the process of change is usually instigated by some out-of-the-ordinary event. Often these events are developmental "milestones" (e.g., marriage, birth, divorce, death). In other cases, they are self-threatening events for which the self is unprepared. When change is in process, we observe it as "reorganization." When it fails to occur, the outcome may be unresolved trauma or loss.

Lack of resolution of trauma and loss[27] is a response to extreme danger. Consequently, the speaker's psychological response to trauma and loss can be analyzed using the same tools that are used for other parts of the interview. In general, speakers use the same strategy for minor and major dangers, that is, A → U(ds) and C → U(p), but, occasionally, the danger is so great (and often ongoing) that the habitual strategy fails to keep speakers safe or to enable them to feel comfortable. In these cases, the habitual strategy may be abandoned. Sometimes it is replaced by the opposite strategy (e.g., a Type A speaker becomes preoccupied with a loss). Sometimes the danger leads to psychological confusion (i.e., disorganization); this is especially likely when several severe threats have similar features and all left the speakers unprotected. Sometimes the danger leads to belief that protection is not possible to achieve (i.e., depression). And sometimes it leads to metacognitive thought that is productive and results in reorganization of previously existing internal representational models.

The terms "trauma" and "loss," as used in this DMM method, are interpreted more broadly than by Main and Goldwyn (1984, 1994). Further, loss is treated as a subcategory of trauma, that is, a specific type of self-threatening event. Additionally, trauma is not limited to abuse experienced directly by the speaker. Instead, it includes nonabusive danger, observed danger, danger to attachment figures and persons at-

---

27. This construct was introduced by Main and Goldwyn (1984, 1994), but is modified somewhat in the DMM method.

tached to the self, and nonpersonal dangers, such as repressive political regimes, terrorism, historical threats, and living in violent neighborhoods. In the DMM method, trauma is not a dangerous event: It is an unresolved psychological response to a dangerous event. Trauma, in other words, is one form of psychological response to self-endangering conditions.

Similarly, loss can include deaths of attachment figures or others, vicarious reactions to deaths experienced by attachment figures, loss of the function of an attachment figure who lives (e.g., in some cases of adoption, foster care, or divorce), and anticipatory loss (when a death is realistically or unrealistically expected).

Lack of resolution can take any of several forms: preoccupying (as in Main & Goldwyn, 1984, 1994), dismissed, displaced, blocked, denied, delusionally repaired, vicarious, imagined, suggested, hinted, delusional revenge or attack, anticipated, disorganized, or depressed. An individual speaker can use more than one form of lack of resolution with different or the same events or persons.

To summarize, the DMM method of discourse analysis addresses abuse and loss as well as other threatening circumstances and permits analysis of events occurring to the self, events experienced vicariously, and events that are anticipated. Lack of resolution implies the failure of the speaker to differentiate aspects of the event or situation that are relevant only to that event (and should, thus, be set firmly in the past) from aspects that are relevant to future safety (and should, thus, be carried forward).

Reorganization of attachment relationships involves modifying or changing mental and behavioral strategies. When the experience of discrepancy leads to awareness of both the limitations of previous patterns and also the possibility of other strategies, reorganization becomes possible. Its successful outcome is a new pattern, one that is different from or more sophisticated than the earlier pattern. The new pattern may be an "earned" balanced strategy that reflects a more balanced and self-protective perspective, but this is not always the outcome. Maturation may also lead to recognition that former dangers are no longer dangerous. This, in turn, can enable the speaker to give up one self-protective strategy in favor of another. Thus, Type A adolescents who recognize that displaying negative feelings will not endanger them any longer may become preoccupied with anger at their parents' injustices. Similarly, Type C adolescents who recognize that they can now survive without their parents may distance themselves from those attachment relationships. (These processes can occur at any age but are particularly frequent in adolescence.) In any case, when both patterns are in active use, including when intellectual understanding is more mature than procedural functioning, the speaker can be classified as reorganizing from one pattern to another. (When the process is complete, the speaker is assigned to the outcome classification.) The direction of change can be from A or C to B or a change from A to C and vice versa.

Depression is treated as a modification of the underlying pattern in which the speaker no longer uses the strategy self-protectively. The reason is that the representations in the various memory systems are not self-relevant; that is, they contain no disposition for the self to respond. Thus, the speaker has the discourse markers of a strategy but not the functional application of them. Indeed, the speaker articulates awareness of the futility of strategic behavior. Often a self-protective strategy is actually possible but only if the speaker can access and use information that is not trusted. In some cases, however, there is no possible self-protective strategy, given the dangers facing the speaker.

Disorientation refers to the speaker's inability to construct a functional self-protective strategy. In this case, however, the speaker has multiple representations from different individuals for which the source is unknown. Consequently, the speaker is disposed to act in ways that are consistent with the self's perspective as well as with others' perspectives. Without access to source memory, the conflicting strategic goals of different persons cannot be differentiated. Thus, action is inconsistent and conflicting and, ultimately, nonstrategic. Depression and disorganization, in other words, reflect opposite processes with regard to source memory. In cases of depression, the associative process of representation to self is aborted such that representations are not self-relevant. In disorganization, there is an overattribution of self-relevance to representations "borrowed" from other people. Both under- and overattribution of self-relevance reduce (or eliminate altogether) the strategic function of mental representation.

Intrusion of forbidden negative affect refers to the unregulated and sudden intrusion of negative affect into a compulsive Type A strategy. It is associated with very serious psychopathology.

Expressed somatic symptoms are nonverbal behaviors that occur in ways that disrupt the conduct of the AAI. They draw attention away from the topics discussed and appear to represent conflict between what the speaker knows or suspects and what is permitted or safe to say.

COHERENCE OF DISCOURSE

In addition to identifying specific transformations of information, it can be helpful for the coder to consider the overall coherence of the discourse and of the underlying thought processes.[28] *Coherence of transcript*[29] refers to the overall coherence of the speaker's discourse. It depends on more than the presence or absence of specific discourse markers. Ultimately, it depends on the relation between the interviewer and the speaker. The interviewer asks questions; the speaker is obliged to respond. Grice's four maxims provide a means of evaluating the relation of the speaker's response to the question asked (Grice, 1975).

The maxim of *quality* refers to the evidentiary appropriateness of the content of the response. When speakers provide adequate evidence to support their statements (which is not contradicted elsewhere), their speech is coherent and likely to be balanced. When the evidence is inconsistent, the transcript is more likely to be that of a Type A or Type C speaker.

The maxim of *quantity* refers to the length of the answer. The length should be related to the sort of question asked, with closed questions producing short, concise answers and open-ended questions producing longer answers. Speakers who say less than is necessary to answer the question are likely to be Type A, whereas speakers who say far more than necessary are likely to be Type C.

The maxim of *relevance* refers to the relation of the answer to the question. Balanced speakers more often direct their answer to the question asked than to what is on their own mind (Type C speakers) or to distracting and irrelevant topics of no particular interest (Type A speakers).

The final maxim of *manner* refers to the way in which the answer is given. When the response is confused, leaping from one topic to another, is out of temporal order, or requires presumed but unstated in-

28. Main and Goldwyn refer to these as coherence of transcript and coherence of mind, respectively.
29. This construct was introduced by Main and Goldwyn (1984, 1994); it is applied without substantial change here.

formation, it is typical of Type C speakers. When it is rigidly ordered but devoid of feeling, the answer is more typical of Type A speakers. Balanced speakers, more than others, actively maintain the relationship with the interviewer by attending to the questions asked and providing relevant and interesting answers of appropriate length, in a manner that is comprehensible to the listener.

Coherence of mind[30] is a more demanding construct than coherence of transcript. Coherence of mind requires that the speakers describe themselves, their attachment figures, and their relationships in ways that are psychologically sound. In the best of cases, this occurs throughout the transcript. For some speakers, however, distorting transformations are used in the early portions of the interview, but these give way to reflective and psychologically accurate thought in response to the integrative questions toward the end of the interview.

---

30. This construct was introduced by Main and Goldwyn (1984, 1994); it is applied without substantial change here.

PART II

THE CLASSIFICATORY SYSTEM

Introduction to the Classificatory Chapters

IN CHAPTERS 5 TO 9, EACH STRATEGY IS DESCRIBED IN GENERAL, STARTING from the most balanced (B3), and proceeding to the cognitively biased (B1–2 and all A strategies) then to the affectively biased (B4–5 and all C strategies). Each strategy is described in detail, noting the specifics of the strategy; the discourse markers in each of the six memory systems, with their psychological functions in protecting the speaker; and the probable history likely to accompany such discourse/strategies. Within the A and C strategies, there is a distinction between their normative forms and the compulsive A and obsessive C strategies, typically developed in more dangerous contexts.

Chapter 10 describes some of the ways in which the A and C strategies can be combined by the same individual, at the same time or in different moments/contexts.

Chapter 11 deals with unresolved traumatic events that can interfere with the basic strategies and Chapter 12 discusses modifying conditions that prevent strategies from functioning protectively.

This book does not replace instruction in the method (any more than a textbook replaces the course for which it is assigned). Instead, we offer generalized descriptions of the discourse patterns and of memory system functions, and functional definitions of the strategies and modifiers. Together, these permit conceptual distinctions to be made among individuals.

The goal is to offer readers a way to think about the constructs in terms of evidence in narrative discourse and researchers a way to evaluate studies that use the method. Experience with transcripts of spoken discourse is necessary to actually discern the strategies. For forensic purposes, these chapters enable trained and certified experts to provide empirical support for their evaluations of adults' attachment.

Chapter 5

Overview of the Type B (Balanced) Strategies

GENERAL CHARACTERISTICS APPLYING TO ALL TYPE B (BALANCED) CLASSIFICATIONS

Overview

THE PRIMARY MENTAL PROCESS OF BALANCED SPEAKERS IS INTEGRATION of affect and cognition, such that each can be used to correct the errors of the other, thus, balancing mental and behavioral responses. Balanced (B) transcripts are typified by speakers' access to all memory systems: procedural, imaged, semantic, connotative, and episodic. Further, there are few distortions or dysfluencies, and when dysfluencies occur they rarely indicate distortions of thought, that is, they do not function to distort or hide important information. In addition, most B speakers are somewhat optimistic, either through minimizing negative past events and maximizing positive experiences (B1–2) or through transforming a minimally adequate past into a better future (B4–5). Bs, in other words, generally look on the bright side of things (Scheier & Carver, 1982; Taylor & Brown, 1988). Finally, speakers using a balanced strategy handle the integrative questions at least adequately and sometimes exceptionally well. That is, they are able to describe how their childhood experiences have contributed to the adults they have become, how their parents' developmental history affected the sort of parents they became, and how they apply these understandings to their current roles in attachment relationships. In particular, they describe experiences in ways that reflect their underlying complexity without becoming unable to draw reasonable conclusions. The answers to the integrative questions, together with information presented earlier in the interview, create a psychologically sound picture of the speaker and his or her family. Thus, we as observers tend to agree with the speaker's conclusions about his or her experience.

Main, Goldwyn, and Hesse (2003) refer to two sorts of balanced speakers: those with supportive histories and those with difficult histories that include anxious attachment in childhood. The latter are labeled "earned" because their balanced and integrated mental status comes in adulthood as a result of personal effort to understand their developmental process and that of their parents. That is, it is the result of mental reorganization. The former are referred to here as "naive Bs." Their mental functioning reflects, in a naive and preconscious manner, the integration of safety and comfort in their developmental context.

Naive Bs are often considered prototypical Bs. It may be, however, that in the context of danger, they would be more endangered than earned Bs. That is, the balance and organization that naive Bs display are the natural outcomes of developing in a safe, comfortable, and organized environment in which things are as they appear to be, that is, that most information is truly predictive and any distortions that are present do not result in danger. Under such conditions, there is no pressure to reach quick decisions regarding self-protective behavior. Therefore, it is safe to take the time to integrate information. Moreover, because information is rarely transformed in misleading ways, it is easy to integrate affect and cognition. Further, the lack of discrepancy among representations means that integration does not often require conscious self-reflective or metacognitive consideration. The outcome is a happy and comfortable individual who is organized around the expectation of safety and supportive people and who is relatively naive to the probability of danger.

Speakers who present transcripts that qualify as balanced in spite of having childhood histories indicative of problems with attachment figures are considered "earned" Bs. Earned Bs have reorganized their childhood anxious pattern of attachment in favor of a more balanced and discerning mental organization in adulthood. Earned Bs tend to be especially thoughtful and self-reflective as a function of having had to integrate difficult, discrepant, and often threatening information. The mental process of reorganizing and resolving difficult histories can facilitate recognition of danger in adult life because such individuals have experience identifying transformations of information that create misleading and potentially endangering appearances. That is, earned Bs know that not everything is safe and not everything is as it appears to be. Being able to discern deception can be highly protective in a world that contains both overt and covert danger. Although adults with difficult histories may be advantaged with regard to knowledge of mental transformations and deception, all adults, including the naively comfortable, have the opportunity to learn this difficult reality. Thus, all adults can become fully integrated earned Bs.

To be fully convinced of the current balanced and integrated status of the speaker, observers need evidence that the speaker functions as a B in all memory systems. That is, a reorganizing B is most likely to achieve integration when fully conscious and focusing on discrepancies related to attachment, for example, in response to the integrative questions of the AAI. Such an individual is more likely to use self-protective mental processing (i.e., to function in a Type A or Type C manner) when functioning is preconscious (i.e., when responding procedurally to the probes of imaged, semantic, and episodic memory). Therefore, a reorganizing B is less likely to display balance in early questions of the AAI (because these do not require conscious consideration) than in the integrative questions at the end. To become fully integrated, this achieved balance must be concatenated through the various memory systems until it becomes procedurally a spontaneous part of preconscious functioning. In addition to displaying balance in all parts of the interview, it helps if the speaker can explain something about how the process of reorganization was accomplished. This facilitates differentiation of pseudointegration (the "right" and "normal" platitudes of Type A speakers and the "jargon" and pseudoreflections and rationalizations of Type C speakers) from true integration.

In the final analysis, when we evaluate the speaker's conclusions regarding his or her history, we tend to agree with the balanced speaker's perspective: We either find the history to be as the speaker describes it or find the explanation of relationships to be psychologically sound.

Affect and Cognition

Affect: Balanced speakers display the full range of human feelings including complex emotional states such as sadness, regret, and compassion. "Emotions" as used here refer to cognitive/affective integrations (Crittenden, 1994). Feelings are evident in all memory systems and are modulated by cognitive information. In particular, Bs are comfortable with the need for comfort and with giving and receiving comfort.

Cognition: Balanced speakers are able to describe complex causal relations, including multiple causation, reciprocal effects, interactive effects, and systemic processes. In spite of recognition of complexity, they do not fall into the trap of being unable to assign personal responsibility. Instead, responsibility is discernible but not simplistic. Further, causal situations are seen to include both acts and feelings. That is, they understand that humans are motivated both by anticipated consequences and by feeling states.

With regard to time, Type B speakers are flexible. That is, they see the past itself as immutable but see one's understanding and use of the past as changeable and the future as under the influence of one's own behavior, but not entirely within one's control. They understand that events can occur that one did not predict or desire, but which one cannot change.

Discourse Markers and Their Psychological Function

1. Procedural memory:
   (a) B speakers use fluent speech in which any dysfluencies that occur are minor, such as hesitations, stutters, and restarts. Major dysfluencies indicative of transformation of information are rare and, when they do occur, they usually alert the speaker to a discrepancy of thought. Consequently, they are often accompanied by self-reflective thought (Fonagy, Steele et al., 1997) or metacognitions regarding the psychological meaning of the dysfluency. In addition, balanced speakers give evidence of their active use of integration through references within the transcript to things said elsewhere in the transcript. In particular, when the information is discrepant, the balanced speaker either actively explains how these two things can both be true or corrects one of the sources of information, often with a metacognitive statement.
   (b) Expressed affect covers a wide range, in tune with the topics being discussed, and generally reflects an overall positive disposition.

(c) Balanced speakers are cooperative with the interviewer and monitor their speech for illogical or inaccurate discrepancies. This functions to identify and correct error as well as to facilitate exchanging information with other people.

2. *Imaged memory*: Balanced speakers use lively images to convey a variety of affective states and are able to tie these overtly to their conscious understanding of their experiences. This functions to maximize the utility of the image in focusing attention and motivation while concurrently minimizing the influence of distortions.

3. *Semantic memory*: Balanced speakers maintain a moderate distance from life experiences, that is, sufficient distance to take account of alternative perspectives (including others' perspectives), together with sufficient involvement to maintain their own perspectives. Their semantic conclusions tend to emphasize the positive. For B1–2 speakers, this means negative aspects of the past are minimized and reliance on the self to improve the future is maximized. For B4–5 speakers, optimism for the future is maximized. Both are forms of "idealization," but, in balanced speakers, they are used to emphasize healthy potentials and reduce the risk of sadness or depression (Scheier & Carver, 1982, Taylor & Brown, 1988); they are not used to deny important aspects of reality.

4. *Connotative language*: Balanced speakers talk in ways that convey very clearly the feelings they also state semantically. They can have different styles in terms of predominance of evocative or denotative qualities of the language, but the clarity of the affective communication is a common feature of their language.

5. *Episodic memory*: Balanced speakers recall a variety of episodes but, like all people, they have more detail for troubling and threatening experiences than for safe and comfortable ones. Therefore, examples of positive characteristics of relationships are more likely to be in the form of scripts with unique details than of full episodes. Episodes when the self felt endangered as a child tend to be reviewed from an adult perspective (i.e., from the safe condition of being able to protect oneself from most childhood threats). The bias toward recall of troubling episodes functions to facilitate preparation for possible future danger whereas reevaluation of the meaning of childhood ex-

perience permits closure of past experiences that are no longer threatening.

6. *Reflective integration*: Balanced speakers integrate all transformations of cognitive and affective information from all memory systems to achieve balanced, self-protective conclusions that can be applied to others, especially one's children. These include the recognition that all people reflect mixtures of desirable and undesirable characteristics, that recurrent conditions are usually maintained on the basis of contributions from all participants (i.e., there is complicity of all participants in the state of relationships, that all people change over time, that different people can experience the same situation differently, and that not everything is as it appears to be). Recognition of these truths enables balanced speakers to construct dispositional representations of self and others that are hierarchical with regard to relationship, conditional, qualified, and open to ongoing revision.

An important aspect of reflective integration as shown in the discourse of B speakers is the use of metacognitions. Metacognitive thinking is thought about thinking itself. Statements that are insightful, evaluative (without being either overly critical or inconclusive), and balanced with regard to perspectives or responsibility are likely candidates for metacognitions (presuming that they are tied directly to the speaker's experience and therefore, are not merely wise sayings that are universally true).

Metacognitive statements that are made as a result of thinking occurring during the interview provide the most powerful evidence of metacognitive functioning.

Fully integrated speakers are aware of their own and others' transformations of information. Moreover, they are aware of their mental strategies, have a wide range of such strategies (from Type A to Type C), and can effectively apply these strategies, with awareness, to appropriate situations without becoming trapped in the strategy.

Regarding Grice's (1975) maxims, balanced speakers offer high-*quality* information, told in an orderly *manner*. They vary in the *quantity* of information but do not greatly exceed or underestimate usual expectations. Further, although some *relevant* information may be very sketchy (B1) or somewhat excessive (B4–5), balanced speakers are sensitive to the organization of their history and present a coherent story that can be understood by the listener. Thus, overall balanced speakers tend to be moderate to high in the coherence of the discourse and often are even higher in their mental coherence.

ASSOCIATED STRATEGIES OR MODIFIERS

B transcripts rarely are paired with other strategies or with modifiers. The one exception is the possibility of U trauma or loss, when these events are very recent.

RISK OF PSYCHOPATHOLOGY

Under safe circumstances, there is little or no threat of psychopathology to those employing a B strategy. The single exception is the intrusion of unexpected tragedies (i.e., loss or trauma). These may, in some cases, lead to reactive forms of psychopathology. Little is known about the functioning of B individuals under substantial, enduring, pervasive, and deceptive sorts of threat. It is possible that Type B is not an adaptive strategy under these conditions and, in its naivete, may even constitute a risk.

Experience/History

Naive Bs have safe and supporting histories whereas earned Bs may have any kind of history.

B3 (COMFORTABLY BALANCED)

Overview

This strategy is the exemplar for the balanced strategy. It is based on Ainsworth's (1973, 1979) B3 infant pattern and Main, Goldwyn, and Hesse's (2003) F3 pattern.

B3 speakers, more than any others, communicate clearly to others their intentions and feelings, listen to others' perspectives, and negotiate differences in these to achieve mutually satisfying compromises that keep both parties safe and comfortable as circumstances permit.

More than other speakers, they avoid distortions of information and are aware of the motivations underlying their behavior.

Discourse Markers and Their Psychological Function

1. Procedurally, B3 speakers have the fewest dysfluencies of discourse and none of these create serious transformations of information. They speak easily and fluently and show few dysfluencies beyond restarts and repetitions.

    They display moderate affect that reflects how they genuinely feel. They neither make too much of their feelings nor dismiss them as unimportant. When an intense affect is unexpected, they use the information to reconsider the subject under discussion.

    They are cooperative with the interviewer, displaying a comfortable reciprocity that neither places too great nor too little a burden on either person. They show few violations of Grice's (1975) maxims, and when there are such violations they are acknowledged and the speakers seek (explicitly or implicitly) permission for the violation from the interviewer. The function is to enable speakers to benefit from both their own potential to think about their circumstances and also others' perspectives on these.

2. They use fresh, lively, and often unique images to enhance their story. These function both to communicate effectively and to enable the speaker to re-experience the event while concurrently re-evaluating it from his or her present perspective.

3. Semantically, relationships with parents are presented as varied and differentiated. This enables B3 speakers to account for a wide range of self and parental attributes and experiences. That is, B3 speakers construct complex representations that are hierarchically structured, contingency based, and contextually variable. They are aware of both the temporal order of events and also the causal relations among them. When information is not known, they are clear about the nature of the confusion. They are also able to differentiate childhood understandings from their adult understandings. In particular, causal relations are seen, in the present, to be complex and bidirectional, rather than uni-causal and unidirectional.

4. Their connotative language is congruent with their stated feelings, so that it enhances their communication, without obscuring its clarity.

5. B3 speakers tend to tell affectively lively and causally ordered episodes and, when the episodes were positive, to enjoy recalling them. When the experiences were painful, they both display and regulate affect. Moreover, even in these cases, comfortably balanced speakers find retelling their histories emotionally satisfying. For daily experiences, such as being loved, they report scripts with sufficient unique details that it is clear that they recall specific aspects of the relationship. These episodes function to provide concrete information upon which the speaker can construct, and reconstruct, new understandings.

6. B3 speakers are comfortable monitoring their own behavior for discrepancies. These tend to bring procedural behavior to conscious consideration. Regardless of the difficulties in their histories, B3 speakers are able to accept multiple perspectives on experience, without losing the validity of their own perspectives. Put another way, B3 speakers are able to express an understanding of how each person is not only embedded in their developmental context but also an active contributor to that context with the possibility to act so as to create change. Sometimes this is a natural outgrowth of a safe and organized childhood. In other cases, the speakers have had to struggle to understand threatening and complex experiences. In these cases, integration may not have been possible until the maturity, independence, and developmental experience of adulthood have been achieved. Access to all (or most) of the information enables B3 speakers to organize their adult behavior flexibly. Facility with the integrative process functions to maximize ongoing reorganization throughout life.

B3 speakers, especially earned B3s, display the widest range of mental, behavioral, and discourse strategies. That is, B3 speakers use all the strategies *when* they are appropriate and *without* mental confusion regarding the underlying true information. Such flexibility is highly protective but can confuse those readers who expect a defense-free, "perfect" transcript.

B3 transcripts have an assortment of discourse markers and display aspects of many classifications but are differentiated from other strategies by (a) the breadth of styles of mental processing of information and (b) the ultimate balancing and integration of these into a psychologically sound perspective on the speaker's experience.

DIFFERENTIATING B3 FROM OTHER STRATEGIES

B3 is most frequently confused with other forms of B and with the compulsive As. Bs can be differentiated from the compulsive strategies (with which they are often confused) by the balanced speaker's maintenance of his or her own perspective, even when displaying compassion for others' perspectives, and by the absence of dismissing discourse markers. Occasionally they are confused with A/C combinations, particularly those with high-numbered strategies that denote deception. The quality of interviewing is of particular importance in differentiating B3 transcripts from A/Cs and ACs. This is because the high-numbered A/C and AC strategies are based on deception. If the interviewer does not press for suitable evidence but accepts superficial responses instead, treating them as adequate, it can be difficult or even impossible to know how the speaker would respond to threat, in this case the threat of exposure.

Experience/History

B3 speakers have all kinds of histories. If, however, there is any commonality, it is probably that somewhere in their histories there has been a model of mature and compassionate acceptance of human variability and fallibility. That is, most B3 speakers have had experience with a balanced person who was accepting of them. This person is often an attachment figure, but that is not necessary. Teachers, neighbors, or therapists can fulfill this function without being attachment figures. Moreover, occasionally there is no such figure and integration was achieved through an extended process of personal mental reflection and reevaluation.

B1 (DISTANCED FROM PAST)

Overview

This is the most distancing of the balanced strategies. It is based on Ainsworth's B1 pattern for infants and Main, Goldwyn and Hesse's (2003) F1 pattern for adults, but it is modified to fit the split between idealizing the attachment figure versus negating the self that differentiates the even/odd-numbered strategies distinction among Type A strategies.

B1 speakers are open and direct regarding their intentions and feelings and negotiate differences in these with others to achieve mutually satisfactory compromises. On the other hand, compared to other Type B speakers, they dwell less on negative features of others' contributions to their functioning and, instead, focus on what they can do for themselves.

Discourse Markers and Their Psychological Function

1. Procedurally, B1 speakers use concise, brief, and distancing speech that is, nevertheless, psychologically sound and does not omit or deny negative information about the parents or the self. B1 speakers' strategy is one of coming directly to the point with few, but clear, words. The discourse frequently uses minimization in phrasing without distortion of meaning.

    Although affect is not emphasized in the pattern of speech, affective states, particularly negative states and states of vulnerability, are described accurately and, often, touchingly. They are clearly attributed to the self but without extended discussion.

    They also cooperate thoughtfully with the interviewer, while, nevertheless, giving relatively little attention to negative information about the parents or their own feelings of being hurt by the parents. They do not, however, omit or falsify this information. The function is to enable them to focus on the present and its positive potentials. Usually, they are self-made, independent people who are not easily led by the interviewer into points of view that do not truly reflect their own experiences. On the other hand, they accept ideas when these improve their understanding.

2. B1 speakers often use clear images to present meaning concisely without having to dwell in detail upon the unpleasant event. The images are embedded in temporally and causally ordered episodes and fit the semantic adjectives that elicited them. The function of images is to make experiences affectively self-relevant.

3. Semantic memory is varied and consistent with episodic evidence, even if it is a bit generous to the parents particularly in terms of legitimate explanatory circumstances. With regard to the self, the emphasis is upon causal contingencies, although sometimes these are overdrawn in ways that put more control in the speakers' behavior than probably existed in reality. (This, of course, is a self-protective strategy that is adaptive, as long as there is some truth

in the contingencies.). These characteristics functioned in childhood to organize the speakers' behavior in self-protective ways and to increase feelings of self-efficacy.

4. Episodes are short, concise, recalled accurately, and support the semantic words. They include negative experiences that are not cut off or otherwise distorted. The function of such clear recall is to provide the speaker with relatively untransformed information that can be reintegrated as the adult reaches progressively more inclusive integrations. Nevertheless, the episodes are usually set at a distance, firmly in the past, thus enabling the speaker to organize a life that is not plagued by past problems.

5. The connotative quality of the language is concentrated in small bits of phrasing that convey affective qualities; otherwise the manner of speech is more focused on the semantic definition of affect rather than on evocative qualities.

6. Integration in B1 speakers was often achieved after some effort. This integration enables them to (a) maintain the maximum positive contact with their parents, (b) protect themselves psychologically from the parents' limitations as parents, and (c) knowledgeably and consciously change their behavior in adulthood. Often the speaker is able to articulate (a) his or her active choice to keep attachment-related topics at a psychological distance and (b) his or her developmental process from childhood to the present, such that changes in perspective or strategy are the outcome of an understood process. Attachment and relationships, however, are treated as being important and are not dismissed.

The criteria for Grice's (1975) maxims of manner, relevance, and quality are all met, although, often, the quantity of speech is only barely sufficient. In evaluating speakers' presentations of their histories, we tend to agree with their perspectives (i.e., we find the histories to be psychologically sound).

ASSOCIATED STRATEGIES OR MODIFIERS

In the case of unresolved trauma or loss for recent events, the most frequent response for B1s is a dismissing form of lack of resolution of the loss or trauma. In addition, more than for other Bs, B1s may have some slight risk of depression.

DIFFERENTIATING **B1** FROM OTHER STRATEGIES

B1 transcripts are differentiated from A1 transcripts by the absence of idealization of negative aspects of childhood attachment relationships and the acknowledged recall of negative episodic information. They are differentiated from B2 transcripts by the relative conciseness of their discourse and emphasis on positive aspects of others.

Experience/History

The histories of B1 speakers vary greatly but usually involve some re-jection of attachment behavior or of the self. Often there are also indica-tions that the speaker was loved (i.e., protected and comforted). If a speaker's history is largely negative or dangerous, there is usually some reference to an attachment figure (or important affiliative figure) who supported the speaker emotionally. If the history does not contain dan-ger, a pattern of emotional reserve that belies tender feelings is usually presented (i.e., the communication "code" of the family is one of re-serve).

B2 (ACCEPTING)

Overview

As presented here, the B1–2 strategies are slightly changed from Ains-worth's (1973) patterns to fit with the theory developed for the Type A strategies. That is, B1 is more idealizing of attachment figures and B2 is more negating of the self. But in both cases, this is a mild process that does not substantively distort the truth. In particular, B2 speakers em-phasize their own contributions to untoward outcomes but they do not consider themselves inherently bad. They also do not accept responsi-bility for the behavior of others or dismiss these outcomes as inconse-quential.

B2 speakers are open and direct; they negotiate differences to achieve mutually satisfactory compromises. On the other hand, compared to other Type B speakers, they dwell a bit more on their own negative contributions to their functioning, setting aside somewhat the limita-tions of others. There is a clear valuing of attachment and familial rela-tionships, even when these have been a source of difficulty.

Discourse Markers and Their Psychological Function

1. Procedurally, B2 speakers appear distancing until they feel comfortable with the interview and interviewer; the function of this slow-to-warm approach is to protect the self from the discomfort of negative feelings.
2. Images are inhibited until the speaker feels at ease; this functions to keep affect under control during the portion of the interview when the speaker knows least well what to expect. After that point, the images are well integrated in the discourse and convey feeling.
3. Although semantic memory is more positive than can be supported by evidence from episodic memory, there is no evidence that it is distorted to the point of being false (thus, it is similar to the semantic memory of B1 speakers). As with the B1 strategy, this functions to keep the speaker from becoming preoccupied with aspects of the past that cannot be changed. In comparison with B1, they are more inclined to acknowledge negative aspects of relationships with attachment figures, but they attribute some responsibility for this to the self.
4. The connotative quality of their language becomes less contained and guarded than B1, once they have warmed up to the process of the interview.
5. Episodes are recalled and function as a reliable guide to how things have worked out in the past. They provide credible evidence for what the speaker says, that is, there is no evidence of unacknowledged discrepancies between semantic and episodic information. The past may be seen with "rosy glasses," but not distorted lenses.
6. In terms of integration, B2 speakers are reflective and on occasion display metacognitions. This functions to draw attention to discrepancy and change, allowing them to keep integrative processes self-relevant as the self and conditions change. They tend to find what good there is in their experiences and consciously focus their attention on it.

ASSOCIATED STRATEGIES OR MODIFIERS

B2 speakers may have some slight risk of depression.

DIFFERENTIATING B2 FROM OTHER STRATEGIES

B2 transcripts are differentiated from A2 transcripts by the lack of exaggeration in the negative portrayal of self and awareness of the self's positive contributions to desirable outcomes. They are differentiated from B1 transcripts by being longer and focusing more on the legitimate responsibility of the self for negative outcomes. They are differentiated from B3 transcripts by the presence of dismissing speech, a slow-to-warm approach to the interviewer, and a relatively forgiving perspective on their parents' limitations.

Experience/History

Naive B2 speakers have histories that are similar to those of B1 speakers, although there is generally a bit more warmth. Regardless of whether it is external conditions or parental personality that limited the comfort given to the speaker in childhood, it was clear to the speaker then and remains clear now that he or she was loved without reserve. That is, the speaker is confident that he or she was not kept at a distance because of personal characteristics. If there was danger in the speaker's childhood, it was usually not the result of parental limitations. On the contrary, it more often involved external or untoward events like wars, deaths, or serious illnesses. These, of course, can be more easily understood and their effects on the parents and oneself more easily forgiven than if there is the appearance that the parents could easily have made other, more loving and protective choices.

B4 (SENTIMENTAL)

Overview

The B4 strategy is based on Ainsworth's B4 infant pattern. It has been modified, however, to reflect the split within negative affect that defines the Type C even/odd distinction among classifications. B4 speakers are focused more on comfort and desire for comfort than B5 speakers who emphasize anger a bit more.

B4 speakers are balanced with regard to affect and cognition although they emphasize affect, particularly desire for comfort, somewhat more than cognition. Furthermore, B4 speakers are able both to connect themselves causally to difficult situations in which they contributed to outcomes and also to distance themselves when the parent was fully responsible for what happened. That is, unlike Type A individuals, they do not overattribute causality to themselves, even when doing so would increase feelings of control. On the other hand, unlike Type C individuals, they do not assign responsibility solely to others for undesirable relationships or events (i.e., they do not blame others). Instead, they are able to describe a reasonable interaction of the self and others in the genesis of their experiences.

Discourse Markers and Their Psychological Function

1. B4 speakers speak freely, if a bit at length, and make few serious errors of speech. When errors of thought are made, B4 speakers tend to notice and correct them. This clarity functions to increase the probability that B4 speakers will have mutually satisfying interactions with others and that they will perceive and correct incongruities. They are clear about temporal and causal relations (i.e., cognitive information). Statements, especially those about feelings, may be exaggerated but they are not inaccurate.

   B4 speakers show feelings easily, in a way that does not interrupt or otherwise hinder the interview. The feeling states tend more often to be tender than angry or fearful. Moreover, as the speaker reflects on the past, compassion for parents' experiences that was not recognized in childhood may be demonstrated.

   They engage cooperatively with the interviewer in an exploration of their past; the openness of communication of their affect doesn't distract the speakers' attention from discussion of the topic or force the interviewer to become involved in regulating the speakers' affective state.

2. B4 speakers use many images and some are a bit "over the top," particularly when positive aspects of relationships are being described. These function to communicate quickly about affective states and contexts, making others feel appreciated; they also focus the speaker's attention on the positive aspects of relationships. The images tend to be embedded in fully elaborated episodes rather than to stand alone.

3. B4 speakers have adequate access to semantic memory and are accurate about the temporal order of events and their causal connections, even if they feel some need to launch into fuller than nec-

essary discussion of their thoughts. Thus, the function of semantic memory to condense information to easily manipulated units of thought is reduced and the speaker becomes somewhat enmeshed in detail. However, the speaker's semantic understanding is that situations have multiple qualities and that these can elicit mixed feelings. B4 speakers can articulate and accept this complexity in both situations and themselves.

4.   The connotative quality of their language shows persuasive, evocative aspects, along with semantically expressed statements of the same feelings evoked. The suggestive functions of the language don't substitute for clear semantic statements of feelings.

5.   Episodic memory tends to be clear, readily available, consistent with semantic memory, and related to both good and bad aspects of the relationships. This functions to give speakers a good source of "raw" data from which to examine, and re-examine, their experiences. In fact they tend to focus on the present.

6.   Integrative processes are active in B4 speakers, with new ideas (new integrations of old information) coming easily. In addition, like all B speakers, B4 speakers generally take pleasure in arriving at new insights, even when these reflect uncomfortable information. They are optimistic, focusing on the value of relationships and finding, within the constraints imposed by the parents, the maximum possibility for forgiveness and supportive relationships in the present. Where this cannot be established with the parent, B4 speakers often discuss their current family as the resolution to past difficulties.

ASSOCIATED STRATEGIES OR MODIFIERS

In the case of especially recent and unexpected losses or exposures to danger, B4 speakers may temporarily show a preoccupied lack of resolution of the threat, but this tends to be quite limited or contained.

DIFFERENTIATING B4 FROM OTHER STRATEGIES

The B4 strategy can be differentiated from B3 by the greater volume of speech, repetition of ideas, and reliance on feelings to explain relationships. It can be differentiated from B5 by the more treasuring approach to relationships (i.e., a focus on comfort) and a lesser amount of angry complaining.

Experience/History

Like all Bs, B4 speakers can have any sort of history.

B5 (COMPLAINING ACCEPTANCE)

Overview

This pattern was first identified empirically by Main and Cassidy among 6-year-olds (Main & Cassidy, 1988). In terms of the theory presented here, the B4–5 pair corresponds in psychological process to the threatening/disarming split of anger from fear and desire for comfort that is seen in the coercive strategies (e.g., C1–2, C3–4). In the case of B4–5, however, there is greater integration and more awareness of the contributions of the self to this process.

B5 speakers are open and direct in their dealings with others; however, they tend to remain aware of negative experiences from the past and their implications for the future more than other Type B speakers. They feel considerable anger and are aware of its source in relationships. They have discovered that, although display of anger can be an effective attachment behavior, anger cannot solve all problems and that, when excessive, it can interfere with personal happiness and adaptation, or even jeopardize relationships. In addition, B5 speakers are aware when they contribute to maintaining the angry quality of these relationships. Therefore, their mental activity is organized around preventing defensive angry responses.

Discourse Markers and Their Psychological Function

1. Procedurally, B5 speakers are cooperative with the interviewer, and when they speak at excessive length they acknowledge this, often humorously (e.g., *"How much time do we have?"*). Thus, they seek permission to violate Grice's (1975) maxims. Procedural memory functions to facilitate engagement with others, thus, increasing the probability that others will support them. The relative absence of errors of thought (i.e., transformations of information) enables B5 speakers to focus their attention and identify relations among events, feelings, and relationships.

2. Images are often used: They tend to be lively and explicitly tied to the speaker. Thus, they are used illustratively rather than as substi-

tutes for semantic understanding or violating the boundaries of time and context. They function to clarify feeling states without obscuring their actual complexity.

3. Semantically, B5 speakers are able to focus on relationships with their parents separately and to summarize each with several unique descriptive words or phrases. These words may be contradictory, but the speaker is able to explain how both qualities existed in the relationship. Often there is a negative flavor to the set of semantic descriptors, but the reflected circumstances are credible, even if slanted toward the speaker's own perspective and, especially, toward his or her childhood perspective. This functions to keep problems at the forefront of attention (where they can possibly be resolved).

4. Connotative language tends to be arousing and to fit the content. The evocative features include long responses, with the use of repetition and striking rhetorical figures to emphasize the anger tied to negative circumstances.

5. Episodic memory is extensive, offering credible evidence of the speaker's semantic overview of the relationship; it is also particularly focused on the present, functioning to improve the possibility for re-analysis of current functioning, thus, creating the possibility for change.

6. Throughout, and especially in response to the integrative questions, B5 speakers are balanced in their review of their experiences. This facilitates the recognition of interpersonal processes. They differentiate people and relationships well, seeing both the positive and negative aspects of each. In particular, they differentiate their parents' contributions to their experiences from their own; thus, they do not place full responsibility for problems in the relationship on the parents. Instead, they acknowledge their own contributions to creating and maintaining each relationship as it was. Moreover, although they still continue to express regret that things could not have been different, they do, in fact, acknowledge that childhood has ended, that the past cannot be changed, and that their parents cannot be changed to fit their desires. Their thoughtfulness during the interview is demonstrated in self-reflective statements. This, in turn, facilitates change. In addition, it enables the speaker to reinterpret parental deficiencies so that they are seen less in terms of unfair treatment and more in terms of the limitations of the parents. One outcome of this process can be the re-

placement of anger toward the parents with compassion for all family members' situations.

In sum, we tend to agree with B5 speakers' evaluation of their situations, including their conclusion that they still tend to be drawn back into the old conflicts but that they have and use strategies to curtail the endless perseveration of the Type C strategy.

With regard to Grice's maxims, B5 speakers often violate the maxim of *quantity* by offering too much and too detailed information, although the information is *relevant* to the topic and consistent in meaning throughout the interview (i.e., the *quality* of the information is consistent). Moreover, B5 speakers relate information in a clear and orderly *manner* so that, in spite of the quantity, the reader is neither overwhelmed nor confused. Overall, the speech of B5 speakers is moderately coherent.

In conclusion, rather than acting coercively, they report hesitating before acting and using the extra time to integrate information in a more balanced manner that will facilitate productive, relationship-maintaining responses. This pattern of mental functioning limits their experience of anger, focuses them on dyadic contributions to the relationship, and enables them to find other means of meeting their need for safety and comfort.

ASSOCIATED STRATEGIES AND MODIFIERS

B5 speakers are generally not associated with other strategies but may have preoccupied lack of resolution of loss or trauma.

RISK FOR PSYCHOPATHOLOGY

B5 speakers have little risk for psychopathology. Under adverse conditions, however, there is a small risk that anger will become a more dominating and distorting state, thus, generating a bit of risk for anxiety disorders.

DIFFERENTIATING B5 FROM OTHER STRATEGIES

B5 speakers are differentiated from other Bs by the complaining tone of their speech and its preoccupied quality as reflected in discourse typical of Type C speakers, for example, long, run-on sentences (without errors of thought). They are differentiated from Type C speakers by the somewhat greater coherence of their discourse, for example, there are few serious dysfluencies indicative of errors of thought (such as involving anger, use of the present tense, or oscillations) and a substantially greater coherence of their thought processes.

Experience/History

B5 speakers tend to have had conflictual relationships with parents who were centered more on themselves and their problems than on the child's perspective and needs. Often the parents were involving with the child and over- or underprotective. Nevertheless, B5 speakers tended not to have been exposed to real dangers of either a physical or psychological sort.

In cases where B5 status is the adult outcome of a history of a Type A or C childhood pattern of attachment, any sort of history is possible. The speaker, however, is able to articulate some of the process through which the current integration was achieved.

BO (BALANCED OTHER)

The BO designation is reserved for transcripts that meet the general criteria for a balanced strategy but that, nevertheless, do not fit the criteria for any of the particular Type B strategies. That is, they qualify as balanced by having balanced patterns of discourse in at least three memory systems. In addition, however, there are several likely forms of incongruency. First, the transcripts do not meet the criteria for any specific Type B strategy. Second, many BO transcripts fit descriptors for both the dismissingly balanced strategies (B1–2) and the involvingly balanced strategies (B4–5). Third, there may be both balanced and non-balanced items checked in the same memory system and for the same attachment figure. Transcripts assigned to Balanced Other do not, however, contain any serious errors of thought that remain uncorrected; specifically, they do not contain errors of thought in a minimum of three memory systems that would permit assignment to some other Type A or C classification.

In addition, BO transcripts meet the criteria for coherent discourse as defined by Grice's maxims and they satisfy the final four comparison questions, that is, the coder agrees with the speaker's evaluation of his or her experience, the information in different memory systems is consistent, there is direct access to all memory systems, and attachment issues are discussed coherently.

Nevertheless, the incongruencies (lack of a coherent pattern, mixed balanced and nonbalanced items, and mixtures of A and C items within a single memory system) leave the speaker with a vulnerability that is greater than expected for a "full" balanced individual.

There are a number of life circumstances that are associated with assignment of a transcript to BO. The three most common are

- Recent completion or nearing completion of psychotherapy;
- Recent major and self-threatening changes in life circumstances (e.g., recent divorce or death);
- Unresolved loss or trauma that is pervasive through the transcript in too great frequency for full balance, but without distorting thought with regard to other attachment-relevant topics.

Chapter 6

Overview of the Type A Strategies and A1–2

GENERAL CHARACTERISTICS APPLYING TO ALL TYPE A CLASSIFICATIONS

Overview

THE PRIMARY MENTAL PROCESSES ASSOCIATED WITH THE TYPE A STRATegy are (a) splitting of positive and negative features of self, others, and relationships and (b) dismissing one's own negative affect from mental processing and behavior, while attending vigilantly to an attachment figure's negative affect. Functionally, this includes (a) distancing the self from one's own feelings, (b) dismissing negative conclusions about attachment figures, and (c) attributing negative features of relationships to the self. The process of "splitting" is a dissociative process involving keeping some information out of further processing while other information is carried forward for further transformation. The Type A strategy omits information about negative aspects of the attachment figure and negative affect of the self from processing. In the absence of this information, semantic information appears absolute (i.e., without exception) and is, therefore, distorted in the direction of idealization or exoneration of the attachment figure. In the absence of displayed negative affect, positive feelings about experience become possible. Within the array of strategies, there is a dichotomy between strategies organized primarily around the positive qualities of the attachment figure (the odd-numbered strategies) and strategies organized primarily around the negative qualities of the self (the even-numbered strategies, see Figure 2.2).

Transcripts of speakers who use a Type A self-protective strategy are typified by (a) discourse dismissing the self; (b) limited procedural engagement with the interviewer; (c) a paucity of images, unconnected images, or obliquely connected images; (d) distorted (idealized, exonerating, or delusionally exulting) semantic memory; (e) limited or distorted episodic recall; and (f) little, banal, or failed integration. Crucially, in all Type A transcripts, there is an absence of the speaker's own perspective and true negative feelings (i.e., anger, fear, and desire for comfort). The means by which feelings are omitted from awareness varies by strategy, but omission is common to all Type A transcripts. (Other feelings and emotions, such as positive affect, shame, and attachment figures' feelings may be included.)

In addition, speakers who use a Type A self-protective strategy tend to use temporally ordered information to generate semantic generalizations, particularly semantic understandings that are framed as if/then statements pertaining to responsibility or the consequences of failing to fulfill responsibility, for instance, *"If you were bad, then you were punished."*

Especially in the A1–2 strategies, the five descriptive words question, the central semantic probe in the AAI, tends to produce stereotyped answers in which the words are synonyms used to describe the single quality of a good relationship (e.g., *very good, loving, very close, supportive, caring*). In addition, because good and bad attributes are split in semantic memory they tend to be stated with greater than realistic clarity, that is, with absolute words like *always* and *never*. Frequently, the adjectives for the mother and father are almost identical with little differentiation of person; this suggests that a mental stereotype is being used to select the descriptors rather than actual recall of the specific relationships. Although there is often a failure to recall episodes, when episodic memory is present, it tends to have more temporal order than affect or images. Further, episodes are better retrieved through the semantic retrieval strategy of the five descriptive words or phrases than through the direct probes of episodic memory contained in the questions regarding the negative conditions of distress, illness, hurt, separation, rejection, and anger. The latter more often produce denial or displacement: *"That never happened. I was never ill. I can't remember being distressed. I recall a time when my sister was."*

In terms of the coherence of speech (Grice's four maxims regarding coherent speech), speakers using a Type A self-protective strategy tend to (a) speak in an orderly *manner* (fulfilling the requirements of manner), (b) offer an insufficient *quantity* of information (particularly about the negative aspects of the attachment figure and positive aspects of the self), (c) fail to support their (positive) generalizations with evidence (thus, failing the requirements of *quality*), and (d) describe their childhood experience from the attachment figure's perspective (thus, failing to meet fully the requirements of *relevance*). Overall, then, speakers who use a Type A self-protective strategy tend to be moderate to low in the coherence of their discourse, but not confusing. That is, their words read clearly and the meanings can be grasped, but both are distorted. Consequently, their coherence of mind, that is, their capacity to reach balanced, integrative conclusions, tends to be quite low. This discrepancy between apparently fluent speech and distorted thought is what deceives the naive reader into thinking that the thought processes are well integrated and is also the process by which the psychological strategy protects the speaker.

In considering all that the speaker has said, the skilled coder ultimately decides that critical information has been omitted and, therefore, that the central conclusions that are offered are inaccurate or misleading.

Affect and Cognition

Affect: Speakers using a Type A self-protective strategy inhibit display of negative affect and have few or unconnected images of danger or safety. They often use nonverbal false positive affect (e.g., laughing at uncomfortable moments). They are, however, able to discuss affect semantically and in a nominalized form.

Cognition: Such speakers organize their behavior around temporal expectations. Because these tend to include the expectation of rejection for displaying negative affect, evidence of feelings tends to be inhibited. When, on the other hand, display of positive feelings is rewarded, these are displayed even if they are not felt, thus, creating false positive affect. Cognitively, therefore, Type A speakers emphasize the predictable rules that guide protective behavior.

With regard to time, speakers using a Type A self-protective strategy conceptualize time as finite and immutable. The consequence is that they believe not only that the past cannot be changed (an accurate belief), but also that its relations extend into the future, that is, that causal relations do not change over time (an inaccurate belief). This has implications for beliefs about the futility of reconsideration of the past and the futility of change in the future. The psychological strategy for coping with this immutability is to distance recall of the past as much as possible, retaining and carrying forward only the guidelines for safe behavior. However, when the context from which these guidelines were derived is discarded from recall, it becomes difficult for the individual to discover ways in which the guidelines are inappropriate for current contexts. Put another way, omitting episodic memory omits source memory as well and this reduces the speaker's ability to evaluate the validity of his or her semantic conclusions. Further, even if they notice that their behavior malfunctions, speakers using a Type A self-protective strategy have procedural routines that they use so automatically that often the strategy is implemented before conscious thought can generate a more appropriate alternative. Thus, new responses need to be both learned and also implemented in place of automatic procedures; it is the latter that is most difficult.

Further, with regard to responsibility, speakers who use a Type A strategy equate temporal order with causation and causation with responsibility. Thus, without regard to age or relative power, such speakers often consider themselves responsible for those things that follow their own behavior. Thus, even children can be held responsible for parental behavior. Of course, defining the beginning of a sequence is a subjective choice. Speakers using a Type A self-protective strategy often begin sequences with their own actions. This creates the appearance, in their minds, of having control over outcomes. Especially in the case of children, who have much less control over their lives than do adults, this can be adaptive when parents are exceptionally threatening. In adulthood, however, it both disposes individuals to an inner sense of shame and also creates an appearance of "grandiosity" or arrogance from the perspective of others.

Discourse Markers and Their Psychological Function

1. Procedural memory:
    (a) Speakers with a Type A self-protective strategy use *distancing* discourse. Markers include omission of the self

from sentences, speaking from others' perspectives, sub-stitution of distancing pronouns for self-referent personal pronouns, extended pausing before answering, clarity of temporal ordering, clarity of causal relations (e.g., when/then and if/then phrasing), minimization of intense nega-tive feelings or threatening experiences, normalization of negative situations, and nominalization of affect.

In their discourse, speakers with low-numbered strate-gies (A1–2) often speak carefully and with many hesita-tions so as to monitor their own speech; thus, those errors that remain tend to be errors of thought. Carefulness func-tions to protect the speaker from spontaneously leaking discrepant or forbidden information.

Speakers with high-numbered strategies (A3–8) are often agitated and show many dysfluencies; these are sometimes noticed by the speaker and covered with failed or incon-clusive metacognitions.

It is important to consider the topics that produce dys-fluence. Dysfluences regarding the self (e.g., stuttering, *I, I, I*) and important attachment figures (e.g., mumbling . . . *th mm my mother*) are common in Type A transcripts.

(b) In terms of expressed affect, *omission of true negative affect* functions to enable the speaker to inhibit behavior that could elicit rejection. Put another way, by deactivating the representation of negative affect, a speaker is less disposed to act on it and, therefore, less likely to be rejected by an attachment figure. On the other hand, display of *false posi-tive affect* can elicit parental caregiving/approval.

(c) In the relationship with the interviewer, speakers using a low-numbered Type A strategy distance themselves from the interviewer in a *neutral* way; this functions to reduce arousal, limits the interviewer's probes, and, thus, reduces the risk of the speaker becoming aware of distress-eliciting information. Speakers with high-numbered Type A strat-egies distance themselves from their own situations by allying themselves *analytically* (and self-critically) with the interviewer; this protects the self from others' criti-cism.

2. Imaged memory: *Omission* of images functions to direct atten-tion away from threatening experiences and feelings. Images, particularly images of place, which are *disconnected* from the

self, function similarly while still making information about dangerous contexts available.

3. Semantic memory: Semantic conclusions are simplified by splitting good and bad (between self and parents or between a parent and stepparent). This speeds decision making and reduces the probability that the individual's action will displease the attachment figure. In addition, by making the rules clear and the self responsible for parental satisfaction or dissatisfaction, distortion of semantic memory increases feelings of self-efficacy in children who feel vulnerable to parental threat.

4. Connotative language: The Type A strategy is best maintained when the language used does not refer to specific people and does not elicit feelings. Consequently, *artificial*, abstract, and intellectualized language is used.

5. Episodic memory: A1 and A2 speakers recount *few* episodes; instead, they more often restate their ideas semantically. When they do tell episodes, they *cut off* or misinterpret them. This creates the appearance of having evidence for their semantic conclusions when, in fact, such evidence is lacking or contradictory. Compulsive Type A speakers do recall episodes but recall them *from the parents' perspective*. This functions to keep critical episodic information available, without leading to personal distress or conflict with attachment figures.

6. Reflective integration: Speakers using a Type A self-protective strategy generally *do not integrate* information from different memory systems. This functions to prevent recognition of personal vulnerability or others' failure to protect or comfort the speaker in childhood. Those speakers who are aware of their negative childhood experiences often claim that their experiences show them what not to do and that they will use this information to reverse the negative strategy with their own children. Many use platitudes to avoid thinking about the issues raised. These, together with refusal to show true feelings to others or to arrive at semantic conclusions that include the influence and effects on the self of others, preclude such individuals from experiencing intimacy. Although they protect children from full awareness of their vulnerability, these functions are often counterproductive in adulthood.

Experience/History

Parents of speakers using a Type A self-protective strategy usually rejected their children's attachment behavior (for A1–2) or the attached child (for A3+). The rejection can range from rejection of attachment behavior when the child is actually safe (e.g., inhibiting crying when scared but actually safe at night in bed) or only mildly hurt (e.g., after the parent has come to bandage a wound) to endangering forms of rejection of the child (e.g., physical abuse or abandonment). The former examples involve protection but denial of comfort. The latter involve actual endangerment without either protection or comfort. Because the rejection was predictable, the child was able to organize a self-protective strategy to prevent it. The parents themselves usually used a Type A strategy in cases of lack of comfort whereas in the case of A3–6 speakers, they often used Type C+ strategies (cf. Crittenden et al., 1991; Hautamäki et al., 2010; Shah et al., 2010). At A7–8, speakers often had multiple dangerous caregivers.

A1 (IDEALIZING)

The A1 strategy is based on Ainsworth's (1973) A1 infant pattern, the preschool A1 strategy, and Main, Goldwyn and Hesse's (2003) Ds1 pattern in adulthood.

A1 individuals tend to minimize or omit their parents' negative characteristics. With only the positive aspects of their attachment figures available to awareness, these are easily exaggerated, making the parents appear ideal. In addition, A1 adults inhibit display of negative affect, emphasizing positive affect whenever possible.

Discourse Markers and their Psychological Function

In the A1 strategy, the function of the discourse style is to deactivate dispositional representations (DRs) of negative feelings.

1. The *distancing* function of the discourse, used for negative events or feelings of the self, is often marked by dysfluence. Typical A1 distancing discourse procedures involve delayed responding, cutting off of discussion, minimizing of negative events and feelings (which are often nominalized), and distancing the self from problems. The functions of dismissing discourse are (a) to give speakers

time to organize their thoughts consciously such that a consistent and logical model of childhood and the relationships with attachment figures can be presented without the intrusion of negative material and (b) to avoid activating DRs that could motivate negative behavior.

Procedurally, the A1 strategy allows for little or no feeling to be displayed during the interview.

The *neutral* relationship with the interviewer is typified by such brevity in the answers that interviewers feel reluctant to press further.

2. Images are generally *omitted* from discourse although some speakers may use images of comforting places. When images are present, they are cut off quickly. This functions to protect speakers from recognition of negative feelings with regard to parents.

3. Adults using the A1 strategy tend to *idealize* their attachment figures (e.g., the five descriptive words). Generalizations are distorted by splitting good and bad and assigning the positive characteristics to attachment figures. In the AAI, however, semantic idealization incurs the burden of supplying episodic evidence. Because the semantic descriptors are distorted, actual experience will not support the generalizations. This has implications for how episodic memory can be used. Idealized parents are often poorly differentiated (because perfection is so undifferentiable!). Moreover, in order to preclude an implied negative attribution, when something good is mentioned with reference to one parent, there is often a quick reassurance that the other was in no way lacking. Semantic idealization functions to keep information that attachment figures were rejecting of the speakers' feelings out of awareness; thus, A1 speakers can maintain the belief that they were safe and loved and avoid feeling vulnerable and uncomforted. It also functions to keep parental rules prominent in guiding their behavior. This is displayed in the frequent use of prescriptive semantic generalizations, often in the form of if/then phrases.

4. The language of A1 speakers is factual, often dry and intellectualized, generally socially desirable in a way that elicits approval, but not feeling. Occasionally, though, a powerful word will slip in. The infrequence and incongruence of such words add to their importance in conveying the negative aspects of the speaker's story.

5. When childhood experience does not support the semantic de-

scriptors, A1 speakers often state that they *cannot remember* early childhood or specific episodes that occurred in childhood (omitted episodic memory). Consequently, to provide evidence to support their semantic words or phrases, they reason *hypothetically* rather than recalling occasion-specific information. This often takes the form of scripts (e.g., *"She probably would . . ."*; *"Of course, she would . . ."*). This reduces the probability that the speaker will be faced with information that is in conflict with idealized generalizations. Generally, such speakers provide fewer episodes in response to the direct probes of episodic memory (e.g., sick, hurt, angry, rejected) than in response to the semantic probes of episodic memory (i.e., the five words or phrases). Indeed, A1 speakers often deny having had troubling experiences at all.

6. A1 speakers offer superficial and impersonal answers to the integrative questions. These answers do not indicate any awareness on the speaker's part of how he or she came to have the adult personality that we observe in the interview. Among well-educated A1 speakers, extensive sociological or cultural explanations may be offered instead of personal, family-specific ones. Frequently, an idealized version of maintaining the parents' good qualities is presented as if no evaluation of the parents' behavior were necessary. Even if the speaker suggests that he or she would like to change in some way, he or she does not pursue the possibility of parental limitations. Consequently, discrepant information is left unintegrated. The *lack of integration* is often covered by the use of socially accepted *platitudes*. In the final analysis, we do not agree with A1 speakers that their parents were "ideal" or that their childhood experiences enabled them to feel comfortable.

ASSOCIATED STRATEGIES OR MODIFIERS

A1 is usually a simple classification without associated strategies or modifiers. Occasionally, however, A1 is applied to one attachment figure and not to others. In addition, dismissed lack of resolution of loss may be present and reorganization is possible.

RISK FOR PSYCHOPATHOLOGY

Under safe conditions, individuals classified as A1 experience little or no threat of psychopathology.

DIFFERENTIATING A1 FROM OTHER STRATEGIES

A1 transcripts are most easily differentiated from A2 transcripts by a greater emphasis on the desirable qualities of the parents and a greater absence of episodic recall and from the compulsive strategies by greater idealization. They are differentiated from B1 by a lack of negative information. They can be differentiated from A7 transcripts by the lack of evidence of serious threats to the speaker's physical or psychological integrity and by the lack of "fantastic" or delusional episodes; strategically, A1 speakers emphasize positive and minimize negative qualities, while A7 speakers deny negative qualities altogether, sometimes transforming them into positive delusions.

Experience/History

Parents of adults classified as A1 tended to be demanding regarding their children's behavior and were more likely to actually punish children for displaying unnecessary attachment behavior or failing to meet parental standards of independence and performance than were parents of A2 adults. The unnecessary display of attachment behavior was often related to threatening, but "safe," separations (e.g., going to alternate caregivers, going to the hospital). The required "performance" could refer either to accomplishments or to good/obedient behavior. Parents of A1 speakers could be approving and rewarding when their demands were met.

Within the range of approved behavior in a physically safe environment, these adults tend to perform well. They are reliable, predictable, and independent. They also maintain relationships well over long periods of time and distance. Their vulnerability becomes most readily apparent in situations that require intimacy and affective reciprocity.

A2 (DISTANCING)

The A2 strategy is based on Ainsworth's (1973) similarly named pattern in infancy, the A2 strategy in the preschool years, and Main, Goldwyn and Hesse's (2003) Ds3 pattern (although it is restricted as compared to Main, Goldwyn, and Hesse).

Like A1 speakers, A2 speakers have had negative affect rejected in the context of sufficient protection. Unlike A1 individuals, in the split between good and bad, they focus more on the negative aspects of themselves that can explain their parents' need to be restrictive or rejecting than on the parents' "ideal" characteristics. The negative self-focus prevents their having to judge their attachment figures negatively, which would elicit the very negative affect that results in rejection.

Discourse Markers and their Psychological Function

1. Individuals using the A2 strategy (a) use self-*dismissing* discourse and (b) tend to be uncomfortable during the interview. As a result, many rush their speech in an attempt to satisfy the interviewer. In any case, they struggle over how to present negative information about their childhood relationships, being neither fully avoidant nor cooperative. The function of the dysfluencies and interpersonal distance is to give speakers time to consciously organize their thoughts (such that negative information will not be intruded spontaneously). The stutters and restarts reflect attempts to control intrusive and unwanted ideas.

    With regard to displayed affect, A2 speakers show anxiety and sometimes annoyance with themselves or *self-disparaging humor*. Like Ainsworth's (1973) A2 pattern in infancy, these are the angry Type A speakers; that is, the anger that all individuals using a Type A strategy actually feel is closest to the surface and less thoroughly inhibited in A2 speakers. The anger, however, is more directed toward the self or the context than toward attachment figures. In some cases, however, the anger can be focused on a distant attachment figure (e.g., a stepparent or an absent divorced parent).

    Speakers using an A2 self-protective strategy engage with the interviewer with relative willingness but often take considerable time to answer questions.

2. A2 speakers tend to use few images, and those that they do produce are often in conflict with their semantic statements. The images function to represent, without conscious recognition, speakers' true negative feelings.

3. A2 speakers distort semantic memory to make their parents appear good in the context of a self that is made to appear bad and without unfulfilled needs. Specifically, A2 speakers split information that is helpful in predicting future parental behavior (especially behavior in response to the self) from information that elicits disapproval. Helpful information receives preferential attention in or-

ganizing perception, behavior, and speech. Therefore, A2 speakers *idealize* their attachment figures and disparage themselves. When negative feelings are mentioned, they are minimized or nominalized; this keeps them psychologically distant and therefore speakers can feel more secure and loved and avoid feeling vulnerable and unprotected. Distorted semantic memory also functions to keep parental rules, as opposed to self-negative feelings, prominent in motivating behavior.

4. Connotatively, speakers using an A2 strategy retain negative information in images of places and activities of the self, but use little, if any, negative language that is tied to attachment figures. This functions to enable speakers to retain some access to negative affect without having it associated with the parent. Their speech often has a rushed, run-on quality that expresses heightened arousal and their episodes can contain poignant images. These features, plus the underlying angry tone, can mislead the listener/coder into thinking the individual is using a Type C strategy. Consideration of whose perspective is being offered can usually clarify the Type A strategy.

5. Episodic memory is *omitted* or partially omitted from consciousness. This functions to keep speakers from being fully aware of the discrepancy between the idealized parents that they imagined they had and the somewhat rejecting parents they actually had. Many of the episodes that are offered are really semantic scripts or "hypothetical episodes" that are constructed from semantic memory. When genuine, occasion-specific episodes are provided, they tend to contradict the meaning of positive adjectives (*opposite* episodes). This is due to the attribution of negative aspects of relationships to the self; this process allows the omission of episodic memory to be only partial, such that some episodes that are incompatible with the positive semantic descriptors can be recalled. Consequently, speakers must use self-protective processes to avoid coming to the conclusion that relationships with parents had distinct negative qualities. These self-protective processes are usually only partially successful because the contradictory information has already been brought to mind. In these cases, A2 speakers may (a) be unaware of this and conclude that they have supported the adjective (i.e., positive wrap-up), (b) distract attention to another topic, or (c) cut off the episode at the point when the attachment figure fails to provide comfort. The need for the abrupt cutting off of episodes pro-

vides evidence that the negative information *is recalled* and also that the mind *is monitoring what is being said* such that, when discrepancies are found, it takes protective action.

6. The integrative process is distorted such that erroneous conclusions about the self are drawn from episodic memory. Although the presence of intruded material creates substantial opportunity for self-awareness, integration is very limited in A2 speakers. Instead, speakers give superficial and normalizing answers to the integrative questions (e.g., *"Why did your parents act that way?" "Because they loved me, because that's the way they were raised, because it was the right thing to do."*). Again, this functions to keep negative information about the speakers' own uncomforted feelings out of consciousness and reduces feelings of being threatened by the rejection of attachment figures. Overall, the reader does not agree with the speaker regarding the positive qualities of the parents, the negative qualities of the speaker, and the speaker's positive relationships with the parents.

Associated strategies or modifiers

A2 is usually a simple strategy without associated strategies or modifiers. Occasionally, however, A2 is applied to one attachment figure and not to others. In addition, dismissed lack of resolution of loss is common and reorganization is possible.

Risk for psychopathology

There is little or no risk of psychopathology among A2 individuals in safe contexts.

Differentiating A2 transcripts from other strategies

A2 transcripts are most easily differentiated from A1 transcripts by speakers' greater willingness to participate in the interview, access to episodic memory, and emphasis on the negative qualities of the self. They differ from B2 transcripts by speakers' limited semantic recognition of the negative character of childhood attachment relationships and unwillingness to consider thoughtfully contributions of their parents to this and the implications to themselves of their experiences.

Experience/History

Attachment figures of speakers using an A2 self-protective strategy usually protected their children from actual danger but failed to provide comfort for psychological threats (e.g., separations or illnesses). Instead, parents taught their children to act independently, without disruptive emotional displays and in predictable and logical ways, and to trust that others would be equally predictable and logical. Consequently, A2 speakers have often experienced rejection of *unnecessary attachment behavior* (but not of attachment per se, nor of themselves) by their attachment figures. On the other hand, they were usually accepted when approved behavior was shown.

The threat experienced by most people classified as A2 tends to be mild (e.g., disapproval or withdrawal of approval when attachment behavior was displayed or when parental standards were not met). Therefore, the splitting off (dismissing) of information about the unloving and unprotective parent and needy self is not complete.

Individuals using a Type A strategy tend to be independent and reliable in their interpersonal relationships; adults using an A2 strategy tend to display more negative affect and to be more resentful than adults using other Type A strategies.

Chapter 7

Compulsive Type A Strategies (A3–8)

Coping With Danger

THE COMPULSIVE TYPE A STRATEGIES (A3–8) ARE DRAWN FROM THE Dynamic-Maturational Model of attachment and adaptation and expand on the patterning described by Bowlby (1973, 1980). They differ in important ways from the Ainsworth-based A1–2 strategies (Ainsworth, 1973). In terms of discourse, speakers using the compulsive Type A strategies (A+) are more willing to engage in the interview than A1–2, that is, there are fewer cut-offs, long hesitations, telegraphic responses, and so forth. In addition, they often create an analytical alliance with the interviewer, thus, distancing themselves from their own perspectives. They do not idealize their attachment relationships (except in A7), relating negative episodes that give substance to semantically described limitations of the parents. However, they often exonerate parents of responsibility for their limitations.

In addition, several critical features preclude these speakers being placed in the Type B or Type C classifications. First, they use dismissing discourse to dismiss themselves, their feelings, and their own perspectives throughout (therefore, they are not self-focused). Second, they distance themselves from negative affect and often substitute false positive affect (therefore, they are not balanced). Third, they use semantic memory in preference to episodic recall and the semantic generaliza-tions are not merely hypothetical (as in A1–2), but more often prescrip-tive of what should happen (A3–6) or intentional regarding what they will make happen (A7–8). Fourth, they tell their stories from the per-spectives of their attachment figures (therefore, they are neither bal-anced nor preoccupied with themselves). Fifth, they are not sufficiently integrated to describe the interactive relations of affect and cognition, of self to others, and of past to present for either themselves or their parents (therefore, they cannot be balanced). Many compulsive Type A speakers claim that their experiences taught them what not to do and that they will use this information to reverse the negative strategy with their own children. Because they are unable to describe a process of change, particularly one that accounts for multiple perspectives, in-cluding their own, there is often evidence that they were unable to im-plement a correction (although they may have instigated a reversal and, thus, raised a Type C child, cf. Crittenden et al., 1991; Hautamäki et al., 2010; Shah et al., 2010). This is an example of "pendulum parent-ing" (Crittenden, 2008).

In terms of history, unlike A1 and A2 speakers, adults classified as using compulsive strategies were usually endangered as children ei-ther by the parents' threatening action or by the parents' failure to act protectively. Moreover, in most cases, the compulsive adult strategy is the outcome of a series of strategy changes or reorganizations that occur across infancy and childhood.

The compulsive strategies are often classified as B or C or Cannot Classify when the Main, Goldwyn and Hesse (2003) method is used. In this way, these strategies are similar to the patterns of behavior of dis-turbed children in the Strange Situation that were originally misclassi-fied as secure (Cicchetti & Barnett, 1991; Egeland & Sroufe, 1981) but would now be considered to be A3, A4, or A/C (Crittenden, Claussen, & Kozlowska, 2007; Spieker & Crittenden, 2010).

A3 (COMPULSIVE CAREGIVING AND COMPULSIVE ATTENTION)

Overview

The compulsive caregiving strategy (A3) is based on observations of preschool children's organization (Crittenden, 1992), clinical observa-tions, and Bowlby's (1973) description of such children in his discus-sion of the effects of maternal anxiety on children.

The A3 strategy exists in two forms: compulsive caregiving (A3) and compulsive attention (A3-). Both involve focusing on others' perspectives by inhibiting the negative affect of the self and giving priority to the needs of attachment figures. They differ in who is the object of attention, but, in both cases, the person using the strategy desires protection.

Compulsive caregiving (A3) is a strategy in which, as a child, the individual pragmatically does those things that draw the attention of withdrawn or neglectful parents to himself or herself. Often, that meant cheering up or caring for the parent (i.e., role reversal). By adulthood, compulsive caregivers feel safest and most comfortable when caring for other people, even to the exclusion of their own needs. They usually exonerate their caregivers from failure to meet their needs.

The "softer" form of the strategy, compulsive attention (A3-), doesn't reach full role reversal, as the child just needs to pay steady attention to the parent to make the parent feel more confident and important. By adulthood, the A3- strategy is focused on being present and attentive for important people and their priorities, with a relative dismissal of the priorities of the self.

Discourse Markers and their Psychological Function

1. Procedurally, speakers using an A3 strategy use self-dismissing discourse and the perspective of the cared-for parent.

   True negative affect is inhibited and *false positive affect* is substituted. Thus, compulsive caregiving speakers tend to show false affect at difficult moments in the interview (e.g., laughing when discussing a loss). This enables them to feel that they are not stressing the interviewer and are without needs for empathy themselves (because this need is not expected to be fulfilled by an attachment figure). The function is to increase the availability of attachment figures and reduce the probability of psychological or physical abandonment.

   Speakers using a compulsive caregiving strategy tend to take an *analytical* stance with regard to themselves, thus, allying themselves with the interviewer; this functions to increase closeness to and approval from the interviewer and to shelter them from criticism. In addition, compulsive caregiving speakers often show sympathy for, or caregiving of, the interviewer.

2. *Displaced* images are frequent in A3 transcripts; they often describe safe places and are substituted for answers that should refer to the

parent (e.g., *Tell me about your mother? We always lived in a big house* . . .). Other images refer to danger and tend to replace dangerous people or endangered/dangerous parts of bodies. These images, containing true negative affect located in contexts as distant as possible from the self, function to retain access to affect-based information, especially information regarding dangerous and safe places and situations.

3. Semantically, compulsive caregiving speakers do not idealize parents; instead, they describe relationships with relative accuracy but *exonerate* parents of responsibility for failures. Specifically, they tend to supply adjectives that express the parents' desires and frailties and to excuse or explain parental behavior in terms of the parents' needs and vulnerabilities. Further, in describing their own behavior, they use *prescriptive* semantic statements about how one should behave. Semantic memory is distorted in ways that make parents' limitations seem forgivable and the self seem responsible for creating and solving the problem. The function is to enable speakers to maintain relationships with attachment figures, which is essential to survival in childhood. It also enables the self to improve the relationship and to feel efficacious.

4. A3 connotative language is *artificial* and dry, although the parents' perspectives may be rendered in less stilted ways.

5. Episodic memory is present and temporally accurate (often in the form of detailed scripts) although self-perspectives are absent (images substitute for self-affect). Instead, episodic memory is distorted to reflect the *parents' perspectives*. The speakers' feelings of fear, anger, and desire for comfort are set aside, dismissed, or left unmentioned. The function is to foster recall of important event contingencies while protecting the speaker from negative feelings that could motivate unacceptable behavior.

6. Integration is pervasively *refused*; instead, the focus is on protecting the parent from blame or responsibility through exoneration. The availability of negative information provides an A3 speaker with repeated opportunities for integration and often these are acknowledged by the speaker. That is, the speaker notes awareness of some discrepancy. The opportunity for integration is, however, allowed to slip away without further consideration. The potential for a metacognition *fails*. In childhood, this functions to keep the self from feeling vulnerable. In adulthood, it maintains the caregiving behavior even when it is not adaptive.

ASSOCIATED STRATEGIES AND MODIFIERS

A3 is often seen in conjunction with A1 or A4 (for a different attachment figure) and, among psychotherapists, A3 is often in a state of reorganization. Lack of resolution of loss (both dismissed and preoccupying or both) is also common. Sometimes there is unresolved trauma in a preoccupied form with regard to abandonment by the cared-for figure.

RISK FOR PSYCHOPATHOLOGY

The risk for psychopathology is relatively low, except under certain circumstances. When caregiving is not possible, individuals using an A3 strategy may become excessively anxious and at times even depressed (e.g., when faced with the loss of a cared-for attachment figure). In addition, many A3 speakers experienced psychosomatic illnesses in childhood or adulthood (or both) but these were minimized and not used to elicit caregiving or control parental behavior. The risk for psychopathology increases as the strategy is applied more pervasively and with increasingly less integration of negative affect to life situations.

DIFFERENTIATING A3 FROM OTHER STRATEGIES

A3 transcripts are differentiated from B transcripts by the absence of the speakers' perspectives and feelings and from A1 and A2 transcripts by the absence of semantic idealization and presence of acknowledged negative episodes. A3 is differentiated from A4 transcripts by the procedural predominance of showing false positive affect over performing or obeying. A3- transcripts are differentiated from A3 transcripts by the speakers showing less affect through images, less anxiety through run-on speech, and less false positive affect; also, A3- speakers appear more inhibited, with less caregiving initiatives than speakers with the full version of the strategy.

Experience/History

The basis for the role-reversing, compulsive caregiving A3 self-protective strategy is the primary caregiver's inability to function in a protective and comforting manner. In mild cases, the feeling of security is at greatest risk; in more severe cases, actual safety is compromised. Alternate caregivers tend to be idealized or derogated, depending on whether they were distant and relatively absent from daily life (idealization) or were present and a threat to the child or primary attachment figure (derogation). Speakers often report that there was a period of adolescent rebellion in which speakers acted coercively and often very angrily, but longitudinal evidence is lacking. In adulthood, speakers maintain a relation with the role-reversing attachment figure by accepting the role of caregiver and excusing parents' limitations.

Compulsive caregiving adults are often particularly adept at working with people who do not know how they feel or who need more than the usual support and structure. In group settings, they often enable others to feel comfortable enough to function productively. At the same time, however, they are not comfortable with expressed negative affect and may seek prematurely to terminate it, that is, before exploring its meaning to the individual who experiences this motivational state.

A4 (COMPULSIVE COMPLIANCE AND COMPULSIVE PERFORMANCE)

Overview

The A4 self-protective strategy is based on observations of infants (Crittenden, 1985a; Crittenden & DiLalla, 1988), preschool children's behavior (Crittenden, 1992), adolescents, adults, clinical case materials, and Adult Attachment Interviews (AAIs).

The A4 strategy consists of taking adults' perspectives, foreseeing their demands, and, without reference to one's own desires or feelings, meeting those demands. It is used when children have been subjected to excessive pressure to do as adults wish them to do. The consequences of failure to meet the demands are attributed to the self being bad rather than to negative qualities of the powerful adult.

The strategy has two forms. A4, compulsive compliance, is the full form of the strategy, based on the attempt to avoid harsh punishment for not complying with others' demands. A4-, compulsive performance, is the "softer" form, in which parents' love and approval, instead of physical punishment, is the means of coercing the individual to perform as others (usually the parents) wish, even if others' goals and standards are too high to be fully met. Usually, the individual's performance is excellent and appears to be its own reward, but the stress to the individual is overlooked.

Discourse Markers and their Psychological Function

1. Procedurally, A4 speakers show discourse markers typical of Type A but without idealization or lack of recall of episodes. A4 speakers focus on temporal order: what precedes violence or rejection and what can prevent it. Dangerous experiences are told with distancing discourse. A4- speakers use the same discourse, focusing on outcomes and whether these meet others' expectations.

   Usually, little affect is displayed (except possibly anxiety) and if negative affect is displayed, it is not directed toward other people. True affect is expressed as anxiety and reflected in dysfluencies of speech, especially around stressful topics. A4- speakers can display mildly falsified positive affect when there is risk of failure; this functions to reduce perception of threat and to disarm disapproval.

   The relationship with the interviewer is analytical in ways that function to elicit approval and reduce criticism. Attention is carefully monitored so as to maintain vigilant observation of one's own behavior with regard to powerful people. Thus, A4 speakers comply with interviewers' requests (that are treated as demands), often in excessive detail; during the AAI, they often anticipate and meet interviewers' requests even before being asked. A4- speakers are excessively concerned with giving a "good" interview and treat the questions as "tests." During the AAI, they often revise their answers, trying to make them more nearly perfect.

2. Imaged memory contains *unconnected images* of frightening experiences (or, for A4- speakers, embarrassing or inappropriate experiences). The significance of these is not, however, acknowledged openly. Safety tends to reside in places (and excessive work) and is evident in the desire to be in a place rather than with a person. The images function to enable the self to feel safe and to identify dangerous contexts.

3. Semantically, the attachment figure's perspective is offered in *prescriptive* form. When the limitations of the relationship with the attachment figure are acknowledged, they are attributed to (a) the inadequacy of the self or (b) unavoidable circumstances of the at-

tachment figure. Thus, attachment figures are *exonerated* for any limitations and the self is held responsible. The function is to enable A4 speakers to focus on that which they can control, that is, their own behavior. A4- speakers rarely understand that their parents required too much; instead they accepted the parents' standard for what they should, prescriptively, do. The function is to enable A4- speakers to be in synchrony with their parents through efforts they make themselves.

4. Connotative language of A4 speakers is dry, rational, and lacking in emotion-activating attributes. A4- speakers have sincere, earnest denotative language, and are sometimes ironic about the "failures" of the self.

5. Episodically, A4 speakers recall negative experiences, especially those that were endangering. They fail, however, to integrate recall of their own feelings into the episodes, tending instead to emphasize if/then causal relationships, focusing on the predictability of events. Often the events are distorted to omit wrongdoing or harsh behavior of attachment figures. The function is to foster recall of important contingencies while protecting the speaker from feeling angry.

   A4- speakers also recall failed attempts and embarrassing moments more than successes; they distance themselves from feelings, focusing more on continuing efforts to achieve as if they were inattentive or otherwise willfully or selfishly unprepared and thus responsible for what was not accomplished. They fail to recall their own motivations and to consider the worth of these. Parental pleasure and satisfaction do not figure highly in the episodes; self-pleasure and satisfaction are absent. The function is to reduce conflict both with their parents and internally among their dispositional representations.

6. The vigilant attention to detail and to relations among events often leads to incipient integration. However, in the moment of recognition of discrepancy, A4 and A4- speakers drop the thought. Thus, these are *failed metacognitions*. Instead bland, self-evident *platitudes* are offered, and these usually fail to acknowledge responsibility as a function of age and status. Other conclusions that may be provided are usually from the *parents' perspective*.

   A4- speakers are excessively aware of others' evaluations of them (both actual and imagined). They are less aware of how others affect them and they are not comfortable stating their own opinions and preferences. Rather than concluding they have done well, they focus on the need to accomplish future tasks.

ASSOCIATED STRATEGIES AND MODIFIERS

A4 and A4- are often seen in conjunction with A3 (for different attachment figures). In cases of very serious and pervasive harm as a child, A4 may be combined with A7 (delusional idealization). Lack of resolution of loss (often vicarious for A4-, dismissed or preoccupying or both for A4) is also common. Lack of resolution of trauma (which may take many different forms) is more common in A4 than in A4-. Sometimes, especially when the strategy is applied very pervasively, it is modified by depression and, particularly in A4, intrusions of forbidden negative affect. In addition, the A4 strategy is sometimes found in conjunction with a triangulated C5–6 strategy, for example, in cases of borderline personality disorder (Crittenden & Newman, 2010).

RISK FOR PSYCHOPATHOLOGY

The risk to A4 and A4- individuals is relatively low if they are able to meet the demands of others and experience satisfaction in doing so. If they cannot meet the demands, anxiety is a possible outcome and, if they cannot experience satisfaction, depression is a possible outcome. In either case, distress may be experienced somatically but it is unlikely that the somatic condition will receive attention or be treated as meaningful information by the individual. On the other hand, when the risk is severe, uncontrollable, or ongoing, compulsive compliance can be associated with very severe psychopathology. Further, it is often an iatrogenic outcome of intense interventions or treatments ranging from pharmacological treatment to institutionalization.

DIFFERENTIATING A4 FROM OTHER STRATEGIES

A4 and A4- transcripts are differentiated from B transcripts by the absence of the speakers' perspectives and feelings and from A1 and A2 transcripts by the absence of semantic idealization, the presence of acknowledged negative episodes, and the persistently negative view of the self. They are differentiated from A3 transcripts by the relatively scarce use of false positive affect and the semantic emphasis on the self's shortcomings. While being very similar to A4, the compulsive performance strategy (A4-) can be differentiated from A4 by the relative lack of fear and for the emphasis on achievement rather than on the risks incurred by lack of compliance.

Experience/History

Children of rigid, hostile, and/or punitive parents often organize a compulsively compliant A4 strategy as children. Such children are highly vigilant to signals of impending danger. The signals may be either their own behavior or an attachment figure's affective state. When these signals go unheeded, attachment figures reject the child in ways that are punitive, violent, and, sometimes, very dangerous. Many compulsively compliant adults appear to have been "too" good in childhood—even though they describe themselves as having been bad. In many cases, a speaker is caregiving with regard to one parent (the weak one) and compliant with regard to the other (the violent one). Sometimes the transition to adulthood creates such conflict between obedience and independence that psychotic breaks occur. In adulthood, the A4 strategy is often combined with the A3 strategy and sometimes with A7.

Adults using an A4- compulsive performing strategy often had anxious parents who felt gratified by their children's performances or feared their children's failures in the competition of life. Many compulsively performing adults appear to have been "too" good in childhood—even though they describe themselves as having been inadequate. In many cases, such speakers are also caregiving with regard to one parent (the weak one) and performing with regard to the other (the demanding one).

Among adults using an A4 strategy, there is often an overt awareness of a desire to do better with one's own children, either by avoiding punishment or by not pushing too hard for achievement. This can lead to a reversal in which the parent is too focused on the feelings of the child and, thus, raises a child with a Type C strategy (note that, in doing so, the parent maintains the strategy of focusing on others' perspectives). The reversal results in coercive strategies in the children, which parents using a Type A strategy are usually unprepared to discern or regulate.

In adulthood, a risk is depression in the face of endless tasks that are not self-satisfying (A4-) or of a general negation of the perspective of the self. Nevertheless, compulsively compliant or performing adults include those who are high achievers and, interpersonally, they are able to work effectively with very demanding or difficult people. The strategy can be associated with both severe maladaptation and extraordinary achievement.

A5 (COMPULSIVELY PROMISCUOUS, SOCIALLY OR SEXUALLY)

Overview

This strategy is based on theory (Bowlby, 1980; Crittenden, 1995, 1997b), clinical case materials, and clinical observations from AAIs. Because this description has been drawn from fewer examples than other strategies, it may require revision and elaboration.

The A5 strategy has two forms: socially promiscuous and sexually promiscuous. Both prefer *distance* from appropriately intimate relationships (such as with protective attachment figures and committed sexual partners) and *intimacy* (both sexual and nonsexual) with distant, inappropriate, or dangerous figures (i.e., "indiscriminate" attachment and masochistic attachment). Put another way, individuals using an A5 strategy give up idealization and exoneration of family members but retain the idealizing process, which is applied to unknown persons (who have not failed the self). In addition, both functionally and in terms of the processing of information, there is a confusion of danger and pain with safety and comfort. This confusion is based on treating perception of discomfort or pain as only marginally relevant to the self, and functions to allow the individual to pursue obtaining comfort from strangers despite the danger that doing this may incur.

The socially (A5-) and sexually (A5) promiscuous forms of the compulsively promiscuous strategy differ in the nature of danger that the individual is strategically biased to tolerate, and therefore also in the extent of the transformation of information used to implement the strategy. The A5- strategy employs idealization of strangers to overcome the pain of separation from attachment figures, and false positive affect to overcome the fear of precipitous approach to strangers.[1] The A5 strategy employs false sexual arousal to overcome isolation and,

---

1. This is similar to Disinhibited Social Engagement Disorder in the *DSM-V*. Unlike the *DSM*, however, the DMM strategy is seen as a meaningful and adaptive organization that is related by information processing to other strategies.

sometimes, the fear and pain of harm associated with intimate relationships.

The compulsively promiscuous strategy usually develops in conjunction with A6 and often has fragments of other compulsive strategies from childhood. For example, the A5–6 speaker may have been (or may now be) role reversing or compliant with regard to one of the parents. These strategies, however, failed to protect the child adequately and have been replaced in adulthood by a preference for intimacy with idealized, but unknown, others.

Discourse and Its Psychological Functions

1. Procedurally, compulsively promiscuous speakers are often more than willing to comply with the interview, with run-on responses, filled with detail, including private detail. The style of speech is dismissing, too concise, acknowledging problems in the family but without distress and with a recurrent juxtaposition of closeness and distance (e.g., a speaker might say, "*I don't remember what kind of relationship I had with Mommy*," thus, juxtaposing distance in the relationship with the affectionate term "Mommy"), and, particularly for the A5 form, the intrusion of sexual content is provided in response to nonsexual questions.

    Little affect is displayed.

    The interviewer is both held at a distance and told very revealing things. Intrusions of intimate information interest others and make them feel special and trusted, thereby, drawing them in to relationships. It also warns astute observers that intimacy will be a problem. The incompleteness functions to keep the source of personal shame private, thus, fostering contact with others without incurring the risks of others' disgust.

2. Imaged memory is crisp but intense, regarding bodies, body parts and actions, but without direct reference to persons: They are *unconnected*, psychologically disembodied. Images are split between those associated with comfort and those with danger, pain, or disgust. The images of comfort are usually associated with dangerous or nonprotective people, particularly people who misused the speaker sexually (as a child) or failed to protect the child from such experiences. In addition, there can be images of sexual contact or places; these are associated with either (unsafe) comfort or overt threat. *Unconnected* sexual images recur throughout the transcript

and are usually not explained sufficiently. In addition, words used in the images may be reintroduced in unexpected ways (that recall the sexual images) at other places in the transcript, that is, they are *obliquely connected images*. The unconnected and incomplete quality of the images protects the self from full awareness of his or her vulnerability while, nevertheless, keeping the speaker focused on relationships and intimacy. Indeed, it may have an autoerotic function that propels the speaker into relationships and, thus, out of the despair of isolation. This provides some comfort and promotes reproduction in otherwise isolated people.

3. Semantic memory is distorted such that the speaker accepts responsibility for the acts, including especially sexual acts, of others, therefore overattributing *responsibility to the self*. Specifically, when the promiscuity is sexual, the speaker accepts responsibility, as a child, for initiating and liking the imposed sexual contact of others. This gives the speaker the illusion of control over the otherwise uncontrollable victimization of self, but the cost is a definition of self that includes, and may even center on, distressing interpersonal experiences, especially self-demeaning and (sometimes) painful sexual activity.

4. Connotative language functions to keep incipient sexuality present through much of the discourse—even if the meanings are not definitive or clear. Sometimes the choice of words is peculiar, with sexual overtones, or words can carry ambiguous double meanings. Sexuality remains as an undercurrent in the transcript, as if waiting in readiness to be activated. Even so, the discourse is bleak in ways that are not titillating at all for the listener. The recurrence of specific words related to images of comfort and danger functions to preserve information despite the incompleteness and distortions of episodic memory.

5. Episodic memory is often distorted to claim that the self chose abusive activities that reflect other people's desires and motivations. The topics of episodes are often obliquely related to sex but are not about sexual contact. For example, episodes may be about toilets, wetting, precocious puberty, menstruation, etc. This functions to reduce both the experience of threat and powerlessness around isolation and intrusive closeness and also the likelihood that current behavior will be evaluated accurately.

6. Compulsively promiscuous speakers show very little integration. Among A5- speakers, lack of integration is covered by intellectual-

ization, in which all the information is presented but is kept distant from the self and superficial, whereas, in other cases, there is little awareness of a need to explain anything. Some extreme A5 speakers, especially those who were most seriously harmed, claim personal control that, by implication, protected their selves or the parents; but these defenses are simple denials of their selves being victimized without plausibility. Alternatively, they may display depression, in which all the facts are known but, because inaccurate causal attributions are made, no life-sustaining solution can be found. As with all the high-numbered Type A strategies, the absence of integration can result in contradictory statements in different parts of the transcripts, such that one or both statements must be considered "lies." Usually, however, the speaker is unaware of these inconsistencies. Because they reflect only an unintegrated, disassociative process, their function is quite different from intentional deception among speakers using a Type C5–8 strategy. The contradictions usually involve the attribution of responsibility to self and the self-demeaning nature of activities that functioned as surrogates of comfort. Leaving this contradiction unresolved is pragmatic in childhood in that it permits the speaker to accept what relationship was available from attachment figures (or their substitutes) while avoiding the feeling of uncontrollable threat. However, continuing to do so later can have self-endangering consequences in adulthood. It can result in a pattern of self-threatening or self-demeaning adult relationships that are not evaluated accurately either in terms of the speaker's true feelings or causal role.

ASSOCIATED STRATEGIES AND MODIFIERS

A3 and A4 are often seen in the history of A5 speakers. Lack of resolution of loss (both dismissed and preoccupying or both) is also common as is lack of resolution of trauma (particularly of sexual abuse), which may take many different forms. Depression is also a frequent state for the A5 strategy and may be accompanied by intrusions of forbidden negative affect and expressed somatic symptoms. In addition, the A5 strategy, together with other compulsive A strategies, may be found in A/C combinations. Overall, A5 is more often found in combination with other A+ strategies than as a primary strategy (cf. Crittenden & Newman, 2010).

RISK FOR PSYCHOPATHOLOGY

The strategy can exist in a mild, compulsively social form (A5-) in which nonsexual, nonintimate relationships appear to replace truly intimate sexual relationships as well as in a more severe, sexually promiscuous (A5) form (as typified by incest victims, prostitutes, pedophiles, even some serial killers). The social form has a risk of relationship dissolution, depression, and somatization of distress, without attention to the somatic signals. The isolated form carries the same risks and, in addition, the physical and psychological risks associated with dangerous sexual contact with strangers, including pedophilia (Haapasalo, Puupponen, & Crittenden, 1999) and masochism.

DIFFERENTIATING A5 FROM OTHER STRATEGIES

A5 transcripts can be confused with B transcripts because speakers seem so open, yet there is an absence of speakers' perspectives and feelings. Unlike A1 and A2 transcripts, there is little semantic idealization and acknowledged negative episodes are present. Unlike A3 and A4 transcripts, there is little exoneration or episodes told from parental perspectives. A5 transcripts are differentiated from A6 transcripts by the frequent intrusion of sexual words, images, and allusions, and by the absence of an explicit valuing of independence from others (i.e., a semantic motivation to keep isolated). A5- and A5 are differentiated by the presence in the sexually promiscuous form of obliquely connected images about sex and danger and, in the socially promiscuous form, of an easy friendliness that could be mistaken for Type B.

Experience/History

The A5 strategy is usually associated with a history of extreme lack of comfort in a context of threat or danger. In some cases of the A5- form, its roots were intense parental demands coupled with threats of loss of parents' love; in these cases, compulsive performance is the underlying strategy, with promiscuous behavior permitting the self to be rewarded with quick comfort.

More often the danger was repeated rejection and abandonment by numerous short-term caregivers. Thus, maltreated children who experienced several different foster placements are at risk for developing an

A5 strategy as are children living in institutions (who often show indiscriminant attachment). In these cases, the children often used both compulsive caregiving and compulsive compliant strategies, but also needed a means to attract and hold potential attachment figures faster than could occur in genuine relationships. Compulsive promiscuity functioned to fulfill this need.

In the most severe cases, children who later employ a sexually promiscuous A5 strategy were subjected to child prostitution and pornography. In those cases in which adults' compulsive promiscuity extends to illegal behavior and especially when there is also criminal or violent behavior, the history is likely to include violent physical abuse from parents or other caregivers. The sexually promiscuous strategy does not fully develop until late adolescence.

A6 (COMPULSIVELY SELF-RELIANT, SOCIAL OR ISOLATED)

Overview

This strategy is based on theory (Bowlby, 1980; Crittenden, 1995), clinical case materials, and clinical observations from AAIs.

Individuals using a compulsively self-reliant strategy inhibit display of negative affect, dismiss self-relevance, and withdraw from close relationships as a way to prevent disappointment or harm to the self.

The strategy exists in two forms: A6-, the social form, and A6, the isolated form. The social form of compulsive self-reliance allows the individual to engage in social relationships, while distancing the self in close or intimate relationships (in which A6 individuals fear rejection too much to seek support or comfort). The more severe, isolated form of the strategy involves withdrawal from all relationships as a means to safety. This eases considerably social and interpersonal demands while concurrently limiting both the protection and comfort received and also reproductive opportunities.

Discourse Markers and their Psychological Function

1. Procedurally, A6 is typified by a style of speech that dismisses the self, acknowledges problems in the family, and emphasizes the speaker's competence to function independently. Thus, the dis-

course is fluent, but the content omits the perspective and vulnerability of the self. Speakers using an A6 strategy tend to display little affect although sadness and a feeling of emptiness may be elicited in the reader. Although there is no complaint about being alone, nor any attempt to elicit caregiving, there is usually a bleak tone to the discourse.

Occasionally, particularly when discussing threatening circumstances in the past, A6 speakers mock or demean themselves to dismiss the import of these experiences. If fear is shown, it is more with regard to others' judgment of them and less to dangerous events.

Finally, A6 speakers are conscientious in answering all questions, they are unexpectedly open in what they disclose, and they can be somewhat analytical in how they think about themselves. This leads others, including coders, to see them as balanced. Their self-derogatory and analytical perspective reduces the threat of criticism from the interviewer. Further, the strategy protects them from incurring the risks of intimacy.

2. Imaged memory is generally absent. When there are images, they are either unconnected to people, including the self, or somaticized. The former process functions both to remove affect from recall and, thus, to protect the self from irresolvable feelings (that is, feelings that could never be comforted) and also to retain important information that can be tucked away safely in the "corners" of the mind. Somatization leaves the speaker exceptionally in need of comfort and may increase the likelihood of use of the A5 (compulsively promiscuous) strategy or of depression. Idealized images of place may substitute for security or comfort in human relationships.

3. Semantic memory is less split and less exonerating than with the lower numbered compulsive strategies. Instead, it is highly pragmatic, as though the speaker were simply acknowledging that this is how things were and always will be. This functions to free the speaker from a need to remain in contact with unsupportive attachment figures or to try to resolve problems with them. Speakers using an A6 strategy generally accept responsibility for what has happened to them (e.g., for their marital troubles or criminal behavior). When they attribute blame to others, they tend to treat such problems as inevitable and not reprehensible. Limitations of the self are seen clearly and treated as intrinsic or immutable.

4. Connotative language, in a displaced form (i.e., addressed to distant and nonpersonal topics), holds information about painful experiences but holds it at a distance where it does not so easily activate behavior. On the other hand, the thorough absence of warmth or feeling in the discourse about personal or family characteristics often evokes a feeling of despair in the reader.

5. Episodic memory is complete but related in a largely semantic manner with only enough details to clarify that specific events are remembered. Stories are told concisely, without lingering over poignant, self-relevant details. Descriptions of feelings are absent. Often, the parents' perspectives are clearer than that of the speakers. This sort of recall keeps speakers aware of why they should remain distant from relationships, whereas the semantic quality of the recall reduces the probability of unsoothed affective arousal.

6. Compulsively self-reliant and isolated speakers show very little integration. In particular, they seem unaware of their feelings, the cost of their strategy to themselves and others, the ways in which their early experiences have affected their adult relationships, and of the developmental reasons for their parents' behavior or their parents' feelings. When affect is mentioned overtly, it is nominalized and treated as an intrapersonal state, rather than as the interactive outcome of an interpersonal exchange or relationship. Most critically, when they can see how things are related and even state causal relations, they do not see alternatives or the possibility of change. Moments of potential insight are dismissed as "*Oh, well, that's how it is.*" That is, there are frequent *failed metacognitions* that hint to an underlying depression. This functions to protect speakers from attempts to reestablish past relationships (that might fail again) and from the regret that would be associated with such failure.

ASSOCIATED STRATEGIES AND MODIFIERS

The compulsively self-reliant (social or isolated) strategy usually develops out of a failed A3 or A4 childhood strategy and is often observed in conjunction with another compulsive strategy. For example, it may be part of a combination (A6, $A3_M$) strategy in which an A6 speaker retains a compulsive caregiving role with regard to the mother. Alternatively, the isolated strategy is sometimes found with the promiscuous strategy, that is, A5–6. Lack of resolution of loss (both dismissed and preoccupying or both) is also common as is lack of resolution of trauma (particularly violence and abandonment), which may take many different forms. Depression is also a frequent state for the A6 strategy.

RISK FOR PSYCHOPATHOLOGY

The strategy can exist in a mild, compulsively self-reliant form, A6- (e.g., in married speakers who are psychologically distant from their spouses, some clergy, and single adults); these individuals may be very competent in nonintimate social and business relationships. Nevertheless, they are at risk for depression, somatic disorders that go untreated, self-distraction with overwork or substance abuse, and suicide. The more severe, isolated form, A6, is typified by loners, drifters, and some criminals. All are prone to depression, untreated somatization of distress, addictive disorders, and suicide.

DIFFERENTIATING A6 FROM OTHER STRATEGIES

A6 transcripts are differentiated from B transcripts by the absence of speakers' perspectives and feelings and from A1 and A2 transcripts by the absence of semantic idealization and the presence of acknowledged negative episodes. They are often misclassified as A3 or A4 because the content of the history describes caregiving or compliance, but the discourse used is more transformed (distorted) than that of A3–4 speakers and suggests the failure of the compulsive caregiving/compliant strategies and their replacement by a bleaker A6 strategy. A6 transcripts can be differentiated from A5 by the lower level of arousal shown by the subject and the relative absence of sexual connotations in the language.

Experience/History

The A6 strategy is most often associated with a history of the child's sense of being rejected. However, unlike the compulsively caregiving and compliant strategies, there was no way for the child to create a false self that was accepted by the parents. Thus, the child was rejected both as an actual person and also as a possible person. Sometimes the rejection was solely through psychological neglect, but it often extended through physical absence of the parents (due to travel, distant work, hospitalization, or the child's placement in an institution or series of foster homes). Thus, the rejection carried with it real danger of abandonment. In those cases in which compulsive self-reliance extends to isolation and especially when there is also criminal behavior, the history is likely to include unpredictable violence from parents or other caregivers that could not be moderated by the child's response.

Because self-reliance requires a minimum level of competence, this strategy is not observed in young children. Instead, its probable precursors include unsuccessful attempts to use the A1, A3, or A4 strategies. Because these are unsuccessful, the related history often includes somatic evidence of childhood anxiety (e.g., sleep disturbance, bedwetting, stuttering). Given this history, it is not surprising that A6 speakers rarely report having childhood friendships with peers; instead, they seem often to have been those unnoticed children who were neither popular nor especially disliked. Some of those who will later become isolated may already in the school years be noticed and rejected by peers as "nerds" or "geeks." The compulsively self-reliant strategy forms during or after adolescence when independence can minimally be achieved. At this point, A6 speakers often report a sudden cut-off of the feelings that reflected childhood anxiety about abandonment or isolation. Indeed, many A6 adolescents report leaving home quite early.

By late adolescence, the isolated form of the strategy is often combined with sexual promiscuity and, sometimes, with sexually violent promiscuity. In all cases, the strategy is one of constructing a self-protective shell against the world of relationships. Hiding behind the shell, compulsively self-reliant adults constrain their behavior to that which they can manage by themselves and without help from others.

The advantages of this strategy are an ability to function alone for long periods of time, to initiate new relationships quickly and easily, and to take responsibility for one's own behavior. In pioneer and former pioneer cultures, this "do-it-yourself," rugged individualism, and self-help approach was highly valued because it was adaptive.

A7 (DELUSIONAL IDEALIZATION)

Overview

The A7 strategy is based on theory and clinical observations from AAIs, and further is consistent with clinical theory and experiences, for example, hostages' "identification" with their captors in what has become referred to as the Stockholm syndrome (Cassidy, 2002; Goddard & Stanley, 1994; Kuleshnyk, 1984). It has been observed most frequently in parents who severely harm their children and in incestuous sexual offenders, violent criminals, and psychiatric patients with diagnoses of psychosis or borderline personality disorder.

The A7 strategy refers to idealization of abandoningly absent or life-threateningly present attachment figures. Critical to determining that idealization is delusional are (a) credible evidence that the individual's life was either threatened (or believed to be threatened) by the idealized person or could have been protected by the idealized person and was not and (b) credible evidence that the idealized rescue events could not possibly have occurred. In addition, both functionally and in terms of the processing of information, A7 speakers deny negative affect, particularly fear, anger, and pain, and they delusionally proclaim safety and caregiving when there was little or none.

Discourse Markers and their Psychological Function

1. Procedurally, A7 speakers are characterized by a dismissingly intellectualized style of speech that is both open and revealing and, concurrently, is cut off at critical moments, leaving great gaps of missing information.

    Little feeling is displayed and it is markedly absent (*denied*) at moments where pain should have been experienced.

    The relationship with the interviewer is characterized by a willingness to engage and an air of thoughtfulness that ultimately explains very little. This functions to mark the need for integration without fully facing the painfulness of the history or current relationships.

2. Imaged memory is minimal but striking in its intensity. The images are split between those associated with comfort and those with danger, pain, or anger (particularly the condition of the self when these feelings were experienced). The *delusionally protective images* of comfort are usually associated with delusionally idealized persons. They appear as impossible occurrences embedded in otherwise realistic episodes; these images refer to desirable or comforting experiences *that did not happen*. They function to represent or elicit feelings of comfort in the context of uncomforted and unprotected danger, the effects of which on the speaker are denied. Few images of danger exist and, often, they are both unconnected to the self

and also obliquely connected to each other. This protects the self from the full awareness of his or her vulnerability while, nevertheless, permitting some access to information about the past danger. Frequently, this becomes the basis for describing how things should be in the future.

3. Semantic memory reflects the usual Type A split between good and bad: The self receives the bad attributions, but nothing good can be extracted from denied painful experiences, so what is semantically good must be constructed delusionally. Similarly, in terms of causality the speaker searches in vain for positive causal explanations for events that cannot be explained positively with reference to temporal order; consequently, the speaker cannot maintain belief in their own causal control over past events. A7 speakers refer often to how things "always" were, but instead of using hypothetical (A1–2) or prescriptive (A3–6) semantic generalizations, they either delusionally *misattribute positive intents* to the dangerous attachment figures or refer to their corrective intentions for the future (i.e., "redeeming" generalizations). This functions to give the speaker hope, an illusion that life has order, and the belief that he or she will succeed ultimately in correcting a past disorder or injustice in the future. Because causality is unknown, the speaker may accept the inevitability of danger.

4. Connotative language may be quite descriptive. Because the speaker is at least partially describing what did not occur, the story can be embellished and told in a more realistic and emotional manner than can the actual episodes of other speakers using a Type A strategy. The language, however, is trite, bland, and common; often the same phrases are repeated, with a stereotyped, mantralike quality. In general, the language describes affective states without evoking them. Descriptions of pain or suffering are attributed to others even when the self would be expected to have suffered more intensely.

5. Episodic memory is often omitted, although fragments of dangerous experiences can appear in misplaced negative verbs or descriptions in a positive episode. When negative episodes are recalled, the self may claim an unlikely decision-making role that would not have represented the true desires of the self (*distorted guilt episodes*). For example, the speakers state that they were institutionalized as if it were their choice. In such negative episodes, the self is viewed as an object from an impersonal perspective; negative affect, in-

cluding physical pain, is *denied* even when the event must necessarily have included it. Positive episodes are recalled, but either they are trivial or they refer to persons other than the attachment figures. In extreme cases, some episodes contain protective or comforting events that could not have happened. In these *delusional idealization* episodes, the delusion provides a sense of safety that replaces denied suffering. This functions to reduce the experience of distress and powerlessness but at the cost of increasing likelihood that current behavior will be maladaptive.

6. Delusionally idealizing speakers may show an intellectualized, superficial integration. This is displayed as a relatively complete presentation of information that is, nevertheless, kept affectively distant from the self. Intellectualization functions to protect A7 speakers from experiencing fully the danger and irrational cruelty to which they have been exposed. It also, however, reduces the probability of change in current or future relationships. Indeed, evidence of similar processes in current relationships is often present but its relevance is overlooked by the speaker.

In addition, however, there are repeated occasions when the speaker discovers a discrepancy, focuses on it, and wonders why it is present. But these articulated comments or questions do not result in productive answers that increase understanding and promote integration. Instead, the gap in understanding remains, the discrepancies appear again, and the issue is rearticulated, still without resolution. The form looks like reflection, but the outcome is not integration. Instead, these *inconclusive metacognitions* mark speakers' inability to carry thought further without accessing denied information. There may also be depression in which all the facts are known but, because inaccurate causal attributions are made, no connection to the present can be found.

Unsuccessful attempts to integrate can result in contradictory statements in different parts of the transcript. One reason may be that the speaker is vigilant to identify what the listener is ready to hear, shaping the response to meet these (presumed) demands or expectations on a moment-by-moment basis. Denial of negative affective information may either abort integration or require production of *delusional* information to fill the gaps and produce responses that appear acceptable. These factors shape the story as it is being told without the speaker being aware of the process. Because these unintentional "lies" reflect disassociative processes and the consequent attempts to preserve coherence and identity, their function is quite different from intentional deception among speakers using a Type C5–8 strategy. Similarly, the overattribution of responsibility and competence to the self can create an appearance of "grandiosity" that resembles Type C5–8 strategies, but A7 speakers (unlike individuals using Type C strategies) continue to live in a prescriptive world in which the demands of others must be satisfied.

ASSOCIATED STRATEGIES OR MODIFIERS

Other Type A strategies, particularly A4, are often displayed in partial form in A7 transcripts. Lack of resolution of loss or trauma, especially blocked recall of violence to the self, is frequent. Depression is also frequent with the A7 strategy. Angry, blaming, and fearful outbursts may be observed as intrusions of forbidden negative affect or alternated as a primary Type C strategy used in conjunction with the Type A strategy.

RISK FOR PSYCHOPATHOLOGY

There is very great risk for psychopathology and criminal behavior among A7 individuals, including extreme anxiety, paranoia, psychosis, substance abuse, sexual offending or violence, and depression and other mood disorders. Parents using an A7 strategy are more likely to maltreat their children.

DIFFERENTIATING A7 FROM OTHER STRATEGIES

A7 transcripts are differentiated from A1 transcripts by the extreme dangers to which the speaker has been exposed, by the insignificance of comfort, and by the apparent absence of distress, including pain when it should predominate. Whereas A1 speakers distort information (minimizing negative and emphasizing positive information), A7 speakers deny negative information and sometimes construct delusional positive information. They can be differentiated from B or reorganizing toward B transcripts by the absence of speakers' perspectives and feelings and by the lack of complete and meaningful integrative conclusions. Further, transcripts assigned to A7 always have unresolved trauma or loss and very often there are both multiple traumas and very complex forms of trauma (see Chapter 11). These transcripts are differentiated from C5–8 transcripts by delusional images or episodes, which protect or soothe, rather than highlight danger or scare the listener. Intrusions of forbidden negative affect are differentiated from a Type C strategy by the lack of dyadic regulation and the embarrassment or shame of the speaker regarding the intrusion.

Experience/History

The A7 strategy is associated with a history of severe danger, including physical violence, child sexual abuse, and repeated abandonment. Psychological maltreatment usually has accompanied the physical threats. Often the individual was abandoned by a succession of potentially protective people. Because the creation of a delusional form of protection does not reflect a truly possible means of protecting the self, individuals using such a strategy remain vulnerable to repetitions of the dangerous patterns of behavior. They are particularly vulnerable to philosophies of life that idealize an unavailable protective figure while stating clear guidelines for achieving acceptability and safety (e.g., some excessively strict forms of religious belief, including both affectively dry belief systems and, their opposite, hypnotically arousing and calming cultlike groups).

A8 (EXTERNALLY ASSEMBLED SELF)

Overview

The A8 strategy is based on theory and clinical observations from AAIs, and further is consistent with clinical theory and the reported experience of severely threatened or abused individuals. Its roots have been observed in children with DMM assessments of attachment and always involve children changing attachment figures many times (i.e., multiple foster placements) or having little or no access to attachment figures (i.e., institutionalization).[2] In such cases, professionals take over the parenting function, thus promoting the delusion that they not only know what is best for the individual but also know the individual. A8 is a severe, avoidable, and iatrogenic strategy.

The A8 strategy refers to loss of self-representation in the context of abandoningly absent attachment figures. Abandonment almost always

2. These are the criteria for Reactive Attachment Disorder in childhood, but there are no data linking this disorder to adulthood. Here we suggest a hypothesis.

began early in life and continued throughout childhood. Critical to determining that the process of construction of a "self" has been negated and curtailed is credible evidence in the discourse that the speaker (a) was pervasively and persistently rejected by attachment figures and (b) cannot now explain critical aspects of his or her own functioning. Further, although there may be a verbal presentation of affect in a nominalized form or in unconnected or obliquely connected images, there is little or no expressed negative affect, especially regarding rejection, in the transcript. What affect is expressed is socially desirable and incongruous with the events being told. Moreover, the painful effect of rejection is denied by the speaker, such that the self lacks personally generated information about childhood experiences. As a consequence, the "self" consists largely of unintegrated information generated by other people, particularly professionals. That is, A8 speakers have little personal source memory; this leaves the speaker almost entirely dependent on others for self-definition.

Discourse Markers and their Psychological Function

1. Procedurally, A8 discourse is dismissing of the self and fragmented, filled with gaps in what is known. The self is viewed as an object and from afar emotionally (some speakers even describe themselves in the third person).

    Little or no affect is expressed; pain in particular is absent in contexts where it would have been both unavoidable and essential to self-protection. Any affect displayed has no interpersonal function, that is, it is merely dismissingly rueful. The effect elicited in readers is often one of sadness.

    Information that is usually kept private is offered readily, prior to establishment of a working relationship with the interviewer. Thus, there is both a willingness to talk and also a paradoxical absence of personal engagement with the interviewer. In addition, the interviewer may be used as a source of information about the speaker, as though the speaker would *defer to the interviewer's* knowledge of the speaker in preference to his or her own recall. This can be considered an extreme form of the "analytical relationship with the interviewer" in which the speaker has no stance, no perspective of his or her own, and defers completely to the interviewer (as a representation of other people) who is treated as having more valid information about the self than does the self. Stable forms of information (such as reports) are referenced by A8 speakers to inform themselves and to guide their personal narratives. The function of their openness is to access as much information as possible in an objective, nonaffective manner.

2. Borrowed images (from photographs or from other people) create or generate a sense of personal history where little is recalled. Sometimes the images are from the perspectives of others and refer to events that could not be imaged by the speaker. Genuine, but unconnected, fragments of imaged information may slip into the discourse without the speaker's awareness. This implicit personal knowledge functions to retain some minimal information about past danger.

3. Semantic memory is distorted such that A8 speakers cannot explain their experiences. The self is presented as a *nonagent* regarding protection and comfort. Thus, the usual cognitive self-protective strategies of Type A speakers have failed. Instead, the speaker focuses on what they intend to do in the future—deluding themselves that professionals can guide them adequately. Considerable emphasis is placed on prescriptive semantic strictures of what one should or should not do, although there is no evidence that following such strictures protected the speaker in the past. Referring to how things "always" were and how they "ought" to be gives A8 speakers the illusion that relationships endure, in spite of repeated experiences to the contrary.

4. The linguistic style uses borrowed speech from professionals, including echoing interviewers' words, phrasing that resembles that of case reports written by professionals, "borrowed" psychological jargon, and terminology associated with medical diagnoses.

5. Episodic memory is often omitted or cut off around repeated rejection that resulted in yet another placement and new attachment figures in early childhood. Other dangerous experiences are presented quite fully and the self's contribution seems distorted in its negativity; this episodic information is usually derived from *external reference* and reflects the perception of caregivers or professionals. Further, the self may be portrayed in negative terms that suggest that the self deserved no better than what was received. This reduces both the experience of gratuitous injustice and powerlessness and also the likelihood that current behavior will be evaluated accurately.

6. Speakers who attempt to assemble a self around incompletely understood rejection and abandonment often show an apparent reflective capacity but it fails to yield understanding, not even recog-

nition that there must be missing information. Thus, bits of relevant information may be scattered through the transcript and pertinent reflective questions may be asked. These are not dismissed (i.e., they are not failed metacognitions). Instead, they are referred to the interviewer or other professionals in the delusion that others know the self better than the self does. The potential metacognitions are, thus, *delusionally inconclusive.* When there is understanding of effects on the self, these tend to be either too global or too narrow to bridge adequately the gap between past and present. Evidence of similar processes in current relationships is generally overlooked by the speaker.

The failure to recall and integrate allows A8 speakers to *deny* the danger and irrational cruelty of repeated abandonment. In childhood, this permits the speaker to accept any relationships that were available while avoiding anger or depression. In adulthood, it can result in a pattern of too intimate or too distant adult relationships (and sudden reversals between these).

ASSOCIATED STRATEGIES OR MODIFIERS

The strategy may be found in the context of other strategies, particularly A5–6, C5–8, and with modifiers (e.g., depression, intrusions, and even reorganization). Lack of resolution of trauma, especially blocked trauma, is very frequent as are intrusions of forbidden negative affect. An alternated Type C strategy may be present when there have been caring figures who have responded to it.

RISK FOR PSYCHOPATHOLOGY

Psychopathology is almost certain among individuals classified as A8. Depression, anxiety, serious somatic disorders, PTSD, substance abuse, and a failure to manage daily life outside of structured settings are common manifestations of the distress accompanying loss of self-representation.

DIFFERENTIATING A8 FROM OTHER STRATEGIES

A8 transcripts are differentiated from A1 or A2 transcripts by the intensely dangerous experiences to which speakers have been exposed, by the dismissal of needing comfort, and by denial of the perception of pain when pain should predominate. They are differentiated from A7 by the failure to idealize real or imagined attachment figures. They can be differentiated from B or reorganizing toward B transcripts by the absence of speakers' perspectives and feelings and by the failure of the reflective statements or questions to reach any conclusions. They are differentiated from Type C transcripts by the lack of involving anger or deception, the inclusion of the negative contribution of the self, and the lack of involvement of the interviewer as either a collusive support or an opponent.

Experience/History

The A8 strategy is associated with a history of repeated rejection by attachment figures and multiple out-of-home placements. Professionals' statements that they were protecting children may have encouraged the children's delusional reliance on authority figures. Often, the only protective action that a child could take was acceptance of inappropriate intimacy when it was available. Finally, when the mistreatment led to verifiably abnormal behavior during childhood, the adult, reflecting back on this, may think that he or she caused the neglectful behavior. Seeking attachment figures who both abuse and protect or comfort oneself *in adulthood* is a possible outcome of the denial and incomplete processing of information that is central to this strategy.

Chapter 8

Overview of the Type C Strategies and C1–2

GENERAL CHARACTERISTICS APPLYING TO ALL TYPE C CLASSIFICATIONS

Overview

TYPE C IS A STRATEGY OF EMOTIONAL COERCION THAT RANGES FROM MILD to intense to deceptive. Unlike Type A speakers who rely on, but simplify, causal relations, Type C speakers experience such complexity of causation that they rely instead on their feelings. Feelings are used both to guide their behavior and also to form the basis of their self-protective strategy. Unlike Type B speakers who comprehend partial, contributory, and shared causation, Type C speakers cannot easily discern either what caused what or their own contributions to outcomes. Being left primarily with their own mixed feelings to explain past events and motivate future behavior, they face the problems of complexity and complicity.

Speakers whose transcripts are classified as C1 and C2 flounder through these problems in ways that create mild confusion of meaning, particularly in semantic representation. This, in turn, affects episodic memory and integrative capacity. Thus, the primary mental processes of low-numbered Type C speakers are (a) using distorted and mixed feelings to guide behavior, (b) involving others in the regulation of their affect, (c) fragmenting the temporal organization of episodes by lack of clarity about their own contributions, while retaining extensive information about their feelings, other participants, and contexts, (d) omitting information about causal relations, and (e) failing to draw conclusions about either themselves or others. The result of so much uncertainty is a reluctance to let go of the past; instead, Type C speakers maintain an entangling present focus on the past. In addition, fluctuating affective states lead to changing and unpredictable behavior that adds to the complexity of relationships. C1 speakers oscillate between competing perspectives whereas C2 speakers display vague uncertainty regarding how things are connected.

On the other hand, under threatening conditions wavering and unclear behavior is neither effective nor protective. Midrange to high-numbered Type C speakers have experienced or perceived threatening circumstances that call for decisive self-protective action, yet the causal conditions remain unclear. This problem is resolved by increasing the split between the invulnerable/powerful affect of anger and the vulnerable/powerless affects of fear and desire for comfort such that one or the other guides behavior with increasing exclusivity as the strategy number increases. Such "obsession" clarifies and simplifies mental representation, leading to a clear disposition to action.

When compared to other approaches to understanding the Type C strategy, the approach described here focuses less on others' reactions to Type C behavior and more on how information is transformed and organized strategically to protect the self. Among the apparently "invulnerable" strategies (C1, C3, C5, and C7), the gradient in anger is from irritation to rage to cold malice. Within the apparently "vulnerable" strategies (C2, C4, C6, and C8), there is a gradient from mostly desirous of comfort (C2) to pervasively fearful (C8). In the lowest and highest numbered strategies, the split feelings are almost integrated, with more extreme splitting in the midrange strategies (C3–6). At C7–8, the almost integrated states are the emotions of "hate" and "dread," blends of anger and fear with the overgeneralized source of danger. The processes for accomplishing these transformations are described in detail in Chapter 9.

Procedurally, Type C speakers talk about their pasts in the form of *involving discourse,* that is, in a rush of arousing words that capture listeners' attention without reaching a conclusion. In the high-numbered

Type C strategies, few but intense words may accomplish the same function. In AAIs, interviewers are both caught up in the tales being told and also required to assist speakers to focus, come to closure, and move forward to the next topic. In addition, Type C speakers often expect interviewers to supply needed words and even thoughts, seek the interviewers' agreement with their perspectives, and, in the high-numbered strategies (C3–8), attempt to engage interviewers in a psychological collusion against others (or suspect interviewers of such collusion against themselves).

In terms of content, Type C speakers tend to address their personal and familial problems before the topics are queried. There is a collapsing of time into a present focus in which the past threats still evoke emotional responses that influence current behavior. Thus, past events may be told in the present tense, stories from early childhood are mixed with recent events, and people from the past are spoken to as if they were present.

Type C speakers often associate strong feelings with contexts. These are represented in images of people or places. Somatic images reflect particularly intense and inexplicit feeling states. Rather than naming feelings semantically (e.g., "*He was very angry*"), Type C speakers communicate with images (e.g., "*His eyes were popping out*").

Lack of semantic understanding of the past is reflected in difficulty both in producing five descriptors of relationships with attachment figures and also in selecting episodes to illustrate the descriptive words. Furthermore, semantic words tend not to have precise meanings as they are used by Type C speakers; instead, they are vague and often contain aspects of other ideas. Finally, Type C speakers do not see clearly temporal and causal relations among events. As a consequence, Type C speakers often blur the boundaries of person, place, and time. This produces confusing discourse, thus, generating a need to involve others in clarifying their thoughts.

Ironically, however, many Type C speakers retain hope for the future; this hope, however, is excessive and idealized, given the absence of any defined process for achieving change. Often they recall sudden and unexplained reversals for the better in their situations and expect similar changes in the future—as soon as they resolve their currently preoccupying problems. Tenacity, rather than specific problem-resolution skills, seems to be the primary criterion for reaching the expected utopia.

Confusion of temporal sequencing is often displayed in the form of *blurred episodes* that slip from one event to another without completion or semantic closure. The "logic" underlying the flow of events appears to be affective, but, even so, odd reversals and juxtapositions of anger, fear, and desire for comfort are frequent. In addition, episodes mix important and trivial details as though the speaker did not know what was important. Given that Type C speakers do not know why things happened, the excessive detail may function to prevent loss of potentially important information. Moreover, episodes are retrieved less well through the semantic retrieval strategy of illustrating the five descriptive words than through the direct probes of episodic memory contained in the questions regarding distress, illness, injury, separation, rejection, and anger. Thus, the speakers' answers to the five descriptive words questions more often produce wandering, vague, and irrelevant discourse than the subsequent direct probes of negative experiences.

Because they find it difficult to maintain moderate psychological distance from past feeling states, it is hard for Type C speakers to think reflectively about their experiences. This limits their integrative capacity. Specifically, they tend not to notice developmental change that occurs over time, causal contingencies that could explain changes in behavior, effects of early development on later functioning, or the validity of other people's perspectives. As a consequence, they often remain trapped in the problems of their childhood relationships. Not knowing the ways in which they are psychologically separate from their parents, Type C speakers find it difficult to become autonomous in adulthood.

In terms of "coherence of speech" (Grice, 1975), Type C speakers tend to speak in a disorderly *manner*, offering an excessive *quantity* of information. They neither support nor contradict their generalizations with evidence, thus, failing to meet fully the requirements of *quality*. Finally, they provide information that is both relevant and irrelevant to the question asked, thus, failing to meet fully the requirements of *relevance*. Overall, Type C speakers tend to be low to very low in coherence of speech, and in some cases they are exceptionally incoherent. Their mental coherence is also low, but not always as low as the discourse would suggest. Nevertheless, when the reader evaluates the nature of the speaker's experience, he or she arrives at substantively different conclusions from the speaker. Specifically, the reader often decides that moderating information, explanatory conditions, and precision of meaning are missing.

Affect and Cognition

Affect: Because, in the past, feelings have been more predictive of future danger and safety than have temporal contingencies, Type C speakers use affect to organize their psychological processes and self-protective behavior. This is displayed in nonverbal indicators of high arousal (e.g., giggling, crying, smirking) and in images of scary, irritating, or comforting contexts.

Cognition: Because, during childhood, the temporal order and the contingencies among events were unpredictable and, for high-numbered strategies, misleading, Type C speakers are confused about causation and tend to either not use or falsify cognitive information. Type C speakers conceive of time as being fluid and impermanent. That is, they believe the past to be correctable (i.e., they think of the past as part of the present) and they also imagine that the future can be fore-stalled or changed as needed or desired. Consequently, they live fully in the present, often focusing their activity on correcting past problems, and have little concern that today's actions could have enduring consequences.

Discourse Markers and Their Psychological Function

1. Procedural memory:
    (a) Type C speakers use involving discourse. For C1–2 speakers, this takes the form of (a) vague and wandering discourse, (b) confusion of persons (particularly through use of pronouns with unclear referents) and time (including present tense and present participle verbs), (c) nonsense words to convey unstated semantic meanings, (d) incomplete semantic statements, (e) oscillations and contradictions of semantic conclusions, and (f) run-on-sentences that make temporal order and causal connections unclear. Erroneous procedural information places people in events where they were not present and disorders events temporally. Such discourse keeps everything self-relevant in the present and also functions to involve others in the speaker's problems.
    (b) Affectively, speakers use a coercive strategy to express intense feelings. Exaggerated, nonverbal affect functions to clarify the speaker's perspective and, often, to elicit involvement from interviewers. Speakers using high-

numbered Type C strategies can distort or omit affect in ways that elicit strong feelings in others.

(c) Type C speakers seek assurance that interviewers agree with them and share their affective states and perspectives. The intensity, openness, and means of coercion vary with the different C strategies.

2. Imaged memory: Images are vivid, with an arousing, affect-laden quality, but are not balanced by other information; consequently, they tend to exaggerate (distort) some feelings while minimizing awareness of others. This functions both to clarify mixed affective dispositions, thus, providing (however briefly) a single, clear motivation to action, and also to retain information about the context, but without full clarity regarding the source or meaning of the affect.

3. Semantic memory: Type C speakers use vague or extreme semantic descriptors. This is one outcome of their distorted displays of affect. That is, telling a Type C child that he is "angry" when he displays exaggerated anger while concurrently inhibiting display of fear and desire for comfort reduces the precision of the semantic language that he learns.

   Similarly, the confusing and oscillating features of involving discourse make it difficult to reach clear semantic conclusions. That is, Type C speakers use *passive semantic thought*. In cases of relative safety, omission of semantic memory (i.e., omission of generalized and linguistic cognitive information) functions to keep the speaker from reaching premature closure in complex situations. In cases of deceptive danger, *false cognition* can keep everything potentially meaningful but in uncertain ways (i.e., the same thing might signal either safety or danger). Among speakers placed in the high-numbered Type C strategies, false cognition is both expected from others and also used to deceive others regarding the speakers' potential treachery. In the very high-numbered C strategies, information that cannot be tolerated may be denied, and, in a few cases, delusional reasoning may substitute for it.

4. Connotative language: The connotative quality of Type C speakers' language conveys their feelings in ways that elicit emotion-based responses from listeners (e.g., soothing, fearful vigilance). That is, affect regulation and self-protection involve others. In the higher numbered Type C strategies, language often has strongly evocative qualities: rhythmic, sonic,

metaphorical, and rhetorical qualities that generate feeling in the listener. This both communicates the speaker's state and also, by involving the listener in the speaker's experience, asserts its validity.

5. Episodic memory: Episodes are distorted by compressing affectively similar events from different points in time into a single unit of recall. Often only the intensity (rather than type) of affect unifies the episodes. This functions to clarify the need for alarm in the context of variable conditions. The contribution of the self to events is generally less understood than the effect of others upon the self.

6. Reflective integration: Being unable to explain causal relations, take the perspectives of others, or keep irrelevant information out of awareness, Type C speakers tend not to integrate information to arrive at balanced conclusions regarding (a) the dangerousness and protectiveness of attachment figures and situations and (b) personal responsibility and competence to protect the self. Instead, they remain excessively alarmed, accept too little personal responsibility for making change, and try to coerce change from others. Many explain or rationalize their behaviors with pseudopsychological jargon that in fact neither explains nor justifies the behaviors.

Experience/History

The history of speakers who use a coercive strategy involves inconsistent availability and response of attachment figures, overprotection from unseen dangers or underprotection from perceived danger, and greater responsiveness to affective signals than to cognitive communications. As the classification number increases, there is increasing experience of actual danger, including parentally inflicted danger, danger from outside of the family, and misleading information about danger and protection.

C1 (THREATENINGLY ANGRY)

Overview

Ainsworth's infant ambivalent pattern (Type C) is typified by mixed feelings of anger, fear, and desire for comfort. In the preschool Type C strategy, these are organized strategically as an alternation of threatening (angry) and disarming (desire for comfort and fear) behavior. Psychologically, negative affect is split. One set of feelings is exaggerated and its opposite is inhibited, then the displays are alternated contingent on the behavior of the attachment figure. This creates a coercive strategy. The C1 strategy emphasizes threat; the C2 strategy disarms threat (Crittenden, 1992). Although the discourse pattern described here is very similar to Main and Goldwyn's (1984, 1994) preoccupied and angry E2 pattern, it differs in being seen as part of a coercive strategy and being limited to transcripts that do not contain specific discourse markers indicative of one of the obsessive strategies. Put another way, the C1 strategy used here is the Main and Goldwyn pattern with limits that exclude risk cases.

The C1 strategy is used in conjunction with the C2 strategy. The speaker's focus is on using exaggerated anger to coerce attachment figures into providing the care and comfort that was desired in childhood, with disarming behavior held in reserve to deal with caregivers' anger. Among C1 speakers, the anger might better be described as chronic irritation that is easily (but only temporarily) assuaged by caregivers' placating behavior. When others defuse Type C speakers' anger by soothing, apologizing, assisting, and so forth, they have been coerced. Because the complaint was distorted and the rescue premature (in terms of a balanced understanding), the underlying problem is not resolved and an endless series of trivial complaints ensues.

Discourse Markers and Their Psychological Function

1. Procedurally, C1 speakers' discourse is involving. It is overlong, often dysfluent and characterized by switches to the present tense (or present participle forms), confusion of general and specific levels of information, use of *contradictory* conjunctions (e.g., but, on the other hand, rather, instead, although) without resolution and confusion of person. Dysfluence is greatest when conclusions (semantic or integrative) are requested.

    C1 speakers express nonverbally mixed and intense affective states that appear as exaggerated anger and inhibited/minimized desire for comfort; fear is almost absent. Affect, in other words, is distorted. This leads to confusion of the exaggerated feeling with equally true, but inhibited, feelings.

    Speakers using a C1 strategy are eager to tell the interviewers about childhood problems but with the intent of eliciting agreement rather than of thoughtfully reconsidering their histories. This functions to extend dialogues, both in attachment relationships and also in superficial interactions like the interview itself. The speaker usually indirectly or nonverbally requests reassurance from the interviewer that things were really as the speaker now feels them to have been.

2. C1 speakers have many images of conflict; in AAIs auditory images of angry speech are especially frequent. Sometimes they appear in such intense forms that the current context seems to be almost lost. The images both reflect an exaggerating distortion of imaged memory and also function to focus attention on the immediacy of the speaker's problems.

3. Semantic memory is vague and confused, so that descriptors and adjectives are not given precise or accurate meanings (i.e., their meanings are vague to the speaker). This confusion regarding the meanings of words is explained by the inappropriate association of the words with inhibited feeling states as well. Semantic memory is also distorted by opposite perspectives that are oscillated without resolution. Although C1 speakers are often aware that there are more moderate perspectives and can even state these, they cannot find validity in them or use them to modify their own perspectives. Instead, they simplify complex situations in an "either/or" manner. Temporal order may be ambiguous and uncertain, but causal relations are not seriously distorted and not intentionally deceptive. The lack of temporal clarity enables speakers to avoid awareness of causal relations, especially regarding their own behavior.

4. The connotative quality of C1 speakers' language functions to enlist listeners' support of the speakers' overt anger and covert desire for comfort. The affective qualities of the language are intense but vague, and the affects elicited are not extreme.

5. C1 speakers recall fragments and details of many episodes without recalling temporal/causal order well. Thus, their episodes often move backward and forward in time and, sometimes, across different events. This functions to retain access to all potentially useful information, keep the speaker from identifying his or her own role in events and relationships, and permit the speaker to blame others for undesirable outcomes.

6. C1 speakers tend to redirect integrative questions into a review of the (biased) evidence or to summarily close reflection with pseudopsychological jargon. True integration is difficult because affective information is distorted and cognitive information is omitted

from thought processes. Thus lack of integration functions to make resolution of the past appear perpetually possible while never actually being accomplished. This leaves Type C speakers with both a sense of complicity and also the feeling of being trapped. To resolve the discrepancy, they seek reassurance from interviewers that they are innocent of complicity and that their attachment figures are responsible.

RISK FOR PSYCHOPATHOLOGY

There is little or no risk for psychopathology in safe contexts.

DIFFERENTIATING C1 FROM OTHER STRATEGIES

C1 transcripts are differentiated from B5 transcripts by the absence of integrative statements that acknowledge the contribution of the self to the maintenance of conflict and empathic understanding of the parents' developmental history to their behaviors. They are differentiated from C3 transcripts by (a) the absence of outbursts of intense anger, (b) the absence of repetition of angry, emphatic phrases, (c) the greater ability of the C1 speaker to exchange turns with, and attend to, the interviewer, and (d) the presence of evidence of vulnerability.

Experience/History

Children who become adults classified as C1 have usually found that anger more effectively elicited parental caregiving than did appealing for caregiving. Thus, protection was achieved by maintaining an angry struggle with the attachment figure. In childhood, parents often responded in similar ways to both important and inconsequential events and also in different ways to the same behavior (e.g., egging on a rowdy boy, then punishing him for disruptiveness). Both parental threats and promises were often unfulfilled.

Another form of the strategy occurs when Type A parents decide consciously to demand less of their children and to be more accepting of negative affect than their parents were. Such parents hesitate to set limits or say "no." Their children, therefore, show negative affect and make demands that are often unreasonable. Because the parents do not feel comfortable with such demands, they sometimes become unexpectedly demanding or rejecting. This confuses and frustrates both parent and child, leading to an alternation of demands with disarming behavior (i.e., the coercive strategy). When the parent rewards Type A inhibition but does not punish attachment behavior, the child may show a mild form of the A/C strategy. To summarize, the parents of C1 speakers were often unpredictable but were usually not dangerous.

Adults using the C1 strategy are often dynamic and tenacious in the face of obstacles; many use humor effectively to disarm their own and others' aggression. They are devoted and loyal in relationships and readily defend those for whom they feel affection or who they feel have been wronged.

C2 (DISARMINGLY DESIROUS OF COMFORT)

Overview

This is the adult form of the C2 (ambivalent passive) pattern identified by Ainsworth in infancy. In the Main and Goldwyn method (1984, 1994), it is labeled E1 and is inclusive of other strategies that are described here as higher numbered strategies.

The C2 disarming strategy is one of eliciting comfort by emphasizing coy or disarming behavior, including humor, and alternating that with brief flashes of mild anger. Failure to reveal precisely the reasons for needing comfort or for feeling angry reduces the likelihood that others will oppose C2 speakers while concurrently making it difficult for them to resolve problems.

Discourse Markers and Their Psychological Function

1. The discourse of C2 speakers is typified by long, wandering, and run-on speech that is held together with *additive* conjunctions (e.g., and then, and, who, that is, in other words). Actors and objects of action are confused as is past and present. C2 speakers seem overwilling to talk but are relatively unwilling to be held to the structure of the interview. Instead, they tend to wander through topics with relatively little attention to questions. This functions to permit oversight of important information.

    There is a vague and unclear focus on the speaker's nebulous desire for comfort, expressed as enacted nonverbal affect (e.g., silly or disarming laughter, sighs); expression of anger is largely inhibited. Fear is rarely present and never extreme.

Speakers using a disarming strategy are engaging with interviewers, inviting confirmation of their often confused perspectives
and, sometimes, guidance on what to say. This functions to establish supportive relationships and to confirm that further exploration of difficult topics is not needed.

2. C2 speakers often have good access to imaged memory, particularly
somatic images related to comfort. Images distort recall to emphasize vulnerability over anger and also clarify speakers' relatively
inchoate feeling states, thus organizing both psychological processing and behavior. This functions to clarify mixed affective dispositions to action, thus, providing a motivation to seek nurturance.

3. Semantically, C2 speakers are left mildly confused by the omission
of semantic information from recall. This prevents them from focusing on the core issues underlying recurrent interpersonal misunderstandings, thereby avoiding overt conflict.

4. The connotative aspects of C2 language include bumblingly child-
ish discourse that elicits support and assistance from the interviewer.

5. Episodically, C2 speakers recall many experiences but find it difficult to associate them with semantic phrases or to relate a sequence
of events accurately. They confuse alternative perspectives and
seem unable to distribute responsibility for outcomes among multiple causal influences. There is a tendency to juxtapose contradictory affects in the narration (e.g., an image of comfort leads into an
episode about anger), suggesting mixed affective states. The episodes often include excessive and trivial detail. The blurring of episodes functions to prevent speakers from focusing on the reasons
for their anger, thus, not threatening their relationships. At the
same time, retention of excessive detail functions to prevent loss of
potentially important information.

6. C2 speakers manage some superficial integrative thought, but
these *"pseudoreflections"* are often commonsense "folk" knowledge,
self-help phrases, and so forth and, therefore, are often phrased in
terms of aphorisms or psychological jargon (i.e., psychobabble).
They function to give C2 speakers the perception of being in control of their lives and relationships. In general, however, C2 speakers are reluctant to integrate, especially if integration would require
acceptance of the limitations, past and future, of their parents and
acceptance of personal responsibility for their own contributions to
their development and current relationships.

Risk for psychopathology

There is little or no risk of psychopathology in safe contexts.

Differentiating C2 from other strategies

C2 transcripts can be differentiated from B4 transcripts by the failure to acknowledge the negative aspects of childhood attachment relationships and one's responsibility for contributing to these. C2 transcripts can be differentiated from C1 transcripts by the absence of evident anger.

Experience/History

Adults who use a disarming strategy have often had anxious, easily aroused, and overprotective attachment figures who conveyed a sense of concern even when there was no discernible danger. At the same time, they were often self-focused and unpredictable in comforting their children when they were distressed. Thus, feelings of vulnerability were associated with both safe and threatening contexts. Children of such parents found that expression of vulnerability elicited attachment figures' caregiving more reliably than either anger or evidence of competence. In the end, maintaining a disarmingly dependent closeness to parents best solved the problem of anxiety regarding unseen danger and unreliable caregiving. Therefore, C2 speakers often mention having stayed close to attachment figures by sleeping with them, or by staying home from school, and so forth. Being unaware of this motivation, C2 adults continue to seek excessive closeness. Further, they often report self-soothing behavior, such as overeating, hypervigilance expressed as anxiety, and nighttime fears of darkness, ghosts, bogeymen, or shadows on the walls.

Nevertheless, because closeness can generate conflict as well as comfort, anger was common. Thus, an enmeshing relationship was created in which proximity generated feelings of both comfort and anger. Feelings of vulnerability were exaggerated while feelings of anger were minimized or denied and individual competence was constrained, all to maintain the relationship with attachment figures. Critical features of the typical C2 history include minimal danger, considerable anxiety, and an unwillingness to consider the sources of anxiety.

C2 speakers are often warm, pleasing, and disarming people who enjoy the company of others and whose company is sought by others. Often they are persuasive or charmingly humorous individuals.

Chapter 9

Obsessive Type C Strategies (C3–8)

Coping With Uncertainty, Ambiguity, and Threat

THE OBSESSIVE STRATEGIES (C3–8) DIFFER IN IMPORTANT WAYS FROM THE Ainsworth-based C1–2 strategies (Ainsworth, 1973). In particular, C3–8 speakers oscillate between perspectives far less than do C1–2 speakers. Instead, they are consumed obsessively by a single perspective, largely to the exclusion of conflicting motivations. In terms of discourse, C3–8 speakers seek to engage interviewers in a collusion against others; their means of accomplishing this range from being demanding to manipulative to deceptive. In many ways, C+ speakers function in the opposite manner from A+ speakers. For example, both use "dismissing" discourse, but C+ speakers dismiss *others* rather than the *self* (A+). Similarly, C+ speakers are preoccupied with *themselves* rather than with *others*.

As with C1–2, the obsessive strategies are affectively organized. Expressed negative feelings are presented with exaggerated intensity as though intensity could eliminate the underlying conflict with other negative feelings (that are not expressed). For example, odd-numbered obsessive speakers (C3, C5, C7) present with a pugnacious veneer of bravado to cover and deny their feelings of vulnerability and desire for comfort. Even-numbered speakers (C4, C6, C8) display such exaggerated innocence and vulnerability that their underlying rage and punitive manipulations may escape notice. Nevertheless, the excluded feelings motivate behavior powerfully, thus placing the obsessive speaker at risk for unpredictable and destructive behavior. For example, anger at a lover's betrayal (or imagined betrayal) can block out information about needing and loving the person, even to the point of enabling attack (with the possible outcomes of loss of the loved person and criminal sanctions against oneself).

A gradient of feelings of vulnerability from desire for comfort to fear results in greater desire for comfort associated with low-numbered strategies and greater fear with high-numbered strategies (see Figure 2.3). By C7–8, the possibility of comfort is dismissed; fear and anger become integrated in the emotions of hate (C7) and dread (C8). The denial of information (the inhibited affects, as well as the contribution of the self to causality) begins to have serious implications for the suitability of thought and behavior *under safe conditions*. (Under dangerous conditions, these transformations have protective value.)

Particular images and episodes tend to provide recurrent themes in the interviews of obsessive speakers and are central to identifying the source of their preoccupation. Furthermore, obsessive speakers use semantic logic in sophisticated and complex, albeit false, ways. In particular, they have an idealized sense of justice, that is, of how things ought to be. Based on their own, uncompromising perspective regarding what is fair, they prepare to fight for their "rights." Again, there is an inversion between the C and A strategies. Type A speakers idealize the past behavior of attachment figures and Type C speakers idealize the future. Idealization of the past offers a pragmatic guide to safe behavior in a context in which there may be no expectation of justice whereas idealization of the future offers a hoped-for release from the injustices of past and present.

In addition, several critical features preclude these transcripts being classified as Types B or A. First, obsessive speakers use involving discourse throughout (therefore, they are not Type A). Second, they omit true cognitive information, often substitute false cognition and sometimes deny all cognition involving the self (therefore, they are not Type B). Third, they tell their stories solely from their own perspectives (therefore, they are neither Types A or B). Fourth, although they do inhibit some negative feeling states (and use distancing discourse for the inhibited affect), they intensify the focus on other negative feelings (therefore, they cannot be Type A). Fifth, they are not sufficiently integrated to describe the interactive relations of affect and cognition, self to others, and past to present for either themselves or their parents (therefore, they cannot be Type B).

Likely history. In terms of history, adults using an obsessive Type C strategy were endangered as children either by the parents' threatening action or by their parents' deception regarding danger. When children do not understand why their parents are not protective, they use the information that they have to construct reasons and, often, this leads to erroneous causal attributions. Because acting on erroneous representations does not yield the desired response, such children increasingly become suspicious of apparent information and use deception themselves. When these processes are underway, children are distorting incoming information to achieve predictable meaning and falsifying output information to avoid negative consequences. Both of these are self-protective in the short term, but the broader consequence is a limited ability to function adaptively under safe conditions with transparent information.

The obsessive adult strategy is usually the outcome of a series of strategy changes or reorganizations that occur across childhood and adolescence. That is, a full obsessive strategy is not possible in infancy, so the infants are generally classified as A, C, and A/C (in the DMM) or disorganized (in the ABC+D system). In the preschool years, the aggressive (C3) and feigned helpless strategies (C4) become effectively organized, but those children with a high probability of becoming C5–8 in adulthood begin to show a pattern of deception that is not yet strategic. Like the pre-A3 or pre-A4 strategies in infancy, the pre-C5–8 strategy in the preschool years has little effective protective value. In the school years, some C3–4 children progress to the more ominous C5–6 strategies. By adolescence, these strategies are both endangering to the self and others and also, in the most threatened and threatening strategies, become the basis for the C7–8 strategies. In addition, after puberty, the C6 strategy takes on characteristics of *sexual* seduction (Crittenden, 1997b).

When the Main and Goldwyn (1994) system is used without modification, the obsessive strategies are often classified as fearfully preoccupied (E3), dismissing (Ds), unresolved/disorganized (U), Cannot Classify (CC), or even balanced/autonomous (B). Ironically, the more devious the use of false cognition, or the more complete the dismissal of information about the involvement of self in causality (i.e., the closer the strategy is to psychopathy), the more likely is the misassignment of the transcript to B. This is consistent with findings of confusion between B and D at earlier ages where the DMM and ABC+D methods are compared (Crittenden et al., 2007; Spieker & Crittenden, 2010).

C3 (AGGRESSIVELY ANGRY)

Overview

This strategy is based on observations of preschool-aged children's behavior (Crittenden, 1992). Like all other Type C strategies, the C3 strategy is paired with an even-numbered strategy to create an alternating angry/disarming strategy. In most cases, C3 is paired with C4, but it could be paired with other even-numbered strategies.

C3 speakers use aggressive displays of anger to coerce attachment figures. The focus of the coercion is often an inconsequential problem that hides the underlying and inexplicit need for safety and comfort. Moreover, although they are aware of being angry with attachment figures, C3 speakers still openly desire closeness to them and feel vulnerable without them. That is, they look angry but also feel vulnerable. Their discourse serves the functions of focusing and maintaining the anger and of reducing awareness of fear and desire for comfort that would interfere with this focus. Rather than oscillating between semantic perspectives, C3 speakers use reductionist reasoning to justify their perspectives. Themes of hierarchy, justice, and strength pervade their transcripts.

Discourse Markers and Their Psychological Function

1. C3 speakers' discourse is eagerly produced and shows features of *involving anger*, conveyed through expletives, profanity, or scatological comments. Although they are not vengeful, their angry displays discourage others' aggression by eliciting fear. There is dysfluence around being strong and independent (which they do not truly feel) as well as around threats and dependency. C3 speakers use repetition for emphasis. There is an overuse of causal conjunctions (e.g., because, so, therefore) when the causal relations are not as stated, which reflects C3 speakers' confusion of causality.

    Along with the outbursts of anger, C3 speakers can also show some *mocking-gotcha! humor*, usually derisive to others.

    The *confronting/collusive* relationship with the interviewer functions to increase the speaker's feelings of strength and confidence. This can take the form of a struggle for dominance in social hierarchies; such a process was begun with parents but now is used in many relationships, including that with the interviewer. Procedurally, C3 speakers are still involved in trying to resolve family relationships and they attempt to involve the interviewer as an ally. When that seems to be failing, they may interrupt the interviewer to continue their barrage against others.

2. *Intense* images tend to be used in place of semantic or episodic information. Auditory images of parents' speech are particularly frequent, but these are introduced in ways that make it clear that, although the speakers are highly involved in their stories, they have not lost awareness of their present context (e.g., they do not speak to or hear from absent people). Auditory images are used illustratively to convince the interviewer that others are as the speaker says they are (i.e., to support the involving collusion). The function of the focus on anger-generating images is to clarify mixed and incompatible feelings (thus, promoting rapid and coherent action) and increase the perceived immediacy of past threats, thus, keeping the self vigilant in the present.

3. Semantic information is transformed by the omission of accurate causal relations, particularly with regard to contributions of the self to outcomes. Instead, feelings are used both as explanations for others' behavior (e.g., *"Because I feel angry, he is to blame"*) and also as justifications for one's own behavior (*"Because I am irate, I have the right to attack"*). Thus the oscillation of evaluative judgment, typical of C1–2 speakers, becomes more extreme, producing *reductionist blaming thought*. This enables the speaker to reverse the roles of victim and perpetrator such that the aggressive speaker perceives himself or herself to be a victim. Throughout, affect is transformed semantically into a theme of injustice to the speaker.

4. Connotative language is *emphatic*, through repetition and intensity. It functions to persuade listeners that the perspective of the C3 speaker is central and absolute. Its aggressive qualities suggest that it would be risky to dissent. It also functions to clarify mixed feelings, highlighting anger and reducing listeners' awareness of the speaker's vulnerability.

5. C3 speakers often repeat their blaming semantic statements instead of telling an actual episode (*lack of a negative episode*). The episodes that they tell tend to be about present events rather than childhood.

Unlike C1 speakers, C3 speakers often have accurate temporal order, especially in episodes involving danger; nevertheless, the temporal order is not complete in that it omits the speaker's early contribution to the problem (*fragmented episodes*). Without awareness of their own contributions, people cannot explain why things progressed as they did. This is especially true when episodes have apparently gratuitous violence in which omission of self-contributions emphasizes the innocent and victimized status of the speaker. This functions to keep the individual alert to the possibility of similar events recurring (i.e., it keeps the "fight" aspect of the fight or flight response primed and justifies the speaker's aggression).

6. Confusion among different perspectives, between past and present, and among different episodes makes the discourse and underlying thought processes difficult to follow. Integrative functioning is very often simply *omitted*. This prevents C3 speakers from identifying the critical missing information: (a) the speaker's own contribution and (b) the reasons that parents behaved as they did. Partly because these outbursts are elicited by others and partly because they are often ineffective, C3 speakers experience themselves in a passive role in which they react to others, thus *rationalizing* away their negative contributions to relationship problems. That is, in spite of their angry verbal behavior, they think of themselves as victims. With regard to understanding others, they use "cop-out" *pseudoreflections* (e.g., blaming parental behavior on "alcoholism"). C3 speakers are still trying to elicit the predictable caregiving and soothing comfort that they desired as children, but they are unwilling to consider the reciprocal and complex causal effects in their relationships. This functions to prevent closure of old disputes and recognition of the speaker's contribution, especially in the present, to events.

FAMILY TRIANGULATION AMONG C3–4 SPEAKERS

Frequently, families that produce children who use a C3–4 strategy pulled their children into the spousal relationship in an effort to resolve adult problems. When children cannot see that one parent is using them against the other, they inaccurately conclude that the parent is responding directly to them. Because this is inaccurate, the children's behavior has unpredictable effects, causing the children to agitate harder to achieve predictability.

RISK FOR PSYCHOPATHOLOGY

In childhood, C3 carries the risk of an array of attention-seeking, acting-out disorders: hyperactivity, attentional problems, conduct disorders, and anxiety disorders. By adolescence, most of these are under control and, instead, relationship difficulties are surfacing; in adulthood, the risk is primarily associated with family and work relationships. That is, the angry quality of C3 individuals both limits their range of response to untoward events and contributes to the occurrence of such events through poor selection of partners, employers, and so forth. The problems displayed include excessive anxiety, familial violence, and child abuse (Seefeldt, 1997) and self-managed ways of reducing anxiety (e.g., through substance dependence and bulimia, Ringer & Crittenden, 2007).

DIFFERENTIATING C3 FROM OTHER STRATEGIES

C3 transcripts are most easily differentiated from C1 transcripts by the increasingly vituperative quality of speech as the interview progresses; from C4 transcripts by the omission of acknowledgment of vulnerability; and from C5 transcripts by the absence of use of distancing or dismissing discourse and of false cognition.

Experience/History

Parents of C3 adults tended not only to be inconsistent but they also actively misled, teased, and tricked their children in ways that were often distressing and sometimes dangerous. For example, they may have encouraged the child's aggressive play and then suddenly punished severely his or her obstreperousness. The reasons for these changes are unclear to both the former child and also the adult speaker telling the story. In most C3 histories, there is some evidence of danger or lack of protection, but not life-threatening danger directed toward the child or danger disguised as safety. The child often showed conduct problems, including aggression, provocative disobedience, and risk taking. Among older children and adolescents, this includes reports of using moody withdrawal to accent the child's anger. Parents of C3 children often triangulated the family to resolve problems between themselves. Throughout family relationships and disputes, there are issues of hierarchy and power. The intensity of aggression is related to the perceived intensity of threat and felt helplessness to protect oneself.

C3 adults can be fiercely protective lovers, spouses, and parents. In addition, when aroused by social causes, they can behave in resolute, daring, and effective ways. When faced with a real threat, they can switch fluidly to the persuasive and charming half of their strategy, thus, rescuing the relationships that their anger challenges.

C4 (FEIGNED HELPLESS)

Overview

This strategy is based on observations of preschool-aged children's behavior (Crittenden, 1992) and is paired with an odd-numbered strategy to create an alternating angry/disarming strategy.

As with C3 speakers, adults who feign helplessness are still engaged in dominance struggles over attaining protection and comfort from unpredictable attachment figures. Exaggeration of fear and inhibition of anger mislead others regarding the individual's actual state with regard to danger and the relationship; specifically, neither the individual nor others are explicitly aware of how angry and competent the individual actually is behind the appearance of fearfulness. Nevertheless, even in adulthood, there can be great power in feigning innocent weakness and claiming the right of the vanquished to be protected by the victor. C4 speakers appear to remain enmeshed with attachment figures in a mutual and reciprocal bond of protection from uncertain danger.

Discourse Markers and Their Psychological Function

1. The discourse is organized around *involving fear*, absolute negatives, present-tense verbs, run-on sentences, and so forth. This keeps the speaker alert to the immediacy of danger.

   The procedural management of expressed affect privileges the clear display of fear, through, for example, barely audible voices, gasps, and other signals of vulnerability and submission. This *arousing nonverbal affect* has strong interpersonal effects.

   The *appealing/submissive* relationship with the interviewer is focused on seeking support from the interviewer. All forms of procedural functioning are distorted to give priority to identifying potential threats and seeking assistance from others. This functions to maximize the probability of identifying danger and motivating others to respond protectively.

2. Imaged memory is distorted by *intense,* vivid images of past fear, often in the absence of evidence of true threat to the self, and of desire for comfort. Often, fearful images from different contexts are juxtaposed. This functions to induce somatic arousal (in the present), which increases the perceived immediacy of threats and focuses attention on self-protection.

3. Semantic memory is distorted to reflect the absence of fully accurate causal relations, particularly multiple and interactive causation: What remains apparent is simple, unidirectional causation, in which speakers appear to be innocent victims when, in fact, there is disguised evidence that speakers are at least partially aware of how they irritate and instigate others' aggressive behavior. *Reductionist blaming thought* prevents closure of old disputes and recognition of the speakers' contributions, especially in the present, to events.

4. The frequent, *evocative* references to fear (*scared, panic, afraid*) dominate the discourse. Evocative words and syntactic constructions increase somatic arousal for the speaker and listener, focusing them both on protection of the speaker.

5. Episodes are present but *distorted.* Many are *fragmented,* with more emphasis on images than on initiating conditions, sequences of events, and specified conclusions. The source of fear is unclear and the outcome is generalized defeat. This functions to prevent C4 speakers from recognizing that the past danger was actually quite minimal. In fact, for C4 speakers, it is more often the absence of clear and predictable safety, rather than the presence of threat, that is the source of arousal.

6. Integration is largely absent. Instead, feelings are used to explain events. This functions to reduce the possibility of comparing past and present circumstances and determining that there is no current danger or that the speaker could now take responsibility for self-protection. They and their attachment figures increase feelings of security by restricting exploration, including mental exploration of ideas.

Complicitous splitting, false idealization, and familial triangulation. When the family context involves triangulated relationships, C4 speakers split good and bad between the parents. This leads to a false idealization of the "good" parent, which involves presuming the preferred parent to be, like the speaker, an innocent victim of the aggression of the feared and blamed parent. This is different from Type A because ultimately even the falsely idealized parent is held responsible for the negative states of the self, which remain the central target of attention.

RISK FOR PSYCHOPATHOLOGY

In childhood, C4 is associated with the risk of victimization and incompetence (rather than aggression). Socially, C4s are often excluded although other children do not actively dislike them. C4 children are often passive daydreamers, many of whom underachieve academically or suffer from psychosomatic illnesses that require considerable adult attention (e.g., allergies). Daydreaming, in particular, can include ruminating thoughts of self-justification, revenge, or fear, which, because they are not spoken aloud, are not readily identified as being generated by the self. Lacking a source "code" of self, the individual may treat the information as being externally valid, rather than being internally generated.

By adulthood, C4 speakers appear vulnerable and needy and easily attract others' care and assistance without actually benefiting from it. Thus, they frustrate those who would help them. They experience heightened anxiety and an inability to make decisions and effectively achieve independence. They also contribute to the possibility of life-event crises by choosing partners and jobs poorly.

DIFFERENTIATING C4 FROM OTHER STRATEGIES

C4 transcripts are most easily differentiated from C2 and C1 transcripts by their "pity me" quality of blame. They contain the same sorts of dysfluency and psychological functions as C3 transcripts except that the dominant affects are fear and desire for comfort, with display of anger being inhibited. Thus, C4 speakers appear pitiful and attempt to charm (rather than intimidate) interviewers into assuming a sympathetic role. C4 transcripts are differentiated from C6 transcripts by the absence of (a) teasing the interviewer with enticing information that is, nevertheless, withheld and (b) the use of false cognition.

Experience/History

C4 speakers often had parents whose moods and behavior were unpredictable; moreover, they tended to be both overprotective and unpredictably threatening. Frequently, these were Type A parents who tried to reverse the way they themselves were cared for. In addition, there was often the occurrence of inexplicable and frightening events that, although they did not directly harm the speaker, carried an ominous feeling of threat; these events could have been traumas to the parents. Often, parents of C4 children felt confirmed in their importance to the child by the child's clinging. Other parents of C4 children tricked them. Common forms of such trickery include warnings about invisible and unreal dangers, for example, warnings about bogeymen or monsters that might harm the child. Nevertheless, when children responded with fear, parents sometimes comforted and often mocked them. When they responded with overt anger or aggression, the parents became punitive in reestablishing the dominance hierarchy. Thus, the parents tended to punish aggressive or angry behavior in severe and predictable ways, whereas they both rewarded and punished passive helplessness. As a consequence, the children often became hypervigilant to the possibility of danger in ways that left them both feeling vulnerable and, sometimes, actually vulnerable to harm. In addition, however, they were often angry and resentful that they could not do things that appeared safe, count on parental support, and challenge parental authority.

Feigned helpless adults use the submissive role to achieve control, but it is at the cost of failing to develop self-protective competence. In childhood, the appearance of being in danger is manipulated by the child to elicit caregiving from reluctant caregivers, whereas, in adulthood, the appearance of incompetence is manipulated to avoid the responsibilities of adulthood. As a result, C4 adults are truly limited in their ability to differentiate safe and dangerous conditions, either temporally or contextually.

When it is used outside the family home, the feigned helpless strategy often leads to mockery by peers, exclusion from peer groups, and, sometimes, actual victimization. Thus, the feigned helpless strategy protects children from parents' anger and elicits their caregiving, but makes children vulnerable to victimization outside of the home. This confirms the C4 individual's sense of injustice. In addition, the strategy carries the potential for covertly oppositional rebellion (i.e., passive-aggressive behavior).

Adults using this strategy are often charming and pleasant to be with while still being very effective in achieving outcomes in contexts where overt attempts at control would elicit confrontation.

C5 (PUNITIVELY ANGRY AND OBSESSED WITH REVENGE)

Overview

This strategy is based on theory (Crittenden, 1995), clinical case histories, and observations of discourse drawn from AAIs, and it is paired with an even-numbered strategy, usually C6, to create an alternating coercive strategy. C5 is one of the most versatile strategies with many presentations. It is used by many people in troubled relationships and, in its failing forms, by people in psychological treatment.

The C5 strategy is organized around revenge against attachment figures. Adults using the C5 strategy are almost completely motivated by anger, but the anger is "cooler" and better regulated than that of "hot" C3 speakers. At the same time, C5 speakers are less clear about its basis. This leads to a pervasive blaming attitude, a "chip on the shoulder." Individuals using a C5 strategy bear grudges over long periods of time and, in the extreme, the desire to punish attachment figures can so overwhelm the desire for closeness that some individuals using a C5 strategy sacrifice their relationships, attachment figures, and even themselves to exact retribution. Angry engagement and revenge, in other words, can become ends in themselves, rather than the means to achieve protection.

There are several major differences as compared to lower numbered Type C strategies. First, the oscillations of C3–4 speakers become *contradictions* in the C5 strategy. These are embedded in the structure of the interview rather than in dysfluent statements. Indeed, the obvious discourse errors of C1–4 speakers are usually absent and the language flows with apparent ease. Instead, information at different points in the transcript is contradictory, without the speaker showing awareness of the contradiction. Common sources of contradiction are (a) perceived threat and experienced danger, (b) idealization of love and scorn for loved people, and (c) boasts of power and claims of being victimized.

The second is the use of deception to carry out the individual's angry motivations. Self-deception functions to justify the obsessive focus on retribution. The duplicity of C5 speakers is not their telling of bald lies, but rather a form of presentation of information that causes listeners to draw inaccurate conclusions. For example, a series of events may be presented without connecting conjunctions. This requires the listener to attribute causality and responsibility; the series, however, may be structured so as to suggest the innocence of the speaker and culpability of others—when these conditions are not accurate. Thus, the strategy is *complicitous* (i.e., covertly involving) because the listener must contribute to the construction of the deception. As a consequence, even if the truth becomes known, the listener is often unclear as to the source of the error. Deception prevents others from preparing for the attack, whereas flips to the disarming, charming half of the strategy (i.e., C4, C6, and C8) protect the self from others' wrath. The joint effect is an irresolvable struggle that confuses partners and observers alike. Usually, only careful coding of transcribed speech reveals such deception.

The third major difference is the response to comfort. Because attachment figures have often appeared available and empathic but acted in unexpectedly threatening ways, individuals using a C5 strategy do not trust comfort. It makes them more uneasy than threat. C5, in other words, is the beginning of the "comfort disorders" (i.e., C5–8).

Discourse Markers and Their Psychological Function

At its simplest, C5 is the inverse of the A1 strategy. That is, it uses dismissing and distancing discourse to achieve the opposite result. Others are distanced, dismissed, and derogated. Attachment is treated as being unimportant. The self is glorified and others are held responsible for the negative feelings of the self. Further, the psychological process of splitting is the same as in the As except that it is used to achieve a *self*-perspective and the distorted semantic conclusions are *positive regarding the self* and negative regarding others. In a reversal of the compulsive A process (in which action creates responsibility), C5 speakers do not take responsibility for their actions. To the contrary, they claim that powerlessness absolves them of responsibility. The crucial differentiating features are not in the discourse markers (which are dismissing in both A and C5), but rather in (a) the pervasive presence of the perspective of the *self* and (b) the emphasis on one's own *negative affect* as motivating behavior for the C5 strategy.

1. The discourse of C5 speakers is terse, focused, hostile, and *dismissing of others*. Omission of extraneous information clarifies the speaker's motivation to behave angrily. Dismissing the perspectives of other people, one's own vulnerability, and others' positive characteristics reduces complexity and maintains the angry focus.

   C5 speakers use distorted, angry affect but in a cooler, more dismissing manner than C3 speakers (e.g., defensive humor, mocking, and sarcasm), including pleasure taken at others' misfortune (*distorted positive affect*). These express the bitterness of C5 speakers' experience. Concurrently, there is near complete omission of vulnerable affects, thus, disconnecting the self from vulnerability and creating an illusion of invulnerability.

   Confrontation (e.g., interruption, delayed responding, spontaneous cutting off of discussion, and long silences) and *triangulated collusion* force interviewers into a nonneutral position of supporting or refuting the speakers. Less obvious tactics include *parrying*. Interviewers' positive affect, especially when conveying comfort, usually elicits an uneasy response as though it was expected to be false; this reduces the probability of being caught unprepared for others' attacks. These procedures suggest the fragility of the mental strategy: If the speaker permitted further discussion, the defense might fail.

2. Images are used sparingly, but when present, are often *animated* and reflect intensely frightening episodes in which the self was unprotected. Therefore, they are cut off quickly and attention is focused elsewhere.

3. Generalizations are *distorted* by the splitting of self and others' responsibility, with assignment of responsibility to attachment figures (in a *derogating* form) and of innocent victimization to the self (i.e., this is the same process as for Type A, but in the reverse). This takes the form of *misattribution of causality* and functions to reduce the probability of the self being unprepared for parents' unpredictable aggression and duplicity. C5 speakers are both confused about actual causal relations and also actively use *false cognition* to deceive others regarding their own intended behavior. That is, the surface of their discourse reflects the usual cognitive structures (e.g., if/then, when/then), but the meanings are inverted (i.e., false). Omitting true cognition about the relations among events and constructing false cognition mislead others regarding one's angry intentions.

4. The linguistic style is bitingly dry with scorn of others captured in a few cutting words, particularly words that connote denigration, trickery, and deception. Language is also used to make the listener experience the subject's negative affective state (i.e., projection).

5. Few episodes are recalled (*lack of negative episode*) although there are usually some in which a speaker gives a believable account of his or her parents' endangering behavior. Nevertheless, these episodes are distorted by the exclusion of the speaker's vulnerability, such that the self appears strong, protected, or physically absent

when in fact the self was present, vulnerable, and hurt (*negative episode without harmful effects on the self*). Other episodes focus on times when the speaker tricked others or felt victimized by their trickery. Focusing on tricking others functions to bolster the speaker's confidence, whereas focusing on past victimization provides support for revenge. A functional outcome is a reduced capacity for trust and increased vigilance. Occasionally, episodes are transformed in ways that change the speaker's role from victim to perpetrator (or vice versa) to protect the speaker from the predictable consequences of his or her behavior (*false innocence/blame*). Such transformations protect C5 speakers from recognizing their vulnerability.

6. Integration is very limited. The function of curtailed integration is to protect the speaker from recognizing the extent of his or her vulnerability and complicity in problems. However, the inhibited feelings (of fear and desire for comfort) remain unchanged. Without an integrative resolution, they cannot be transformed into the more mature and less dangerous feelings of regret, sadness, and so forth. Instead integration of falsified cognition with negative feelings leads to intense, complex, and negative affects such as jealousy, envy, resentment, and vengeance. Consequently, there is risk that the adult will act on feelings he or she had as a child. Justice is *rationalized* without consultation with others, thus, protecting the speaker from others' deception and from the need to account for, and adapt to, others' perspectives. C5 speakers simplify the complex situation of being both victims of others' treachery and also angry perpetrators of treachery by perceiving themselves as victims. This clarifies their right to take offensive action. Under dangerous circumstances, these transformations are adaptive; under safe conditions, they are maladaptive in that they both prevent the self from experiencing comfort and also endanger others.

COMPLICITOUS SPLITTING, FALSE IDEALIZATION, AND FAMILIAL TRIANGULATION

Some obsessive Type C speakers split good and bad between their parents, idealizing one parent and derogating the other. The idealization is not, however, that of a Type A speaker because the speakers always maintain their own perspectives and are motivated by their own negative affects. Instead, false idealization allows C5 speakers to vilify one parent by comparison with the other.

The central problem leading to "false" idealization (with the notation [A]) is that children could not understand their relationship with each parent because of hidden parental discord. Thus, the parents sometimes interacted with the child while being motivated by the unseen discord. When the child drew self-relevant causal attributions, they were erroneous. To simplify the inscrutable process, the child split good and bad, treating one parent as innocent and holding the other responsible for both the child's and the innocent parent's distress. The hidden spousal discord prevented the child from conceptualizing troubled relationships as reciprocal and organized around complicitous victimization and impotent aggression. For example, arguments between the parents that were kept hidden could result in a parent suddenly punishing a child in a particularly vindictive way. Because the child was unaware of the argument and found the parent's behavior capricious and cruel, that parent was vilified.

Speakers who as children were triangulated into parental conflicts are unable to articulate anything substantive to explain their maladapted functioning. Sometimes traumas are sought, but they tend to melt away under scrutiny; at best, they qualify as "imagined" (see Chapter 11). Being without explanation, some clam up, fall silent, and enter a stuck form of the C5–6 strategy, which appears in the AAI as the C5–6 speaker "stonewalling" the interview. That is, the individual feels bad and acts inappropriately, but the only explanations that can be offered are grossly insufficient to explain the situation. Still the effects, which can range from pervasive negativity to eating and personality disorders, are too substantial to be ignored. By saying nothing, speakers avoid ridicule for saying something inadequate. However, by refusing an interpersonal dialogue, they preclude learning anything useful. By suffering so long and without relief, while inhibiting explicit expressions of rage, they convince themselves that they are caregiving, compliant, or self-reliant. This then forms the surface of their story: a caregiving, compliant, or self-reliant speaker who lacks a sufficiently neglectful or abusive history to account for a compulsive strategy. The reality is of a resentful, coercive, and angry speaker who cannot and will not articulate complaints and who dominates the interview itself. This suggests that "stonewalling" speakers display a modified version of the C5–6 strategy. The stuck and nonstrategic quality of the strategy, along with the speaker's awareness of its failure to protect the self, suggests the possibility of a depressed modifier. On the other hand, the high arousal and the speaker's continuing active struggle do not fit the criteria for depression. Possibly in the future we will define a new modifier that explains this form of C5–6.

Particularly when comfort has been received from one parent in a triangulating process that undercut the other parent, the child may implicitly discern in adulthood that the comfort was not truly meant for him or her, but rather that the child was a tool in the dispute between the parents. Providing comfort in such cases will elicit anger from the speaker.

DIFFERENTIATING C5 FROM OTHER STRATEGIES

The C5 strategy is most easily differentiated from the C3 strategy by the greater control over anger displayed by the speaker, by the presence of dismissing discourse with regard to personal vulnerability and the value of others' perspectives, and by the use of deception, especially with the interviewer. Further, instead of the run-on sentences with obfuscating irrelevant details that characterize passive thought (C1, C3), there is an economy of carefully selected detail, with omissions of relevant information, which leads both speaker and listener to inaccurate conclusions about the past. This functions to justify the speaker's angry involvement in present struggles. Unlike the C6 strategy, there is direct evidence of anger and a valuing of power. Compared to the C7 strategy, there is a clear focus on a specific person who is the object of anger, even though the focus may be both expanded beyond the actual threat to other related specific people and also narrowed to reduce the contribution of the self. Moreover, unlike C7–8 transcripts, contradictions are readily apparent when different parts of the transcript are compared, and the form of deception used is less involving. Further, there is not the menacing quality of allusions to very dangerous behavior (e.g., murder) and the pervasive distrust of the interviewer. Finally, unlike C7–8, there is not a complete denial of self-responsibility.

C5 is similar to Type A strategies in that distancing and dismissing discourse markers are used; C5 differs in the function of the discourse markers. For example, Type A speakers make clear causal attributions of an if/then sort in which the self bears responsibility for negative outcomes, whereas C5 speakers often present temporally ordered information without causal attributions and with the implicit assumption that the self is (irrationally) not responsible for negative behavior. In addition, Type A speakers emphasize the positive features of attachment figures, acknowledge others' perspectives and feelings, and use these as the basis for self-organization, whereas C5 speakers dismiss the feelings and perspectives of others and transform the desirable aspects of others into their weaknesses. For the compulsive A strategies, vulnerability of the self is assumed and dismissed as not worthy of consideration, whereas for C5 speakers vulnerability of the self is denied. For all Type A strategies, anger is distanced or denied, whereas C5 speakers display preoccupying, present-tense anger. Type A speakers minimize or exonerate attachment figures' faults whereas C5 speakers highlight these. For triangulated and stuck C5–6 "stonewalling" speakers, the distinction between their strategy and a Type A strategy is most easily made by the Type C speaker's unwillingness to provide socially appropriate responses that take the attention *off* the problem; to the contrary, the silence of "stonewalling" speakers focuses attention on themselves and on the presence of an (insoluble) problem.

RISK FOR PSYCHOPATHOLOGY

The C5–6 form of the strategy carries considerable risk for mild to moderate psychopathology, particularly the anxiety disorders (Hughes, 1997). There is also risk for familial violence, petty criminal behavior, and addictive disorders. Much of the risk is realized as a result of poor life decisions made under the influence of the mental distortions that typify the strategy. See below for further discussion of C5+, "stonewalling" speakers. The extreme splits among the negative affects and within semantic memory create a risk of strategic failure and, therefore, of maladjustment. Not surprisingly, the proportion of individuals using C5–6 strategies in psychological treatment or who are involved with the legal system is substantially greater than for individuals using C3–4 strategies. Common problems among individuals using the C5 strategy include bullying, gang activity, delinquency, drug and alcohol abuse, and partner abuse as well as all the attentional, conduct, learning, and anxiety disorders associated with the developmental roots of the strategy. Among individuals with a nonstrategic, "stonewalling" form of the C5 strategy, common symptoms and diagnoses include some personality disorders, some restricting eating disorders (Ringer & Crittenden, 2007), suicide and threats of suicide, and so forth.

Experience/History

As children, speakers classified as C5 often experienced lack of comfort and support in the context of an inexplicit feeling of threat. Their families were often characterized by secrets or unclear, but potentially dangerous, incidents or conditions (e.g., marital conflict, alcoholism, parental mental illness, hidden marital infidelity). Attachment figures tried often to protect the children from these conditions by being silent, but the effect was to distress children without giving substance to the distress. When, in addition, the parents involved the children in parental conflicts, the outcome was often an intense struggle without clarity regarding the focus of the struggle. The parents themselves often appeared to be in opposition as aggressor and victim in the marriage; the children tended to side with and idealize the victimized parent without seeing that parent's complicity in the family problems. This left children feeling psychologically and physically vulnerable in ways that were often more harmful than the threatened danger. Thus, there is a general failure of the events of the history to match in intensity the behavior of the speaker. Under these conditions of ambiguous threat and uncertain comfort, apparent safety and comfort carried risk of deception and danger. As children, C5 speakers often displayed agitation, hyperactivity, sleep disorders, conduct or disciplinary problems, and so forth (i.e., the problems associated with C3–4). By school age, most (future) C5 speakers themselves used false cognition to trick others about their aggressive intentions. As struggles with parents intensified, children became stubbornly unwilling to admit vulnerability or responsibility. Nevertheless, most report being the repeated victims of parents' or peers' harassment, persecution, or ostracism (e.g., name-calling, taunting). Frequently this included bullying behavior in which feelings of weakness were transformed into feelings of strength by comparison with the fear and submission of the victim.

In adolescence, their covertly aggressive acts could have long-term and dangerous consequences. For example, some C5 adolescents participated in gang violence, used violence in dating relationships, became pregnant out of wedlock (especially when their parents would be horrified and socially shunned), or refused evidence of parental affection and concern (e.g., not accepting food in some cases of anorexia). Peers often were perplexed by the combination of aggressive and protective/charming characteristics of C5 adolescents.

Many C5 adults jealously and obsessively protect (idealized) love relationships using a strategy of deception; when their partners protest, their fears of infidelity (i.e., victimization) are activated and some seek revenge, thus, becoming themselves sources of danger to their partners.

C5 adults can be powerfully attractive leaders, lovers, and spouses;

can rally almost fanatical support for social causes; and may have the disregard for personal danger that is an essential component of heroism. The strategy can be intellectually seductive such that it easily deceives both others and the individuals using the strategy. As Elie Wiesel (1960) noted, "I have one request: may I never use my reason against truth." C5 speakers, and those using higher numbered Type C strategies, often do this without awareness.

C6 (SEDUCTIVE AND OBSESSED WITH RESCUE)

Overview

This strategy is based on theory (Crittenden, 1995), clinical case histories, and observations from AAIs. Like all other Type C strategies, it is paired with an odd-numbered strategy, usually C5.

In transcripts assigned to this strategy, information about attachment or sexuality is used to lead, mislead, and involve the listener in a collusion against (presumed threatening) important figures in the speaker's life. Careful consideration of the evidence, however, makes clear that (a) these figures are deemed excessively powerful and threatening (i.e., there are no supportive people), (b) even powerless people (such as infants) are construed as powerful and scheming, and (c) trivial threats are often given more emphasis than substantive threats.

Individuals using the C6 strategy attempt to entice others into a chase, the conclusion of which is kept undefined and elusive. Indeed, if the interviewer tries to help by focusing on some specific issue and exploring concrete ways to resolve it, the C6 speaker adroitly shifts the focus, changes the complaint, or thrusts forward a new obstacle that itself requires attention. Metaphorically, the ground of the interview keeps slipping, with only the threat of danger and need for rescue remaining constant. Furthermore, although there is a superficial appearance of desire for some form of rescue or protection, the collusion of the interviewer against others suggests that the ultimate yield might be inadvertent support for an attack. Overall, C6 speakers present themselves ingenuously and often manipulate unwary interviewers into a contributing role in a strategy that seems more focused on the process of rescuing than on the creation of safety. Indeed, comfort is often the most unsettling of affective states because trust in comfort could lead to vulnerability in the event of covert danger.

Discourse Markers and Their Psychological Function

1. C6 speakers try procedurally in several covert ways to involve interviewers in rescuing them from insoluble problems. Their discourse presents information in incomplete and ambiguous ways that *tantalize* and attract the listener. *Involving fear* is prominent but not in ways that are as blatant as in the C4 strategy.

   Arousing nonverbal affect is displayed intensely, to elicit in the interviewer a desire to protect, help, or rescue the speaker. The display of vulnerable affect is exaggerated and fragmented, together with omission (inhibition) of anger. This begins to dissociate the self from anger (i.e., one ceases to be aware of having the inhibited feelings).

   The relationship with the interviewer, as well as being *appealing/ submissive*, also becomes *seductive* when information is dangled teasingly in the discourse such that the listener feels obliged to inquire further, thus often changing the direction of the interview and extending it beyond its natural conclusion. Occasionally, silence functions to draw interviewers into mind-reading games or the supposition that the speakers' silence reflects traumatization, thus, eliciting extensive caregiving from interviewers. Procedural functioning is distorted to elicit help rather than enabling the speaker to help himself or herself. Further, there is a subtle manipulation in the speaker's bids for support that functions to make it difficult to refuse to collude and difficult to identify the collusion explicitly. In addition, as noted for C5, some C6 speakers refuse to respond to the interviewers' questions, thus, "stonewalling" the interview.

2. Images are often *animated* and generally distorted to convey the appearance of hierarchical power relations in which the speaker appears powerless; these belie the underlying complexity of true power relations. The images function to keep both others and the self from realizing the power of the speaker, thus, increasing their power.

3. *Misattribution of causality* and *false cognition* conceal the true causal relations among events and people, often by subtle shaping of the presentation of information, for example, by using passive verbs for the self and active verbs for others' power. There are themes (often in the form of complaints) of others being advantaged (by being together, safe, and successful), whereas the speaker (and

sometimes his or her family) is excluded, unfavored, or picked on. False cognition is used to portray the speaker as helpless and unable to influence these untoward events. Concurrently, however, there is a theme of chronic anger, even obsessive anger, toward everyone.

4. Language can be powerfully evocative, in poetic and beautiful ways that motivate the listener to ally with the speaker, who appears needy and vulnerable but is also able to enchant and seduce with his or her speech.

5. *Fragmented* and *false innocence/blame* distorted episodes emphasize threat to the vulnerable self and fail to provide the full sequence of events; concurrently, however, they provide the justification for anger.

6. C6 speakers refuse to integrate information; this functions to clarify one set of feelings while permitting a hidden set, which initiates rumination, to influence behavior and to obscure self-contributions to outcomes. In the place of integrated information, distorted affective motivation makes complex, reciprocal interactions seem mysterious and beyond control.

RISK FOR PSYCHOPATHOLOGY

The C6 strategy does not develop until the school years and often is used by those C4 children whose strategy was ineffective at eliciting the comfort and protection that they felt they needed. The C6 strategy heightens the demand and adds both false cognition and sexual seductiveness to the set of tools used to coerce others. The emphasis on incompetence and fearfulness leaves C6 speakers vulnerable to anxiety disorders (Hughes, 1995), victimization by family members and strangers, addictive disorders, and mood disorders. In its extreme forms, when it is becoming nonstrategic, the C6 strategy (alone or in combination with other strategies) is associated to some personality disorders, bipolar disorders, some eating disorders, and some forms of panic disorder as well as an array of quite desperate bids for attention, including self-harm and suicide threats and attempts.

DIFFERENTIATING C6 FROM OTHER STRATEGIES

Compared to C4 speakers, C6 speakers are ingratiatingly submissive and cloyingly self-pitying. They present themselves as overwhelmed and yet are able to manipulate the process of the interview quite effectively; indeed, they seek to hold the interviewer's attention as long as possible. This is accomplished frequently by twisting the interviewer's words to make them seem hurtful in ways that then induce guilt and elicit caregiving from the interviewer. Compared to C5 speakers, C6 speakers display little anger, especially semantically and procedurally, focusing instead on their fearfulness. Compared to C8 speakers, they are better able to maintain the appearance of rationality and to appear confident in their interactions with interviewers. In particular, they are able to focus their fear, even if the focus is too great, rather than fearing potentially everything and everyone.

Like the C5 strategy, the C6 strategy can be confused with some Type A strategies because of the presence of distancing discourse markers. It is important to note that C6 speakers dismiss their own anger while emphasizing vulnerability, that they are cognitively distorted, and that they dismiss the desirable qualities of others (whereas Type A speakers dismiss the negative qualities of others). Like C5 speakers, they condemn others more through the absence of others' extenuating circumstances and their own complicity than through the presence of overwhelming negative detail.

Experience/History

Parents of speakers classified as C6 tend to be inconsistently rejecting; they had both rewarded and punished passive and submissive behavior without using differentiating forewarning conditions, and they consistently punished angry behavior. Often they tricked (or failed) the child regarding safety. Often there were family secrets, to which the child was not privy. Consequently, they could not apply this information to predicting future events. In addition, many C6 children felt intentionally abandoned because of separations from their parents (e.g., parental death, early entry to boarding school, placement in foster care); such separations tend to be especially powerful when children cannot understand how they "deserved" the separation or could not change it, and, especially, if dangerous things happened during the separation from which the children could not protect themselves. C6 speakers often report severe psychosomatic conditions (e.g., asthma, nightmares, allergies, frequent illness or accidents) both as children and as adults. In addition, some report various forms of childhood victimization (e.g., being bullied, incestuous sexual abuse) and ongoing victimization (e.g., a violently domineering spouse). Families with a C6 member often have triangulated relationships in which alliances are forever shifting in unpredictable ways.

The seductive quality of C6 adults and their apparent desire to please others can be very attractive. On the other hand, they can also move quietly and without attracting attention through complex and sometimes treacherous social contexts while, nevertheless, accomplishing their goals. This can make them formidable adversaries.

GRADATIONS WITHIN C5–6

The C5–6 classification covers a wide range of interpersonal functioning from chronically angry and engaging to life-threatening incapacity to function (in which the threat to life can be either to the self or to loved ones). The clarity of the threat, from the speaker's perspective, provides the basis for differences in strategy and, thus, in the adaptiveness of strategy. The clearer the threat (and the source of the threat), the more directly the individual can organize around it. Thus when one or both parents were overtly and pervasively dangerous, the attached person can disavow the relationship and despise the endangering person, or focus on the rescue by the other parent; the strategy, in other words, is highly focused, even if extreme. The more obscure the threat or the source of the threat, the less focused the individual's strategy can be. Thus when the threatening attachment figure is also caring and involving (i.e., if the attachment figure uses multiple strategies, including C-odd, C-even and A+) and, especially, if there is some deception, the speaker may organize a C5–6 strategy (with varying proportions of C5 or C6). When the individual feels or becomes party to a threat that is neither explicit nor directly self-relevant (e.g., marital discord), it becomes difficult for the individual to focus his or her anger. Three subgroups, differing for decreasing clarity of threat, suggest the range of functioning among C5–6 individuals.

1.   Sometimes C5 is a partial and transient derogating strategy.[1] That is, it is too openly angry to be fully C5 but, at the same time, is too dismissing to merely be C3. The only deception is the self-deception of claiming not to care about or want comfort from the

1. The Main and Goldwyn Ds2 pattern is included here.

derogated figure. The intensity of expressed anger makes interpersonal engagement impossible, thus, removing the flexibility from the strategy. Used in the derogating form, C5 is the explicit repudiation of an attachment figure who harmed the speaker greatly in the past, but whose protection and affection is still (covertly) desired. The strategy, therefore, is an attempt to protect the current psychological self from both the unpredictable and uncontrollable danger experienced in childhood when the self had little or no physical protection and also the recognition of current needs for comfort. Therefore, it is often seen in complex combinations in which derogation is used with one parent, but the other parent is idealized or a minor figure is delusionally idealized. Derogation is most likely during adolescence and the transition to adulthood or during the process of reorganizing mental representations (e.g., Type A adults who begin to hold their parents responsible for their limitations may flip to derogation). Used this way (i.e., without the alternation with C6), derogation is a brittle defense that usually is replaced by or combined with more productive and stable strategies.

2. Usually, C5 is found in alternation with C6. In this form, it is a functional strategy that permits flexibility and variation within a relationship; as a consequence, it can endure indefinitely, such that struggling without resolution becomes the way of engaging. C5–6 speakers generally are engaging with interviewers, have some characteristics of C3–4 speakers (i.e., clear involving characteristics), and provide responses to the questions (albeit distorted responses). This form of the strategy is associated with histories of family complicity; current relationships that are jealous, entangling, and unstable; and risk of violence (e.g., spousal violence, child abuse).

3. In extreme cases, a C5 or C6 speaker refuses to let the interview proceed in a meaningful way. The speaker, in other words, closes the interviewer out or "stonewalls" the interview. This effectively keeps others from knowing or resolving the problem. The most likely reason for this is that the speaker does not know what the problem is; instead, they have only minor complaints that seem trivial and are, therefore, concealed. In these extreme cases, the primary information available to the coder is from procedural memory, particularly the relationship with the interviewer. It comes in two forms: the discourse (in which the self is foremost and others

are distanced) and the relationship with the interviewer (which focuses on the speaker having problems through either noncompliance or helplessness). Managing such an interview poses special difficulties. In all cases, the interviewer should avoid (a) using closed questions (using instead open-ended, positively framed questions), (b) helping the speaker through gratuitous interpretations, and (c) taking sides in described family disputes. In addition, the coder should carefully consider those bits of speech that contain anything more than minimal responses. These cases, where the strategy is failing, are denoted as C5–6+: The relationship with the interviewer and the distorted integration provide the best evidence of the pattern. Careful review of many such transcripts suggests that C5–6+ speakers are not clear about what happened in the past, how they felt about it (i.e., they usually report generalized arousal, rather than specific and motivating feeling states), how others contributed to it, or how they contributed (and still contribute) to it. C5–6+ speakers have become so focused on winning the interpersonal battle that the struggle itself becomes the goal. Under these conditions, the self may be sacrificed to make the point.

In the C5–6+ form, the strategy has lost its flexibility and is becoming rigidly nonstrategic. This bodes very poorly for adaptation and (alone or in combination with other strategies) is often associated with severe psychiatric diagnoses (e.g., some personality disorders, Rindal, 2000), restrictive eating disorders (Ringer & Crittenden, 2007), some postnatal depression, and so forth. Most notable, these disorders are as resistant to psychotherapy as the speakers are regarding engaging productively in the AAI.

C7 (MENACING)

Overview

This strategy is based on theory (Crittenden, 1995), clinical case histories, and observations from AAIs and is paired with an even-numbered strategy, usually C8, to create an alternating all-powerful/utterly vulnerable strategy. C7–8 speakers deny information about the role of the self in causing negative outcomes (denied cognitive information) and are motivated by unfocused anger and fear (distorted negative affect combined with the omission of desire for comfort). When faced with the discrepancies created by denial, they can respond by producing delusional "integrations" of made-up cognitive information and extremely distorted affective information. This has two kinds of effects. The first is that C7 speakers experience very high anxiety and that motivates action. The second is that they have limited awareness of the probable consequences of their actions and even less awareness of their responsibility for the outcomes of their actions. If they were aware of consequences and their responsibility, they might be less disposed to act, but, being unaware, they often engage in dangerous actions.

Individuals using a C7–8 strategy perceive threat to be pervasive and no longer imagine that help or comfort is possible. Therefore, the oscillation is solely around anger and fear. Moreover, the extreme splits in self that typified the C3–4 and C5–6 strategies are reduced, such that C7 and C8 become more similar strategies with respect to the emphasis on anger and fear as the crucial organizing affects. At the same time, however, the differentiation between self and others is increased. C7, as compared to C8, is more organized around anger/hate than fear/dread.

As to the focus of the anger and fear, individuals using a C7–8 strategy have a wider scope than those using a C5–6 strategy. C5–6 is characterized by a distinction between "me and my gang" and "you and your gang." At C7–8 it becomes "with me or against me" (i.e., the middle ground of neutral people disappears). In extreme C7–8, "me and my gang" delusionally becomes "me against the world." Everyone becomes a potential enemy and, therefore, a potential target. Thus, for C7–8 the source and focus of danger become very wide and very nonspecific. The basis for such radical and delusional differentiation between the self and the world is the denial of all cognitive information about the self as participant or initiator of causal sequences, resulting in danger and denial of vulnerability of the self. This leaves the world as aggressor and the self as rightfully protecting against the world.

C7 individuals believe that others intend to harm them and will deceive them regarding this intention. Because C7 individuals fear a preemptive and deceptive attack, they, themselves, plot such attacks. Thus, although they deny feeling fearful, both anger and fear motivate their covertly aggressive behaviors. The focused punitive revenge that motivated C5 functioning becomes, in the C7 strategy, a much more generalized retribution, with a looser causal connection and distinct irrational, even delusional, qualities. Given C7–8 speakers' probable past experiences with treacherous attachment figures, they interpret their own actions as self-protective, rather than as gratuitous attacks. Such thinking depends upon fusing time, people, and places (such that past treachery motivates current retribution toward all people in all places) in a self-protective, rationalizing process. Further, in order not to elicit attack, C7 individuals intentionally inhibit evidence of their anger. Thus, C7 individuals are preoccupied with anger and fear and are dismissing of their feelings of desire for comfort.

In addition, menacing adults, usually based on actual childhood experiences, perceive others as being impervious to their pleas and perspectives. Consequently, they perceive others as lacking both true feelings and compassionate intentions. This perception enables menacing individuals to behave sadistically. That is, they deny both the veracity of evidence that others have tender feelings and also causal information about their responsibility in inflicting pain and harm. Instead, suspecting treachery and deception and denying all culpability of the self, they can feel contempt for others' (presumed) manipulative use of weakness. This helps to explain both their failure to feel empathy and their ghoulish delight in being able to *contingently* cause their victims to express pain.

Discourse Markers and Their Psychological Function

1. Procedurally, the discourse of C7 speakers is highly dismissing of others' feelings and perspectives.

   Displayed affect is *cold*, controlled, and distant or anxiously arousing, specifically, fiendishly playful (*sadistically cruel*) while images sometimes betray the hostile feelings that motivate behavior (see imaged memory below). This positive affect in the context of others' suffering is discordant and unsettling for the listener. Unlike "affectless" depressed speakers, C7–8 speakers are vigilantly, sometimes even playfully, alert. Seductive displays are still possible when the speaker feels in control, particularly in socially nonthreatening moments.

   Interviewers often feel "toyed with." C7 speakers play an involving and suspicious cat-and-mouse game with interviewers who are neither trusted nor avoided, but warily monitored for their intentions. This, together with the sadistic affect, creates an *intimidating/ spooky* relationship with the interviewer, in which the listener participates in the speaker's discomfort.

2. There are unsettling images in the discourse of C7 speakers. Some

are explosively *animated* (such that they startle or frighten the interviewer) whereas others have a *generalized* or *delusionally threatening* quality. Irrelevant sensory aspects of a context associated in the past with danger are taken erroneously as evidence that similar sensory conditions, in the present, also represent danger. These tend to evoke fear in both the speaker and the listener and can be juxtaposed with images of delusional power of the self. Often these images include places and people that should give comfort or that appear comforting. The images function to keep the speaker focused on the danger of letting down one's guard, especially when things appear safe and comfortable. Comfort, in other words, is treated as being more dangerous than obvious danger. The images are part of an intense associative process that connects experiences on the basis of feelings even when there is no logical or causal connection.

3. Semantically, accurate cognitive information is missing. Instead, the causal contribution of others is distrusted (presuming their use of deceptive false cognition), and information about the causal contribution of the self is *denied.* These distortions lead to confusion regarding temporal sequences and regarding the role of individuals in those sequences, up to delusional explanations. The outcome is that C7 speakers often connect unrelated events in ways that preclude temporal closure, and they often see people as fulfilling similar roles, leading to a lack of person-specificity. Because each aggressive act of the self leads to a response from others (often a coordinated response from victims and law enforcement), C7 speakers often misconstrue this as an unjustified conspiracy. This twisting of semantic attributions often results in conclusions that are the opposite of what others conclude. Nevertheless, these conclusions dispose the self to revenge, sometimes in the form of long-delayed or displaced retribution. These transformations function to keep the C7 individual perpetually vigilant with regard to (apparently) potentially imminent danger.

4. Connotative language contains viciously inappropriate words and active verbs for inanimate objects (whereby such things appear to be part of life's conspiracy to harm the speaker).

5. Because recalled episodes often involve treachery, critical causal events that implicate the speaker are omitted. Only *fragmented* images of violence remain. Further, the temporal sequence of the episodes suggests that the speaker was an innocent victim even though

information elsewhere indicates that the speaker may well have been the aggressor. Thus, the episodes are distorted in the direction of *false innocence*, even reaching *delusional revenge*. In addition, episodes of mysteriously dangerous (and unsatisfactorily explained) events frequently come to mind.

6. In the long delay between perceived threat and vengeful response, individuals using a C7 strategy often engage in considerable reflection. When the thinking only intensifies the misattributions and discards discrepant information (thus creating no opening for reconsideration), the reflective process is considered *rumination*. Denial of cognitive information about the self reduces the possibility of accurately evaluating one's own behavior. To maintain their denial of self-responsibility, C7 individuals actively seek evidence for the need for self-protection, or sometimes they construct it delusionally if it is not found. Based on the erroneous conclusion that they are threatened, C7 speakers plan their revenge, *skillfully misleading* listeners to false conclusions that vindicate the speakers and minimize their dangerousness. When this is successful, external confirmation of the C7 speaker's *rationalization* reinforces the speaker's feeling of innocent victimization and prevents alternative perspectives from initiating reflection.

    Because unpredictable aggression is extremely dangerous and usually separated temporally from the events that instigated it, it is not only ineffective at eliciting protective and loving behavior from attachment figures, but it also threatens individuals and relationships. The discourse of C7 adults serves the function of hiding the speakers' intentions while trying to elicit evidence of the true intentions of others.

RISK OF PSYCHOPATHOLOGY

The strategy of C7 speakers is highly distorted in ways that increase the probability of identifying danger, especially deceptive danger. Thus, it is an adaptive strategy for contexts that contain deceptive danger (e.g., Nazi Europe, Stalinist Russia, Cambodia, or the former Yugoslavia). Under safer and more transparent conditions, the menacing strategy is both dangerous to others (through the overidentification of threat) and to the self as well (as a result of others' need to be protected from such people). Delusional ideation is frequent. In addition, because the strategy is based on fear and anger, all symptoms of intense anxiety are associated with this strategy. In safe societies, most individuals classified as C7 are in prisons and mental hospitals: in societies marked by pervasive and deceptive dangers, people using a C7 strategies may sometimes hold powerful positions.

DIFFERENTIATING C7 FROM OTHER STRATEGIES

The C7 strategy is most easily differentiated from the C5 strategy by the presence of misleading statements that covertly carry the implication of very dangerous activities, by the juxtaposition of safety/comfort and danger, and by a denial of desire for comfort.

Experience/History

Menacing adults often have histories of pervasive childhood danger, usually life-threatening, carried out by attachment figures. Furthermore, the danger was unpredictable and often occurred in the context of apparent safety, when the attachment figures did not appear to intend harm. Moreover, as children, menacing adults were unable to reduce or effectively modify their parents' violent behavior. The critical events, therefore, are (a) danger from attachment figures, (b) unpredictability of danger, (c) deceptive intentions of dangerous people, and (d) implacability of the danger, even in the face of the child's agony. School-aged and adolescent peers usually identify these children as "creepy."

C8 (PARANOID)

Overview

This strategy is paired with an odd-numbered strategy (in most cases, C7). The description of this strategy, however, has been drawn from fewer examples than other strategies and is, therefore, both sketchy and more in need of revision and elaboration.

The C8 strategy involves the denial of all cognitive information about the active role of the self in danger-related sequences. This prevents awareness of what the self could do to prevent harm. As a consequence, doubt and apprehension about danger become generalized dread, with expectation of overwhelming danger and great uncertainty regarding its source. Once the responsibility of the self is denied, "dread" becomes the alternate side of the cognitive-affective emotion of "hate"; in C8, the fearful aspect is dominant. Thus, the C8 strategy is one of overzealous preparation against being attacked. Anxiety is at extremely high levels on a constant basis, but, because evidence of the anxiety could tip off attackers, paranoid speakers inhibit, as much as possible, the overt display of anxiety. For similar reasons, they inhibit evidence of underlying anger and intent (past or present) to attack others. Desire for comfort is denied and evidence of anger is inhibited almost completely. When they feel safe, most C8 individuals display menacing behavior.

Discourse Markers and Their Psychological Function

1. Procedurally, C8 discourse shows evidence of both hesitations and monitoring of others and also dysfluencies indicative of anxiety and alert calculation that are associated with the Type C pattern.

    Any affect shown is likely to be scornful or mocking of others and others' distress.

    C8 speakers want both to engage the interviewer in rescuing them and also to avoid the (potentially treacherous) interviewer; this generates the sense that C8 speakers are "spooked" by the interview itself. This functions to keep the speaker from trusting others as well as from being protected by them.

2. The images of paranoid speakers sometimes include *delusionally threatening* and *generalized* images, in which present reality becomes associated in inexplicit ways with fearful experiences in the past and expectations of the future. The images are drawn from both true experiences and erroneously associated contexts (especially those in which evidence of comfort has been misleading). In other words, something true adheres delusionally to other things that may bear some sensory relation, but not a meaningful one. In this sense of active expansion and generalization, the images almost take on lives of their own, expanding outside of the conscious control of the mind of the speaker. These images are highly motivating but not clearly explained to the listener; they function to warn and arouse the speaker, but in an overestimation of the probability of danger. That is, they are overinclusive and, therefore, decrease the probability that real danger will be overlooked while concurrently increasing the probability that safety will be mistakenly identified as danger. The function is to maintain vigilance in all conditions, but this precludes feeling comfortable at any time.

3. Semantically, the *denial of self-related cognition* helps C8 speakers to

focus on their fear of the use of false cognition by others (in the form of unexpected and dangerous attack that may appear as comfort or rescue). Their construction of causality is completely focused on the others as initiators of causal sequences regarding danger. This confuses the roles of aggressor and victim by obscuring any active responsibility of the self, while clarifying the priority of protecting the self. All activity of the self is then framed as rightfully protective even when this appears irrational or hostile.

4. The language of C8 speakers is hesitant and wary with sudden and surprisingly ominous fear-eliciting qualities. This leaves both the speaker and the listener sharing a state of vigilance and distrust in the possibility of comfort.

5. Episodes are almost entirely lacking and replaced by perseveration on distorted images. When episodes are recalled, denial of the role of the causal self leaves important omissions in the temporal and causal linkages between events. This prevents the self from acknowledging contributions to events.

6. Integration is in the form of *skillful misleading*; this causes others to derive false conclusions, which, when acted upon, convince the speaker that he or she was right all along (i.e., the listener's false conclusion confirms the speaker's deception for the speaker). By this point, deception has become reciprocal and involving.

RISK OF PSYCHOPATHOLOGY

The strategy of C8 speakers is highly distorted in ways that increase the probability of identifying danger, especially deceptive danger. Thus, it is an adaptive strategy for contexts that contain deceptive danger and can, in fact, be highly persuasive when others feel frightened and disempowered. Under safer and less deceptive conditions, the paranoid strategy is dangerous both to others (if paranoid individuals should mistakenly feel the need to protect themselves) and also to paranoid persons. In safe societies, many individuals classified as C8 are in prisons and mental hospitals, whereas, in pervasively dangerous societies, paranoid individuals may function as leaders.

DIFFERENTIATING C8 FROM OTHER STRATEGIES

The C8 strategy is most easily differentiated from the C6 strategy by the absence of social facility (charm, seductiveness), by the procedural uneasiness of the speaker, and by the pervasiveness of fearfulness, including discomfort with the interviewer. It is not easily differentiated from the C7 strategy and, indeed, often occurs in the paired form of C7–C8.

Experience/History

C8 speakers generally have been repeatedly and deceptively victimized by attachment figures when they were young and vulnerable. Although they emphasize their fearfulness and innocence to others, C8 speakers are very dangerous. This strategy is an extreme and very dangerous form of passive-aggressive behavior.

Chapter 10

Combination Patterns

A/C and AC

In this chapter we describe the integrated and unintegrated combinations of Type A and Type C. A/C strategies are of interest because they reflect processes found also in Bs. That is, exposure to danger enables one to construct ever more sophisticated and condition-specific self-protective strategies. Such strategies bring forward from the past what is relevant to the present and discard (leave in the past) that which is relevant only to the past. Thus, the most adaptive person has access to all the behavioral strategies without distorting their mental processing of information. Earned/mature/wise (nonnaive) B3s can act in any manner (strategically), but they know what they do, why they do it, and, crucially, they can stop doing it. That is, they can deceive others, but they do not deceive themselves and they cease to deceive when it is no longer needed for self-protection. This is what differentiates earned (or mature) B3s from a gradient of A/Cs that culminate in psychopathy. Like B3s, psychopaths use all of the behavioral strategies, but they do so on the basis of distorted, falsified, denied, and delusional information. They use deception, particularly involving and reciprocal deception. Often they look most like B3s when they are in the context of explicit and clear threat for which they have effective strategies and least like Bs when confronted with safety and comfort, which, in their experience, could actually hide the presence of danger.

TYPES A/C AND AC

These Dynamic-Maturational Model (DMM) classifications are based on observations of infants and preschool-aged children (Crittenden, 1985a), theory (Crittenden, 1995), and clinical observations from AAIs. An important distinction can be made between A and C combinations that use only the Ainsworth-based classifications (i.e., A1–2 and C1–2, Ainsworth, 1973) and compulsive-and-obsessive combinations that contain strategies from the DMM classificatory system (i.e., A+ and C+; this notation refers to all A3–8 and C3–8 classifications). The latter tend to be associated with greater psychopathology and with histories of both greater danger and less comfort and also greater deception with regard to danger.

It should be stated clearly that (a) A/C and AC are classifiable, organized strategies, (b) any A and C patterns can be combined (e.g., A1/C1, A3/C4, A7/C5), and (c) only the A7–8C7–8 combination is truly psychopathic.

Overview

Some adults use both Type A and Type C strategies to defend themselves from perceived danger. The combination may be either alternating (A/C) or blended (AC). The strategies may use any combination from both the low- and high-numbered patterns (e.g., A2/C1, A3/C2, A4/C6). Moreover, the alternation may reflect the use of specific strategies for different attachment figures (e.g., $A3_M$ /$C3_F$) or it may indicate the use of specific strategies for different situations, for example, C1–2 for mild threats and A3–4 for serious threats.

The blended combination is more integrated and constitutes a gradient from the integration of true affect and true cognition (B3) to the integration of true affect or cognition with some omitted information (A1–2C1–2) to the integration of distorted information together with some omitted information (A3–4C3–4) to the inclusion of falsified and sometimes denied information (A3–6C3–6) to falsified, denied, and sometimes delusional information (A7–8C7–8). The culmination of this gradient is a psychopathic integration (see below) which, like an earned

B3, includes all possibilities, but emphasizes, in contrast to B3, false, denied, and delusional affect and cognition.

All the discourse markers and related psychological processes described above for the Type A and C strategies may be combined, in any manner, for the A/C and AC strategies. Described in terms of memory systems, procedurally, A-and-C speakers use both cut-offs and also involvement of the interviewer to (a) prevent exploration of threatening topics and (b) focus on and enlist the interviewer's support around these topics. In terms of images, they both avoid affectively rousing descriptions and, when it is not possible to fail to recall, they also use sensory images of desired comfort or vivid images of the things that they fear or that elicit anger. Both processes activate physiological arousal. Semantically, A/C and AC speakers idealize (and sometimes exonerate) whenever possible, but when they cannot, they use passive or blaming reductionist thought, oscillation of thought, or false cognition to avoid coming to obvious self-relevant negative conclusions. Connotatively, the discourse can swing between denotative and evocative extremes, or it can appear generally dry with occasional outstandingly arousing constructions or phrasings. Episodically, A/C and AC speakers use lack of recall or parental perspective wherever possible, but when this fails, they use blurred, fragmented, or distorted episodes as well as delusional pseudoepisodes.

By combining the two self-protective strategies, A/C and AC speakers both double the range of possible defenses and also gain access, at different times, to all of the information. The information is not, however, integrated. Thus, A/C and AC speakers answer the integrative questions in the AAI in superficially complex, but ultimately unsatisfying, ways. Nevertheless, these distortions, when discovered by the speaker, can also be the impetus to integration (Crittenden, 1997a). Identifying the lack of true integration may require the reader to consider carefully the underlying premises of the speaker's story and their veracity. That is, the "anti-integration" of psychopathic ACs is very coherent and presents few, if any, directly false statements. It is the overall representation of self, others, and the relationship of self to others, particularly as represented by listeners (and coders), that is false.

A/C AND PSYCHIATRIC DIAGNOSES

A number of psychopathological conditions are associated with the combined A and C strategies. It should be noted, however, that psychiatric diagnoses often cluster a wide range of symptoms and, from an information processing or functional perspective, may reflect a clustering of several disorders. Thus a one-to-one relation of psychiatric diagnosis to attachment classification is not to be expected.

Bipolar depression is an obvious example of a possible relation, with many individuals with diagnoses of bipolar disorder displaying a range of A3–6/C3–6 combinations. Borderline personality disorder is also often associated with a heavily modified A/C organization (see Crittenden & Newman, 2010).

PSYCHOPATHY

Psychopathic AC speakers (A7–8C7–8) deny their own negative affect (including physical pain) and their own contributions to eliciting danger. The remaining information is so strongly biased toward the perspectives and motivations of others, that its integration creates a strategy in which the observer's perspective is very well understood, but their intention to act is grossly misunderstood or even constructed delusionally.

Consequently, the speaker is able to construct an appearance that so closely matches the observer's expectations/desires (cognitively in values and affectively in feelings) that the observer is ultimately manipulated into participating in his or her own deception. In most cases, lying is avoided (because that kind of deception is easily uncovered).

To the contrary, in order to establish credibility, psychopaths quickly and openly reveal negative information that is likely to be known already by the listener. The presentation of psychopathic AC speakers is very like that of balanced speakers, that is, smooth, fluent, and engaging. Psychopathic AC speakers appear cooperative and have relatively few dysfluencies. However, while both B3 and psychopathic AC speakers seem very conscious and monitor what they say for coherence, psychopathic ACs are highly vigilant and nonspontaneous. Indeed, their speech often has a rehearsed quality to it and functions, in all memory systems, to organize information so as to deny all self-generated dangerous information (both affective and cognitive) and focus on the others, whose perspectives are at the same time both used and distrusted.

The perpetually anxious AC speaker longs for comfort and seeks closeness with appealing and apparently safe people. But the speaker so grossly overestimates the probability of threat, particularly presumed threat hidden behind benign appearances, that attack and escape are perceived as the only safe options. Thus, the central functions of identifying and approaching safety and identifying and avoiding danger are inextricably confounded. This confusion focuses all transformations of affect and cognition on the goal of denying all negative information about the self while maintaining a wary attention to possible negative information about others (sometimes including delusional information).

The organization of nonverbal affect and the relationship with the interviewer are particularly important to identifying these individuals. Slips in which inappropriate affect occurs (e.g., fear during discussions of comfort, or pleasure during discussions of distress, especially others' distress) should be noted carefully and included parenthetically, by the transcriber, in the transcript itself. Similarly, psychopathic speakers easily create a collaborative appearance; the cues to falseness can sometimes be found in their too-ready willingness to reveal intimate information, their too-ingratiating demeanor, or an out-of-focus, anxious, "creepy" quality to their interactions. For interviewers (and coders), this sometimes creates an almost imperceptible discomfort that, if made conscious, leads to an inability to decide how to perceive the speaker.

To discern this, all bids to interviewers for confirmation, authority, or comfort should be carefully considered. In order to identify deception, it is important that the interviewer ask unexpected questions that surprise the mind; only when forced into spontaneous responses will the speaker be unable to use prepared, "pat" answers. Another indicator of the possibility of a psychopathic organization is a psychologically perplexing history, particularly one that includes past deceptive danger in which the speaker's "recovery" or reorganization is insufficiently explained.

Themes of sexuality are almost always intruded into high-numbered AC interviews. Finally, themes of aggression in not fully connected episodes (i.e., episodes in which there are temporal or causal omissions or errors) can suggest the presence of a high-numbered AC organization. Thus, there may be small slips in which a history of unethical behavior can be glimpsed. Such AC speakers also tend to juxtapose incompatible information, particularly about danger and safety/comfort. Thus, in their self-presentation in the AAI transcript, there is an asynchrony between the apparent cognitive and affective integration of psychopathic speakers (together with their interpersonal skills, including empathic awareness of others' perspectives, i.e., high theory of mind) and their negative histories (or the absence of sufficiently supportive histories to explain the positive aspects of the discourse).

Experience/History

A/C and AC speakers have a variety of histories that reflect both predictable, self-rejecting dangers and unpredictable dangers that cannot easily be attributed to a specific cause or agent. Sometimes A/C speakers use a specific strategy for a specific parent; in such cases, the parents differed in the nature of the danger that each presented to the child. In other cases, the strategies are combined with respect to the same parent; in these cases, a parent's behavior was variable, that is, sometimes the parent behaved like the parent of a Type A child and sometimes like the parent of a Type C child. In these latter cases, both A/C and AC combinations are possible. Alternatively, it may be the type of circumstance that determines the selection of an A or C strategy. For example, the speaker may speak with preoccupied discourse about nonthreatening topics, but then switch to dismissing discourse when discussing severe threats. Finally, changes from A to C or the reverse often accompany developmental change and the outcome can be an A/C strategy (e.g., $A3_{childhood} \rightarrow C3_{adolescence} \rightarrow A3/C5\text{--}6_{adulthood}$). It should be clearly noted, however, that the AAI cannot establish this developmental trajectory.

Psychopathic ACs have experienced danger, usually at the hands of attachment figures, that was recurrent and cognitively and affectively deceptive. The danger usually began early in life and continued throughout childhood. Further, there were no consistently safe people or places; those protective persons who were available at some point failed to protect the child. Nevertheless, the child learned that there were strategies that could be protective at least some of the time and these strategies included both Type A and Type C organizations and, when they became possible as a function of maturation, the compulsive and obsessively coercive strategies. With development, future AC children became better able to protect themselves, but the cost was isolation from enduring, intimate, and comforting relationships. Instead, the psychopathic AC organized himself or herself as a mirror of others' expectations while concurrently doubting everyone and everything, restlessly seeking closeness, preparing to defend against treachery, and seeking retribution from treacherous people who withheld needed and "deserved" love and protection. Thus, for the psychopathic AC, the most desired person would be a balanced Type B. However, a balanced Type B could be the most feared and (in a blurring of the boundaries of time, place, and person) the most hated for the past treachery of other desired attachment figures. To the extent that a balanced individual in the company of a psychopath was not aware of the transformations of information that could be used to falsify appearances, the naive B would become the natural prey of the psychopath.

A/C combinations are also common in the process of psychotherapy. As Type A speakers become aware of inhibited affect, they often become preoccupied with their own feelings; this can lead to A/C combinations. Similarly, as Type C speakers become aware of the negative semantic conclusions that can be drawn from their experiences, they may display both types of strategy. The course of therapy should, however, reduce the oscillation between strategies as integration becomes more frequent and extensive.

INSECURE OTHER (IO)

The final types of transcripts that may be identified are those with important dysfluencies of speech or distortions of thought that are not described by this method. That is, important elements of the discourse are outside of the method as described here (i.e., they do not fit B, A, A+, C, or C+ patterns or their modifications or combinations). Transcripts with truly unrecognized elements and patterns should be classified as IO, with a "forced" best guess as to the best-fitting DMM classification and a written description of the incongruent elements. These transcripts should be set aside for periodic reconsideration. As other transcripts that are similar are identified, it may be possible to identify their organization.

Further, just as this manual represents an expansion of the array of organizations described by Main and Goldwyn (1984, 1994), it is presumed that other organizations remain to be identified. The literature in future years should be consulted for these.

Chapter 11

Conditions That Reflect the Disruption of Interpersonal Self-Protective Strategies

Unresolved Trauma (Utr) or Loss (Ul)

THIS CHAPTER IS ABOUT SOME CONDITIONS THAT INTERFERE WITH THE successful functioning of a self-protective strategy. These conditions are related to specific dangerous events in the history of an individual and can, on occasion, temporarily interrupt the ability of the individual to protect the self, promote safe reproduction, or protect one's progeny.

These conditions reflect *traumatic* psychological responses to specific past dangerous events (loss of attachment figures and other threats to the self or to attachment figures). These responses involve maladaptive processing of information. Either too much irrelevant information is retained (and used to organize behavior), or too much relevant information is discarded, or other errors of thought are made regarding the dangerous event. Events treated in one (or more) of these ways are considered *unresolved*. These errors can interfere with the general strategic functioning. By analogy, the effect is similar to that of a land mine. One walks safely, strategically, over the ground most of the time until something triggers preconscious recall. Information in procedural or imaged memory is usually the underground, preconscious trigger. When evoked preconsciously, recall of unresolved events changes the individual's dispositional representation (DR), causing behavior to become maladaptive under a narrow set of conditions. The impact of these instances on the self-protective strategy used by the individual can vary in extent. Some traumatic responses have very circumscribed and limited effects on strategic functioning. Others, especially if due to the interaction of multiple transformations of information regarding several dangerous events, have more widespread effects.

Lack of resolution of exposure to danger and loss is often an indicator of increased risk for psychopathology (i.e., thought and behavior that is not well adapted to the current situation). That is, each of the strategic patterns and combinations of patterns is adaptive in some context and, therefore, not inherently indicative of psychopathology. Lack of resolution, however, specifically implies that the self-threatening event has not been integrated with respect to current functioning. The lack of integration has implications for current and future functioning that create risk.

OVERVIEW

RESOLUTION

To understand lack of resolution one must first define resolution of loss or exposure to danger. The function of mental processing of information is to glean useful information about dangerous events while discarding irrelevant information. Because surviving danger is crucial to life, psychological adaptation is first and foremost about using the past to prepare for future danger.

Humans have only two sources of information about danger and how to stay safe: that which is genetically transmitted and, therefore, innate to our central nervous systems and that which is learned, from our own experiences or vicariously from others' experiences. This discussion of trauma and loss focuses on the interaction of innate potentials with unique experiences to generate information about how to stay safe and how to protect people who are attached to oneself (e.g., children, spouses, parents).

Danger focuses perception and attention on the threatening situation; this increases the probability that we will identify the signals that will predict future danger and the self-protective responses that can be taken. Such a preoccupying focus is adaptive for as long as both (a) the signals and protective responses are unknown and also (b) there remains a possibility of similar danger in the future.

Danger is also psychologically disruptive, such that one wants to forget about it and move on to happier, more productive topics. This dismissing process is adaptive when the danger is unlikely to recur and when the signals of impending danger are easily recognized and lead to protective responses.

Psychological resolution of threatening or dangerous experiences is defined as either identification of the signals of danger and learning of self-protective responses or determination that there is very little probability of a recurrence of the event, together with the integration of this information into current functioning. Resolution involves retaining predictive information and setting in the past nonpredictive information. It permits the transfer of attention and mental processes away from the threat and onto other aspects of life while maintaining the advantage of what was learned from the endangering experience. Individuals can be considered resolved if they

- Have extracted predictive and protective information from past dangerous experiences;
- Can apply this information to future experience to differentiate probable dangerous situations from probable safe ones with reasonable accuracy;
- Have developed preventive strategies for use in the event of signals of possible danger;
- Associate information about the past danger that is *not* relevant to future safety only with the past (i.e., they dismiss it from future self-protective functioning);
- Have developed strategies for protecting the self in the event of unpreventable danger;
- Have accepted and accommodated to changes in the self and others that occurred because of the past danger;
- Have transformed the intense negative feelings associated with the experience to more complex and variegated emotional states, specifically states that include cognitive information, such as sadness, regret, acceptance, and increased contentment with what remains;
- Have accepted the ambiguity and uncertainty inherent in life and, nevertheless, found ways to attend to other aspects of life in addition to preparing for danger; and
- Find some redeeming or satisfying outcomes that have resulted from the event.

LACK OF RESOLUTION

Having reliable information about very dangerous situations is crucial to mental functioning and physical safety. Until one understands past threats sufficiently to be able to protect oneself in the future, there is a strong tendency to maintain self-protective responses to the event. In the best of circumstances, the threatening information causes mental alertness, which results in integrative mental activity and the construction of new and more sophisticated mental and behavioral responses and, when necessary, revision of DRs of self and others. In this case, the threatening information tends to be available for conscious recall.

In less satisfactory situations, threatening information pervades mental processes but without eliciting the integrative mental activity that would enable construction of more effective strategies for protecting the self in the future. Instead, information is split, distorted, or manipulated to keep some truth, which is deemed even more dangerous, out of awareness. Specifically, unresolved speakers using a dismissing psychological process (with regard specifically to the past danger) refuse to acknowledge the ongoing risk of life; their lack of resolution involves a continuing effort to exclude this information from awareness and from strategic behavior. In contrast, unresolved speakers who are preoccupied with a past trauma or loss refuse to acknowledge the irreversibility of the event and the possibility, in the future, of safety and comfort; their lack of resolution involves a continuing effort to exclude that information from awareness and from strategic behavior. It should be noted that, for a speaker who had dismissed a self-endangering event, "not remembering" is an active process that is present and pervasive in mental functioning, even though it is not accessible to conscious review, to integration, or, therefore, to resolution. In other words, *unresolved-dismissed* [U(ds)] and *unresolved-preoccupied* [U(p)] are actually two hierarchically and functionally parallel constructs that function in opposite ways, that is, the process is different, but the outcome of lack of resolution is the same.

The central question regarding lack of resolution is *does the danger (or dangerous loss) affect mental functioning in general, either through what is omitted from psychological processing that is needed or what is retained that is not needed for identification, prevention, or protection from future danger?* Put another way: The function of "resolution" is to (a) take forward into the future information that can help to predict, prevent, or protect from danger (including danger of death) and (b) leave in the past that which is related only to the past and not relevant to the future. If too much is taken forward, it is preoccupying lack of resolution; if too much is left in the past, it is dismissed lack of resolution. Resolution is the right differentiation of this information.

Lack of resolution has a number of important implications for daily functioning. Lack of integrative activity precludes being able to connect the various aspects of others' personality into a single whole or, more important, the various aspects of self across relationships, time, and contexts into a whole. Without such integrations, relatively inaccurate predictions of self and others, particularly in interaction with external conditions, will be made. Under conditions of safety, this will adversely affect comfort and, thus, the ability to maintain intimate attachment and reproductive relationships. In extreme cases, where threat is greatly overpredicted, the individual's self-protective activity may even create or elicit danger. Under conditions of threat, lack of resolution may affect safety either by generating too much anxiety for effective thought and action or by failing to direct sufficient attention and arousal to the threat.

The George et al. AAI (1985, 1996) is more effective at identifying evidence of preoccupying lack of resolution than evidence of resolution or dismissed lack of resolution. For this and other reasons, a modification of the George et al. interview is recommended for use with the DMM method (Crittenden, 2007). Whichever form of the interview is used, the coder must decide whether the speaker is resolved. There are several forms of lack of resolution, all of which imply an inability to differentiate unique aspects of the past danger from aspects that are relevant to the future. In order from the most dismissing to the most preoccupying, these forms of lack of resolution are:

Dismissed forms
a. dismissed trauma or loss, Utr/l(ds);
b. displaced trauma or loss, Utr/l(dpl);
c. blocked trauma, Utr(b);
d. denied trauma or loss, Utr/l (dn);
Preoccupying forms
d. preoccupying trauma or loss, Utr/l (p);
e. vicarious trauma or loss, Utr/l(v);
f. imagined trauma or loss, Utr/l(i);
g. suggested trauma, Utr(s);

h.   hinted trauma or loss, Utr/l(h);
i.   anticipated trauma or loss, Utr/l(a);
Other forms
j.   delusional repair, Utr/l(dlr)
k.   delusional revenge, Utr/l (dlv)
l.   disorganized trauma or loss, Utr/l(dx);
m.   depressed trauma or loss, Utr/l(dp).

Dismissed trauma or loss is most common among speakers with a basic Type A strategy. In this case, the speaker dismisses the importance of the event to the self both in terms of preparing for future danger and in terms of feelings. As a consequence, feelings such as sadness or even pleasure and satisfaction become impossible. Such speakers appear dry and unresponsive.

Displaced trauma or loss is a form of dismissing in which information about the actual eliciting event is both omitted from processing and also transferred to some other, presumably less threatening, event or person. Thus, one's own abuse by a parent may be dismissed whereas one's sibling's sufferings may occupy an inordinate amount of attention. The strategy, in other words, involves both dismissing and preoccupying components, but these are split with regard to referent.

Blocked trauma or loss refers to the presentation by the speaker of otherwise inexplicable details that, taken together, strongly suggest a traumatic experience that the speaker does not acknowledge. That is, no trauma or loss is claimed by the speaker (and none is hinted), but the observer both finds evidence for such an event in the speaker's style of discourse and the facts of history, and also finds that, by including this hypothesized event, the speaker's history and pattern of discourse become psychologically sound. Previously, other theories have assumed that memories of such events were repressed (i.e., present in the mind, but not recalled). Current understandings from the cognitive neurosciences suggest that lack of elaborative recall may result in the absence of facilitated neurological pathways. That is, some possible memories may never have been consolidated through elaborative processes and, in that case, would be neurologically absent (Schacter, 1996).

Four conditions are necessary to code blocked trauma in an AAI:

1.   There must be opportunity in the events related by the speaker for the potentially blocked event to have occurred.

2. The event must seem probable, given both what the speaker has said and how (in the discourse) it was stated.
3. There must be several "oblique" markers that, linked across disparate parts of the transcript, point to the potentially blocked event. These markers are often images or evocative language. When a sexual act is the potentially blocked event, double entendres may convey the meaning but such terms are not by themselves sufficient to code blocked child sexual abuse.
4. The event must be necessary to make the speaker's story and self-protective strategy psychologically coherent.

Denied trauma or loss occurs when very serious and inescapable threats to the speaker's physical or psychological integrity appear to overwhelm the speaker (e.g., being frequently and inappropriately included in discussion of other topics, arousing the speaker intensely, even in [ina] or [ess] forms; see Appendix and Chapter 12). Nevertheless, when queried directly, the speaker denies either the event or its ongoing negative effects. This complex form of response involves errors of association. Implicitly, there is an overassociative process, with procedures and images reflecting a functional preoccupation with the threat. Explicitly, however, the threat is disassociated from the self, being verbally described as irrelevant to the self. Utr/l (dn) is differentiated from the simpler dismissed form because the denial is only semantic, with an abundance of information about the threat being processed implicitly; both DRs hold the potential to affect the speaker's behavior, but in incompatible and often maladaptive ways. Utr/l(ds), on the other hand, involves a consistent functional dismissal, with the dangerous event being rarely discussed at all; its omission from the DRs that regulate behavior is the basis for risk. The discrepancy between activated and inactivated processes in Utr/l(dn) is sometimes "resolved" with a delusion.

Preoccupying trauma or loss involves the taking over of mental processing by the self-threatening event. This can be limited to the event itself or the event can be associated with such a wide range of stimuli that it pervades all functioning.

Vicarious trauma or loss is a form of response in which the speaker neither experienced nor witnessed the endangering event. Instead, this event occurred to an attachment figure and directly affects their behavior and mental construction of reality. When describing this event, the vicariously unresolved speaker uses dysfluencies typical of lack of resolution without being able to associate these explicitly with the attachment figure's experience and, often, without essential information about the event.

Imagined trauma or loss occurs when the speaker provides credible evidence that the event occurred but makes an attribution of psychological trauma that is unwarranted (i.e., the speaker makes an erroneous causal attribution).

Suggested trauma is coded when the *interviewer* imagines a trauma and inadvertently feeds the speaker ideas and words that the speaker accepts as real. This is particularly problematic in that "false memory syndrome" must be differentiated from active deception in which the speaker knows the truth but, for a variety of reasons, feels the need to make false assertions of past victimization. This distortion reflects "borrowed" information that the speaker attributes to the self when the source is actually the therapist (or another authority figure).

Hinted trauma or loss is assigned when the speaker's cunning placement of details, usually accompanied by submissive ingenuousness, leads the observer to conclude that others have greatly harmed the speaker (or the speaker's attachment figures). Put another way, the speaker plants the idea in the interviewer's mind while implicitly denying that it happened. In all cases, the speakers themselves display deception (false cognition) within the interview and with regard to other topics. Moreover, the presumed perpetrator is always someone who harmed the speaker and who is still, at the time of the interview, feared. The function of this form of lack of resolution is to engage the observer in the process of accusation of the presumed perpetrator.

Anticipated loss or trauma reflects fear that is exaggerated in an irrationally preoccupying manner, for example, fearing that one will lose one's child because of the loss of one's mother during childhood. The basis for the fear of death may be displaced (for example, from a fear of one's own death to a fear of one's child's death) or transformed (for example, from a desire to kill to a fear of the death, i.e., reaction formation).[1]

Delusional forms of unresolved trauma or loss occur when the speaker imagines, from a semantic or affective base, episodes that appear to have occurred but in fact cannot have occurred as reported. Frequently, the speaker marks this by saying "as if" or "like" but then

---

1. Fearfully anticipated death of a child that is cut off from the source of fear is treated by Main and Goldwyn as a pattern within dismissing (Ds4); here, it is treated as one form of lack of resolution of danger [Ul(a)$_{child}$].

goes on to quote "actual" dialogue, and so forth. The error is that the speaker fails to recognize that his or her own mind is the source of information.

Delusionally repaired trauma or loss involves speakers' delusionally constructing an explanation for endangering events that otherwise would seem to the speaker to be unforgivable, inexplicable, and unrelenting, even into the present. The delusional frame placed around the events makes them seem meaningful, or even inevitable, in a just and rational world, thus, reversing unrelenting distress resulting from gratuitous trauma and loss. The false resolution can involve expected future happiness beyond this life or, in a more self-aggrandizing form, can transform the victimized self into a sacrificed savior or powerful figure in control of chaos.

As with all forms of lack of resolution, danger and protection are central to delusions. With regard to cognition and affect, the delusion functions to add cognitive, rational meaning where there was no contingency or justification for what occurred and, because what occurred could only elicit intense and irresolvable negative affect, the delusion helps to lower arousal that cannot motivate useful action. Such delusions, based as they are on distortions of cognitive temporal reasoning, often include the speaker's feeling that he or she can foretell the future.

Delusional revenge or attacks involve similar transformations as delusional repair, but instead of focusing on future reward for the self, they emphasize punishment of perpetrators. Consequently, they pose greater danger to others.

Depressed is assigned when the dangerous events (or losses) are perceived by the speaker to be (a) beyond his or her control, both in the event itself and in the process of recovery and reorganization around them and (b) essential to his or her welfare, physically or psychologically.

Disorganized trauma is assigned under two conditions: (1) when the person displays multiple psychological responses to a single traumatic event that is, at various points in the transcript, dismissed, preoccupied upon, displaced, etc. (a minimum of three different responses is needed) and (2) when there are multiple events or deaths that (a) have markers of lack of resolution, (b) do not fully qualify as traumatic events (usually because some are quite minor), and (c) are confused in ways that are irrational (as opposed to connected in meaningful, albeit excessive ways). The point is that no particular trauma accounts for the psychological effects on the individual, but rather an array of real and imagined attributes of the experiences are connected to almost any other experience that, even tangentially, shares that characteristic. The effect is to make a very wide range of events a potential trigger for intense emotional response.

WHO OR WHAT CAN BE RESOLVED OR UNRESOLVED?

"U-loss" (Ul) is reserved for attachment figures, attached persons (i.e., the speaker's children), and substitutes for the self (e.g., siblings). Only these figures can receive Ul(p), Ul(ds), and Ul(v) (preoccupied, dismissing, and vicarious, respectively). A judgment must be made as to whether nonparental relatives (e.g., stepparents, grandparents, or aunts and uncles) functioned as attachment figures; this is done on a person-by-person basis and not for the class of such figures. In addition, siblings (who bear the same relation as one's self to one's attachment figures) may also be attachment figures or attached persons to oneself. There are also cases in which a pet is an attachment figure or even a self-substitute, but this should not be probed unless the speaker introduces it. An event can be a loss without there being a death, for example, divorce or placement in foster care. It should be noted, however, that such events involve separation from actual attachment figures and from the state of having an attachment figure.

Both attachment figures and other, more inconsequential persons can receive classifications of Ul(dpl), Ul(a), and Ul(i) (displaced, anticipated, and imaged, respectively).

With dangerous experiences, only threats to the self or threats to others that the speaker observed directly can receive Utr(p) and Utr(ds). Utr(v) is reserved for threats to attachment figures or attached persons when the speaker was not present at the event. Utr(dpl), Utr(a), Utr(i), and Utr(h) can be applied to any person or event. When there is evidence of lack of resolution regarding a person whose life was relatively unimportant to the speaker, both Ul(dpl) and Utr should be considered as possibilities. Ul(dpl) is used when the loss is the critical factor, but is displaced away from a more important loss. Utr is used when the death seems to threaten the speaker's confidence regarding his or her own personal safety. Particularly violent deaths (e.g., suicide or murder) may be given both Ul and Utr.

MATCHING AND MESHING LACK OF RESOLUTION AND BASIC STRATEGY

In concluding this discussion of lack of resolution, it should be noted that there is an interaction of an individual's primary strategy with the strategy for dealing with the self-threatening event. When these are the same (i.e., when they match), assigning the speaker to a "U" category seems redundant. Nevertheless, if the speaker is not resolved, lack of resolution is noted. The advantage of this is that the clinician has a note that it is there, waiting like a little land mine to explode at some future time.

More interesting are cases of reversal or differences in degree of dismissal or preoccupation. Examples of the meshing of opposite strategies include Type A speakers with a preoccupying trauma/loss or, conversely, Type C speakers with a dismissed trauma/loss. Patterns that involve reversal of strategy are most likely to occur when minor threats have been of one sort (cognitively or affectively), but a major danger occurs that calls for the opposite predictors and self-protective strategy, for example, $Ul(ds)_F$ C3, for an aggressively Type C speaker (C3) who dismisses the import of the death of his father, or $Utr(p)_{fall}A1$, for an idealizing Type A speaker (A1) who is traumatized by a childhood accident. The latter organization is one of two organizations often associated with panic attack symptoms (Heller & Pollet, 2010). Reversals are clinically significant and worthy of note.

On the other hand, there may be a difference in the extreme use of the strategy, such as when a mild Type C speaker (C1–2) displays obsessive or false cognitive qualities with regard to a dangerous event or loss. An example is $Utr(v)_M C2$, for a disarming Type C speaker (C2) who was vicariously traumatized by her mother's unexplained amputated legs, $Utr(v)_M$. Exaggeration of a Type C pattern around a traumatic event is often associated with another form of panic disorder (Crittenden, 1997a).

Finally, while lack of resolution of trauma or loss indicates a lack of integration of information and functioning around the trauma or loss, it does not imply that other aspects of the individual's functioning are unintegrated. Consequently, one can have Utr and Ul states associated with a predominant Type B pattern. Indeed, it is normal and expected that following many self-related deaths or traumas there will be a period of reorganization. During this period, the Type B individual is unresolved.

Consequently, in the DMM method, all nonresolved traumas and losses are listed, without regard to the dominant pattern.

CONTAINED VERSUS UNCONTAINED LACK OF RESOLUTION

The breadth of effects of lack of resolution on an individual's functioning is important. The opening questions of the AAI contain no threat or challenge. If there is evidence of psychological trauma in them, it can be expected to be quite pervasive in the speaker's functioning. Following that, questions about relationships with attachment figures may elicit evidence of childhood threat that is tied to a specific parent. Because this section is under the speaker's control, that is, the speaker chooses the words and episodes, intrusion of the trauma or loss is relevant. The section about normal dangers in childhood is even more likely to identify threat and, therefore, trauma. The issue becomes how well the psychological response is limited to the eliciting event (e.g., is it dismissed, displaced, confused with other events?). The section on traumatic danger and loss is most likely to uncover lack of resolution. However, this is less critical to adaptive functioning if distortions of thought are limited to this section instead of being in less directly related parts of the interview. Finally, the integrative questions suggest the extent to which the endangering experience colors the speakers' interpretations of their life experiences. Of particular concern in very disturbed speakers is confusion among traumatic events (i.e., disorganized lack of resolution). Trauma responses that appear only when the topic is probed are considered "contained" whereas those that appear spontaneously are "uncontained."

Discourse Markers and Their Psychological Function

There are a number of indicators of *preoccupation* with loss or traumatic events and, as would be expected, these are identified by involving discourse markers. Images are particularly important. Lack of resolution is indicated by images of agents of danger that are not connected to the dangerous person or experience, that preoccupy attention, and that, especially, are spoken of as though they were occurring in the present.

The indicators of *preoccupying* lack of resolution of trauma or loss involve intense affective arousal and cognitive confusion or uncertainty. All bring the threatening event closer in time and space (i.e., they distort *when* and *where* there might be danger). These indicators have been described in detail by Main and Goldwyn (1984, 1994) with regard to the M&G unresolved/disorganized category and are repeated here:

- An erroneous belief, in at least portions of the interview, that the past is not immutable, that is, that the danger may still be prevented or that the deceased person is not really or entirely dead (usually in procedural or episodic memory).
- Temporal confusion such as confusion regarding the time of death or a dangerous event or placing the dangerous event or death, in at least portions of the interview, in the present (procedural or episodic memory).
- Confusion of person, for example, reversing the pronouns for the self and the perpetrator of harm or for the self and the deceased (procedural memory).
- Erroneous placement of the self at the dangerous event or death when one was, in fact, absent (imaged or episodic memory).
- Psychological confusion regarding the causes or implications of the death (procedural or integrative memory).
- Overly simplified emotional responses, including intense and uncontrollable affective arousal around the topic of the danger or death (procedural or imaged memory).
- Overly simplified reasoning about responsibility for the causes of the danger, particularly one's own complicity in the array of causes, that is, reductionist blaming thought and magical thinking (semantic or integrative memory).
- An irrational belief in the high probability of repetition of the event, for example, anniversary effects (procedural and semantic memory).
- Hypervigilance regarding contextual indicators of the danger, for example, intense imaged recall (imaged memory).

The function of *preoccupying* lack of resolution is to (a) reduce the distance between the self and the event (thus, keeping the event in the present with the apparent potential of being available for resolution), (b) maintain vigilant awareness of all details so as to increase the probability of recognizing a recurrence of the event soon enough to mount a defense, and (c) avoid awareness of the causes of the danger, particularly causes that the self could influence. The benefit of the preoccupied response is that it increases the probability of predicting and preventing similar events in the future; when the causal conditions are unclear (or more threatening that the endangering event), it retains as much "raw" sensory information (both contextual and somatic) as possible, permitting later reconstructions of the event. Further, by keeping the affect associated with the event aroused and by refusing to change behavior patterns (i.e., by refusing to change), it falsely creates the appearance that the event has not actually occurred.

The costs of the preoccupying response are *overprediction of danger and underattribution of responsibility*, leading, therefore, to an inability to take responsible and self-protective action. In addition, there is an inability to move forward in life and an inability to release oneself from the pain associated with the event.

The indicators of *dismissed* lack of resolution include all the usual dismissing markers, but, in addition, include the following:

- Omission of the dangerous event or of the deceased person from early parts of the transcript and from all but the most direct probes of the event (procedural and episodic memory).
- Extreme brevity (more than elsewhere in the interview) regarding the danger or death (procedural memory).
- A noticeable absence of affect about the danger or death when affect would normally be expected (procedural memory).
- Overt claims that the event had no importance to the self (semantic and integrative memory).
- An erroneous belief that the self caused the danger or death, or is guilty for some aspect of it (semantic or integrative memory).
- Placing the self distant from an event for which one was actually present and endangered (episodic memory), including displacing the event onto some other person.

Dismissing forms of lack of resolution function to keep danger away from the self by placing it in the past, at geographic distance, or in other people (Pynoos & Nader, 1989). The benefit of the dismissing response is protection of the self from feeling pain that cannot easily be assuaged. In addition, when display of affect has, in the past, been strongly castigated and led to rejection, dismissing trauma or loss may protect the speaker from further (imagined or real) threat.

The cost of this strategy includes the failure to attend to important predictors or protective responses and, thus, *underidentification of threat of danger*. (This is demonstrated in those individuals who "never saw it coming" when everyone else did.) This can leave the self vulnerable in the future, particularly to events over which the self could have some influence. *Overattribution of responsibility* functions to enable the self to feel in control of events and, thus, leads to a false belief that one can protect the self in the future.

The other forms of preoccupied and dismissed lack of resolution share the respective markers. The disorganized forms mix these markers. The depressed forms are characterized by the same discourse markers as the depressed modifier (see below).

Experience/History

The speaker's history can include any form of perceived self-endangering event. Because children are vulnerable to a greater range of dangers and are less able to understand them than adults, they are more vulnerable to psychological trauma and are at greater risk in the event of the death of an attachment figure. Moreover, because they are less able to store, retrieve, and integrate information, they are more vulnerable to unresolved trauma or loss. Thus, danger that occurs early in life is more likely to produce trauma than later occurring danger. A particularly important aspect of the history is whether or not an attachment figure was able to protect and comfort the child.

Two forms of trauma are especially threatening. One is early danger that is repeated at later ages. Loss of an attachment figure in childhood that was followed by loss of other attachment figures would be an example of an extremely and repeatedly traumatizing set of dangers that would require extensive effort to resolve, that is, to enable the individual to feel safe. The effect might be to exaggerate use of the individual's existing strategy by making it more rigidly self-protective. The second form of trauma may be found in those who had experienced little threat of danger and for whom attachment figures had always been protective and comforting. These individuals might find it difficult to resolve the experience of deceptive danger. That is, individuals using a Type B strategy could be at greater risk of trauma under extreme and dangerous conditions than individuals using the Type A or C strategies, especially the high-numbered patterns.

ADVANTAGES OF
DMM CONCEPTUALIZATION OF
LACK OF RESOLUTION

The treatment of lack of resolution in the DMM method is complex, far more complex than the single preoccupying unresolved/disorganized category of Main, Hesse, and Goldwyn (2008). Nevertheless, articulating these ideas permits clinicians to specify critical features of distressed individuals' responses to dangerous events.

In the DMM method, danger is the central issue around which all strategies are constructed, with loss of an attachment figure (or attached person) being considered one sort of danger. Therefore, theory about response to danger, particularly traumatizing danger (Crittenden, 1997d), forms the basis for the conceptualization of lack of resolution of both trauma and loss. Of these, loss is the universal and ultimate danger. Loss of an attachment figure during childhood threatens personal survival whereas loss of an attached child threatens genetic survival. Thus, these two events are particularly dangerous. However, because loss is an inevitable and universal event, humans must find ways to accommodate the unpleasant and sometimes dangerous reality of losing an attachment figure. When this occurs while one is still dependent or when one is unable to protect an attached child, resolution can be especially difficult to achieve. Nevertheless, everyone must find a way to adapt to loss, whereas other dangers, although common, are not universal.

In the DMM method, resolution is treated explicitly. This leads to specification of the function and process of achieving resolution, which, in turn, permits evaluation of exactly which aspects of resolution have not been accomplished by the speaker. *The function of resolution is to enable the individual to take forward into the future information that is relevant to future protection and comfort and to keep in the past that which was unique to the specific event.* Unresolved individuals are unable to differentiate these two classes of information, particularly in the context of a changing self that faces changing challenges.

The central effect of the DMM approach is that lack of resolution is no longer considered a categorical state but rather is seen as a *process* that is observed both as a gradient and also as affecting a narrower or broader range of functioning. Thus, although a resolved/unresolved distinction is maintained at this point in the development of the DMM method, this distinction may become dimensional with further development of the thinking used here. Even now, however, clinicians will find it useful to record not simply whether dangers have been "resolved" but specifically which aspects of resolution need further integration and which portions of the interview are affected (i.e., how general or specific the lack of resolution is).[2]

As conceptualized here, lack of resolution is a psychological reaction to a *perceived self-endangering circumstance* (see Crittenden, 1997d). This reaction occurs both mentally and behaviorally and also is displayed in discourse in the AAI. Framed in this way, *the psychological response to the event is the critical feature rather than the event itself.* Indeed, the event may only have been observed, may be expected in the future (anticipatory trauma), may be wrongly attributed to another event or person (displaced trauma), may not actually have occurred (suggested trauma), may have occurred to an attachment figure and not to the self (vicarious trauma) or, in some cases, may have occurred without the individual being consciously aware of it (blocked trauma). Thus, self-threatening events like divorce, foster placement, injury to a parent, or "forgotten" child sexual abuse can be considered in terms of resolution or lack of resolution.

Lack of resolution of trauma in the DMM method is not inherently an extension of the Type C strategy. Instead, dismissing, preoccupying, and combined dismissing/preoccupying forms of response to threatening events all indicate a lack of resolution. Specifically, 14 forms of lack of resolution were proposed here (but others may be identified in the future): dismissed, displaced, blocked, denied, anticipated, preoccupying, vicarious, imagined, suggested, hinted, delusional repair, delusional revenge, depressed, and disorganized.

The DMM strategies and types of lack of resolution are particularly attuned to the danger implicit in deception. When parents deceive their children about their dangerousness, the children suffer far more debilitating psychological consequences than when parents' threats are open

---

2. There are both similarities and differences between this and a "stage" model of recovery from loss, with the primary difference being that an order of accomplishing aspects of resolution is not implied here. Indeed, resolution of a particular aspect at one point in time may be changed by some other issue later. This dynamic and systemic perspective on the process of resolution could account for the "reversals" seen in recovering individuals. Possibly some reversals are actually concatenations of old information with newly generated understandings. In addition, the perspective taken here permits the possibility that Type A and Type C individuals might differ in the aspects of resolution that were attempted first or achieved most successfully.

and fulfilled. Similarly, when reproductive partners deceive about sexual activity, it endangers progeny both physically and psychologically.

These features of DMM lack of resolution represent an advantage over simpler conceptualizations. Although empirical studies have only scratched the surface, evidence is accumulating that simple preoccupation with loss or trauma is not strongly associated with psychological disorder whereas dismissed loss and trauma are, as are particular distortions (e.g., imagined trauma with eating and personality disorders, suggested trauma with anxiety disorders, hinted trauma with paranoia) and combinations of responses (dismissed-and-preoccupied trauma with PTSD, disorganized trauma with borderline personality disorder). The studies reporting these findings are summarized in Chapter 15.

Chapter 12

Conditions That Reflect the Failure of Interpersonal Self-Protective Strategies

A Move to the Intrapersonal and Extrafamilial Levels

IN CHAPTER 12 WE DISCUSS CONDITIONS THAT REFLECT THE FAILURE OF A strategy to protect the self, promote safe reproduction, or protect one's progeny. *Modifiers* have a pervasive influence on psychological functioning, creating a general and chronic lack of fit between the individual's strategy and the context to which it is applied. In addition, on first reading, the modifiers render the interview difficult to understand in a way that is quite different from the misassociation of unresolved trauma and loss with posttrauma contexts. We describe five modifiers: depression, disorientation, intrusions of forbidden negative affect, expressed somatic symptoms, and reorganizing.

OVERVIEW

Continuing the metaphor of land mines introduced in Chapter 11 for unresolved loss and trauma, modifiers are like a full-fledged, unlimited (by time or space) war. Nothing is safe or comfortable and the individual has no self-protective strategy. Each modifier changes the strategy in ways that make it nonstrategic for at least a while. In terms of discourse, this means that none of the classificatory criteria for any strategy are fully met. In terms of life experiences, modifiers indicate a state of being stuck (i.e., not in dynamic application of the strategy to experience), of being unable to define the context (i.e., irregularities in application of strategy to an unchanging context that render behavior relatively unpredictable), or of being unable to fully differentiate a previous context from a changed one (i.e., new life conditions that require reorganization).

In the case of *depression* (Dp), the speakers know that the strategy is ineffective. They know how the situation is and believe (whether accurately or not) that there is nothing they can do to protect themselves. Thus, they have accurate information but consider it not to be self-relevant in the present. Nevertheless, in the absence of an effective strategy, the speaker has only the failed strategy available and so continues to use it, even with the certainty of its failure. Thus, the verbal presentation of the strategy fails to distort, omit, or intrude information. Instead, all is open, apparent for us to see. The openness suggests Type B but the sadness, lack of self-relevance, and lack of productive reflective thought confirm that Type B is impossible.

In the case of *disorientation* (DO), speakers do not perceive that the strategy is not functioning. Instead, they believe that they are behaving strategically, but because they mix representations from incompatible sources, their behavior becomes an incoherent mix of other-protection and self-protection—and such a mix is neither self-protective nor protective of progeny. Put another way, for disoriented speakers, everything is self-relevant. Disoriented speakers are confused about the source of information, thereby combining information from many sources as if they were all equally relevant to the self in the present. All are jumbled together, thus rendering current behavior diffuse and misdirected.

Intrusions of forbidden negative affect [ina] interrupt an inhibitory A+ strategy, letting the person behave in unusually affectively intense, wildly forbidden, and apparently maladaptive ways. Unlike lack of resolution, the intrusion of forbidden and formerly inhibited negative affect appears not to be contingent on input from outside the self, neither from contingencies nor from others' display of feeling. It should be made clear, however, that this is the acceptable appearance; in reality contingencies are usually present but are not permitted to be acknowledged. Any of several negative affective states can be intruded but all are action-motivating states (i.e., desire for comfort, anger, fear, sexual desire, and desire for pain). Of these, only desire for pain needs explanation. This desire probably occurs when the speaker's inhibition of affect is so nearly absolute that only life-threateningly intense stimulation can permit the individual to feel at all; it is more often self-inflicted than sought interpersonally (i.e., masochistically). During the intrusion, the compulsive strategy is rendered useless. This occurs only among extremely inhibited and compulsive Type A speakers whose strategy is no longer tied to its eliciting conditions but instead is applied pervasively across all conditions.

Expressed somatic symptoms [ess] are nonverbal, somatic disruptions of the interview that cannot be explained medically (e.g., excessively slow speech, falling asleep, excessive coughing). The symptoms chronically disrupt the strategy at intermittent times. The modifier of expressed somatic symptoms is the newest addition to the DMM-AAI method and, at present, is the least well defined and understood of the modifiers.

Reorganizing (R) speakers are changing from one strategy to another. In such cases, neither strategy functions fully and, thus, the classificatory criteria are mixed and not fully met. Often a non-B strategy is becoming more balanced through a reflective and integrative process. Because no strategy is fully "in charge," the individual is particularly vulnerable—at just the time when new psychological skills and functions are developing. Although reorganization can also occur between Types A and C, criteria for change between the non-B strategies have not been defined.

DEPRESSED

This is one of the DMM method modifiers and is based on theory (Gut, 1989) and clinical observations from AAIs (Crittenden, 1995). It has parallels in all other DMM assessments except the CARE-Index.

Overview

Depression (Dp) can modify any of the patterns, but, when conditions are actually safe, higher numbered patterns are more likely to be classified as depressed than lower numbered patterns. Conversely, dangerous conditions are more likely to result in depression for individuals using low-numbered A, B, or C strategies. The reason for this counter-intuitive relation is tied to the definition of "depression" that is used here.

Clinically, the diagnosis of depression is very broad and includes a wide range of relatively dissimilar symptoms. A narrower focus is used here. *Specifically, Dp, as a modifier of an AAI classification, refers to the failure of the strategy to resolve the problems to which the strategy is applied, combined with the speaker's awareness of this.* This failure implies that neither the cognitive transformation of sensory information nor the affective transformation yields *self-relevant* dispositional representations (DRs). To the contrary, the representations that are offered carry the implication that the self and actions of the self are irrelevant to outcomes. Put another way, everything is apparent and nothing makes any difference. The discourse markers address the failure of both types of transformation (i.e., cognition and affect) to yield any disposition to act.

Discourse Markers and Their Psychological Function

Depression is recognized in AAI discourse by the presence of discourse markers, associated with an underlying strategy, that do not fulfill the function of the strategy. For example, distancing speech that does not dismiss the danger, balanced speech that does not reach an integrative and productive conclusion, and preoccupied speech that does not (a) elicit assistance in solving the problem, (b) generate fury that could motivate attack, or (c) augment fear that could lead to flight from threat. Instead, all the information is present with relatively few distortions and, yet, a self-protective strategy is missing. Thus, there is adequate imaged, semantic, connotative, and episodic information. Procedurally, the speaker cooperates adequately with the interviewer but fails to use that relationship to think productively. Reflective functioning, even when it seems accurate and insightful, carries no self-relevant meanings that could promote adaptive organization of behavior. Furthermore, such possibilities are not only missing but are also not expected by the speaker. *This, indeed, is the central point of all the forms of information: They all place the speaker in a position of nonagency with regard to self-protection and comfort.*

It should be noted that depression is easily mistaken for reorganizing or even Type B because all the information is available, in a relatively undistorted form, and the speaker reflects upon it. The information is not, however, integrated to yield new and more adaptive understanding and behavior.

1. Procedurally, depressed speakers with an underlying Type A or C strategy use many of the discourse markers associated with their strategy. Further, dysfluence marks distressing topics. Many speak of themselves in a distant manner, that is, as objects upon which others acted; often this involves use of the passive voice. Nevertheless, critical information is present in a relatively undistorted form; therefore, procedural functioning fails to preclude awareness of unpleasant information.

   Displayed affect tends not to motivate action and instead (a) conveys the speaker's vulnerability together with the futility of action (e.g., sighs, deep breaths), (b) is absent altogether where it ought to be present (but without being dismissed or transformed into false positive affect) (e.g., flat or sad affect, diverting the subject's attention from possible changes in the probability of danger), or (c) is intense but is undifferentiated, generalized negative affect that is undirected, that is, it focuses on nothing or leads to inaction (e.g., intense sobbing in response to apparently trivial things and without possibility of comfort or relief).

   In terms of the relationship with the interviewer, depressed speakers neither withdraw from the interview nor manipulate the feelings of the listener. Superficially, they cooperate with the question-and-answer format, but they make no attempt to establish a working relationship with the interviewer and do not use the presence of the interviewer as an opportunity to think freshly. They appear both available for interaction and unconnected to the interviewer. That is, the relationship is not used by speakers to block recall and feelings, to develop further understanding, or to involve the interviewer in agreement or problem solving.

2. Imaged memory is reduced to a few images that are impersonal and idiosyncratic: They do not elicit feeling in the listener/reader, being unconnected and desiccated or unique and bizarre such that their meaning is not easily communicated to others (or to the self). The images are therefore rarely self-relevant, not uniquely and personally meaningful, and told in ways that are not evocative of specific feeling states or tied to life events in easily recognizable forms. This distances the self from affect or the motivating function of affect.

3. Semantically, depressed speakers say things that are true but that also close off any possibility of change. For example, random or uncontrollable events from outside the family system (e.g., war, infectious disease) are the cause of irreparable damage to the child. Frequently, the emphasis upon some obvious and unchangeable condition obscures recognition of other causal conditions that are amenable to strategic influence. For example, recognition of the effects of parental handicaps can obscure the responsibility of parents for other aspects of their behavior. In the face of the immutable condition, depressed speakers conclude that action is *futile* or that *fate* has already determined all outcomes. Alternatively, the framing of a situation may make it appear static and immutable when a reframing could identify a range of self-generated responses. Sometimes this is accurate to the past situation, but more often inclusion of new information could change this semantic conclusion, as it relates to the future. Overall, semantic memory (a) is overgeneralized and (b) retains generalized information about lack of protection and comfort, but, by including exonerating or blame-deflecting information, it reduces self-protective organization.

4. Connotatively, the discourse is neither drained nor filled with affect; instead, a sense of unavoidable heaviness or sadness settles over both speaker and listener.

5. Often, recalled episodes are suitable, or minimally suitable, as support for semantic judgments. That is, the history is believable as presented and fits the strategy that the speakers are almost using. On the other hand, the content of the episode provides no guide for actions that could be taken that would effectively limit or change the problem, and it does not elicit feelings that have generated effective behavior in the past. In the episodes, the self is vulnerable, an acted-upon object that neither elicits the action nor responds to it by eliciting protection, fleeing/escaping, attacking, or comforting the self. That is, the episodes have neither protection nor reaction to being unprotected. Consequently, these, too, lack present self-relevance. In most cases, in spite of there being credible evidence, it is difficult to classify the episodes properly.

6. Integration is minimal but is easily confused with true integration. That is, depressed speakers provide clear statements of their problems, including highlighting discrepancies, and they neither dismiss these nor treat them as mysteriously inconclusive. Instead, many depressed speakers simply recognize the problems as *intrin-*

sic to the situation and neither expect nor seek resolution. They also recognize the indicators that signaled risk and the causal conditions that generated the danger, but they do not see how these are tied to their own behavior. Speakers give evidence of feeling helpless to change their situation, in spite of being able to describe the situation accurately and without substantial distortion. For example, depressed speakers may say that they can't change the way things are or that they didn't want to behave in a particular way, but that they, nevertheless, did so. Thus, they integrate information to articulate the problem but are not able to use the integration to generate new or creative solutions. As a consequence, they do not see how changes in their own behaviors could change their own safety and comfort in the present.

Consequently, depressed speakers often fail to meet fully the criteria both for any overall or specific strategy. These failures often preclude assignment to a specific classification. That is, the speakers do not use a thorough-going strategy with its self-protective transformations of information. Instead, one often classifies such transcripts as A+ or C+ to indicate the generic compulsive or obsessive form of the strategy without assignment to a particular and complete strategy. In general, the pattern of discourse is more clearly reflective of the strategy than the discordance among memory systems. That is, depressed speakers use remnants of the strategy effectively against minor, ongoing (procedural) threats, but the strategy fails against the substantive threats of their lives. For these, they appear unprotected and vulnerable. A particular problem is experienced by depressed A/C speakers. Often, acceptance of one or the other strategy would end the power-depleting stalemate, but this would require a distortion of reality. Because this is recognized by the depressed speaker, strategic behavior appears impossible.

DIFFERENTIATING DEPRESSION FROM TYPE B

Because all the information is present in a largely undistorted form and because we generally agree with the speaker's version of his or her past experience, depressed speakers are often misclassified as Type B. Nevertheless, they differ from Type B speakers in the too-accurate attribution of responsibility and causality and the diffuseness of their feelings, keeping in mind that adaptation is promoted by having an optimistic outlook (Scheier & Carver, 1982; Taylor & Brown, 1988). In sum, there is little self-relevance in speakers whose AAIs are assigned the depressed modifier. They differ from disoriented speakers in that their speech is generally coherent and a psychologically sound developmental history can be constructed from the histories that they provide.

Experience/History

Type A depressed speakers have usually had a childhood history that included unavoidable danger. In many cases this involved punishment for display of negative affect in the context of cognitively predictable and preventable danger, followed by a dangerous or threatening event later in life that could not be resolved without access to affect. In other cases, individuals were the object of danger that changed their lives in irreversible ways and that provided no compensating opportunities.

Depressed Type B speakers have usually grown up in a safe and nondeceptive environment and later experienced dangerous conditions that required a change in (a) their DRs of external reality, including recognition of danger and deceptive information about danger, (b) their strategies for processing information and organizing behavior, and (c) their self, including their own capacity for distortion and deception and their willingness to harm others in order to protect themselves, their attachment figures, and their progeny. Put more directly, naive Bs often have to face the unpleasant reality that they and the world are not as "nice" as they had imagined. Usually, beliefs about being safe and protected are challenged in irrefutable ways that demand undesired changes in the self for recovery. Naive Bs are more vulnerable to depression than earned Bs, who may be the least vulnerable to enduring depression, that is, they have earned their resilience.

Type C depressed speakers have usually experienced a childhood history that included unpredictable dangerous events whose outcomes could be modified by intense affective displays, together with a dangerous or threatening event later in life that was unaffected by affective displays and that could not be resolved without access to cognitive information.

DISORIENTED

Disorientation (DO) is a high arousal state that functions in a nonstrategic way because of a source memory problem. It occurs when the source of information is omitted from representations, leading to an overattribution of representations to the self in the present. That is, DRs of other people, particularly attachment figures, and of the self at younger ages are lumped together with currently self-relevant DRs. The result is too inclusive a set of representations in which everything becomes self-relevant. The absence of source memory also hinders evaluation of the veracity and self-relevance of the DRs, thus, permitting contradictory representations to be treated as equally relevant to the self in the present. This prevents individuals from resolving discrepancies and selecting the representation that best serves their current interests. This is most critical when the other persons are attachment figures and when the needs of self and attachment figures are in conflict. Under such conditions, both discourse and behavior may become incoherent. This can lead to incomplete strategic behavior that is sometimes counterproductive to the self. The term "disoriented" is chosen because the individual is oriented in conflicting directions around competing dispositions. The resulting behavior is nonstrategic, that is, neither self-protective nor comfort-eliciting.

Like depression, disorientation can easily be confused with reorganizing or even Type B because all the information is available, in a relatively undistorted form, and the speaker reflects upon it. The information is not, however, integrated to yield new and more adaptive understanding and behavior.

Developmental Antecedents

Several conditions might account for deficient source memory. First, critical learning might have occurred before the capacity for source memory had developed. However, all young children lack source memory, so age alone is insufficient to explain the deficit.

When parents' and children's needs are in conflict and when children cannot discern the conflict, the natural tendency of children to rely on parentally given information may lead to self-detrimental behavior. This is particularly likely when parents feel very threatened themselves, act on their own behalf for reasons that children cannot discern (e.g., in triangulated relationships that function without children's awareness), and semantically tell their children that they acted on the children's behalf or for their benefit. Parental feelings of being very threatened are critical because they cause parents to use self-protective strategies, rather than child-protective strategies. However, this should not create disorientation if the child can perceive the conflict and the choices made by the parent. This condition alone merely leads children to construct complementary self-protective strategies (e.g., the compulsive child of an obsessive parent). The essential component is the parents' use of secretive involving strategies (i.e., obsessive C strategies or child-centered compulsive A strategies). These can confuse children regarding when the perspective is their own and when it is an attachment figure's.

Finally, any condition that causes the parent to behave toward the child in ways that are only partially related to the child favors children's disorientation. Such conditions include parents' responding to their own psychological trauma, parents' behaving toward children in ways that they know are inappropriate and unrelated to the child (e.g., child sexual abuse), and triangulated spousal relationships (in which important causal conditions that affect children are not visible to the child). Cases in which the parent's behavior is totally unrelated to the child are easily identified by children and do not lead to causal confusion. For example, inebriated or psychotic parents are understood by even very young children not to be responding to the children and children do not become confused (or disoriented) regarding whose thoughts and feelings are whose. In the situation of confused perspectives, children are likely to make erroneous self-attributions of causality and to implement strategies based on this erroneous information. The consequent failure of these strategies will further confuse children with regard to the nature of reality.

Discourse Markers and Their Psychological Function

All transcripts assigned to DO have the following attributes: The interviewing is adequate to have enabled the speaker to present a coherent history if he or she were able to do so. The distortions of speech and thought that are used by the speaker are among those described by the DMM method, that is, the elements of the transcript are familiar and have been defined. The elements of the discourse appear in conflict, that is, there appears to be a struggle within the speaker regarding how to present the history and changes in presentation seem to undermine the speaker rather than to provide the flexibility of multiple strategies. There is no self-protective function evident in the presentation of the elements, that is, they neither protect the speaker from self-perceived danger nor mislead others regarding the dangerousness of the speaker. Moreover, unlike depressed speakers, disoriented speakers seem unaware that their strategies have failed and will continue to fail. The psychological profile of the speaker and his or her attachment figures is incoherent, that is, we, the observers, cannot construct a psychologically sound description of the speaker's psychological history.

Transcripts assigned to DO also have the following markers:

1. An A/C or AC strategy.
2. Lack of connection between different parts of the interview as though different histories were being discussed at different times and as though the speaker was unaware of the shifts and inconsistencies.
3. Unacknowledged and erroneous connections are made between unrelated events.
4. Sentences and episodes change meaning midway through, without the speaker being aware of the discrepancy, such that the whole becomes incoherent. This is not an oscillation in which the speaker knowingly changes his or her mind, but rather he or she substitutes one version of an experience for another. It is the unacknowledged juxtaposition in one sentence or episode of two different DRs.
5. Responses that shift from one topic to another without apparent associative connection and without addressing the question at hand. The shift points appear to come when the topic becomes uncomfortable to the speaker, that is, when clarity would be achieved if the thought were completed. Instead, the speaker's mind darts from topic to topic. The function may be to avoid focus and ensuing awareness.
6. Orienting intrusions that seem not to be under the control of the speaker. Three sorts of intrusions are most common:
   a. Requests for reorientation by the interviewer when the speaker has forgotten what was being discussed. This is the least indicative of disorganization because the speaker has awareness of the mental confusion and because the questions can serve other functions.
   b. Self-talk in which speakers try to reorient themselves, as one does mentally, but this is spoken as though the interviewer were not listening. This indicates greater disorientation than requests for help.
   c. Pervasive indicators of arousal (excessive and inappropriate laughter, stuttering, repeated interruptions that do not function as power struggles, or intruded sounds such as

tut-tutting) that do not serve a motivating or strategic function but rather only mark arousal.

7. In some cases, these three features are limited to discussions of dangers or losses. In such cases, multiple contradictory strategies are used. That is, the strategic response is confused, but not the events themselves. In this case, the confusion is limited to trauma or loss and is noted as Ul/tr(dx). More commonly in cases of disorientation, there is no specific danger evident in the history nor is there psychological trauma indicated in the adult speaker's discourse. Instead, the history has troublingly incoherent elements and a lack of clarity. Psychologically, the strategy of the speaker cannot be discerned although the elements of several patterns are generally present.

Differentiating DO from A8: A8 speakers turn to others for information, whereas DO speakers presume that they themselves have the information, but lack an efficient means of accessing it, evaluating it, and attributing it to its source.

INTRUSIONS OF FORBIDDEN NEGATIVE AFFECT

Intrusions of forbidden negative affect ([ina]s) are the sudden and unexpected use of language or forms of address that are unacceptable in the AAI context. They mark a sudden and brief change from an inhibited state to a state of high and disinhibited arousal. Intrusions of forbidden negative affect occur only with pervasively applied compulsive Type A strategies, in which self-as-source has been forbidden and other-as-source has regulated the entire self-organizing process.

Overview

CONDITIONS UNDER WHICH [INA]S OCCUR

Intrusions of forbidden negative affect may occur when the self as a source of information has been rigidly excluded from explicit processing and then bursts into behavior in an unregulated manner. The Type A strategy must be both excessively "complete" (i.e., all negative affects are forbidden) and also pervasive (i.e., there are no occasions when their display is permitted). Because these conditions do not pertain to A1–2, intrusions of forbidden affect are not seen in that strategy. They become possible for the compulsive As (A3–8) but even so are quite rare, except in contexts calling for imposed restraint or protection.

FORM AND PROCESS OF INTRUSIONS

Any negative affect (desire for comfort, anger, fear, sexual desire, or pain) can be intruded. Intrusions involve a sharp increase in arousal that precipitates action. In an AAI, these actions can be inappropriate words, gestures, or sounds, or activities such as walking out; in daily life, intrusions include sudden use of foul language, explosions of violence (especially against objects), inappropriate sexual behavior (from the perspective of the individual himself or herself), self-harm, and suicide (or attempts at suicide).

This intense arousal reverses the lower arousal (e.g., depression) that pervasive inhibition generates. If one conceptualizes negative affect as information about danger that motivates self-protective action, then excessive inhibition may enable an individual to tolerate dangerous conditions without evident reaction. This, of course, is unnatural and unsafe as well: One should act in the face of danger. Intrusions, therefore, can be conceptualized as a "last-ditch" attempt to save the self from danger.

PSYCHOLOGICAL PROCESS

Current thinking about cortical processing indicates that it consists of two opposite processes of inhibition and association (see Chapter 3). Although both processes are essential, they must be coordinated. In cases of intrusion, the inhibitory process has dominated functioning to the exclusion of the associative process. Moreover, the specific function of the inhibitory process has been to exclude self-generated information, especially negative affect and consequent behavior. Thus, the problem is not with source memory; instead, self-as-source is used as the criterion for exclusion. The problem is with integrative processing. The term "intrusion of forbidden negative affect" is used because the inhibitory organization breaks down.

FUNCTIONAL PROCESS

Intrusions of forbidden negative affect are nonstrategic at the interpersonal level, that is, dyadic and family relationships. One problem with extreme inhibition of negative affect is that the individual does not learn to regulate negative affect. Therefore, once expressed, it might no longer be containable or tied to contextual contingencies. This can be intolerable in some relationships or families. Having no *interper*sonal solution to interpersonal problems, the intrusion shifts strategic functioning to both the *intra*personal physiological level and also the *extra*familial, community level. Intrapersonally, the intrusion raises depressed arousal, thus reestablishing physiological homeostasis. Concurrently, it attracts assistance from outside the family (e.g., mental health professionals, law enforcement, religious authorities). Given the Type A organization of the individual, it is crucial that the negative behavior not be associated with the self, that is, the behavior must appear "mad" or "crazy" or otherwise beyond the control of the individual. (If it were construed as being under personal control, this behavior would challenge the "right/wrong" split of the compulsive strategy.) The response of the community outside the family (including professionals as representatives of the community) is often to use medication to constrain arousal, provide therapy to reinstate inhibition, or to move the individual to a more restrictive context (e.g., hospital, prison). When the intrusions do not harm others, they are often treated as extrinsic to the self and become the province of the mental health system. When the intrusions are harmful to others, they are often treated as the essence of self and the individuals displaying them are shunted to the criminal system.

This conceptualization suggests the following:

- Depression with intrusions mimics normal context-contingent and life-maintaining variation in arousal, but at more extreme levels. That is, it reflects a form of bipolarity that is often seen in individuals diagnosed as having psychotic-like episodes.
- Intrusions should occur when danger seems incipient and escape seems mandatory. That is, intrusions both correct the excessively low arousal of the individual and also draw others' attention to the individual's need for protection.

It also suggests that, in spite of appearing "disorganized," intrusions of forbidden negative affect function self-protectively at the intrapersonal (biological) level and at the extrapersonal (societal) level.

In AAIs, [ina]s have been associated with moderate to severe disorders, including diagnoses of psychotic, schizoid, mood, bipolar dis-

Assessing Adult Attachment

orders, and violent criminal behavior. Such disorders are usually of unknown etiology but are most commonly attributed to genetic, neurological, or chemical imbalances. The combination of diagnosis, protective residential circumstances, and pharmacological treatment effectively changes behavior, removes individuals from their daily circumstances, and modifies the mental processes that organize the individuals' behaviors. Given these outcomes, intrusions of forbidden negative affect may reflect use of extreme destabilization to permit, under very limited conditions, the representation of forbidden feelings and experiences for which the source of information is the self. The cost to the individual of this adaptation is very high.

Discourse Markers and Their Psychological Function

Transcripts are assigned an [ina] only when the interviewing is adequate to have enabled the speaker to present a coherent history if he or she were able to do so, the distortions of speech and thought that are used by the speaker are among those described by the DMM method, the procedural elements of the discourse appear in conflict, the behavior appears counterproductive, and the psychological profiles of the speaker and attachment figures are incoherent.

Transcripts assigned an [ina] also have the following markers:

- Pervasive use of compulsive Type A strategy, particularly A4 and A7, including excessive vigilance to others' perspectives and requirements.
- Inappropriate negative language or comments that appear unexpectedly and without explanation.
- Ignoring of an intrusion, as if it had not occurred, or attempts to cover it as if ashamed. The intrusion is not, however, alternated with disarming speech (which would suggest use of a coercive strategy).
- Incomprehensible words around inadmissible negative behavior and threats too great to be articulated.
- Repeated use of a "trigger" word or phrase that represents both the danger and the intrusion (e.g., "nervy" and "nervous" when a murder is explained by the killer having had bad "nerves").
- Distortion and displacement of negative behavior and its consequences onto a self-substitute.
- There are no intrusions during the AAI, but possible intrusions are described in the history and may be denoted as historical, [ina]$_h$.

DEVELOPMENTAL PATHWAYS

Intrusions are sometimes associated with a childhood history of harsh or demanding caregivers who tolerated no exceptions to their standards. This left children with no options but to accept such standards, inhibiting any negation of them. To do otherwise would be to risk punishment or rejection. At some point, however, the children's failure to evaluate parental standards and develop and act on their personal perspectives caps development. The point is often reached in the transition to adulthood. Alternatively, children placed in care, especially more than once, often have intrusions. In video SSP procedures, they tend to occur when a rejected/neglected child approaches the stranger in an intrusion of desire for comfort, then loses muscular control and falls to the floor, overwhelmed by the intruding fear of the unknown, potentially dangerous, strange person.

When a child has learned an inhibitory compulsive strategy and when semantic information from attachment figures denies the validity of the child's perspective, the child may give up all self-generated information in order to use other-directed procedures and other-generated semantic and episodic information exclusively. This is strategically adaptive while the child is dependent upon attachment figures, but it is vulnerable to a loss of prefrontal cortical focus, that is, to loss of inhibition.

Loss of inhibition and intrusion of forbidden negative affect and self-derived semantic attributions seem most likely when affective experiences become overwhelmingly intense and in conflict with the inhibitory strategy. This could occur (a) under great threat, especially when the threat was irresolvable with a Type A response or (b) when developmental progress required forbidden behavior. Periods of developmental transition, particularly when they involve both neurological and environmental change, would seem to place very tightly controlled individuals at greater risk of loss of inhibitory control than would more stable periods. Possibly because puberty adds sexual desire to the array of experienced affective states and also changes hormonal regulation, the period following puberty seems to have particular risk for intrusions of forbidden negative affect into extremely pervasive inhibitory strategies. If, in addition, the individual needs to achieve independence outside of the family of origin (in the transition to adulthood) and the family cannot manage that process, both depression and intrusions may increase.

DIFFERENTIATING [INA]S FROM OTHER CLASSIFICATORY POSSIBILITIES

Intrusions of forbidden negative affect and behavior are easily confused with a Type C strategy. They differ, however, in crucial ways that affect both coding and, more important, treatment. When the negative behavior is escalated until it elicits anger and then is disarmed but reinstigated as soon as the other backs down, then the negative behavior is not an [ina] but is instead part of a coercive strategy.

The A/C pattern and Dp modifier overlap with [ina] and, if they can account for all the evidence in the transcript, then [ina] should not be used as a modifier. In all cases, Dp indicates excessively low arousal and [ina] indicates uncontrollably high arousal, such that this becomes an important means of differentiation. However, Dp and [ina] co-occur frequently, and the arousal of the individual swings accordingly in different parts of the interview.

EXPRESSED SOMATIC SYMPTOMS

Expressed somatic symptoms ([ess]) are nonverbal behaviors that interfere with the interpersonal process of the AAI. Although sometimes they are unusual, more often they are ordinary behaviors that occur in excess and disrupt communication. It is thought that [ess] represent conflict between what is known or suspected and what one is permitted to know or say. This is one of the most recent additions to the DMM array of constructs and, as such, it requires more examples before the construct and its coded application can be fully defined.

Overview

Expressed somatic symptoms are noted in an AAI when nonverbal behavior that is usually marked parenthetically becomes an active part of the interpersonal process and can be seen to perform a repeated function in the dialogue. Expressed somatic symptoms can occur in any high-numbered strategy (A+, C+, A+/C+). Unlike [ina]s that occur infrequently in an AAI (often only once), [ess] are very frequent during the interview, sometimes occurring almost continuously, thus providing evidence of a near constant state of changed arousal. Because they are experienced in a specific bodily organ, [ess] are readily associated with the state of the whole self, but because they are entirely nonverbal, their meaning, that is, precisely what they represent, remains vague. As a consequence, misattributions are easily made and difficult to refute. Functionally, the speaker's meaning is not communicated unambiguously and explicitly in the AAI. The conflict between knowing or suspecting important information and not being allowed to know or express it disrupts strategic functioning. The speaker's strategy, therefore, appears in an incomplete form that doesn't fully meet the criteria for any classification.

According to Kozlowska (Kozlowska, 2007; Kozlowska et al., 2008; Kozlowska & Williams, 2009), there are several types of somatic symptoms: those that we have labeled [ina]s, those that indicate arousal (e.g., scratching, coughing, hyperventilating), but are neither forbidden by the strategy nor uncontrollable, and those that exaggerate a somatic symptom strategically (usually part of an even-numbered Type C strategy, Kozlowska, 2009).

FORM AND PROCESS OF [ESS]

The form of an [ess] can vary greatly, including such behaviors as moaning from stomachaches, coughing, breathing with difficulty, inability to walk, falling asleep, going excessively to the toilet, snorting, rapidly kicking a foot, twisting of the body, tics, and so forth. The form may suggest a function (e.g., "I can't stomach it"; "It suffocates me"; "It cripples me"; "I cannot attend to that at all"; "I must escape"; "It disgusts me"). It is not the case, however, that [ess] always match their meaning morphologically. Particularly crucial symptom types may be those tied to what is taken into the body (i.e., respiratory and gastrointestinal symptoms) or allowed to reach the body (e.g., skin disorders) because these organs define the boundary between self and non-self.

When the [ess] has no auditory component, the interviewer will need to signal its presence and such behaviors as tics can only be mentioned parenthetically in the transcription. Videotaping of AAIs can add to clarity regarding nonauditory [ess] and is recommended.

All these forms of [ess] are related to a change of state, which usually marks high arousal. In a few cases, though, the [ess] can lower arousal (e.g., repeated falling asleep during an AAI by a distressed speaker). Yawning is a particularly interesting behavior. In infancy, it functions to enable an infant to lower arousal and retreat from an overly intense interaction. In adults, it is often interpreted as tiredness but when used excessively it may function to reduce stress by achieving distance.

PSYCHOLOGICAL PROCESS

Expressed somatic symptoms represent without entering the individual's psychological process. This is crucial to their function of representing without communicating what is being represented. For example, symptoms can represent the individual's desire to be released from something he or she would otherwise be obligated to do, to elicit attention and concern from family members or to receive assistance from professionals, or even just to express intense arousal.

It should be noted that the central feature of an [ess] is the conflict between knowing and expressing with clarity and not knowing and expressing obscurely. The [ess] straddles an uncomfortable boundary between the mutually incompatible states of communicating and not communicating.

FUNCTIONAL PROCESS

Expressed somatic symptoms disrupt the interview process by redirecting the focus of the interview from psychological and interpersonal issues to the speaker's physical state and comfort. That is, intruded somatic symptoms deflect attention away from the content of the interview and its meaning to the speaker. In that way, an [ess] functions like illness; out of consideration for the sick individual and with awareness that ill people cannot easily attend to conditions outside themselves, care is given to such people and any problems that might need their attention are held in abeyance until they feel better. In the case of [ess], both individuals and their family members actively avoid attending to the underlying problems, albeit without awareness of this avoidance.

Discourse Markers and Their Psychological Function

SPECIFIC MARKERS

To qualify as an [ess], the behavior must disrupt the flow of the AAI without there being an accepted organic reason for the behavior. Thus, coughing when one has a cold, even if it disrupts the AAI, is not coded as an [ess], although the coughing of some asthma attacks may be. The behavior must occur several times and there must be a functional pattern to the behavior. That is, its occurrence must vary in specifiable ways with the content of the AAI.

Imputing a Meaning to Somatic Representations

Nonverbal behaviors that could function as [ess] should always be analyzed in terms of their effect on (a) the interpersonal process of the interview and (b) the relative attention given to some information as compared to other information. The distribution of the [ess] can signal which topics are most threatening to the speaker, that is, high frequencies of [ess] signal high threat and the absence of [ess] signals safe topics (from the speaker's perspective). Usually, ordinary discourse markers vary similarly, thus marking unspeakable and "speakable" topics. Noting the topics under discussion when the rate of [ess] increases can help to identify what unspeakable information is being represented organically. Expressed somatic symptoms can be thought of as maximizing expressivity at the expense of specificity. That is, the speaker "lives" the representation and imposes it strongly on the listener, but neither is clear about what it means or even that it can convey useful information.

Developmental Pathways

A working hypothesis is that nonverbal somatic representations reflect information that is not known sufficiently for verbal representation or that can create danger if represented verbally. Therefore, family secrets are often associated with nonverbal somatic representations. Such secrets certainly include sexual behavior but also illegal activity, "forgotten" parental history, and so forth. The secret is defined by the adult's inability to carry on if the information were known explicitly. Younger children are probably more vulnerable to this type of somatization, but this is an empirical question.

Differentiating [ess] from Other Classificatory Possibilities

The primary difficulty with coding [ess] is treating ordinary non-verbal behavior as an [ess]. All speakers occasionally cough, sigh, or yawn, but this is not indicative of an [ess]. Whenever there is a range of such markers that occur occasionally and are scattered through the transcript, that do not interfere with the AAI itself, and that either have or do not need a verbal representation, they are not to be coded as [ess]. Further, if the AAI is comprehensible and fits a strategy well, the markers are unlikely to indicate expressed somatic symptoms. That is because expressed somatic symptoms are crucial representations of something important that the speaker could not or dared not put in words. Lacking this important representation, the AAI with an [ess] makes little or no sense; something more is needed to understand the speaker's experience and self-protective strategy. That is not the case when the nonverbal indicators are just the normal sounds and movements that accompany all communication.

REORGANIZING

This is one of the DMM method modifiers and is based on theory (Crittenden, 1990, 1995) and clinical observations from AAIs.

Overview

Reorganizing (R) speakers are actively changing their understanding of their past and current experiences. The following list contains hallmark features of reorganization in the direction of balance:

1.* A history consistent with a self-protective strategy for regulating relationships.
2.* Use of a self-protective pattern of discourse (either Type A or Type C) *together with* the speaker's at least implicit awareness of the strategy and some of the reasons for it.
3. A cooperative relationship with the interviewer in which the speaker actively engages in the process of reviewing his or her history *for the purpose of finding meaning*.
4.+ Self-monitoring such that some discrepancies, inaccuracies, and slips into the old self-protective pattern are noticed and commented upon (i.e., they are licensed) or corrected.
5. Behavioral evidence in the discourse that the dominant pattern is being reversed, that is, that compulsive speakers are taking their own perspectives and acknowledging negative affect, especially toward unsatisfying attachment figures or that obsessive speakers

are taking other people's, especially attachment figures', perspectives and moderating their affect-motivated behavior. Reflective functioning that is compatible with the speaker's basic pattern (e.g., a Type A speaker's recognition of his or her own responsibility or a Type C speaker's recognition of the deception of others) is not evidence of reorganization.

6.+ A reflective stance in which there is evidence of (a) taking in and using new information to arrive at new understandings, (b) weighing and considering alternative perspectives, or (c) active efforts to tie past and present together in a psychologically sound manner.

7.* Overt awareness that appearances are not always synonymous with reality.

8. Statements of self-efficacy that are supported with evidence.

9. Overt articulation of change, including past misunderstandings and reasonable current understandings, changes in perspective, or descriptions of active efforts to change and the process of change (but not jargonized pseudoreflections).

10. Credible evidence of change in the way speakers live their lives.

11.* An optimistic outlook in which the past is acknowledged, but the future is seen to hold the potential to be different (but not magical thinking).

*These features are essential to the designation of reorganization.
+One of these must be included.

Many of these features are indicative of mental balance (B). Unlike a balanced B speaker, however, substantial discordance remains. Frequently, Grice's maxims of quantity (too much or too little), manner (in a distancing or involving manner), and relevance (omission of critical information or inclusion of trivial detail) are repeatedly violated. The maxim of quality, however, is rarely violated; that is, reorganizing speakers generally have evidence for what they say. In addition, proximal causes for events are often more clearly understood than enduring patterns of behavior or their psychological functions. Particularly, under the pressure of threatening events, the old strategy is used at least initially (even if the speaker catches and corrects it). Further, the basic Type A or Type C strategy still precludes the speaker from both retaining the important predictive information from past events and also letting go of that which is specific to those events.

Discourse Markers and Their Psychological Function

There is evidence of current use in the reorganizing transcript of the former pattern, together with at least partial or intermittent recognition of this fact. In most cases, however, the form of self-protective discourse is used more than its function; for example, run-on sentences may be used excessively, but the causal relations among the sentence elements are accurate. Thus, there is a failure to maintain the newer pattern but without the slips into defense that would reflect particularly serious or pervasive disorders of thought or feeling. There is also some level of unresolved incoherence, but the speaker seems to be progressively reducing this. Indeed, many reorganizing speakers indicate that they will probably continue to think about the topics discussed in the interview.

Procedural and imaged memory are more closely associated with ongoing use of the defense than are semantic or episodic memory. Put another way, with the luxury of time for reflection, reorganizing speakers are able to engage productively in cortical analysis of information. But when threatened in the old ways, procedural or imaged information triggers premature, self-protective, defensive responses. Care should be taken, therefore, when evaluating semantic and integrative statements to confirm that they (a) address what has been said by the speaker in the interview, (b) do not merely state universal truths, but rather, tie conclusions directly to the speaker's unique experience, and (c) correct the distortion inherent in the speaker's original strategy. Thus, if the speaker was Type A, the integrative conclusions must attribute some responsibility to the parents, be forgiving of the self, and not dismiss the impact of events on the self. Conversely, if the speaker was Type C, the integrative conclusions must assign some responsibility to the self, acknowledge good aspects of the parents' functioning, and accentuate neither vulnerability nor invulnerability. In both cases, the speaker should be able to articulate the need for comfort in his or her childhood and accept it during the interview from the interviewer.

The most striking feature of the discourse of reorganizing speakers is their attention to discrepancy. When what they say is not consistent or psychologically sound, reorganizing speakers notice this and attend to its implications. All use reflective statements (Fonagy, Steele, et al., 1997). Many also use some metacognitive thought and there are few instances of pseudoreflections or failed metacognitions.

Experience/History

The experiences of reorganizing speakers support both the defensive pattern that is being reorganized and also provide some evidence of the conditions that facilitated reorganization. These can include the presence of an alternate and balanced attachment figure, a dramatic event (e.g., a death) that makes the former defense futile, simple distance (temporal or geographic) from past events and people that now makes self-initiated reorganization possible, or therapy.

PART III

FROM THEORY TO APPLICATION

Chapter 13

The Classificatory Process and Classificatory Guidelines

CLASSIFICATION OF AN ADULT ATTACHMENT INTERVIEW TRANSCRIPT IS a pattern-recognition task. Researchers and clinicians learning to classify AAI transcripts often feel overwhelmed by the detail to be learned and ask (quite futilely) if there isn't some single, sure indicator of the correct strategy. There isn't. Instead, there is a process that increases the probability that all the information will be considered and that discrepancies in the transcript and in the mind of the coder evaluating the transcript will be identified and consciously considered. Put another way, an incremental and concatenated process of mental consideration (and reconsideration) of information is used to examine speakers' mental process of using information. This process yields the best representation of the speaker's mental organization with regard to the protective or endangering aspects of relationships.

GENERAL ISSUES REGARDING CLASSIFICATION

Coding a Transcript

Every AAI should be read at least twice; some will need additional reading or at least a second review of specific sections (generally those involving danger). From the first reading, the coder learns important facts about the speaker's history, identifies the discourse style (dysfluencies of speech), and forms a cursory impression of the speaker's ability to organize information in an easily communicated form. In the second reading, one looks for discrepancies of thought. Knowing, as one does on the second reading, the entire history, the coder determines whether the speaker presents the information logically, with foresight of what will follow, or whether the speaker slips, speaking at one moment as though the history were one way and, at a later point, changing the assumptions. These sorts of errors require knowledge of the whole transcript and, therefore, become most apparent on the second reading.

Throughout, the reader annotates the transcript, that is, "codes" it. The annotations reflect the constructs introduced in Chapter 4 and the specific discourse characteristics introduced in Chapters 5–12.

Overall, three steps are involved in reaching a final classification: (1) reading and interpreting the history, (2) identifying and comparing representations in different memory systems, and (3) evaluating the speaker's coherence and integrative ability. Each step depends on the others in a recursive, concatenating set of parallel and interactive processes that reflects the process of mental integration itself. A linear or quantitative approach to pattern recognition won't yield the correct classification.

Identifying Transformations of Information

INFORMATION, TRUTH, AND SAFETY

Information is uncertain. There is an external reality, but the sensory signals that make information about it available to our minds are:

- incomplete (i.e., there is missing information),
- ambiguous (i.e., the information can be interpreted in more than one way),
- irrelevant (i.e., there is distracting, meaningless information), and
- misleading (i.e., the information seems to mean one thing when, in reality, it means another).

Thus, the mind cannot simply extract the true information from the environment. To the contrary, it must apply mental processes to the array of sensory stimuli to construct a representation of reality. This involves constructing multiple dispositional representations (DRs), each consisting of a unique neurological pathway. The alternative representations can be compared cortically. Representations with lower probabilities of being accurate are combined or eliminated until one representation, the one with the highest probability of being true, is accepted and acted upon.

A critical issue, however, is the meaning of "true." As used here, representations are accepted or eliminated to the extent that they are believed to be truly predictive of future danger or safety (or reproductive opportunity). Thus, a veridical representation of external reality in the past might be irrelevant to prediction of future danger or safety. In this case, the "true" past representation might be eliminated in favor of a distorted DR that is more truly predictive of future danger and safety. This distinction underlies the difference between the balanced (B) representations and the distorted (i.e., self-protective) Type A and C representations. Each representation functions to predict future danger and safety, given some history of experienced danger and safety.

Coders attempt to identify the distortions in the speaker's representations. Speakers, on the other hand, try to keep both themselves and the interviewer unaware of the transformations. To do so they use ambiguity, omissions, irrelevancies, falsifications, denial, and occasionally delusions. Moments of dysfluence in speakers' discourse indicate times when information may have undergone self-protective transformation.

Put metaphorically, asking speakers who have been endangered to respond to the questions in the AAI is like asking them to go waltzing through a minefield. Their knowledge of the locations of the mines and their expertise at avoiding them while continuing to dance are evident in the difficulty that coders have in identifying the flaws in the discourse. Because the mind is always seeking discrepancy and coherence, the distortions function to reduce discrepancy and increase the appearance of coherence. The speakers' representations of reality and their mental processes for maintaining and implementing these representations are, indeed, self-protective.

USING DISCOURSE MARKERS TO IDENTIFY TRANSFORMATIONS OF INFORMATION

Discourse markers indicate points where discrepant information may be found, where the tongue or mind has stumbled and lost coherence. Dysfluencies are analyzed for evidence of transformation; this is particularly important around the topics of danger versus safety and comfort versus negative affect.

The DMM approach emphasizes the *function* of the dysfluency more than its morphology. Put another way, when too much emphasis is put on the presence of discourse markers, the morphology of discourse may be substituted for its psychology. Thus, although the DMM method is generally consistent with Main and Goldwyn's (1984, 1994) interpretation of the meaning of particular discourse markers, it differs when one morphology can serve different functions, for example, dismissing the self (Type A) versus dismissing others (Type C). Where there is ambiguity, the best support for any particular interpretation lies in the *patterning* of the full array of discourse markers.

The DMM method involves the search for places in the discourse where information is discordant and possibly transformed. If there is no transformation (e.g., a simple restart), neither Type A nor C is implied. On the other hand, if the dysfluency involves a transformation and, especially, if it occurs in an endangering context, it is particularly important. It is annotated and reviewed with other annotations to understand how the speaker represents reality and protects the self. When the danger is mild and attachment figures were supportive, the Ainsworth patterns are generally applicable. When the danger is severe and the individual was unprotected or felt unprotected (i.e., survival was at risk or felt at risk), the DMM strategies often fit better. Evidence of transformation, in turn, instigates reconsideration of the history.

INTERPRETING AND USING THE HISTORY IN THE PROCESS OF CLASSIFICATION

History does not determine classification. That is, no event or combination of events determines how individuals will organize their mental processes or behavior. Knowing aspects of the history is essential, however, to identifying self-protective processes and evaluating the psychological coherence of the narrative. To be psychologically coherent, speakers must be able to explain the developmental process by which their childhood experiences coalesced into their adult personality. Particularly when the experiences were self-threatening and speakers appear or claim to be largely without distortion, they must show us how they achieved mental and behavioral balance.

A common error is to confuse historical information with current functioning. For example, some speakers describe themselves as caregivers who took care of their parents. To be classified as A3 in the AAI, however, they must act now, in the discourse, like caregivers. That is, they must use general Type A discourse markers (e.g., distancing and minimizing of self) and specific A3 markers (e.g., exoneration of the parents, taking the interviewer's perspective) *in* the AAI. Consequently, it is not sufficient to report having acted like a caregiver as a child. To the contrary, such reports are often made by speakers using Type C discourse markers and taking their own perspectives of having been misused and denied appropriate caregiving.

Similarly, reporting that one is always alone is insufficient for the A6 classification. There must be the general discourse markers of the Type A strategy as well as the specific markers of A6 (e.g., a minimization of the importance of being alone, evidence of having been alone, assertion of self-competence that enables the self to manage being alone, and exoneration of the rejecting parent). Confusion can result when Type C speakers *complain* repeatedly of being alone but use preoccupying discourse markers and give historical evidence of not being alone or rejected. This is not evidence of A6 because it is spoken with the discourse of a Type C speaker.

Likewise, historical evidence of having had false cognition used against the self by attachment figures is not evidence that the speaker now functions as a C5–8. Evidence that the speaker used false cognition in the past is more relevant but still insufficient. The critical evidence is (a) Type C discourse, (b) evidence of having used false cognition without acknowledging it, and (c) false cognition used to mislead the interviewer. The last is the clearest and most definitive evidence.

To conclude, the coder must reconstruct the speaker's history. Without some notion of what happened to the speaker developmentally, it will be difficult to evaluate the speaker's interpretation of the events. Instances of danger, sexuality, triangulation, and deception are especially important because they indicate an elevated probability of distorted information processing and high-numbered strategies with lack of resolution and modifiers. Of course, speakers do not necessarily relate histories with veridical accuracy. To understand how the speaker perceives his or her experience, the discourse must be examined to identify and attribute meaning to dysfluencies.

COMPARING DISPOSITIONAL REPRESENTATIONS IN DIFFERENT MEMORY SYSTEMS

Memory systems are probed systematically by specific sets of questions. Evaluation of these and of the suitability of the speaker's responses can be used to ascertain how speakers manage classes of information that reflect different sorts of mental processing. Does the speaker access the appropriate memory system when the probe is clear and properly directive? Alternatively, which memory system does the speaker offer when the probe is open ended or when not accessing the probed memory system? The first question permits the coder to ascertain whether the speaker has access to all memory systems and the second reflects the speaker's preferred source of DRs.

In the sections below, we go through the AAI sequentially and describe how meaning is derived from the various sections of the interview.

Orientation to the Childhood Family

The opening question of the AAI asks the speaker to orient the interviewer to the speaker's family situation in early childhood. This is the speaker's first opportunity to frame his or her experience as a child. It is also an opportunity to demonstrate a willingness to participate cooperatively with the interviewer in the process of examining the past. Finally, a successful first response requires that the speaker think ahead to what he or she is likely to say and take the interviewer's perspective so as to identify what the interviewer needs to know before the story is begun. This is, in other words, the speaker's opportunity to demonstrate psychological integration. Failure to think ahead or to take the interviewer's perspective will result in too little, too much, or inappropriate information.

The content of the opening statement should be considered in terms of (a) the completeness of the answer, (b) its relevance to the question, (c) the logic of the order of its presentation, and (d) dysfluencies accompanying its presentation. After the entire interview has been read and evaluated, the initial response should be reconsidered in terms of its quality, given the history that actually follows.

Type B strategy

Balanced speakers tend to provide basic information regarding who was in the family, what the parents did for a living, and where, generally, the family lived. They are unlikely to provide irrelevant details, like first and last names of family members, street names, and so forth, or to give excessive detail about one person or period of life while ignoring others. Instead balanced speakers offer a general overview from their own perspectives, that is, they place themselves at the center of their stories. In addition to the facts, balanced speakers often provide some feeling about what it was like to grow up in their family and seem pleased to have listeners for their tales. Finally, they show good perspective-taking by not presuming that the interviewer knows things that are, in fact, unknown to the interviewer and by clarifying reasonable misinterpretations that the interviewer might make.

TYPE A STRATEGY

Type A speakers tend to be brief, to give only essential facts, and to give no "flavor" of their family experiences. In addition, they give no evidence of being pleased to talk about themselves and their families. Instead, information is offered in the way that one might fill out a demographic questionnaire—without complete sentences or descriptive information. A more loquacious Type A speaker might speak at length about trivial and impersonal details, for example, a full catalogue of where the family lived with little attention to the family, or a long discussion of the father's jobs with little discussion of other family members or of relationships. The function of this is to comply with the interviewer's request while still keeping the focus off relationships.

TYPE C STRATEGY

Type C speakers seem confused about what should be said. They often start in the middle, as though the interviewer already had basic information, and often focus on trivial and irrelevant details. Put more conceptually, Type C speakers seem unable to differentiate generalized information from supporting detail; all information is treated as equally important and relevant. In addition, Type C speakers often blurt out family problems that the more balanced speaker would introduce only later (after a relationship has been established with the interviewer and after basic information about the context of the problems has been presented). Type C speakers also tend to be confusing in the ordering or articulation of their experience; they jump around in time and provide contradictory information (e.g., "*We were four children . . . all three of us . . .*"). Simple things like who was in the family, the order of the children's birth, or the place of the speaker in the sibling order may be unclear and, often, are not readily clarified.

The reader should use the information in the introductory response to form an initial hypothesis regarding the classification of the interview and should also note carefully information that does *not* fit this hypothesis. Based on this hypothesis, expectations can be formulated regarding how the speaker will respond to the next questions. These expectations are tested when reading the next sections of the interview. At this point, the hypothesis is based on very little information. Its function is to enable one to critically examine information and to create little hypotheses that can be "tested" with further reading. To be useful, it must be treated as a working hypothesis, open to change and revision. It is not important whether the initial hypothesis is correct or not. It does matter that it is continually tested against new information and revised as needed. The final hypothesis should be both parsimonious and also account for as much of the information as possible. Ill-fitting information should be highlighted, not brushed aside.

Evaluating Images

Imaged memory can be informative regarding how the speaker uses affect. The question about the earliest memory provides a good opportunity to evaluate imaged memory. When a speaker does not recall an early memory or when the memory that he or she offers has no sensory qualities, there is the possibility that the speaker omits affect from processing (i.e., Type A).

When an early and imaged memory is recalled, it can be examined for its affective quality. Sometimes, but not always, this memory is informative regarding dominant feeling states and associated safe or dangerous contexts.

To interpret the set of images provided throughout the interview, the coder should note in the margin the presence of images. On a rereading of the transcript, the images should be reviewed as a group. Do they tend to reflect a single feeling state or are a variety of affects imaged? Is there variation in the sensory modality that is imaged? How are the images used? For example, do they substitute for other forms of communication (e.g., semantic statements or episodes)? Are they associated with people (suggesting Type B) or do they substitute for people from whom the speaker is estranged or of whom he or she is afraid (suggesting Type A or Type C)? Are they used illustratively to bring life to a story, a place, or a person, and are they embedded in a temporal, episodic context (Type B)? Or are the images themselves the motivation for behavior, that is, do they "live" and "act" independently (compulsive or obsessive)? Are they lively and fresh (Type B), stereotyped (Type A), or static and recurring (Type C)?

The answers to these questions assist one in interpreting the meaning embedded in the speaker's use of images. For example, Type A speakers might use images to represent denied anger or desired safety. Type C speakers might use images to keep anger and resentment from the past as actively experienced feelings in the present.

The Relationship with the Parents

Coders should consider whether the speaker can focus on the *relationship with* the parents or only on the *characteristics of* the parents. In addition, it is important to note whether the two parents are differentiated. Finally, the coder should note whether a generalized statement is offered and how realistic it sounds. Some speakers, particularly those who are Type A, describe the relationship or parents in terms that are too positive to reflect ordinary people. Other speakers, particularly those who are Type C, find it difficult to provide generalized, semantic, descriptors or provide unrelentingly negative descriptors.

This information can be compared to that gained from the initial response and used to modify the working hypothesis accordingly. Any discrepant information should be identified and marked clearly.

Five Descriptive Words (or Phrases)

The five descriptive words (or phrases) that characterize the relationship, first, with the mother and, later, with the father, represent probes of the speaker's *semantic* memory.

TYPE A RESPONSES

If the descriptive words are too good to be true, the speaker may be *idealizing* the relationship. Determining this, however, will depend upon the support offered for each word (see below). In general, the more positive the semantic description (for example, *"very close"* versus *"fairly close"*), the greater the obligation to provide unequivocal validating evidence. Thus "fairly close" requires only some evidence of some kind of closeness (in a relationship that may have some distance as well) whereas "very close" requires clear, direct, and not contradicted evidence of closeness.

The coder should also consider whether the picture offered by the five descriptors, considered together, is reasonable and balanced, that is, is it psychologically sound? Because every relationship has some drawbacks or limitations, there should be some words that refer to un-comfortable aspects of the relationship. Idealization functions to di-chotomize the relationship into good and bad aspects and to emphasize only one of these: the good parent or the bad self.

In addition, the descriptive words should be varied. Five words that mean the same thing are not indicative of a thoughtful stance with re-gard to the relationship. Compulsive speakers tend to select words that reflect problems in the relationship, but these are presented from the attachment figure's point of view. Thus, they retain the information about danger, but they remove the self and exonerate the parent.

Type B responses

A more balanced approach is to realize that no relationship (or person) is either perfect or entirely without redeeming value and, thus, a bal-anced speaker will describe relationships with parents in a complex, varied, and integrated manner. The descriptive words provide a coher-ent, balanced, and psychologically sound description of the relation-ship that "hangs together." Needless to say, the relationship does not have to be a "good" or "secure" relationship.

Type C responses

Some speakers find it very difficult to articulate the characteristics of the relationship. Sometimes, the speaker oscillates between two alter-natives as though they were mutually exclusive, whereas, in other cases, the speaker finds it difficult to think of descriptive words. Both situations suggest limited access to semantic memory and are frequent among Type C speakers who often say that they *"can't remember."* (The latter situation should not be confused with lack of recall of *episodic* memory that is associated with Type A.)

Like compulsive speakers, obsessive speakers retain information about the problems in the relationship, but, unlike compulsive speak-ers, they blame the parent. When the words are too terrible to be true, the speaker may be derogating the parent. In the DMM, derogation is indicative of a Type C strategy. Type A and C speakers are similar, how-ever, in dichotomizing reality into stark positive and negative features and associating these with different people.

In summary, the coder should ask whether the individual has access to semantic memory. Is it distorted? How much? Is the speaker aware of the distortion? Can he or she explain the reason for the distortion?

Finally, the information derived from the descriptive words should be considered in the light of prior information and hypotheses. Ambiguities and discrepancies should be noted.

Examining the Episodes Used to Validate the Descriptive Words

THE INTERVIEWER'S QUESTIONS

The probes of episodic memory should ask for a memory of a specific instance or occasion when the relationship fit the selected word or phrase. (When the probe is poorly constructed, the speaker cannot be held responsible for supplying a proper episode.) The responses constitute episodic evidence that can be used to validate the semantic representation. In some cases, an interviewer who does not understand the intent and process of the AAI asks, "*Why* did you choose _____?" Because the word "why" calls for an integrative response, it should *not* be used at this point in the interview.

THE RELEVANCE OF THE RESPONSE

Assuming an appropriate probe has been provided, the response can be examined. Is it relevant to the word or phrase? That is, can the evidence in it be used to confirm or refute the word or phrase? If so, it is a likely Type A or Type B episode. If not, it is potentially indicative of a Type C strategy.

CREDIBLE EVIDENCE

Does the episode provide credible evidence? That is, does the nature of the response indicate that the speaker is actually accessing episodic memory and reporting on something specific that is recalled? Credible evidence has five characteristics: (a) it occurs at a specific time and place, (b) it is unique to the speaker (i.e., it is not a common experience for most children or would not be told this way by other people); (c) it contains temporal order or contains images or evocative language specific to the situation (phrases that are common in the culture are not to be treated as personal images or evocative language); (d) it is offered spontaneously (i.e., details that must be dragged out of the speaker are treated with greater skepticism than details that are offered spontaneously); and (e) it is self-relevant.

TYPE B

Coders should consider whether the episodes actually support the descriptive words. Balanced speakers organize their presentation of the episode in three parts as (a) a generalization referring to the word, followed by (b) a supporting story, and closed with (c) a summation in terms of the word. Although it is not always used by balanced speakers, when this "perfect" form is used it is strong evidence of coherent thought.

As always, dysfluencies are important. Does the speaker omit or distort information? Among balanced speakers, dysfluencies highlight emotionally important moments, but information is not lost or distorted.

Balanced episodes have both temporal and causal order as well as the language that is lively and connotative, employing sensory images to convey meaning. Particularly clear evidence that affect has been integrated with cognition is reflected in episodes that combine temporal order with lively images.

TYPE A

Many Type A speakers claim that they cannot remember any episodes. Sometimes they construct hypothetical "episodes" by reasoning, from semantic memory, what would have happened if the parent had fit the descriptive word; of course, the speaker is not consciously aware of the constructed quality of his or her answer. Words like *"probably," "certainly," "must have,"* and *"would have"* suggest hypothetical episodes. In other cases, the episodes contradict the positive words without the speaker seeming aware of this. Alternatively, the speaker may cut off the negative conclusion of the episode or conclude inaccurately that the story provided evidence of the positive semantic description.

TYPE C

The episodes used by Type C speakers often seem only tangentially related to the descriptive words. An episode may take on a life of its own as the speaker's focus becomes more the story itself (and associations within the story) than its evidence in support of the descriptive word. In the clearest cases, the answer wanders far from the interviewer's question, slipping from one partial episode to another without conclusion and without awareness of the focus of the question. The "logic" holding the array of stories together is the underlying affective content of the stories. Temporal and causal logic, on the other hand, are absent, confused, or in error.

For all types of speakers, careful annotation is essential in enabling the coder to determine what information is missing and what distortions of information have been used. Based on this, each episode is described as noted in Chapters 5–12 (e.g., parental perspective, credible evidence, blurred).

Examining the Episodes Elicited by Probes of Threatening Experiences

The AAI employs two strategies for retrieving episodic information. The first is a semantic retrieval strategy in which the semantic words are used as stimuli to access episodic memory. When the speaker has good access to both memory systems (as balanced speakers tend to have), this approach works well. But when semantic memory is itself a "weak" memory system, its limitations may interfere with episodic recall. This often happens with Type C speakers. They first have difficulty identifying five descriptive words and, then, when asked for corresponding episodes, they announce that they *"can't remember."* This should not be interpreted as lack of episodic memory if (a) they had difficulty identifying five descriptive words, (b) they spontaneously offer episodes (or episodic fragments) at other points in the transcript, (c) they have access to negative episodes when probed directly, and (d) indicators of Type C discourse are present.

The second strategy for accessing episodic memory is using direct probes for negative and threatening episodes (i.e., when the speaker was hurt, sick, distressed, or angry). Speakers who respond more fully to direct probes of episodic memory than to the semantic "five-word" probes tend to use a Type C strategy. They have access to episodic memory but not when semantic memory must be accessed to retrieve episodes.

Type A speakers respond to the two sets of questions in the opposite manner. They tend to provide more and fuller episodes to fit the words that they have selected (often positive words) than to episodes of threatening experiences. In addition, they often fail to recall, or even deny having experienced, the negative conditions. Comparison of these two retrieval strategies can help to differentiate Type C and Type A speakers.

In summary, the coder should ask whether the speaker has access to episodic memory. Is it distorted? How much? Is the speaker aware of the distortion? Can he or she explain the reason for the distortion?

Resolution of Trauma and Loss

The specific probes of danger and loss in the George et al. (1996) interview have been expanded in the modified DMM interview to include a wider range of dangers, including nonfamilial and sexual dangers. Nevertheless, wherever information about danger occurs, it should be treated as critically important to identifying the speaker's mental processes.

There are several possibilities regarding the relation between the low and high danger portions of the interview. There can be little evidence of transformation of information anywhere (although there is likely to be dysfluence around danger). There can be an intensification of the basic self-protective strategy or a change in the response to severe danger as compared to ordinary events. In some cases, this is a reversal of strategy whereas in others it is a different form of response. For example, a Type A speaker may demonstrate intense preoccupation around a specific recent danger or a Type C speaker may deny the importance of the most dangerous of his or her experiences. Changes in response indicate more traumatization than simple intensification of the basic strategy.

The coder should examine carefully the discourse around all instances of threat, including both loss and danger. It is particularly important, on the second reading, to be certain that errors of thought are not made prior to the introduction of the danger or loss, for example, is a parent introduced in the present tense and then, much later, found to be deceased? Evidence of both dismissal and preoccupation is important. When there are severe inaccuracies around danger, they are noted with the designation of "Ul" or "Utr." The type of lack of resolution (e.g., displaced, anticipated) may or may not correspond to the speaker's basic strategy, but, in all cases of U, it does not resolve the threat psychologically. This means that the speaker's response does not properly set in the past that which was unique to the endangering experience and carry forward that which could be helpful in the future.

The coder should consider the possible losses and dangers. Are they of attachment figures or were the attachment functions of protection and comfort disrupted? Figures whose loss did not create danger to the speaker are not properly the basis for lack of resolution. Is there anything irrational about the discourse or thinking about these events? Does it affect other parts of the transcript (beyond the direct probes of loss or danger). The more pervasive the omissions and inclusions, the more likely the assignment of lack of resolution will be. If the information is only present when directly probed and not included elsewhere, it must be clearly irrational to result in U. Even then, however, it is a "contained" lack of resolution. If it is omitted or included inappropriately throughout the transcript, it needs to be less explicitly irrational to result in an assignment of U; such lack of resolution is considered "uncontained."

Procedural Functioning

Procedural memory is assessed throughout the AAI in three ways: in preconscious dysfluencies in the discourse, in expression of affect, and in the relationship with the interviewer. Analysis of each of these clarifies the classification.

DYSFLUENCE

Dysfluencies of discourse, particularly those involving self-protective transformations of information, are procedural indicators of the speaker's defensive strategy. Dysfluencies should be marked throughout the text. Their interpretation has been discussed in previous chapters.

EXPRESSION OF AFFECT

Affect occurs spontaneously when people speak with each other. Often this appears parenthetically in the AAI as notations about the speaker's affective display. These notations can be evaluated for tone, function, and appropriateness. When positive affect (e.g., laughter) is noted while the speaker discusses difficult topics, anxiety may be interpreted. When such positive affect occurs while the speaker denies sad, angry, or frightening events in the discourse, false positive affect may be interpreted. Both of these uses of affect are consistent with a Type A strategy. Appropriate affect is likely among balanced speakers whereas Type C speakers may show open anxiety, anger, or fearfulness or, in higher numbered classifications, positive affect at others' discomfort. Attention should be paid to somatic expressions of affect because they often suggest the presence of a modifier.

RELATIONSHIP WITH THE INTERVIEWER

The way that the speaker responds to the interviewer can be very informative. When the speaker is cooperative and engages in an open-ended exploration of the speaker's childhood relationships, there is evidence that the speaker trusts the interviewer and expects a supportive listener. Such a dispositional representation is typical of *Type B speakers*. When the speaker is reticent to discuss emotional relationships and provides an overly positive picture, there is evidence of distrust and the expectation of approbation, censure, or rejection. Such expectations are typical of *Type A speakers*. Alternatively, when the speaker behaves as though he or she shared a confidential relationship with the interviewer, one in which the interviewer could read his or her mind and would serve as an ally against the parents, that representation is typical of the *Type C strategy*.

Other speakers display *compulsions* with regard to the interviewer (taking care of the interviewer, being excessively obedient or deferring excessively to the interviewer's perspective). Others may *obsessively* threaten, seduce, or mislead the interviewer. These procedural responses are indicative of A3–8 and C3–8, respectively.

Seeking Evidence of Patterns of Sexuality and Attachment

The Main and Goldwyn (1994) method does not focus on sexuality and George et al.'s AAI (1996) does not contain questions about sexuality. In most cases, therefore, speakers do not discuss sexual issues. Consequently, when such issues are brought up, they may be presumed to have special meaning. Indeed, references to sexuality, sexual images, or episodes involving sex or the possibility of sex occur with greater than random frequency in the interviews of people in psychotherapy. Sexual allusions should be noted throughout the AAI and, when found, patterns of meaning should be explored. When questions about sexuality are asked in the modified DMM version of the AAI, the speaker's ability to address this directly or only as a pattern of innuendo can be examined. Early or inappropriate intrusion of sexual material is often indicative of an A5, a C5–6, or a higher classification.

Evaluating Integration

The closing questions of the interview are especially powerful at identifying mental coherence, the hallmark of Type B. They present an opportunity for speakers who are somewhat dysfluent because they would prefer not to look closely at family situations in order to rise above this tendency and demonstrate that they have a sound understanding of their experiences. In particular, the integrative questions permit speakers to consider alternative perspectives, the motivations underlying behavior, and the implications of their childhood experiences for adult life (personality, selection of a partner, and the rearing of children). Thus, the integrative questions provide the thoughtful speaker with an opportunity to clarify errors made in unthinking ways during the early portions of the transcript.

TYPE B

For speakers to be considered *balanced*, the answers to the integrative questions must be psychologically sound and consistent with the rest of the interview. Further, speakers must have access to untransformed imaged, semantic, and episodic information or be able to identify and correct significant transformations. However, procedural behavior is crucial. That is, in the contemplative environment of the interview, some speakers will be able to function better than in the pressure of living relationships, whereas others will say all the right things in general but be unable to engage in a balanced way.

Coders should consider whether speakers (a) understand with reasonable accuracy the roles of both temporal predictability and feelings in motivating behavior, (b) identify the probable effects of experiences on themselves, (c) have some understanding of their parents' situation and some compassion for them (but without self-denying exoneration), and (d) use the information gleaned from their childhood experiences to guide their adult behavior. Balanced speakers should offer acceptable (although not necessarily profound) answers to each of these topics. Further, information of various sorts and about different relationships should be integrated into one representation that is hierarchical, with regard to relationship, and conditional, with regard to behavior under specific conditions (Bowlby, 1980; Crittenden, 1990).

If his or her childhood experiences were felicitous, the balanced speaker's answers may be *naively* simple. If, however, childhood presented substantial challenges, these must be dealt with in the integrative questions. Thus, the speaker with a difficult history cannot offer simple platitudes or unrealistic dreams. To the contrary, such a speaker both has the obligation to give solid evidence of integration and also the opportunity to display an *earned* awareness of the sometimes dangerous ambiguity of reality and the need for defensive processes.

Particularly when speakers use self-protective processes during the early portions of the interview and then show some substantial, but incomplete, evidence of understanding of their situation during the closing sections of the interview, they may best be considered *reorganizing* toward B. A key to identifying reorganization is that the interview concludes in a manner that leaves the defensive process intact with reference to current functioning. For example, a formerly compulsive caregiving speaker who (a) used self-dismissing discourse with A3 markers, (b) described herself knowingly, in the integrative questions, as a caregiver and identified the need to center on her own perspective, but (c) concluded the interview by talking about delaying a major life decision until her mother was ready for it would be considered reorganizing toward B (rather than an earned B).

Type A

Some speakers respond to the integrative questions by (a) asserting that their experiences had few effects on themselves, (b) showing little interest in their parents' experiences or motivations (for A1–2) or exonerating the parent of responsibility for their behavior (A+), and (c) maintaining self-protective strategies during the interview. Any attempts at self-reflection are cut off with changes of topic or platitudes. This suggests that two incompatible representations of attachment figures exist in the mind of the speaker: a "good" representation that is consciously presented by the speaker and a "bad" representation that is kept out of consciousness because acknowledgment of it would threaten the speaker's relationship with the attachment figure (Main et al., 2003).

Type C

Other speakers are unable to view their experiences from a moderate distance, instead getting caught up in details and in wishful thinking or impossible demands. That is, they make their future satisfaction contingent upon things that are beyond their control, thereby carrying past problems into the future. Type C speakers often shift among more than one DR without recognizing the presence of others or they may confuse representations of different relationships.

MISLEADING RESPONSES TO THE INTEGRATIVE QUESTIONS

Coders should be wary of apparently balanced and wise answers to the integrative questions that (a) do not address substantially less integrated responses made earlier in the interview and (b) reflect the world as it "should" be. The latter often echoes what teachers, parents, or therapists said. The question about selecting a partner is particularly good for exploring whether the ideas offered reflect the speaker's integration or merely the repetition of others' answers because the question has rarely been addressed in prior discussions.

The coder should ask whether the speaker can integrate procedural, imaged, semantic, connotative, and episodic information. Does the integration make psychological sense? Does it yield new information, that is, is the sum greater than the parts? Does this process occur during the interview?

REACHING A CLASSIFICATION

Once the annotation is complete, the interview should be considered as a whole. We offer two perspectives.

Grice's Maxims

The now-familiar discourse can be evaluated in terms of Grice's four maxims (1975) regarding coherent speech: quantity, quality, manner, and relevance. Violations of these maxims should be noted and considered in terms of the topic that produced the violation. When the speaker is aware of not being fully coherent and warns the interviewer or seeks mutual agreement that a temporary violation be sustained, the violation should not be treated as detracting from coherence—presuming that the speaker ultimately becomes coherent about the topic. Awareness that one cannot be fully coherent in spite of clear effort to consider the issue is often a sign of the process of reorganization.

Although coherence should be evaluated throughout the transcript, the introductory questions provide a particularly informative context. The initial question is open ended, leaving to the speaker the opportunity to decide what constitutes a sufficient and useful answer. The next questions are often follow-up questions that ask for very specific information. Speakers who find it difficult to discuss relationships often provide too-brief responses to the open-ended question and curt responses to the factual follow-up questions. On the other hand, speakers who find it hard to focus their thoughts wander at excessive length including irrelevant detail throughout the open-ended questions and respond to the closed, fact-eliciting follow-up questions in the same overwhelming manner. Because these responses occur at the beginning of the interview before the interviewer could have influenced the speaker greatly, because difficult experiences have not yet been addressed (and, therefore, do not require self-protective responses), and because the content of the response is under the speaker's control, the initial responses can be very informative regarding the speaker's coherence of mind.

The Comparative Method of Classification

Main and Goldwyn's (1984, 1994) classificatory method is based on two comparisons. These are drawn from Bowlby's chapter on information processing (1980) in which semantic memory and episodic memory are contrasted and Grice's work in theater in which the close-up and distant perspectives are compared (Grice, 1975). In addition, one might also ask whether the speaker and coder agree about the speaker's experience and psychological processes, whether cognitive or affective probes function more efficiently for the speaker, and whether speech is substantively transformed when the content refers to threat or danger.

The underlying function of these comparisons is to focus the coder's attention on identifying and comparing *true* and *transformed* information. When these comparisons yield a consistent picture of the speaker's attachment experience, it is likely that the transcript will be classified as Type B. When there are significant discrepancies, it is likely that the interview will be classified as Type A or Type C.

Classifying the Transcript

It is important to remember that classification using the AAI generates an approximation of the speaker's psychological functioning based on a sample of verbal behavior derived from an interview. Error, therefore, can be generated at two points: between the "true" classification of the transcript and the one that the coder assigns and between the "true" psychological process of the speaker and the sample of it in the interview. Thus, the *transcript* is assigned to a classification and this permits attributions about the functioning of the speaker. It is not accurate, therefore, to say that the speaker "is" Type A, B, or C. The accurate phrasing is that the transcript was "assigned to" a specific strategy. Further attributions of meaning are just that: attributions. This is, of course, true of almost all psychological assessments (e.g., I.Q. tests, personality measures), but in common usage, this point is not often remembered.

Few transcripts are pure examples of their classification. Indeed, there may be a scattering of responses that suggest more than one pattern. The strategy selected should be *the strategy for coping with dangerous circumstances*. This strategy should be displayed in at least three of the six memory systems, several times and in several places. If the highest strategy to occur at any single point in the transcript were not used for dangerous circumstances, it would not generally be included in the final classification. Instead, the strategy (or strategies) used for danger would appear in the final classification.

The classification should be kept as simple as possible with inclusion of only those elements that are necessary to understand the speaker's functioning. *Simple classifications* are those in which the transcript is assigned to a single group selected directly from Figure 1.1. *Combined classifications* have both a Type A and a Type C component (e.g., A1/C2 or A3/C3). Whenever possible, the specific pattern should be designated; at a minimum, the distinction between the Ainsworth-based strategies and the compulsive and obsessive strategies of the DMM method should be made. *Multiple group classifications* can be used, especially when they are assigned to specific attachment figures (e.g., $A1_MA4_F$ or $C3_MC4_F$). In general, lower numbered patterns that are in the same major strategy as the modal strategy do not need to be listed. When strategies are *failing*, the classification may indicate lack of resolution of loss or trauma, or one of the modifiers, or both (e.g., Utr C1 or Dp A3). *Reorganizing classifications* should include reorganization, plus the classification from which the speaker appears to be moving with an arrow indicating the classification to which the speaker appears to be moving, for example, $R(A3 \rightarrow B1)$.

The most common misclassifications are between truly balanced speakers with difficult past histories and those who (a) use both Type A and C strategies (A/C), (b) integrate false affect and false cognition in a smooth, perpetually defensive strategy (i.e., AC), and (c) are depressed (Dp). Thus, the most balanced strategies are occasionally confused with the most distorted strategies.

In conclusion, the coder should remember that all information is imperfect and, ultimately, no source of information is without ambiguity. To reduce ambiguity, various sources of information must be compared. Recursive comparisons of information derived through different processes and vulnerable to various sorts of error provide the best possibility for reducing the error. This is true for humans who must construct representations of their past experiences to organize future behavior and it is true for coders who must construct representations of others' mental processes.

RELIABILITY

Mastery of the DMM method takes repeated practice, on a wide variety of transcripts, upon which one receives feedback regarding accuracy. For most people, 100 or so transcripts must be coded and classified before classification of both normative and clinical transcripts can be accomplished reliably.

Extent of reliability is calculated on the basis of a standardized reliability set. The tests are culture- and language-specific and include a wide range of strategies that reflect both normative and atypical organizations. Calculation of reliability is made separately for major strategy classification, pattern, the presence of modifiers, and the lack of resolution of trauma or loss. Different levels of reliability are appropriate for screening, coding, and forensic applications.

Reliability is subject to degradation over time; consequently, certificates of reliability have a defined duration, after which they must be renewed. The ways to maintain reliability include coding frequently with feedback, attending advanced AAI courses, and recoding important transcripts.

Aside from the loss of proficiency over time, there are other threats to reliability. Coding with less reliable coders lowers the skilled coder's accuracy, as does coding too many transcripts at one time or coding when tired. Working in small and cohesive coder groups tends to increase internal agreement but to lower external reliability. In addition, coding carried out over a long period of time without reliability checks can lead to "coder drift" of which the coder has no awareness. Coding similar assessments concurrently and coding with any kind of external information available reduce accuracy of classification. Further and quite disconcertingly, it would appear that there is no correlation between coders' confidence in their classifications and their actual accuracy. The risk is that false confidence, combined with interpersonal persuasiveness, will mislead other coders. Coders should be aware of these threats and make active efforts to prevent them.

PATTERNING AND PROCESS

We began this chapter by stating that coding attachment is a pattern-recognition task. We then pointed to the relevant information to gather and offered a process by which its meaning for the individual could be discovered. We repeatedly said that each bit of information and each part of the process of analysis interacted with other parts and that none was definitive in isolation.

The process of arriving at a classification is, we think, very dynamic. It has specifiable steps and constructs, and many examples of these could be offered. But a central point is that the examples are ultimately unique for each individual.

Humans are so limited! They can only do a few things psychologically and behaviorally. But with those few psychological processes and behavioral acts, they can build a near infinite world of interpersonal meaning. Humans are so gloriously variable that the same behaviors almost never recur twice. It is the contrast between what we have to work with and the wide array of combinations we can generate that makes any clustering of human behavior difficult.

Functional patterning is a means by which we can reduce the infinite variety of human behavior to workable subunits that enable us to carry information from previous experience to our current experience. We wish to close by emphasizing that no single bit of information determines the pattern. We can count the bits of data, but they do not yield predictability. The patterns do, but they are harder to identify reliably. The task requires a balance between recognition of the pattern and evidence to support the pattern (gut-level recognition that is not open to observable evidence is not sufficient). Using the memory systems approach, we can usually get near the pattern, but the pattern itself eludes a checklist or numerical approach. At this point, one must consider the function of the discourse—and implied self-protective strategy. Ultimately, we need pattern recognition with both evidence and function. This, of course, is where humans really shine: We are better at pattern recognition than any other species, including computers.

In the next chapter, we take the notion of functional patterning beyond assessment to consider how an assessment is connected to an individual's life, both in the family of origin and in the present. We also demonstrate how a functional formulation of attachment can assist clinicians to design helpful treatment in cases of psychological distress.

Chapter 14

But What Shall I Do?

*Transforming an AAI Classification
Into a Plan for Treatment*

RESEARCHERS ARE HAPPY WITH A RELIABLE CLASSIFICATION, BUT NOT SO psychotherapists and others who must guide troubled individuals and their families. They need an action plan. In this chapter we describe how one uses an AAI classification, combined with information about the history and current functioning of the speaker and his or her family, to derive a *functional formulation*. The functional formulation is the professional's dispositional representation (DR) of the relation between the service structure and the individual in his or her relationships. Like all DRs, a functional formulation is dynamic; it is always changing as new information is integrated into the existing set of information.

This might suggest that functional formulations are too amorphous to be written down, but actually it is quite the contrary. Without a written formulation, the treatment is likely to be amorphous and possibly also inefficient and ineffective. We describe how to derive functional formulations that can guide treatment both at its onset and, with feedback and updating, across the course of treatment.

The raw materials for this reflective, integrative process are (a) the transcript itself, in terms of its content and patterning of discourse (or the behavioral, information processing, and strategic aspects of attachment) and (b) the classification of the transcript compared with (c) the context of the speaker's life. That is, functional formulation consists of a move from the dyadic conversational system of the AAI to larger systems in which the speaker actually lives.

In the next sections, we first consider the meaning of the classification, working in reverse from the general state of adaptation (the modifiers) through sporadic loss of adaption (the unresolved traumas and losses) back to the basic self-protective strategy. Then we describe combining the AAI information with information from the history to create a functional formulation. Next the formulation is used to derive a preliminary treatment plan. We close with a case example.

ADAPTIVE AND NONADAPTIVE
STATES OF STRATEGIES

An AAI classification has several components. In all cases, there is a basic strategy, expressed as a classification or a combination of classifications. In some cases, there are unresolved traumas or losses. In a few cases, there are one or more modifiers. Some combinations of modifier, unresolved trauma and loss, and basic strategy occur more frequently and are theoretically more meaningful than others. Therefore, certain patterns of these components are expected, while others tend to be quite unusual and unexpected. Experienced AAI coders look for expected patterns and pay close attention when they encounter unexpected combinations.

Modifiers

The first step in the functional analysis of an AAI is to consider whether there is a *modifier* to the basic strategy. The presence or absence of a modifier suggests how adapted an individual is to his or her current circumstances. If the basic strategy is not modified, the individual is likely to be functioning with at least minimal adequacy in the present circumstances. The presence of a modifier suggests that the basic strategy is not fitting well and professional help may be required.

DEPRESSION AND DISORIENTATION

The presence of a depressed or disoriented modifier (the two are usually mutually exclusive) means that the basic strategy has been ill-fitting for enough time that the speaker has come to expect its usual effect. Consequently, the speaker has down- or up-regulated arousal. Depression indicates that the speaker is aware of the futility of the strategy (and down-regulates arousal) whereas disorientation indicates that the speaker is anxious to select an effective strategy and does not know how to do that (and up-regulates arousal). The presence of a modifier suggests that risk is already evident in maladaptive behavior, distress, or clinically relevant behaviors, in either the speaker or in attached persons.

INTRUSIONS

Intrusions of forbidden negative affect ([ina]) are only found in speakers who have a compulsive A strategic component, very often modified by depression. Sometimes there is no evidence of such intrusions during the interview itself, but the recalled episodes contain suggestions of past intrusions (which can be noted in the classification as [ina]$_h$). Intrusions of forbidden negative affect can actually promote adaptation for a speaker whose interpersonal strategy is ineffective. This can occur either at the physiological level of arousal by temporarily reversing excessively low arousal or at the extrafamilial community level by precipitating professional intervention, for example, medication, psychological treatment, hospitalization, and detention or other forms of externally imposed restraint. Individuals who have intrusions often experience them as being external to themselves and are perplexed about their origin. Sometimes their state of psychological disarray is "resolved" by delusional explanations for the events.

Expressed somatic symptoms ([ess]) can also be expressed in an AAI. These can occur in any high-numbered strategy (A+, C+, A+/C+) and function to disrupt the interview process by redirecting attention from psychological and interpersonal issues to the physical state and comfort of the speaker. That is, [ess] deflect attention away from the content and meaning of the interview. Often somatic symptoms represent information that preceded verbal awareness, denied information, or information about which there is irresolvable conflict. Although the coding of

[ess] entered the DMM method more recently than other constructs described here, nevertheless it appears that the combination of inexplicit meaning and strongly expressed somatic distress suggests chronic maladaptation that gives little indication of the underlying problem.

The probability of risk when intrusions and expressed somatic symptoms are coded is moderate to high, in terms not only of distress of the individual, but also of the potential for danger to the self or others. Consequently, treatment planning should consider reducing these and restoring at least partially the efficient functioning of the basic strategy as a priority. This can be accomplished through a range of interventions, from protecting the individual in an out-of-home context to medication to psychological work with the person or the family or both.

In general, a sense of self-efficacy is an inherent feature of an effective strategy; thus, modified, nonfunctional strategies may indicate diminished motivation to participate in treatment, thereby also decreasing the chances of success. This, too, requires immediate attention before other aspects of treatment can be expected to function productively.

Reorganizing

The presence of a reorganizing (R) modifier suggests a very different set of processes. This modifier implies active reflective functioning that promotes integration of formerly omitted, distorted, falsified, denied, or somaticized information in the speaker's representations. This suggests that the speaker already recognizes that the currently used strategy is not functioning well and also is actively attempting to update the strategy through metacognitive self-instruction. This indicates much lower risk to the speaker and to those around him or her. It also has implications for possible interventions. Directive and massive interventions will probably not be needed; instead, interventions that leave the individual in direct control of the majority of his or her life circumstances are indicated. Reorganizing speakers are usually able to ask directly for what they need or can be helped to reach clarity on this relatively quickly. It is worth noting, however, that individuals are vulnerable during a period of change and may need more support of a steadying or comforting sort than at other times. The function of the therapist for reorganizing individuals may be thought of as keeping the long-range process in sight when the individual is buffeted by the currents of daily life.

Unresolved Losses and Traumas

A second step in the functional analysis of an AAI classification is consideration of unresolved (U) dangerous events. The presence of unresolved losses (Ul) or traumas (Utr) can be seen as a very condensed history of those past dangers that still adversely affect the speaker's strategic functioning. Therefore, Us in a classification are invariably related to a higher risk of maladaptation, even if the risk can vary greatly depending, in part, upon immediate conditions.

This is stated categorically because, by definition, experiences of danger that have been resolved are subsumed into overall strategic functioning. The very mention of an unresolved danger implies that the speaker is still processing information about the event based on an inability to differentiate relevant from irrelevant information. Errors of self-relevance reduce the protectiveness of behavior and may also reduce the efficiency of processing if too much information is considered relevant.

Unlike modifiers, Us indicate context-elicited disruptions in strategic behavior. Thus, the more Us there are in the classification, the more likely it is that one or more U will be activated by the context. The type of lack of resolution specifies the probability of extreme responses once representations of the traumatic event are activated. A simple "preoccupied" or "dismissed" lack of resolution will have a predictable, discrete effect whereas more complex types can be expected to have less defined and more variable effects, with "disorganized" functioning like a wild card in its unpredictability of activation and variability of response. The extent of functional interference also depends upon how limited to specific probes the evidence of lack of resolution is: If the U is "contained," that is, shown only when the conversation is directed by the interviewer to the topic of the past dangerous events, the functional impact is lower than when the speaker spontaneously reacts to a variety of apparently unrelated topics.

Some types of lack of resolution have almost as much impact on behavior as modifiers. Specifically, the delusional forms of lack of resolution point to a need to find solutions to danger that still seems so active and threatening that the speaker has to make up protective information. Depressed lack of resolution indicates that the impact of the danger is both crucially important and also inescapably destructive, making current strategic functioning irrelevant to the self. Disorganized lack of resolution can effectively stop coherent strategic functioning by eliciting varied and incompatible responses to current conditions.

The patterning created by unresolved dangerous events in the history, by the traumatic psychological response to these events, and by the relation between the type of strategy and type of traumatic response is very complex and unique to each person. There is no obvious and general procedure regarding how to make meaning of this patterning, apart from the idea that in treatment unresolved traumas and losses need to be addressed early on, particularly when aspects of the treatment or the person's daily life activate them. The specific work needed varies, but a guiding principle could be the need to establish appropriate boundaries between past dangers and current risks, addressing openly the risks of the interference and prioritizing effective current protection.

Basic Strategies

Taken together, the modifiers and Us give a picture of how the speaker's functioning fits (or fails to fit) current life circumstances. If there are no modifiers or Us, the speaker's strategy is probably working adaptively. If modifiers or Us are present, depending on how extreme and complex they are, the speaker's strategy is likely to be nonprotective, either physically or psychologically or both.

This might appear to imply that, because strategies represent the distillation of the speaker's developmental experience for coping with danger, including essential distortions of information, the basic strategy does not necessarily need to be addressed in treatment. This would be highly discrepant with the widespread view that B is the only adaptive strategy, with all the other forms of strategic functioning, including A1–2 and C1–2, deemed unhealthy. Both perspectives are based on empirical data and neither is inaccurate; nevertheless they are probably too simplistic to guide practical application. We suggest a gradient of risk, from B to high-numbered A and C strategies. From that perspective, A1–2 and C1–2 experience only low risk and even most people who use an A3–4 or C3–4 strategy get on, even if a bit uncomfortably. If you add lack of resolution or modifiers, that changes, of course.

The last step in the functional analysis of an AAI classification is therefore a careful consideration of the meaning of the self-protective strategy used by the individual. This meaning will be fleshed out more completely (or significant discrepancies will be revealed) when the life history and the circumstances that led to the AAI being administered have been considered.

The basic strategy that an individual uses can be considered like a central processor that defines the most fully consolidated protective process drawn from the speaker's experience. The strategy colors many areas of personal functioning, including information processing and management of attachment relationships. It defines what is dangerous and what is safe, what information to attend to, what attributions of meaning to give it, ways to regulate action, and when to stop processing and initiate action.

The basic strategy gives insight into the innermost workings of the protective functioning of individuals, starting from the crucial question of what danger they are protecting themselves from. Use of a B strategy suggests that dangers provided a basis for learning, with the support and comfort of loving attachment figures. Use of an A strategy suggests predictable dangers related to rejection by, and isolation from, attachment figures. Use of a C strategy suggests entangled relationships with unpredictable dangers that are ambiguous, hidden, or invisible. Use of combined A and C strategies suggests a complexity of dangers, predictable and unpredictable, that were urgent enough to discourage the use of integrative reflection.

These general statements are just a hint of the precision of the possible answer to the question "What is the danger?" Moreover, except for B speakers, we expect to have different answers from the speaker and coder. This implies that therapists will very often frame the problem differently from their clients or patients.

In the DMM method, each strategy implies a specific pattern of information processing. These have been described in the previous chapters. Here we focus on how the classification process of identifying specific discourse markers and assigning them to constructs and memory systems adds detail to the picture of the speaker's protective functioning. As the classification is defined, details become available regarding the relative dominance of (a) cognitive versus affective information (the basic A versus C distinction), (b) implicit representations (somatic, procedural, imaged) versus (c) explicit representations (semantic, connotative, and episodic), and (d) integrative functioning in moments of threat and the time following action. It is also possible to specify what sort of information is omitted from processing, what is distorted in terms of over- or undergeneralization, and what is falsified, denied or even delusional. Each has implications in terms of what kind of statements are believable and what is likely to be inaccurate, as presented by the speaker.

FUNCTIONAL FORMULATION

Comparing the AAI Patterning with Life History

This is the moment when, after the "blind" coder has extracted relevant information from an AAI and constructed a coherent strategy from it, knowledge of the history and current problems can be used to inform treatment. This integrative process may be carried out by the coder or by another professional or collaboratively, but it is probably best managed by someone who knows the transcript intimately, in terms of both content and transformations. The functional formulation is the outcome of the professional's reflective integration and constitutes his or her DR of the individual's functioning and relationship with the interviewer.

A functional formulation consists of two sets of hypotheses: those about the relation of past experience to current strategies and those about the relation of current conditions, including the strategy, to change processes. That is, the functional formulation gives meaning to the individual's past behavior, including how clinical symptoms were generated and are maintained, while narrowing and ordering the possibilities for treatment. The formulation leads to ideas about which interventions could enable the individual to pursue the goals of self-protection, reproduction, and protection of progeny more adaptively. The formulation also facilitates purposeful ordering of treatment actions.

To understand current maladaptation, one should understand the adaptive value of specific behaviors in the past and why they are not functional anymore. Which changes in the individual or the context or both have precipitated the current maladaptation? Maturation can render early strategies obsolete, as can new events that are beyond the scope of the existing strategy. Alternatively, past dangers could have been so substantial and faced so early in life that extreme strategies are relied on invariantly, despite their high developmental cost and even when the dangers are no longer present. In such cases, erroneous information is quite likely; it, of course, was never adaptive, but that has not been noticed by the individual. These circumstances are usually marked by modifiers and Us, but that is not always the case: When the basic strategies are very extreme (A5–8, C5–8), they can protect the individual but only at the cost of forcing the person into a very narrow ecological niche.

The purpose of functional formulation is to generate person-specific hypotheses and questions to be explored during the process of treatment. In other words, this is the point at which a standardized process becomes attuned to personal meanings and histories to generate individualized treatments. Therefore, even if it were possible to generalize this phase of the process, it would not be advisable to do so. Instead, we turn to treatment planning and then offer an example of a functional formulation.

Functional Formulation and Treatment Planning

Danger is the first concern. Is the individual endangered now? If so, in what way (physically, psychologically, in their home, outside of home)? In addition, one must consider whether the individual is a source of danger to himself or herself or to others (such as their spouse or children or strangers). If the danger is substantial, it must be reduced before other aspects of the intervention are addressed.

Dangers associated with intervention should be considered. We suggest two issues as being relevant to all interventions and worthy of early consideration:

1. How is the proposed intervention dangerous from the recipient's perspective, therefore creating "resistance" to the intervention or to parts of it?
2. How is the proposed intervention actually dangerous in ways that the recipient can't see and protest, creating risks of iatrogenic damage?

The latter might surprise some therapists. Consider, for example, the risk that a marriage is maintained by active inattention to some information. Could treatment that made this issue explicit precipitate a divorce? Alternatively, some Type A strategies bias individuals to absorb therapists' words and ideas, thus appearing "cured," but without managing any inner change whatever. Indeed, in such cases, the true thoughts and feelings of the individual can become buried under yet another layer of acquired self. (In the case of individuals whose AAI was assigned to A8, this effect has already occurred.)

A clear functional formulation can prepare the therapist to address these issues and to work with the individual's response. If the general aim is to establish an open and cooperative relationship, then the therapist must take respectful account of the speaker's current strategy. For a person using a compulsive A strategy, there will be an automatic component of obedience and deference to a treatment provider, combined with inhibiting negative affect and accepting blame. For someone using a Type C strategy, there will be confronting or persuasive complicity with the therapist, combined with exaggerating negative affect and blaming others. Neither should be worrying to the therapist if the overall plan is clear, and if stages of the treatment are arranged so that full cooperation and straight processing of information are not needed until they are feasible. That is, the treatment should assume a transitional process that begins where the individual is and moves, always in the zone of proximal development, toward more inclusive adaptation.

Each nonbalanced strategy implies a different pathway to a balanced state of functioning. If we had empirical evidence on how treatment techniques affected information processing, then each of these pathways would suggest a possible therapeutic course of action. Although the field of psychotherapy is not yet sufficiently empirically undergirded or unified to provide that, nevertheless the functional formulation can suggest specific goals for the different memory systems and a path to reflective integration.

For example, the speaker may need access to omitted information if more balanced functioning is to be achieved. Treatment strategies that promote discovery of discrepancies created by the omission are needed and, when successful, need verbal articulation. This move to the metacognitive, reflective level can happen only if the individual feels safe enough to suspend his or her self-protective strategy and engage in exploration. If the therapist is sufficiently informed about the individual's strategy to be able to function as a transitional attachment figure by making the treatment context tolerably safe, then conscious work on information processing itself can begin. The progression of therapeutic work will start from the "ordinary language" used by the individual, on known and easy territory, then move to the gradual discovery of the omitted information and of the complementary distortions of familiar information.

This framing of the therapeutic process allows specification of what goals are likely to be premature at intake, but can be set as long-term, ultimate objectives, while more proximal goals are pursued. Proximal goals often include the individual's stated reason for seeking treatment.

This discussion seems to imply that the ultimate goal of psychological treatment is to bring the individual to a B strategy. This might be possible in theory, but, in practical terms, the question of efficiency is relevant. Once we account for the individuals' actual context, it could be that restoring a specific strategy to functionality might be sufficiently adaptive. Once this goal was reached, further treatment might be suspended by either the client's or therapist's choice. This might also fit the resources available and represent an acceptable outcome of treatment. If needed, a prediction of potential relapse conditions could be made, mapping vulnerabilities and planning further related interventions. More optimistically, once the process of attending to and resolving discrepancy was under way, the individual might be able to proceed without ongoing treatment. Indeed, this is what adequately functioning people do all the time.

MAKING SENSE OF STRATEGIC FUNCTIONING

An example can illustrate how the meaning of a DMM-AAI classification becomes clearer when it is considered in the light of external information about the individual.

The AAI patterning for this transcript is explained in terms of the current adaptiveness of the strategy (i.e., are there modifiers or Us that obstruct its function?) and the functioning of individual memory systems within the basic strategy. Then we discuss the circumstances leading to the administration of the AAI. This provides the history or context for the functional formulation, which in turn suggests hypotheses regarding how treatment could be planned and implemented in this specific case.[1]

Timothy's AAI

Timothy is a man in his early forties and he is married with three children. His AAI was classified as follows: (Dp) $Ul(dx)_F$ $Utr(dx)_{PA\&DV}$ $A1?,4/C5\Delta_{M,F,Uncle}$ $[ina]_h$.

---

1. All names and many details within this case example have been altered to conceal the identities of the individuals.

The classification means that the basic strategy is a combined alternating A and C strategy (A1?,4/C5$\Delta_{M,F,Uncle}$). The A component consists of a clear compulsive compliant (A4) strategy and a less clear inhibitory A1 strategy (that does not completely fulfill the A1 criteria because the idealization is missing). The C component is a punitive triangulated (Δ) strategy (C5) used for mother, father, and uncle. Timothy's mother left home with his uncle after his father died; this may also have left Timothy with implicit doubts about the nature of these relationships even when his father was still alive. This basic strategy is modified by partial depression (Dp); in the interview there was no evidence that the depression was balanced by intrusions of forbidden negative affect, but Timothy spoke about historical events that could be conceptualized as intrusions ([ina]$_h$). There was also lack of resolution for the loss of the father (Ul) and a lack of resolution for physical abuse (PA) and domestic violence (DV) that Timothy experienced as a child (Utr). Both of these are in a disorganized (dx) form, which means there is evidence of multiple and incompatible attempts to deal with information about these past events that are confused among them and with other events.

Overall, the patterning of the classification suggests moderate maladaptation: The depressive modification of the strategy is not complete and the intrusions of negative affect are not current (probably because negative affect can be used strategically in the C component of the strategy). What appears severely stuck is the state of lack of resolution about physical abuse and domestic violence and about the loss of the father. These Us might interfere with a basic strategy that is complex and, in the C component, fairly extreme. The basic strategy suggests that experience with predictable danger is manageable with inhibition or compulsive compliance and also that complex involvement in unclear family relationships, where the self might feel involved in complicitous alliances for unclear purposes, is managed in a triangulated way. The latter component of the strategy could potentially be active in Timothy's current family. Timothy's C5 suggests he is very attentive to hierarchy and power. Could he become vindictive if he perceived slights from present family members (tapping into his vengeful anger that is kept active by the ongoing preoccupation with past offenses)? On the other hand, the inhibition of the A strategy might hamper his ability to communicate his negative feelings more directly if there were family problems.

In addition, however, this first overview of the classification suggests that Timothy may be motivated to reconsider or reorganize his behavior because he is aware that his strategies are not working. This suggests that there might be an opportunity to consider (a) some individual work with him to assess his interest in reviewing his experiences of abuse and loss (to circumscribe and define their influence on his current functioning) and (b) some spousal and family work to consider how the A/C strategies interact with his wife's and children's strategies. The active C5 component suggests that Timothy might have trouble in attributing causality within relationship events; this could affect his family's functioning significantly.

The following list was created by analyzing each memory system for information about how to approach possible treatment with Timothy:

Procedural memory:
1. Discourse—A1: Brief around topics that are threatening to self (*but not idealizing*), distancing, delayed responding; A4: dismissing without idealization and without lack of episodic recall, sibilance indicating anxiety; C5: distancing of his own vulnerability and the perspectives of others, cuts off discussion, long silences.
2. Expressed affect—A1: little affect; C5: bitingly dry humor.
3. Relationship to interviewer—Part I, A1: speaker provides few semantic descriptions of attachment relationships; C5: stonewalling. Parts II & III: generally cooperative, with no negative affect (anger, fear, or desire for comfort).

Imaged memory:
1. Part I—Largely omitted.
2. A+: Unconnected image (*"leather belt"*).
3. C+: Intense images (*"rip his head off"*; *"just use the belt"*).
4. C+: Weak animated image of involving speech (*"I tried to explain to him, 'I didn't do it, one of the others did' and he called me a liar and then started with me, with his leather belt"*).

The implicit memory systems seem focused on avoidance of danger and dismissal of vulnerability. The images of abuse and violence suggest that if avoidance is not possible, intense images of fear and anger could motivate sudden action. The relationship with the interviewer seems to alternate between extremes of avoidance and cooperation. The latter state seems more likely on topics of victimization of self.

Semantic memory:
1. A1: Few words.
2. A1: Splitting of good attachment figure (in respect of grand-mother) from the bad self.
3. A4: Exoneration (partial) of mother and father; parental perspective.
4. C: Passive semantic thought.
5. C5: Splitting of responsibility with attachment figures held responsible, while the self is seen as powerless.

Connotative language:
1. Part I—A1: Dry.
2. C: Evocative language.
3. A4: Repeated phrases to reduce anxiety.

Episodic memory:
1. A1: Lack of memory.
2. A1: Positive episodes for grandmother.
3. A: Scripts.
4. A4: Negative episodes described but the speaker's feelings are distanced.
5. C5: Fragmented episodes demonstrate speaker's innocence and powerlessness.
6. C5: Lack of episodic comfort.
7. C5: Triangulated episodes.
8. C5: False innocence.

Reflective integration:
1. A1: Lack of integration.
2. A4: Incipient integration regarding a suicide attempt (*"I thought 'What am I doing?' and I went round to a friend's . . ."*) and replicative parental script (*"I made a big mistake . . ."*).
3. C5: Rationalization.

The explicit memory systems seem to function to simplify troublesome topics as much as to avoid them. Issues are framed either to reduce arousal and obey attachment figures or to raise arousal around the ideas of a powerless self and bad attachment figures. There is little room for pure description, which probably would be too arousing and without clear dispositions for action. The lack of clear and explicit DRs may be due to the lack of causal clarity connected with triangulation with his parents (which Timothy managed through a resentful C-like alliance with his mother). The clearest part of his story is the abuse by his father and this organizes much of the A-explicit functioning.

The A/C alternation is a robust way for Timothy to regulate his arousal: It can be done implicitly through alternating inhibition and arousing images, explicitly through the different semantic and connotative strategies, and through different kinds of recalled episodes. Even if all his strategies fail, there is a more extreme alternation of depression and intrusions available.

Negotiation of shared procedures explicitly aimed at regulating Timothy's arousal could be one of the early steps in treatment (using, for example, relaxation or imaged techniques). This would allow Timothy to deal with sensitive issues without precipitating his usual automatic A/C alternations. Although such strategic alternations could look like reflection or integration to the therapist in real time, appearing as a satisfactory outcome, little real exploration would be achieved and, consequently, they should be prevented as much as possible.

Depression:
1. Speaks of self as "we," in a distanced way.
2. Sighs, flat, no affect.
3. Nonagency.
4. Futility: grandmother's loss: *"There was nothing I could do."*
5. Lack of productive thought.

Intrusions:
1. Shows the interviewer scars on his arm where he *"cut [his] arms up"* during a period of depression in early adulthood.

Trauma and loss:

$Ul(dx)_F$: Multiple psychological responses around his unresolved loss of father in adolescence; run-on structure and preoccupation; the funeral is dismissed from memory; the distress is displaced to mother; generally, disorganized. The speaker emphasizes his disorganized or "weird" feelings about his father's funeral.

$Utr(dx)_{PA\&DV}$: Multiple psychological responses to traumatic physical abuse and domestic abuse; preoccupation on both topics together in the discourse; a vicarious response to domestic abuse; a displaced response to the beating of self and cousin; generally a dismissively dry and unresponsive reaction to the physical and domestic abuse.

Timothy's awareness of the failures of his strategies, especially around the unresolved traumas, creates the opportunity for a therapist to explicitly discuss these topics. This would allow exploration of ways to establish a working therapeutic relationship.

Why Was Timothy Interviewed? The Family History

After extracting this much meaning from Timothy's AAI through coding and classification, the circumstances that led to the interview itself can be examined. This allows exploration of how the information drawn from the AAI can be integrated with Timothy's history and the current situation of his family to yield a functional formulation. The functional formulation uses information from several DMM assessments (including Timothy's wife's AAI and their oldest son's School-Age Assessment of Attachment) to achieve an understanding of the presenting problems and the possible approaches to treatment beyond what we have already considered about working with Timothy individually. The goal is to formulate how the family functions, both as a system and as the developmental context for each individual. This understanding should assist the therapist to refine the treatment choices more precisely.

THE HISTORY

Timothy and his wife, Valerie, have been together for 14 years. They have three children (Nathan, 13 years old; Sarah, 9; and John, 6).

Valerie has a difficult relationship with her mother who she says favors her older sister. Valerie thinks she is not favored because her parents wanted a son rather than another daughter. In any event, Valerie finds it easier to relate to men and prefers male company to the company of girlfriends. Valerie also has a 17-year-old son, Adam, who she had with her first partner, Brian. Brian was physically and sexually violent to her, and social services determined that he presented a significant risk to Adam and prohibited him from seeing Adam. Placed in the position of having to choose between Brian and her newborn son, and without the felt option of returning home to the care of her parents, Valerie chose to remain with Brian. Adam was adopted by a different family and Valerie now has infrequent contact with him. Valerie eventually separated from Brian; however, this only happened because of the support of her second and current partner, Timothy.

Valerie's AAI was classified as (R) C1(3)Δ. Her C strategy is not extreme, but there is a theme of triangulation in her family of origin around the possibility of infidelity between her parents. Valerie doesn't mention it, but the information she brings to the interview opens the possibility that her paternity was in question. This could explain her being treated differently than her sister. The partial reorganizing modifier describes Valerie's readiness to reformulate her family story, but the missing information about her triangulated relationship with her parents prevents her from doing so.

Timothy is a chef by trade, but for the last few years he had been the children's main caregiver, while Valerie went to work and built a career. She had worked as a cleaner before gaining a promotion, then she worked and studied for vocational qualifications with the aim of becoming a manager. In the course of her work, she developed new friendships including, about a year ago, one particularly close relationship with a male colleague, Alex, to whom she lent a significant amount of money. Valerie gave Timothy a number of different reasons for providing this loan. Timothy wasn't able to resolve the discrepancies among the reasons or to discuss his feelings about this with Valerie for several months.

THE PRECIPITATING CRISIS

One evening about 4 months before Timothy was given the AAI, Nathan phoned his mother, Valerie, at work, complaining his father, Timothy, had sent him to his room without dinner. Valerie rushed home and an argument ensued about appropriate discipline. The next day the argument resurfaced after Valerie received a text, which Timothy thought had come from Alex. Feeling undermined, Timothy lost his temper and assaulted Valerie and Nathan, injuring both of them. Valerie and the children fled. Timothy was arrested, excluded from the home, charged, and convicted of the assaults.

In accordance with social services' restrictions, Timothy is required to live separately and he has twice-weekly supervised contact with his children. In addition, as part of his probation order, Timothy is attending anger management and domestic abuse programs. Children's services have reluctantly accepted the parents' wish to get back together. Furthermore, the children have told their independent advocate that they want their father home. Valerie has had to give up work. She is being assisted to be more assertive with her husband and to provide the children with more structure at home. Individual therapy for both parents and couples therapy have been recommended as next steps.

The family requested an independent counseling service for Nathan because his behavior toward his mother and siblings was deteriorating. The AAIs with Timothy and Valerie and Nathan's SAA were conducted in this context.

Nathan's view of the family

Nathan's SAA was classified as (Dp) $Utr(v)_M$ A3–4-. His basic strategy, a combination of compulsive caregiving to his parents and compulsive performance to please them, shows some suspension around themes of paternity tied to his mother (picking up vicariously a central theme in her functioning). There's also partial depression; in fact, his strategy didn't spare him from his father's attack or from the subsequent events, including a separation from his father, who up to then had been the primary source of reference for Nathan's externally based compulsive strategies. To manage the triadic relationship among himself and his parents more smoothly, Nathan would have needed a C component that both his parents practice extensively, but which he lacks. Instead, despite his relying heavily on their perspectives, he cannot figure out, as demonstrated in the SAA, why his parents do what they do or why he himself does what he does. His avoidance of the peer-related themes in the interview is very strong. Thus, the developmentally salient issues of awareness of the reasons for behavior and of dealing with peers seem not to be under Nathan's control.

Pulling information together

This overall picture allows us to make some sense of the precipitating event. Nathan, by his phone call, triggered a cascade of associations in his father, which ultimately generated a DR of acting violently. Specifically, the call created a situation in which he could have been perceived by his father as allying with his mother. Timothy probably feared, without stating it verbally, that Valerie might be cheating on him with Alex; this, in turn, triggered implicit associations with what his mother might have done with his father, which was tied to representations of violence. These became motivating in the present because his disorganized lack of resolution failed to tie affect that originated in childhood to its temporal conditions. Had these memories been resolved, that is, held discretely in his mind, Timothy could have recognized his fear and consciously considered it, based on his past experience. In that case, he could have decided whether or not to address it explicitly with Valerie. Instead, the associations were "disorganized" in being attributed to too wide a range of circumstances while also being denied. Being saturated with fear, the past associations grabbed priority in regulating his behavior in that unfortunate moment. Moreover, having an A strategy of inhibiting clear expression of negative affect, he had not discussed his suspicion earlier with Valerie; instead, it had simmered silently until the random (i.e., unpredictable) confluence of their fight and the arrival of the text message. In that moment, his current suspicion and past experiences came together, creating a state of fear and anger. Timothy lashed out at both wife and son with explosive, unregulated, and destructive aggression. His childhood pattern of intrusions under intolerable conditions was replayed.

Treatment focused on anger management for Timothy is likely to reinforce his A strategies, leaving both the unresolved traumas and the C strategy untouched. This could be counterproductive if it left him vulnerable to future intrusions. On the other hand, the treatment currently being offered to Valerie seems to aim at increasing her self-focus and her ability to express herself on the basis of her affective states, which, given her current strategy, seems redundant (or even counterproductive) in comparison with the option of focusing on interpersonal causality and her possible (triangulated) role in it. Currently Nathan seems to be the person who is most unsettled by the recent events. In fact, Timothy's previous distress didn't precipitate a request for help on his part; instead treatment was mandated after he had acted. On the other hand, after the separation from his father, Nathan functions in ways that are not recognized by the family as typical for him, and negative feelings that he previously had inhibited seem to be displayed in disruptive ways.

The Functional Formulation for Timothy's Family

The first set of ideas in this functional formulation is focused on the relation of past experience with the strategies of the family members. Valerie's past experience informs her that to manage complex family situations, she should re-focus attention on herself by using angry displays. This is likely to interact with Timothy's past experience (and strategy based on it) of inhibiting any evidence of negative feelings to prevent violence and disruption. This seems to imply that, in the family dominance hierarchy, Valerie is in a higher position than Timothy. As long as themes of cheating and loss are not salient, this setup can theoretically be stable. In fact, the family history shows stability for about a decade, during which Valerie gradually became the primary economic provider and Timothy the primary caregiver for their children. Nathan's strategy tells us that his parents have been predictable with him, demanding from him both appropriate performance and attention to their perspectives and needs. However, they haven't been able to attend to his perspective, particularly his need for comfort. We don't know about the other children in the family: They could be organized similarly to Nathan; alternatively, if he fulfills the parents' requests sufficiently well, the siblings might have organized different strategies to make themselves visible. C strategies with a predominance of angry displays would seem to work well to get Timothy's attention (based on his wife's functioning).

As Valerie became more successful at work and began to explore new social relationships, she probably overlooked Timothy's perspective. It is interesting that the loan (i.e., the indication to Timothy of her possible cheating) functions as an unresolved problem between them, but it did not precipitate Timothy's violence. Potentially, this event could still be subsumed in the usual balance of Timothy not defining and expressing anything that he experiences negatively and of Valerie simply going ahead with her plans, justified in doing so by her previous bad experiences. When Nathan fails to be "a very good boy" who caters to his father, the family balance starts to break down. The next event, the mere arrival of a text message, is perceived by Timothy as evidence of cheating: His negative feelings can't be inhibited anymore, and Valerie and Nathan are attacked together, as enemies allied against him.

Is such violence likely to recur? Considering Valerie's growing interests outside the family, and Nathan's growing potential for independence (we don't know about the other children), the answer must be yes especially if the overall situation of the family doesn't change in some critical ways.

A Treatment Plan

With this understanding, we now offer some hypotheses about how change could be accomplished, based on what we know about the current functioning of the family.

The whole system could change in terms of more reciprocity and more causal clarity between the spouses if Timothy can recognize and express his negative feelings and concerns clearly, but without accusation, and if Valerie can recognize how her own behavior contributes to Timothy's fears. It seems that currently some of this information is still dangerous enough to precipitate unregulated consequences. Therefore some work in protected circumstances, either within individual treatment or couple treatment, might be useful in facilitating such changes. A crucial point, of course, will be whether Timothy's fears are grounded in reality.

What can Timothy change? When, in the AAI, Timothy was asked how his childhood experiences might have affected his adult personality, he said that he is *"trying [to] treat his family differently to what my dad did with his."* For most of the last 14 years, it appears he has in some ways succeeded by using alternate A and C strategies. Recently, though, he experienced a significant replication of his family of origin dynamics; these tapped into the parts of Timothy's history that are less clear to him. The result was an explosion of violent anger toward his wife and child, just as his father had done to him.

There are two changes that could help Timothy to pursue his stated goal. First, he needs to recognize the impact of dangerous events in his past on his current functioning (i.e., "resolving" the Us). This could be pursued both in an individual setting and also through enlisting Valerie's help in understanding and managing the effects of his lack of resolution through her not behaving in ambiguous ways. Second, Timothy could learn to express negative affect, especially fear and desire for comfort, in communicative ways (lessening the A inhibition, and clarifying the causality hidden behind the blaming C triangulation). This second change is more complex and deserving of careful planning. After all, an unregulated display of anger precipitated damage for the family (separation, plus Valerie's loss of a job), so the dangers related to this goal will need to be addressed and regulated by therapists. Gradually, Timothy will need to practice displaying moderated anger, first with a professional functioning as a "transitional attachment figure," then with his wife. Possible triangulating effects that could be very dangerous for Timothy and his family need to be foreseen and managed with special care. This suggests that the children should not be involved in this work until some significant change in the stated direction is already under way.

Valerie seems already disposed to change. Our formulation identifies areas where she needs help: focusing on causal sequences and on other people's perspectives. One theme seems both crucial and hidden for her: The reason why she was treated differently could be tied to her mother's infidelities and potentially to her paternity. The exploration of these themes could occur in individual counseling or in a couples setting; the choice depends on whether Valerie feels this issue is private or prefers to share it with her husband. Both choices have advantages and disadvantages. An interesting exercise for Valerie could be to try and foresee Timothy's perspective on both possibilities, focusing on what she knows and doesn't know about him. This is not what her current strategy advises, so she would have to practice new types of information processing and relationship management procedures to accomplish the task (in a more balanced way than what she is used to).

Nathan, in the meantime, seems to be so focused on his parents' perspectives that his own development seems stymied, especially in his relationships with peers. As adolescence is approaching, this seems inauspicious. The goal of learning to recognize and express communicatively his own negative feelings (thus, reducing the bias toward inhibition and false positive displays that is implicit in his current strategy) seems appropriate for him, as well as for his father. This seems best addressed in a separate, individual setting at first, then some family therapy work could help check whether the changes Nathan is ready to make are best reserved for an out-of-home context or can be accommodated by the parallel changes in his parents' functioning.

This plan for change allows for a relative and temporary independence of treatments offered to Nathan as compared to those for his parents, but it requires careful coordination of the treatments offered to Timothy and Valerie. We lack information about the other children, which is highly relevant to a prediction about the possible recurrence of violent events in the family that could be triggered in similar ways to the previous crisis. We also do not know which, if any, of Timothy's concerns are accurate. If Valerie is having a romantic relationship with Alex, that will have dramatic impact on the family and the therapy. But that cannot be known until communication between husband and wife is clarified.

Overall, the changes we propose seem fairly easy for Valerie, who is already disposed to reflect on her experiences, and for Nathan, who is on the verge of a massive developmental transition anyway. Timothy has more work ahead of him, work that has been made even more difficult by the threatening circumstances created by the social services' effort to protect his family from him. If the treatment doesn't create further risk, however, it is not an overly difficult task, especially with the strong motivations that Timothy has to return to his family and to protect his children adequately.

APPLICATIONS OF THE AAI TO ASSESSMENT AND TREATMENT

This case example touches on almost all the clinical applications of the AAI.

Planning Treatment

Perhaps the most obvious clinical application is to assess adult functioning as a preliminary part of intervention, whether focused on an individual or on a family. The pattern of attachment, as assessed by the DMM-AAI, gives an indication of the cognitive, emotional, and relational functioning of the speaker. This is relevant to all the approaches to treatment that consider individual differences in human functioning crucial to treatment planning. If administered at intake by the professional who is expected to deliver the intervention, the AAI has the added advantages of implicitly establishing a working relationship in which the speaker is actively part of what is happening; is allowed to talk about experiences in the form that is most congenial to him or her; is encouraged to review and interpret all forms of information, thinking, and behavior; and is able to find a listener who doesn't summarize, interpret, or respond with statements that can be considered judgmental. If the clinical approach used considers these features desirable, then the AAI can be a way to begin the therapeutic process during the assessment.

A particularly important conclusion to be drawn from this example is that the family member who presents with problems is rarely the only person in the family with problems. Further, resolving the issues of the presenting individual may require change on the part of family members – or dissolution of the family. Because maintaining the problem and dissolving the family are both negative outcomes, it seems wise to assess family members directly (i.e., not through a presenting individual's report) before initiating service.

It is also crucial to note that formulation involves both prescribing treatment strategies to try and also proscribing treatment strategies that are likely to be ineffective or, worse, harmful. Although a formulation cannot assume that these judgments are accurate, failure to consider which treatments might be helpful, ineffective, and harmful—and the bases for these hypotheses—can unintentionally harm people who seek help.

Using the AAI During or at the Close of Treatment

The AAI format is based on the assumption that the speakers relate their experiences to unknown interviewers, therefore having to rely mostly on their strategies to make predictions on how to best deal with the task. If the AAI is used later on in a course of treatment, having the therapist or a central worker in the case deliver the interview will give more information about the history of relationship between interviewer and speaker than about the speaker in general. In that case, it would be advisable to involve a professional who hasn't yet had any contact with the speaker for the role of interviewer.

If the AAI is administered at the end of a treatment that aims to affect the behavioral, emotional, or cognitive functioning of an individual, it can be used as a tool to assess treatment effects. If the AAI was already given at intake, learning effects will have to be taken into account. The AAI questions, if not new to the listener, can be answered in pre-thought ways; this will be detected through the discourse analysis, but the chance for the speaker to express his or her current state of functioning will be lost. To reduce this problem, the DMM-AAI has been modified to create an alternate form (Form B, Crittenden, 2006). Form B retains the format of the interview in terms of systematically probing memory systems and gradually increasing stress, but it changes the topic or focus of the questions so that they are new to the speaker. For all uses of the AAI that involve repetition of the interview, it is recommended that the two different forms are employed.

Forensic Applications of the AAI

Family assessment is becoming increasingly important in forensic settings focused on the adequacy of parenting. The AAI, used in combination with attachment assessments designed for other family members, can provide an assessment of individual functioning in terms of intra- and interpersonal strategy. The various strategies of all the family members can then be compared and connected as part of the family system, allowing predictions of how the family as a whole is likely to face threats, tasks, and demands, specifying the functional roles of the individuals.

The forensic applications of the AAI so far have been mostly focused on child protection and parenting issues, probably in the tradition of the AAI being considered first and foremost an assessment of adults' states of mind regarding attachment. The AAI, however, can be of interest in all cases in which a general look at adult functioning can be of interest to legal systems. It could integrate or substitute for personality inventories or projective tests, depending on how the validity of each for specific purposes is empirically demonstrated.

Using the AAI with Substitute Caregivers

A possible use of the AAI that falls between assessment and intervention is to assess how adult strategies are compatible with possible adoptive or foster children's strategies. This is slightly different from an approach based on finding out which adults are suitable to function as foster or adoptive parents. Rather than attempting to exclude some potential parents on the basis of the AAI result, this approach presumes that most strategies can be accommodated in foster parents, even when there are unresolved past threats. Preparing substitute parents to cope with their own biases and matching compatible strategies with an awareness of the possible vulnerable points in particular parent-child relationships might promote better use of resources in terms of placement decisions and support.

Selecting Personnel

An altogether different field of application, not particularly widely explored so far, is the application of the AAI to selection of personnel: The AAI could help whenever a dynamic assessment of strategic human functioning is useful. For assessing management abilities, especially in terms of facing specific sorts of danger, the AAI could add valuable information to decision making.

Research

Finally, a word about the AAI research applications: The widest use of the AAI has been in basic research on attachment and human development. The DMM-AAI validation process described in the next chapter is already extending this to clinical research about psychopathology. The applications suggested here imply the possibility of using the AAI in studies about various forms of intervention, based in clinical or policy-based settings.

Chapter 15

Validity and Clinical Implications of the DMM-AAI

IN THIS CHAPTER WE ADDRESS THE VALIDITY OF THE DMM-AAI. UP TO now, the validity of the AAI has been tested using the Main and Goldwyn method of discourse analysis and corresponding classificatory system. Although derived from the M&G-AAI, the DMM-AAI is based on somewhat different theory, discourse analysis, and classificatory options. Consequently, an alternative validation process is needed.

Here, we review the differences between the DMM and Main and Goldwyn approaches to the AAI and a comprehensive analysis of the M&G-AAI. Then we describe a plan for the validation of the DMM-AAI, followed by reviewing studies that used the DMM-AAI classificatory method, including the few studies that compare DMM-AAI and M&G-AAI classifications. We conclude with a discussion of steps to be taken in future research to understand better the contributions and limitations of the DMM approach to the AAI.

DIFFERENCES BETWEEN DMM AND M&G

The theoretical and empirical differences between the Dynamic-Maturational Model and Main and Goldwyn methods justify their treatment as two separate entities. The differences are summarized in Figure 15.1.

Figure 15.1. Differences between the Dynamic-Maturational Model and Main and Goldwyn methods.

The Dynamic-Maturational Model method (Crittenden, 1999a) for analyzing AAIs differs from the Main and Goldwyn (1984; Main et al., 2008) method in several ways:

1. Intent: The intent of the DMM method is to describe the self-protective strategies and patterns of mental processing of speakers; the intent of the Main and Goldwyn method is to predict infants' patterns of attachment.

2. Outcome classifications: The set of outcome classifications is larger in the DMM method and permits greater differentiation among individuals with psychological disorders than the set of classifications used by the Main and Goldwyn method.

3. Treatment of non-Ainsworth classifications: The DMM method uses six compulsive Type A strategies (A3–8) and six obsessive Type C strategies (C3–8), plus a full array of combinations of these. In the Main and Goldwyn method, most nonnormative individuals fall in three classifications (E3, U/E3, and "Cannot Classify").

4. Patterns versus ratings: The DMM method depends on patterns within and among memory systems, whereas the Main and Goldwyn method depends on ratings of constructs.

5. Functions versus defined meanings: The DMM method uses the function of discourse markers to define meaning, whereas the Main and Goldwyn method assigns meanings to discourse markers.

6. Memory systems: The DMM method systematically assesses six memory systems (procedural, imaged, semantic, connotative language, episodic, and reflective integration), whereas the Main and Goldwyn method considers three (semantic, episodic, and working).

7. Modifiers: In the DMM method, there are six modifiers (depressed, disoriented, reorganizing, intrusions of negative affect, expressed somatic symptoms, and unresolved with regard to trauma or loss), with 14 different forms of lack of resolution of trauma or loss (dismissed, displaced, blocked, denied, delusionally repaired, preoccupied, vicarious, anticipated, imagined, suggested, hinted, delusionally vengeful, depressed, and disorganized); the Main and Goldwyn method has only preoccupied lack of resolution of loss or trauma.

8. Validity: The validity of the DMM method is primarily based on clinical samples and differentiation among disorders; validity for the Main and Goldwyn method is primarily based on normative samples and prediction from mothers to infants.

Intent of the M&G-AAI

It is particularly important to be aware that the different intents of the two methods lead to different validity issues. Main and Goldwyn (1984, 1994) constructed a classificatory method for the AAI with the intent of matching mothers' "state of mind with regard to attachment" to the known 12-month Strange Situation Procedure (SSP) classifications of their infants. This was based on Main's belief that quality of attachment was "transmitted" from mother to infant and that quality of attachment was largely unchanging across the life-span (Main et al., 1985; Main et al., 2008). Consequently, in the M&G-AAI coding system, the array of classifications is almost identical, in number and patterning, to that in infancy.

Coding guidelines were constructed to produce a maximally congruent fit of the mothers' AAI classification with the 12-month SSP classifications of their infants. Then the AAIs were recoded blindly: The M&G-AAI matched SSP coding of security versus insecurity in 75% of cases (Main et al., 1985). A robust empirical link between M&G-AAI and SSP classifications has subsequently been demonstrated in multiple studies (Fonagy, Steele, & Steele, 1991; van IJzendoorn, 1995). However, because of the way in which the coding method was developed, the M&G-AAI may be biased to identifying indicators of infant attachment in mothers as opposed to unique aspects of adult attachment (Thompson & Raikes, 2003). This might limit the validity of the AAI if applied outside the field of infant development studies.

Construct and Discriminant Validity

As the applications of the AAI have expanded beyond the issue of transmission of attachment from mother to child, the range of questions that might be addressed has increased. Here we focus on the findings of the Bakermans-Kranenburg and van IJzendoorn (2009) analysis of 10,000 AAIs classified with the M&G-AAI method.

With regard to construct validity, they found the relation proposed by Dozier and her colleagues (2008) of an association of dismissing attachment with externalizing disorders and of preoccupying attachment with internalizing disorders. We find this puzzling from the perspective of attachment theory and its constructs, noting that Crittenden and Ainsworth (1989) proposed the opposite relations. The dismissing category (except for the derogating Ds2 pattern) involves idealization and, in infancy, inhibition of negative affect. We do not understand how this leads to externalizing disorders (e.g., conduct disorder). We think the finding is best explained by the inclusion of the dismissing-of-others Ds2 category, which we think is conceptually and functionally an extreme of the angrily preoccupied category (i.e., E3 in the M&G-AAI and C5 in the DMM). Similarly, the relation between preoccupied and internalizing seems inconsistent with the tendency of preoccupied individuals to display intense negative affect. Possibly in this case, there are two explanations. First, role reversal, which is an inhibition of self-motivations in favor of attending to parental perspectives, is placed in "preoccupied" when conceptually and functionally it might better be placed in "dismissing" (of self). Second, inclusion of cases of borderline personality disorder in the preoccupied category when Crittenden and Newman (2010) have found them to contain both dismissing and preoccupying processes may have confused the analyses. In both cases, the results were significant but accounted for relatively little variance, again suggesting that the M&G categories might be imprecise and "contaminated."

Within the 10,000 AAIs, some were given to adolescents as young as 14 years old. Reduced secure and increased dismissing classifications were found for adolescents. The authors attribute this to the incomplete "working through" of adolescents. Using that argument, all infants should be anxiously attached. Having found the same effect in other research (reduced security and increased A/C classifications among adolescents, Black, Jaeger, McCartney, & Crittenden, 2000), we concluded that the AAI was not attuned to the developmental competence and interests of adolescents and chose to develop a related instrument, the Transition to Adulthood Attachment Interview (TAAI, Crittenden, 2005), which focused on identity, partner selection, and current (rather than past) episodes.

Clinical applications of the AAI depend on discriminant validity. Although significant differences in the distributions were found for clinical and normative samples, the overlap of the groups was too great for clinical use. Specifically, in normative samples, 44% of AAIs were assigned to an insecure category, with 18% being unresolved with regard to loss or trauma. Conversely, in clinical samples, 21–27% of AAIs were assigned to secure, with only 43% being unresolved. In other words, approximately one third of transcripts were classified counter to the hypothesis and a bit more than a third were found resolved or unresolved, again counter to the hypothesis. Having a third of cases on the two central variables misclassified is not clinically useful. Moreover, many of the findings are inexplicable; how does one explain security in extremely maladapted individuals (e.g., incarcerated violent criminals, adults who harm themselves or others)? How does one explain the absence of unresolved trauma or loss in depressed individuals, given our knowledge of loss as a major contributor to depression (Brown & Harris, 1978)? Similarly, the majority of clinical AAIs (57%) showed no unresolved loss or trauma. Beyond that, the M&G-AAI was unable to discriminate among psychological disorders, finding only marginally higher rates of dismissing, preoccupied, or unresolved/cannot classify categories. In sum, the M&G-AAI significantly discriminated the normative and clinical groups, but not diagnostic groups within the clinical group. We conclude that its discriminant validity was limited in ways that cannot be explained by theory and render it inadequate for clinical application. We think such findings challenge (a) attachment theory itself, (b) the method used to derive the data, or (c) the relevance of attachment theory to clinical practice.

Finally, Bakermans-Kranenburg and van IJzendoorn's analysis of 10,000 AAIs found no cultural or gender differences. As they note, almost every major psychological variable, except attachment, demonstrates cultural and gender differences. With regard to culture, they concluded that "the current set of AAI studies does not falsify the idea of the universality of attachment theory" (2009, p. 252). Finding individual differences in the distribution of the categories among groups of people defined by either risk or culture would not invalidate the universality of attachment theory. Only finding a culture in which there was no attachment—and no corresponding deficit in functioning—would invalidate the theory. We conclude that the lack of differentiating qualities in the M&G-AAI so constrains and sometimes distorts the results that cultural and gender differences that are easily perceived in daily life cannot be discerned using the M&G-AAI. Any assessment that is to be useful for generating knowledge and theory and of utility for intervention must differentiate gender, culture, and adaptation.

VALIDATION OF THE DMM-AAI

Crittenden's application of the M&G-AAI to a wide range of adult populations led to progressive changes in the coding and classification of

AAIs that culminated in new life-span theory (Crittenden, 1995, 2008) and the new classificatory procedures for the AAI, first published in 1999 (Crittenden, 1999a, now expanded and updated in this book). Over a decade, Crittenden, together with approximately 250 clinicians taking the DMM-AAI course, coded and classified almost 3,000 AAIs from normative, distressed (in treatment), and endangered/dangerous (in hospital or prison) populations from different cultures. After blind coding, case-by-case feedback permitted both theory and discourse analysis procedures to be refined progressively. A particular goal was to add information beyond a simple replication of the psychiatric diagnosis. Specifically, the potential of the DMM-AAI to yield a functional explanation of the strategic mental and behavioral processes observed in discourse has been explored.

The DMM-AAI focuses on adults' self-protective strategies—without the assumption that these will match their children's strategies. Further, the array of patterns and modifiers in adulthood is much larger in the DMM-AAI than in infancy, making a one-to-one matching from parent to child impossible. Rather than being predicated on infancy, the DMM-AAI was intended to reflect the complexity of functioning relevant to adult adaptation and maladaptation. Therefore, it is best validated in terms of different populations that show different qualities of functioning.

Further, the DMM encompasses the life-span and aims for clinical utility. The process of validation for the array of DMM assessments must therefore address the specific processes of each developmental phase and the individual differences in these that are relevant to clinical distinctions.

Rather than investing early on in large-scale studies, the process of validation has progressed from case discussions to case studies of clinical utility; to small, focused studies of concurrent validity; and now to comparative studies. These studies suggest a direction for more comprehensive and longitudinal studies to validate the DMM-AAI.

In terms of formal studies, there are three relevant types of validation of the DMM-AAI:

1. Longitudinal validity (from prior age periods to adulthood);
2. Concurrent validity (from the AAI to diagnosis, other clinical measures, and adult functioning in the present);
3. Predictive validity (from the present to functioning in the future, including the functioning of the adult's children).

Among the hypotheses that can be derived from the DMM, the following seem especially important to validity:

1. Attachment at younger ages would be related to the AAI, albeit not necessarily in a direct one-to-one manner. In other words, the AAI would show developmental coherence, taking into account both maturation and life events.

2. The AAIs of adults would be related to the attachment patterns assessed in their children, that is, the AAI would show transgenerational continuity for Type B, but complementarity for Types A and C.

3. AAI classifications would be related to measures of depression and anxiety, to psychiatric diagnosis, and to deviant behavior. The AAI would therefore be clinically relevant, with a specific relevance of extreme deviations in arousal.

4. Because attachment is systemic, AAI classifications would be related (albeit not necessarily on a matched way) to assessments of adaptation in parents, partners, and children of the speaker.

5. Adults in normative settings would be more often classified as B, A1–2, and C1–2 than adults drawn from clinical settings. When adults drawn from normative populations do not fall within these classifications, a higher incidence of evidence of distress or maladaptation is predicted (on individual, spousal, or familial levels).

6. Adults in treatment or correctional facilities rather than in normative settings will more often be classified as A3–8, C3–8, or A/C, and will more often have modifiers of depression, disorientation, somatic expressions, and intrusions as well as unresolved loss and trauma.

7. Because the same behaviors can serve different functions, adults showing similar symptoms are not necessarily expected to use similar self-protective strategies (i.e., psychiatric diagnosis will only partially predict DMM strategy).

8. Differences in strategy within diagnostic groups suggest different threats as well as important neurophysiological differences in the DMM functional clusters, especially in A versus C comparisons. These differences are expected to have implications for differential treatment.

9. Delusional information will be seen as an attempt to achieve coherence (internal coherence) when episodic information creates discrepancy and denied information is not accessed.

STUDIES USING THE DMM-AAI

Clinical doctoral theses and dissertations provided early empirical tests of the emerging model and DMM-AAI classificatory method by comparing specific psychiatric diagnosed groups with the general population. More recent studies have tested specific aspects of the hypotheses stated above. Taken together, these studies of almost 700 individuals suggest that the DMM-AAI (a) differentiates adaptive and maladaptive individuals well, (b) differentiates among types of disorder in theoretically and clinically meaningful ways, (c) offers a way to formulate maladaptive behavior in psychological terms rather than solely by symptom clusters, (d) may differentiate subgroups within single psychiatric diagnoses that differ in information processing, and (e) may be able to tie discourse about threat to self-protective behavior and underlying information processing. Moreover, in all of the studies discussed below, at least two coders were able to reach satisfactory inter-coder agreement.

Studies on Normative Populations

INFORMATION PROCESSING

Attachment theory hypothesizes both that the ABC strategies reflect different neurological processing and also that mothers' strategies will affect their infants' developing strategies. Strathearn, Fonagy, Amico, and Montague (2009) tested these hypotheses in an elegant study of 30 mothers seen at three times: during the third trimester of pregnancy (for the AAI), then at 7 months postpartum (for an fMRI), and again when the infant was 14 months old (for the Strange Situation). The researchers tested the relation of the mother's AAI to the fMRI difference between her response to seeing her own baby as compared to that of seeing another baby and the relation between her DMM-AAI and the DMM-SSP classification of her baby. Because the sample lacked sufficient Type C mothers, only the A and B categories were compared. Normative Type A and B mothers displayed strikingly different fMRI patterns of neurological activation when looking at pictures of their own babies and of unfamiliar babies in happy and sad conditions. For mothers using a Type B strategy, activation of brain reward regions, including the ventral striatum and the oxytocin-associated hypothalamus/pituitary region, involved processing related to a *gratifying* quality of experience. By contrast, mothers classified as using a Type A strategy showed greater insular activation in response to viewing photographs of their own infants' sad faces. These results suggest that individual differences in mothers' attachment strategies may be linked with different development of the dopaminergic and oxytocinergic neuroendocrine systems. The findings provide evidence that the DMM has neurofunctional correlates, validating both DMM theory about patterns of attachment as information-processing patterns, and the DMM-AAI as having predictive validity with patterns of neurofunctional activity.

ATTACHMENT WITHIN NORMATIVE FAMILIES

The same sample, extended to 47 mothers, was also used to test the transgenerational hypotheses that Type B mothers would have Type B infants, and Type A and C mothers would have infants with the opposite pattern (Shah et al., 2010). The results supported the notion of both matching of Type B (secure) attachment and also meshing (i.e., inversion of pattern for anxiously attached dyads). These findings add to existing data because the DMM method was not designed to produce an association between the AAI and SSP. Also, in the DMM framework, previous mismatches become theoretically meaningful: Infants' adaptation can be increased by the use of a strategy that is the opposite of their mothers'. For example, some mothers using a Type A strategy tend to be underresponsive; when their infants organize an affectively intense Type C strategy, the infants increase the probability of their mothers responding. Conversely, when mothers use a Type C strategy of angry or helpless demands, their infants may benefit by employing an affectively muted Type A (cognitive) strategy. This framing of the functional relation between mothers' and infants' strategies has implications for the management of cases of risk, maltreatment, or psychopathology.

   A Finnish three-generational study followed 34 firstborn children of volunteer women whose husbands and mothers agreed to participate in the study (Hautamäki, Hautamäki, Neuvonen, & Maliniemi-Piispanen, 2009). The mothers, their husbands, and the maternal grandmothers were all given DMM-AAIs during the third trimester of the mothers' pregnancies. The DMM-Strange Situation procedure and the DMM-Preschool Assessment of Attachment (PAA) were conducted when the firstborn children were 12 months old and 3 years old, respectively.

There was a predominance of Ainsworth strategies (A1–2, B, C1–2), with a particular bias for A1–2, especially in children (51.5%) and maternal grandmothers (42.4%). The proportion of B strategies was lower than in similar Anglo samples. These data suggest culture-specific differences in the distribution of the normative strategies. In terms of prediction of children's patterns, mothers' AAI classifications predicted 1-year-old infants' strategies in 76% of cases, and 3-year-olds' strategies in 58% of cases. Grandmothers' AAI classifications predicted 3-year-olds' PAA classifications in 72% of cases. Continuity was observed in 47% of the grandmother-mother-children triads, mainly for Types B and A1–2. There were also reversal reactions (meshing) in the triads: 22% showed A/C/A (more frequently) and C/A/C combinations. These results replicate Shah and colleagues' research (2010) and extend it to three generations.

The couples in this Finnish sample showed 11 matches (B with B), 12 A/C meshes, and 9 secure/insecure combinations, without any significant relation between the mothers' and the fathers' strategies (Hautamäki et al., 2010).

The hypothesis of meshed adult relationships and parent-child transformations of strategies had already been supported in an early, transitional study (Crittenden et al., 1991). This study used the M&G-AAI coding method applied to the Parents Interview (Crittenden, 1981) in which couples were interviewed about their experiences as former children and currently as parents. The sample consisted of 53 mother-male partner couples, each with a 1- to 4-year-old child, who had been assessed with the SSP or PAA. The families varied in the quality of childrearing (results were adequate, marginally maltreating, and maltreating).

All couples (except three who displayed secure/insecure combinations) were either matched in pattern or meshed (i.e., Type A and C combinations). Empirically, meshed partnerships were associated with abuse and neglect, partner violence, and A/C patterns of child attachment. Even this early study already supported the more complex notion of the adult strategies creating a context that provides information from which children structure their own strategies. This notion includes the possibility of children adapting to complex environments, in which parents use opposite self-protective strategies, by producing combined A/C attachment strategies.

PARENTS, PATIENTS, AND PSYCHOTHERAPISTS

Hughes, Hardy, and Kendrick (2000) interviewed 16 clients engaged in psychological assessment or therapy, comparing their AAIs with those of 11 third-year clinical psychology trainees. Within the following 3 weeks, a "clinically orientated interview" was administered. Both interviews were coded and classified with the DMM-AAI method to explore whether an ordinary clinical session could yield the same attachment strategy as the AAI. The results indicated that (a) coders could reach agreement on the AAI but not on the clinical interview and (b) the two interviews didn't match on A, B, C, or A/C patterns. This suggests that the systematic increase of danger in the topics of the AAI and the orderly probing of the various memory systems make the AAI procedure more reliable.

They also found (not reported in the published paper, but of crucial interest here; Crittenden, from the classifications submitted to Hughes et al., 2000) that the classifications attributed to the clients were well differentiated from those of the clinical psychology trainees. For the trainees, 35% were assigned to Type B, and 55% were reorganizing; also unresolved loss was present in 18%. On the other hand, none of the clients used a B strategy or was reorganizing toward B. Instead, almost half used an A/C strategy in which at least one of the components was a high-numbered strategy. Thirty percent were assigned a C+ strategy and 40% had unresolved loss or trauma or a modifier. The clients and student trainee distributions did not overlap at all. This adds to the concurrent validity of the DMM-AAI, especially in terms of its clinical discrimination.

Drawing from an Italian sample, the DMM-AAIs of 40 parents of child patients were compared with those of (a) 79 parents who were themselves in mental health treatment and (b) 128 parents (not in treatment) of nonpatient children (Crittenden & Landini, 2009). The parents of child patients differed from the normative parents, but not from the patients. Among the adult patients and parents of child patients, there were no Ainsworth classifications (B, A1–2 or C1–2) whereas half of the normative parents were assigned to these patterns. The two nonnormative groups showed slight differences in the distribution of the DMM patterns: The parents of child patients were more often Type A+ (A3–8) or A/C than the adult patients, who were more often Type C+ (C3–8). In addition, the parents of child patients had more unresolved losses than the patients. Both nonnormative groups differed markedly from the normative group in unresolved trauma or loss and depression.

Because the data are concurrent, it is not possible to state a direction of effects between parents and children. The results are nonetheless coherent with the DMM in that family members' strategies are expected to be related. If one family member needs treatment, it would be probable that others would as well. The preponderance of extreme strategies, unresolved losses and traumas, and modifiers found in this sample of "asymptomatic" parents of identified child patients supports DMM theory and suggests that the DMM-AAI may be useful in identifying situations of distress that are not yet clinically evident. The prevalence of a compulsive A component in the strategies of the parents of child patients suggests that dismissing of negative affect and compliance with external standards may normalize the appearance of these families.

Another study compared the DMM-AAIs of 51 experienced Italian psychotherapists to the same comparison groups of 128 normative adults and 79 psychiatric patients (Lambruschi, Landini, & Crittenden, 2008). Almost a third of the psychotherapists used an earned (i.e., reorganized) Type B strategy with another 10% reorganizing toward B. The remaining two-thirds had a prevalence of compulsive Type A strategies (A3–6) and A+/C+ combinations. Unresolved traumas were found in one third of the psychotherapists, as were unresolved losses; the majority of these were of complex forms of lack of resolution (e.g., displaced, imagined, depressed).

When compared with the normative group, the psychotherapists' distribution of strategies showed a slightly lower proportion of Type B, a much lower proportion of Type C, and a much higher proportion of Type A+ and Type A+/C+. On the other hand, the depressed modifier was equally frequent in the normative and psychotherapist samples. When compared with the patient distribution, the patient sample had no B classifications, less reorganization, and a C component only slightly higher than the normative population (especially in the C5–6 range). Otherwise the psychotherapist and patient distributions were almost identical (Lambruschi et al., 2008). This suggests that about one third of the therapists demonstrated evidence of integrative skill that is compatible with functioning as a transitional attachment figure for troubled adults. The other two-thirds show strategies that suggest compulsive caregiving to patients or not fully conscious attempts at using work to repair personal lack of resolution of past experience.

Studies on Clinical Populations

The next group of studies used comparisons of normative samples with clinical samples, defined on the basis of abnormal behavior or psychiatric diagnoses.

FOSTERING

Gogarty's doctoral thesis (2002) reported descriptive data on the DMM-AAIs of 16 adults who as children had been in long-term foster care, of 10 of their foster parents, and of 4 of their birth parents. The former foster children had only one individual using a B strategy (6%). Type C strategies at the C3–4 level were used by 19% of the participants, 30% used A/C strategies, and 45% used highly compulsive A strategies, at the A5–6 level. Fifty-five percent also showed unresolved losses or traumas. The foster parents showed a relatively normative array of strategies (50% B, 30% C, 10% A, 10% A/C) with a bias toward unresolved childhood losses. Three of the four biological parents showed compulsive A strategies; two had unresolved traumas.

The results suggest that the traumas and losses involved in the separation from the biological family often remain unresolved into adulthood. One explanation could include the influence of the foster parents' own lack of resolution of childhood loss on their foster children. Replication on a larger sample and further published research are clearly needed.

EATING AND PERSONALITY DISORDERS

Zachrisson and Kulbotton (2006) classified the AAIs of 20 women with anorexia nervosa using the DMM method. All were assigned to A+, C+, and A/C, with modifiers and Us; none had an Ainsworth classification. Despite the lack of a normative comparison group, the distribution of patterns resembled other clinical studies. Apart from a high frequency of unresolved childhood losses and traumas, no specific strategic functional patterning was discerned as specifically related to the symptoms of anorexia.

Another study of eating disorders (Ringer & Crittenden, 2007) used the DMM-AAI in a sample of 62 Anglo-Australian young women with an eating disorder (19 with anorexia nervosa, 26 with bulimia nervosa, and 17 with bulimic anorexia). All the AAIs were classified within the

DMM categories (that is, there were no A1–2, B, or C1–2 classifications), but were not in the most extreme categories (not A5–8 or C7–8). About half used a coercive Type C strategy while most of the others combined a triangulated Type C3–6 strategy with a compulsive Type A strategy. The women in this sample had been exposed to very little danger or death of family members, thus precluding the assignment of lack of resolution in most cases. Nevertheless about one third of the AAIs had unresolved traumas based on (a) fighting between the parents, (b) vicarious experience of a parent's trauma or (c) an imagined relation between a childhood event and the eating disorder. None had modifiers. The women appeared strategically stuck and lacked an adequate explanation for this state, possibly because triangulation around family secrets regarding discord or parental trauma disrupted causal processes. There was no relation between classification and eating disorder diagnosis.

Discriminant analysis identified three clusters of women with an eating disorder. Cluster 1 contained four cases of Type A strategies without a Type C component; the compulsive caregiving/compliant strategies were directed toward parents who appeared preoccupied with their spousal relationships to the exclusion of their parenting role. Cluster 2 contained the C3–4 strategies whereas Cluster 3 contained the C5–6 and A/C cases. Both Clusters 2 and 3 had cases of imagined unresolved trauma, that is, noncausal but actual events that, in the absence of accurate information about parental problems, were thought by the women to have caused their eating disorders.

The DMM-AAI appears to add information to the symptom description; it remains to be investigated how each type of information (symptoms diagnosis and information processing) is best used for guiding treatment. In almost all cases the women were confused about how parental behavior was tied causally to their own behaviors and they also were very reluctant to talk in the interviews. Based on a combination of discourse and content, it appeared that the parents were often especially close to their daughters, but became unavailable when traumas/losses exerted their interfering effects, and this happened in ways that were unpredictable and inscrutable to the daughters. The daughters attributed causal responsibility to themselves when more accurate information was not available.

The treatment implications highlight the complexity of at least two important ironies. First, family problems were kept secret to protect the children. Although clarity or "disclosure" should probably be pursued in treatment, it should be carried out with careful attention to the possible adverse effects of premature or excessive clarity on various family members. Second, the clarification of causality should be pursued in ways that acknowledge both the complexity of family relationships and also the need for independence among older adolescents and young women. In other words, the treatment process should not strengthen maladaptive bonds within the family of origin. The next step is testing of treatment implications.

A Norwegian study of avoidant personality disorder (APD, Rindal, 2000) compared 12 DMM-AAIs of participants diagnosed with APD with age- and gender-matched normative participants. The clinical sample had no simple Ainsworth classifications whereas these classifications accounted for 60% of the classifications in the normative comparison group. The participants with APD also had a higher incidence of unresolved losses/traumas and modifiers. The "signature pattern" for APD consisted of unresolved childhood trauma, explicit claims of idealization and compliance that were belied by the discourse analysis, and a coercively punitive strategy (Utr(p) [A1,4]C5). This pattern is closely related to the way Type C strategies are used by some women with eating disorders. The small sample size requires replication before the results can be generalized, but the interesting suggestion here is that disorders presenting differently (APD and some of the eating disorders) might be functionally similar. If so, they might benefit from the same kind of intervention.

PSYCHOLOGICAL TRAUMA

Crittenden and Heller (under review) compared 66 adults in three categories: DMM-AAIs of 22 adults with chronic posttraumatic stress disorder (PTSD) with 22 adults receiving psychological treatment for mixed diagnoses (non-PTSD), and with 22 normative adults not in treatment. They found that the PTSD group was differentiable from both comparison groups. With only one exception, the classifications used for the clinical groups were DMM-specific and included 10 out of 11 possible classifications, reflecting a wide range of functional variation. Only one third of the normative cases were assigned to the DMM strategies. This fits epidemiological predictions that 25–30% of a normative population is diagnosable with some form of mental illness (Kessler, 1994). There were also differences in the number of unresolved traumas (PTSD was highest, and normative the lowest), with type of lack of resolution (PTSD showing the most complex types, normative the simplest) constituting the "signature" of PTSD.

Over all, participants diagnosed with PTSD (a) were generally strategic in their functioning, using most often a coercive punitive/seductive strategy (C5–6), (b) had a high number of childhood traumas or losses, (c) displayed nonstrategic alternation of dismissing and preoccupying processing around specific childhood traumas or losses, (d) confused traumas with one another, and (e) tended not to use illusory forms of response to childhood trauma and loss. Further, the DMM-AAI data suggest that the alternating quality of the DSM-IV diagnosis of PTSD probably refers to the response to trauma or loss and not to individuals' basic self-protective strategies.

The results suggest that the DMM-AAI can not only discriminate among diagnostic categories, but can also find different functional groupings within single descriptive categories. For example, the "signature pattern" for chronic PTSD appears to differ from those for the eating and personality disorders.

Again, discriminant analysis found three clusters that suggest clinically relevant hypotheses. Clusters 1 and 2 were similar, being primarily organized around a coercive Type C strategy together with unresolved trauma in an incompatible dismissing-and-preoccupied or disorganized form and no modifiers. Cluster 3 had compulsive A classifications, very often modified by depression, and one or more unresolved traumas that always included a dismissing process; these adults appeared to have been very seriously harmed as children, with almost no protection or comfort from attachment figures. Individuals in Cluster 3 were nonstrategic, whereas those in Clusters 1 and 2 were strategic except when dealing with current situations that triggered representations associated with the unresolved childhood event. If replicated on a larger sample, these cluster differences suggest that both the focus and methods of treatment for PTSD for adults in Clusters 1–2 might need to be different from those for adults in Cluster 3.

Four cases drawn from the PTSD sample were discussed in detail with reference to clinical implications by Heller (Heller, 2010; Heller & Pollet, 2010). Heller observed that the traumatizing event in adulthood shared both morphological similarity and psychological meaning with the childhood event; she emphasized the lack of comfort and protection in childhood as creating vulnerability for an unresolvable response to particular sorts of danger in adulthood.

SEXUAL OFFENDING AGAINST CHILDREN

Thirty-three Irish men convicted of sexual assault and in prison were given the AAI before and after cognitive behavioral treatment intended to reduce recidivism (O'Reilly, 2010). The transcripts were coded by five blinded and reliable coders. Here we describe only the pretreatment AAIs. The classifications were distributed evenly among A+, C+, and A+/C+; there were no B, A1–3, or C1–4 instances. The A+ components were almost uniformly A4 (compulsive compliance) or A7 (delusional idealization of an endangering parent) or both. The C+ component was usually C5–6 (punitive and seductive), with a small number of C7–8 (menacing and paranoid) classifications. Depression was rare, but when it was present, it was associated with A4 or A7. Intrusions of negative affect were also rare. About half the men had unresolved losses from childhood, usually of several family members. Essentially all the men had unresolved trauma from childhood; moreover, the type of lack of resolution included a dismissing or disorganized component. In all cases, the danger consisted of physical violence against themselves or their mothers or both; in about half of cases, the dangers also included being sexually abused. As a whole, the set of interviews was bleak and distressing in the accumulation of violations of safety and comfort during childhood and the current inability of the men to have compassion for the boys that they once were.

This distribution appears different from that of cases of familial sexual abuse that have been brought to AAI courses. These, almost uniformly, were classified as A4/A7, with unresolved loss and trauma, but without depression, intrusions, or past child sexual abuse. That is, the familial cases that we have seen fit one subgroup in the O'Reilly sample. It should be noted that, among these cases, the sexually abusing fathers expressed the desire to raise their children differently than they were raised, specifically by being less violent and more affectionate than their fathers (cf. Crittenden, 2008, cases of John and David).

Comparing DMM and Main and Goldwyn Classifications

CHILD MALTREATMENT

Seefeldt (1997) sought to discriminate among 31 abusive, neglectful, and low-income adequate mother-infant dyads in terms of maternal attachment and parenting behavior. The mothers were single and Caucasian, with infants ranging from 6 to 24 months in age. The maltreating mothers were under child protection supervision for substantiated or high-risk reports; the adequate mothers had no child protection referrals. Both AAIs and videotaped feeding and play interactions were gathered.

The AAIs were initially classified with the Main and Goldwyn method. Because 15 of the 31 transcripts in all three groups were identified as Cannot Classify (CC), the data could not be used to test group differences.

The AAIs were reclassified using the DMM. The AAIs of mothers in the abuse group were typified by idealization of their parents together with dismissed traumas in their childhoods.[1] Neglectful mothers were characterized by depression, idealization, and dismissed traumas. Normative low-income mothers received balanced and mildly anxious classifications (i.e., B, A1–3, and C1–4) without lack of resolution or depression. There was a significant difference in ABC classification between the maltreating and nonmaltreating mothers' AAIs and between the abuse and neglect groups on depression. Parenting groups, in turn, predicted mothers' caregiving behavior, as assessed with feeding and teaching rating scales applied to the videotapes.

This study demonstrated that maltreating parents can be differentiated from adequate parents by their self-protective attachment strategies, but only when the DMM-AAI is used. Further, the predictive validity of the AAI classification regarding parenting behavior was suggested, but a larger sample is needed to elaborate on this relation.

BORDERLINE PERSONALITY DISORDER

Crittenden and Newman (2010) compared the AAIs of 15 mothers with borderline personality disorder (BPD) to those of 17 normative mothers. Both the Main and Goldwyn and DMM methods were used to classify the AAIs. This allowed not only comparison of the functioning of mothers with BPD to that of mothers without psychiatric disorders, but also a comparison of the two classificatory methods. As predicted by the DMM, the mothers with BPD recalled more danger (five times as often), reported more negative effects of danger, and gave evidence of more unresolved trauma than the normative mothers. All but one

---

1. Because the A7 classification was not identified at this time, it cannot be said whether the idealization was delusional or not, that is, whether the classification was A1 or A7.

mother with BPD was classified as depressed with unresolved trauma in an A+/C+ strategy whereas none of the normative mothers were classified as A/C or with a strategy in the lower upper half of the DMM circle and none had depression or intrusions. They also showed a DMM "signature" pattern different from the eating and personality disorders and PTSD, but containing components of both: preoccupying unresolved trauma with a coercive C5–6 strategy (the component similar to both APD and eating disorders) and depression with multiple dismissed, disorganized, and blocked unresolved traumas (as in PTSD). There was also a compulsive A strategy with destabilizing intrusions of forbidden negative affect (a patterning observed clinically in cases of psychosis).

When the same AAIs were classified with the M&G method, 40% of mothers with BPD lacked coherent, integrated representations (i.e., E3, the least integrated classification in the system), but so did 18% of the normative women. On the other hand, 47% of mothers with BPD (and 41% of normative mothers) had Ainsworth insecure classifications (Ds1, Ds3, and E2). None of the mothers with BPD and 35% of the normative mothers were classified as secure. All of the mothers with BPD had lack of resolution as did 25% of normative mothers. These findings produced both a significant group difference and also an overlap in strategy among more than half of the mothers in each group.

The classifications in the two methods matched in about half of the cases. The DMM classifications produced more significant findings and accounted for more variance overall.

Although both methods differentiated the groups of mothers, the M&G classifications showed considerable overlap. That is, the representations of borderline and normative mothers were not strikingly different, thus, providing a less clear explanation for BPD mothers' dangerously maladaptive behavior. Instead, the DMM classifications of the mothers with BPD were substantially more complex than the M&G classifications, reflecting the clinical complexity of the condition. Specifically, the A/C structure with swings in arousal between depression and intrusions seems coherent with the theoretical expectation of an alternation between denial of perception of danger and very high perception of danger; this is also compatible with the descriptive diagnostic criteria. These strategic components might require precise targeting of treatment components, with a substantial risk that failure to differentiate and sequence the various treatment components properly could augment the psychological distortions.

Summary of empirical results

Overall, these studies show that

- There is almost no overlap in DMM-AAI classifications between normative and clinical groups.
- Descriptive diagnoses and DMM-AAI classifications are related, but are not the same thing.
- Some DMM constructs cross diagnoses and may explain behavior more than the descriptive diagnoses (for example A7, CΔ, [ina]).
- The psychologically different subgroups (with similar symptoms) identified within several descriptive diagnoses by the DMM-AAI classifications might need different treatments.

Case Studies of Treatment

Clinicians who applied DMM theory and formulation to patient care, by using DMM-AAI classifications for shaping treatment plans, published their findings as case studies. These are reviewed to explore both the etiological hypotheses that they suggest and also how the functional formulations based on the DMM-AAI can inform treatment.

Disorientation and attention deficit hyperactivity disorder (ADHD)

A 10-year-old Norwegian boy, diagnosed with ADHD and treated with psychostimulant medication, was given a School-Age Assessment of Attachment; his mother was given the AAI (Crittenden & Kulbotton, 2007). The mother's AAI was classified as disoriented compulsive A and obsessive C (i.e., DO A+C+). Disorientation was the crucial feature of the transcript, because it rendered the mother's behavior nonstrategic. The boy's SAA was classified DO Utr(ds)$_{mother}$ A+(8)C5. Both mother and son appeared similarly disoriented, with the mother's disorientation tied to her own childhood, and the son's tied to the mother, especially to her marital traumas. Based on her attachment classification, the mother's behavior could be expected to be highly anxious and unpredictable. This, in turn, would make the strategic attempts of her son ineffective. This would close the circle by making the mother more anxious and confused. The whole process was characterized by an inability to connect feelings and actions to their proper sources. This suggests that a child-focused treatment for ADHD might not address parental factors that contributed to the child's condition. The presence of a partial A8 component in the boy's classification suggests that treatment may be adding to the boy's source confusion by supplying him with therapist-generated perspectives that he confuses with his own and those of his mother. The outcome would be shifting, unpredictable, and frequently maladaptive behavior.

Dismissed lack of resolution of loss and
factitious illness by proxy

A case of factitious illness by proxy in which a 6-year-old Australian girl was removed from her home due to concern about the parents' management of her health care had, as part of the assessment, administration of the DMM-AAI to the parents (Kozlowska, Foley, & Crittenden, 2006). The parents were both nurses; of their five children, the youngest child had had respiratory problems that led to the issues investigated by the services.

The mother's AAI classification was $Ul(ds\&p)_F (p)_{ex\text{-}patient} (dx)_{friend\ in\ Bali\ bombing} A1(A3/4)$. The outstanding feature of this classification is not so much the A strategy (which would nonetheless explain the compulsive focus on the health of the daughter), but the array of unresolved losses. The loss of her father in her childhood was treated in opposite ways and still appears actively unresolved. The more recent and less personal losses of a former patient and a friend who died in a terrorist attack were spoken about with great arousal. The death of the former patient was especially interesting because she discussed it in the present tense with bodily agitation. The breathing problems that led to this death (and were also a key factor in the death of her father) were also perceived by the mother in the focal daughter, leading to attempts to have her undergo neurosurgery. These misguided child-protective actions were motivated by the preconscious representations connected to the mother's past unresolved losses. The father's classification was $Ul(p)_{M\ \&\ F} A1$: an idealizing strategy, with a strong preoccupation on what the father could have done to prevent his parents' deaths.

The parents' strategies and unresolved losses appear very similar, so that the misattributions of one parent were unlikely to be identified and corrected by the other. To the contrary, each parent was primed to support the other in overattributing threat to mild signs of respiratory distress in their children. Both used Type A strategies to distance them-selves from their feelings, making reciprocal comfort unlikely. Instead, they channeled their feelings into action aimed at protecting their children, even to the point of causing the children to have unnecessary and possibly harmful medical procedures.

The parents considered the DMM-AAI a major step during treatment: The mother especially began to understand how her experiences with loss had motivated her to behave in specific ways with the medical services. The main contribution of the DMM-AAI in this case was the opportunity it afforded professionals to make sense in protective ways of what could have been framed as malicious and absurdly dangerous parenting behavior. With the DMM-AAI, compassion, guidance, and change became possible.

PREOCCUPIED UNRESOLVED LOSS AND
CHRONIC URINARY RETENTION

The mother of a preschool-aged Australian girl showing medically unexplained chronic urinary retention was given the AAI as part of a family assessment to investigate factors contributing to the condition (Kozlowska, 2010). The mother's transcript was classified $Ul(p)_{cousin, grandmother}$ $(a)_{self}$ A6(7). The compulsive self-reliance (A6) appears with a delusional idealization of her parents who were alcoholic; their violently abusive relationship pervaded the mother's childhood home. The mother had been unable to implement the Type A strategy of inhibition of negative affect in the context of her preoccupation with (a) the death of her cousin, who had died from cystic fibrosis at 11 years of age, (b) the death of her grandmother, and (c) the anticipation of her own death. The PAA showed that the daughter used a self-protective strategy of compulsive performance with intrusions of forbidden anger, along with evidence of unresolved trauma around medical procedures (displayed in unusual doll play).

The withholding of urine first appeared in the context of separation from the distressed and ill mother. It seems to have been interpreted by the mother as unrelated to herself or the family and, instead, triggered fear of chronic illnesses (associated with the death of the cousin and with previous experiences of her own mother's pain). The mother's anxiety was mirrored in the high levels of arousal in the daughter, either extremely inhibited or displayed in outbursts, all related to previous traumatic experiences associated with somatic disorders. The AAI focused the mother's attention on similarities between various negative events in her experience. This awareness led to intervention focused on supporting the comforting qualities of the mother-daughter relationship and on limiting the protective actions of the mother, which were motivated by past dangerous experiences rather than by the daughter's current health.

REASSESSMENT AND TREATMENT OF AN ADOLESCENT WITH "OBSESSIVE-COMPULSIVE DISORDER"

After 13 years of unsuccessful treatment, a 17-year-old girl was referred to an inpatient adolescent psychiatric unit (Wilkinson, 2010). The descriptive diagnosis was obsessive-compulsive disorder.

The girl no longer lived at home because she had intense angry outbursts. Some years ago, she had physically attacked her mother, scaring both parents greatly. She was hospitalized then, but her famly would not accept her home when she was discharged. She had lived alone since she was 15. Outpatient cognitive behavioral treatment combined with medication had followed, but progress had stopped, leaving some "behavioral rigidity." Admission to a hospital was seen as a way to foster further progress.

Before accepting her as a patient, Wilkinson insisted on a functional formulation to show how hospitalization could accomplish what 13 years of treatment had failed to do. Assessment showed that the girl did not fulfill criteria for a current obsessive-compulsive disorder (OCD) diagnosis or for any other axis I diagnosis.

The whole family was interviewed with DMM procedures. The girl's Transition to Adulthood Attachment Interview was classified as Dp Utr(ds)$_{hospitalization}$ A6 [ina: anger]. Her failing strategy of self-reliance couldn't prevent intrusions of forbidden anger. She denied feeling angry, didn't recognize the feeling as part of herself, and was ashamed of her behavior. She dismissed the negative impact of the former hospitalization, including the resulting separation from her family. The mother's AAI was classified as Utr(ds)$_{hospitalization}$ A4-. She evaluated her own performance through the performance of her children. As a child, she herself had been abandoned by her parents during a long hospitalization; she dismissed the importance of this (therefore making abandonment of her own child more likely). She saw no personal or communicative meaning in her daughter's anger, interpreting it as a "symptom" of the "sickness." Any other meaning would have been incompatible with her prescriptive semantic values, contradicting her need to perform well as a mother. The father's AAI was classified A1–2, without any unresolved loss or trauma: He was less uneasy with negative affect than his wife.

The functional formulation focused on

- describing the current salient problem for the girl, her trouble living on her own, rather than the former diagnosis or the sporadic aggressive episodes;
- reframing expressions of anger as meaningful and normative for all family members; and
- valuing affective information as potentially clarifying previously unpredictable occurrences.

The treatment discontinued the previous emphasis on predictable contingencies (which would have been appropriate if the aggressive behavior had occurred in the context of a C strategy). Instead, the "symptoms of OCD" were framed as the only form of communication that could break through the misunderstanding among family members regarding the girl's need to be cared for and her parents' need to be caregivers. The former hospitalization was now seen as having had a destructive effect through initiating separation of the girl from her family and leading to dismissal of its importance by everyone. It was redefined as important and the separation as needing to be reversed. Visits back home, in increasingly long periods of time, were initiated, with guidance for communicating through and managing feelings.

Two years later, the 19-year-old girl lived at home, worked part time, and was about to move voluntarily into independent lodgings (Wilkinson, personal communication). The parents were still anxious about the girl's signs of growing independence and desire for privacy, but she had been able to convey her perspective to her parents using regulated, but clear, expressions of anger. The parents communicated with the therapists less about the diagnoses and more with questions about interpersonal meanings.

CHILD SEXUAL ABUSE, DRUG ABUSE, AND POSTTRAUMATIC STRESS DISORDER (PTSD)

A young Italian mother, living with her husband and 3-year-old daughter in a community for treatment of alcohol and drug addiction was diagnosed with PTSD (Crittenden & Poggioli, 2008). The traumatizing event was repeated rape by the clients of her prostitute mother when she was 10–12 years old. She was then institutionalized for neglect and abuse, ran away from the institution, used drugs, and lived on the streets. At 17 she married and had a child. After the birth, she became very depressed and attempted suicide. As a consequence, the family moved to the treatment community, where husband, wife, and child lived separately in different sections of the community. The mother had regular daily contact with the daughter who was cared for by others.

Her TAAI was classified Dp Utr(ds)$_{\text{domestic violence, physical abuse and neglect, sexual abuse}}$ Ul(ds)$_{\text{fatherlike friend}}$ A5. This classification suggests that the young mother seriously distorted her understanding of her experience by (a) denying true negative affect, (b) doing whatever other people required in order to elicit their caregiving, and (c) holding herself responsible for what happened to her. Specifically, she displayed false sexual interest and engaged in partner-pleasing sexual behavior; these superficial relationships appeared to substitute for the failed attachment to her parents. Her inhibition of negative affect was probably adaptive when she was a child and could not change the dangerous conditions of her life. In adulthood, however, inhibition prevented her from establishing close and enduring attachments with her husband and daughter and, in addition, prevented her from using her feelings to avoid dangerous situations. To protect herself and her daughter, the mother needed to attend to the alerting and warning function of negative affect. She also needed to recognize that sexual feelings sometimes indicate a desire for comfort.

The PAA showed her daughter to use a depressed Type Dp A strategy with her mother. The mother did not initiate positive affect and the daughter, probably because she was not fully dependent on her mother for her basic care and protection, had not acquired a potentially adaptive compulsive caregiving strategy. If she had, this might have provided a way for mother and daughter to relate to each other.

Framing the problems of this family in this way suggests that the perceived threat of intimacy is reinforced by the treatment plan that requires the family to live apart. This fails to provide a chance for exploration of feelings within a family setting. Instead, the treatment community's resources could be construed as protecting the participants from themselves, thus supporting and maintaining the distorted strategy used by the mother.

Denied Desire for Comfort and Sexual Offending Across Two Generations

A Finnish recidivist violent sexual offender, with a history of antisocial behavior, was given the AAI (Haapasalo et al., 1999). His classification reflects the early stages of development of the DMM-AAI, in that he was classified $A3_M A4_F \rightarrow A5$–6, without specific mention of unresolved traumas or the possibility of A7. In fact, the files and the participant's written account of his own life history indicate that his father physically abused both him and his siblings, was often violent toward his mother with the violent episodes often ending with sexual intercourse, and at least once sexually abused him in ways that closely matched the morphology of the subsequent six violent sexual crimes the participant committed (usually under the influence of alcohol and cannabis).

The dangerous experiences with sexual components are not mentioned in the AAI, which leaves open the possibility of a dismissed form of lack of resolution around these events. There is also no mention of modifiers: Given the nature of the patterning and of the history, there would be reason to question whether depression and intrusions could be present. Modifiers, however, were not yet part of the DMM method at the time of publication.

Nonetheless, the classification contributes a possible functional formulation of this man's behavior. His basic strategy was compulsive self-reliance, alternating with compulsive promiscuity, growing out of the failure of compulsive compliance to the father and compulsive caregiving to the mother to protect him. This strategy indicates that he believed that all negative affect must be inhibited, with a special denial for desire for interpersonal comfort. Sexual contact may have been his way to overcome this intense inhibition. However, in the man's experience (both witnessed and experienced), sexual acts were connected to violence. It is possible that intrusions of unregulated desire for comfort underlie his criminal acts. When the inhibition of negative affect was reinstated, he was unable to recall his affective motivation for the violent rapes, and, instead, expressed only the "appropriate" semantic shame and guilt.

Alcohol Abuse and Personality Disorder

In this case, the AAI was used to re-focus a course of treatment (Tone Flo, 2009). A 35-year-old man, after about 10 years of alcohol abuse and recurrent hospitalizations for psychotic symptomatology, entered both individual psychotherapy and a course of treatment for alcohol abuse, leading to his being an active member of Alcoholics Anonymous (AA). His diagnosis at intake was emotionally unstable personality disorder with alcohol abuse. The AAI was given to him after 3 years of psychotherapy, after the patient had showed an increased desire to further his understanding of himself. His therapist had trouble reconciling the history (which seemed "all C") and the attitude of the patient in the sessions ("never angry or critical, always prepared and on time").

The DMM-AAI classification was Ul(a)$_{father}$, R (DO A1+C3, 4, 5–6, 8? → B). The originally disoriented state of the patient's strategies was coherent with his feelings of "confusion" when dealing with his family history in the initial stages of treatment. One of the potentially complex features of the therapeutic setting, having parallel individual and group (AA) therapies, was shown to be helpful by the functional formulation through the AAI. The combined therapies allowed the patient to experience differences in the treatments, pushing him to find a way to integrate their usefulness for him. Presumably the process was helped by the extreme clarity of source for various representations related to treatment: As the patient summarized to the therapist at the end of treatment, *"They (AA) tore me down, and you picked me up."* After the AAI, the patient concentrated on specifying sources of his knowledge about his past and extending his inquiries: This process included the discovery of a family secret (the suicide of his maternal grandfather) that seemed to explain his previous attempts to use C5–6 strategies.

RECURRENT DEPRESSION

Pre- and posttreatment DMM-AAIs were given to a 40-year-old Norwegian man with recurrent depression who received four-times-a-week psychoanalysis for 3 years (Gullestad, 2003). The first AAI was given before starting treatment, and the second was given 6 months after termination. The patient's mother was alcoholic and had attempted suicide several times, being repeatedly admitted to psychiatric institutions. His parents separated when the man was 6 years old, and he spent periods of time at an orphanage. In all, he was estranged from his mother for 12 years, until he was 25. He was unhappily married with three children at the time of the AAI.

The pretreatment AAI classification was: Dp Utr(ds)$_{abandonment\ by}$ $_{father}$ A4,6 C3. The posttreatment AAI classification was B2. The patient's own account of the changes that occurred in therapy included a change from his awareness of his life history as "mere facts" to the memories acquiring "movement, color, and smell." This seems to be coherent with a depressed modifier, which lowered arousal and reduced the power of dispositional representations to motivate behavior, that later changed to a fully strategic state. He also spoke about a change in the "me-versus-them" to a "we" attitude; again this was paralleled in the change of strategy, from a blended AC in which all information is present, but not integrated, to a B strategy that opened up the possibility of cooperation.

SUMMARY OF CASE STUDY FINDINGS

Overall, these case studies show the following:

- The DMM-AAI classifications reframe problems in ways that are acceptable to families and engage their participation in change.
- The DMM may identify psychological conditions that pass unnoticed using either DSM or ICD, but which have implications for adaptation of adults or their children (for example, disorientation).
- Parents of child patients bring psychological problems to the treatment of their children.
- Addressing the parents' problems helps children to get better.
- The DMM case formulation identifies some common treatments as inappropriate or even harmful for specific families.

FUTURE DIRECTIONS FOR THE TESTING OF DMM-AAI VALIDITY

Overview of Existing Results

Up to now, most studies of the DMM-AAI have addressed concurrent validity and used small samples that required limited investment of resources. The main concern has been to establish the clinical relevance of the DMM-AAI. We believe that the set of studies reviewed above is sufficient to establish preliminary reliability of coding, validity of classification, and utility of the findings, for both individuals and groups of similar individuals. It is now time to consolidate and expand these results.

Recommendations for Future Studies

Larger normative comparison groups are needed to establish cultural-specific normative distributions. Larger samples of clinical groups could allow replication of the findings described above, and theoretically guided selection of other diagnostic groups could allow more direct testing of hypotheses drawn from the DMM. A broader range of validating variables, particularly variables using several different data-gathering procedures, is needed. That is, it is time for theory-based studies using a multimethod, multi-informant design. This, of course, will require funding and the best argument for funding may be the potential of the DMM and DMM-AAI to improve treatment effectiveness.

Potential of the DMM-AAI for Clinical Research

The DMM-AAI can be thought of as striking a useful balance between the general descriptive diagnoses and the unique details of a case, but whether this balance is useful for planning and implementing intervention is an empirical question. To determine whether the effort required by the application of the AAI is clinically justified, studies that test the relevance of the information about attachment strategy for treatment are crucially important.

We think that the development of DMM theory and DMM-AAI methodology has now progressed sufficiently to support study of even very severe disorders such as psychoses, violent criminal behavior, and sexual abuse. The application of the AAI to these issues could offer theoretical understanding and can also inform treatment approaches and allow observation-based testing of treatment-related changes. In addition, DMM theory can easily support studies of clinically relevant topics, such as adult couples (e.g., pair matching, conflict resolution, divorce), immigration, sexuality (including sexual disorders and offending behavior), and family relationships.

The DMM-AAI in Basic Research

Existing longitudinal samples could be recoded to determine whether the DMM-AAI explains more variance in life-span and intergenerational effects or finds different outcome effects using the same measures as were used with the original ABC+D analyses. Longitudinal effects are also relevant for clinical studies, for example, in establishing direction of effects in the process leading to disorder. Thus, a major yield in information could come from a relatively small input of new funding.

Studies addressing the development of individuals over time and across several age ranges, all using DMM assessments, could address the issue of predictive validity. This would be especially relevant to forensic applications of the DMM-AAI (predicting parental functioning or dangerous behavior). For example, systematic follow-up of the outcomes of the expert recommendations to courts based on family assessments using the DMM-AAI could be of special value.

Overall, the DMM-AAI shows relevance to clinical issues, both psychopathological and therapeutic. Its observational nature has the potential to inform new approaches in areas of human functioning that are not yet sufficiently understood. The formalized and replicable procedures of the DMM-AAI offer an empirical means of investigating some of the complex effects of human relationships on mental and behavioral functioning.

Chapter 16

Conclusions

THE ADULT ATTACHMENT INTERVIEW IS POSSIBLY THE MOST EXCITING clinical assessment tool to be developed in the last several decades. It generated enthusiasm even before it was well known: An assessment described as investigating adults' state of mind regarding attachment sounds full of promise. The early data were powerful: Personal history in the context of the family of origin, distilled as a current mental state, influences current behavior that, in turn, becomes the developmental context for one's children (Main et al., 1985). Adults who successfully reproduce are in a pivotal phase of the life cycle, one that holds immense potential (both positive and negative) for the next generation. Any assessment able to capture useful information about such a moment will be extremely valuable.

We think the AAI can do that and more. It can inform us about psychological distress and disorder, the effects of exposure to danger on development and adaptation, developmental pathways to becoming a source of danger to oneself and others, the effects of psychological intervention, and the process of change. Interpreted with DMM theory and discourse analysis, it may even offer a diagnostic alternative to *DSM* or ICD symptom-based diagnoses. Given the concerns that the latter have failed to identify coherent clusters of patients and that diagnoses alone do not predict which treatment strategies will succeed (Angold & Costello, 2009; Denton, 2007; Dignam, Parry, & Berk, 2010; First, 2009; Frances, 2010; Goldberg, 2010), we wonder whether the DMM method's emphasis on danger and sexuality, behavioral strategies, and individual differences in information processing might be more useful to clinicians. Indeed, the suggestion for personality domains in *DSM-V* (see www.dsm5.org) seems to be a step in this direction, given the personality facets that are viewed as occurring together in each domain. These are beginning to map onto attachment strategies. With this in mind, in this final chapter, we summarize some of the advantages of the AAI, describe its limitations, consider its applicability to treatment and forensic settings, and suggest directions for future research.

CONTRIBUTIONS OF THE AAI

The power of the DMM-AAI lies in its (a) focus on the organizing function of exposure to danger or sexual opportunity, (b) basis in information processing, and (c) comparative process in classification. In clinical applications, its power goes beyond simply generating a classification to initiating a potentially therapeutic process.

Exposure to Danger and Sexual Opportunity

FOCUS ON DANGER AND SAFETY, REPRODUCTION, AND SEXUALITY

The DMM-AAI focuses on danger more thoroughly than the original AAI and includes threats other than separation and loss. It also addresses sexuality and threats tied to sexuality. Thus, the DMM-AAI explores individual differences in strategies for self-protection, reproduction, and progeny protection. Because these functions are essential to human survival (both individually and as a species), including them creates a more comprehensive assessment from which one can expect to understand adult functioning more thoroughly. Further, it returns attachment theory to its roots in evolutionary processes and Bowlby's dedication to ameliorating psychological suffering.

MAKING MEANING

Everyone wants to be understood accurately and favorably. For adults who use Type A or C strategies, these can seem contradictory. Because they do not know why they do what they do and what they do seems unfavorable, they present themselves with distortions, then ask, "D'you know what I mean?" By addressing danger and sexuality, the DMM-AAI both recasts their behavior in a favorable and adaptive light and also penetrates layers of self-protection to reach core issues that are the basis of psychological and behavioral organization.

This can assist both troubled adults and therapists to see beyond presenting issues in order to more effectively guide patients to generate meaningful explanations for their behavior. Although any meaning is better than no meaning, we think meanings tied to self-protection, reproduction, and protection of progeny provide an enhanced opportunity to improve the quality of life.

Information Processing

MULTIPLE DISPOSITIONAL REPRESENTATIONS

By addressing somatic, cognitive, and affective dispositional representations (DRs), each in preconscious (implicit), conscious (explicit), and integrative forms, the DMM-AAI has the breadth and flexibility to account for the complexity of human behavior. By tying DRs to neurocognitive research, the DMM-AAI method of discourse analysis remains open to revision to bring it in line with our most current scientific understanding.

TRANSPARENCY AND SUBTLETY

Unlike self-report measures that confine respondents to predefined responses and are vulnerable to both self-deception and wishful thinking, the AAI permits speakers to present themselves in their own voices. At the same time, it assesses discrepancies among self-representations. Unlike projective assessments that try to capture complexity through ambiguous stimuli, the AAI discusses its central topic directly with the individual who is being assessed, providing an opportunity to frame his or her perspective explicitly. The coding addresses subtleties of meaning that cannot be processed fully by either speaker or listener while actively participating in the interview. That is, the DMM-AAI achieves both transparency and subtlety.

Comparative Process

COMPARING MEMORY SYSTEMS AND CONDITIONS

The idea of comparing representations drawn from different sorts of information to extract psychological meaning was introduced to attachment theory by Bowlby (1980). He proposed comparing semantic and episodic representations to indicate an individual's degree of psychological coherence. In the DMM-AAI method, that idea has been up-dated to include six memory systems as well as source memory and, most recently, somatic representations. The notion of slowly increasing threat while offering the support of a temporary attachment figure comes directly from Ainsworth's Strange Situation (Ainsworth, 1979) when the stranger functioned as a temporary substitute attachment fig-ure. This permits comparison of behavior under conditions of safety, threat, and support. Main and her colleagues adapt these ideas to adult-hood and verbal expression.

The inherent soundness of this comparative process facilitates ex-ploration beyond the focus of the original work by Main and her col-leagues and makes the AAI amenable to modification, expansion, and adaptation. As a consequence, it has the potential for both broad appli-cations in clinical and forensic settings and also for generating new em-pirical findings about human functioning and adaptation.

EVIDENCE AND INTERPRETATION

A particular advantage of the AAI is that the observational nature of the interview permits behavior to be preserved in its natural form. The interview keeps evidence gathering, theory, and method of interpre-tation separate. This enables users with new perspectives to draw meaning from existing data and methods. It enables courts and other evaluative settings to keep the evidence clean, untransformed by inter-pretation, thus, promoting an evidence-based and transparent ap-proach to evaluation. By allowing speakers to express themselves in their own way, observers are able to either recognize well-known pat-terns or identify new behavioral elements and patterns. In other words, the AAI permits exploration of not-yet-known—or even imagined—organizations of behavior. This potential has raised considerable inter-est from clinicians, whose task involves making sense of sometimes inscrutable behaviors.

Clinical Applications

USING THE INTERPERSONAL PROCESS

In the DMM method, the AAI creates a brief relationship, one that mim-ics crucial aspects of genuine attachment relationships in the opportu-nity for shared engagement around topics tied to threat. The analysis of

such transitional relationships has deep roots in psychoanalytic treatment (Freud, 1927; Lichtenberg, Lachmann, & Fosshage, 1996); in the
DMM-AAI method of discourse analysis, it is refined in terms of individual differences in self-protective strategy. This interpersonal process
permits a shared construction of meaning and, in fact, the ability to
share meanings with another individual is part of what is being assessed. The individual has a choice of cooperating or not, and the process of this choice is one of the most meaningful parts of the assessment.
That is, the DMM-AAI offers the speaker the opportunity to know and
to be known. The dialectic between speaker and interviewer becomes a
coded part of the DMM-AAI process. Indeed, it may be the best indicator of how the individual actually functions in relationships.

ESTABLISHING A PROCESS FOR WORKING TOGETHER

Each individual involved in the AAI (speaker and interviewer) has a
specific role: The interviewer poses relevant questions, listens carefully
to the answers, and responds with thoughtful follow-up questions; the
speaker provides the content information and takes the leap of integrating it, either spontaneously or when probed by the interviewer to
do so. The speaker is the expert in his or her own experience and its
meaning; the interviewer knows how to listen and carry the dialogue
either deeper on the same topic or forward onto other topics. As a consequence, instead of keeping "subject" and "therapist/scientist" hierarchically separated, the AAI opens the possibility of equality and
collaboration.

   A particular advantage of the AAI is that it offers therapists an opportunity to understand without having to act, without having to "fix"
speakers in a therapeutic way. This moment of reflective calm before
the storm of treatment is unleashed promotes comprehension and
compassion; the success of the whole venture depends on these being
present.

REACTIVE AND NONDIRECTIVE

Regardless of how the speaker deals with the questions and the relationship with the interviewer, the process itself activates the speaker's
mind, surprising it with unexpected thoughts and feelings. The juxtaposition of representations from different memory systems facilitates
discovery of discrepancies. These perturbations, in turn, modify the

mind's inherent self-organizing processes in ways that often continue even after the interview has ended. This is advantageous for all speakers but especially for those whose DRs are out of tune with their current contexts. This includes adults engaged in psychotherapy. Put another way, when delivered properly, the AAI is a therapeutic assessment.

EXPANSION AND INTEGRATION OF THEORY

Although the original AAI is developmentally constrained to early parenthood, Crittenden's modification addresses adulthood more generally. The AAI is compatible with all the major theories of psychological treatment such that most mental health professionals can find meaningful information in it. Further, the breadth of topic and applications promotes communication across disciplines and theories. The AAI is, in other words, an assessment that lends itself to integrative approaches to treatment.

Contributions from Research to Understanding Human Adaptation

THE MAIN AND GOLDWYN AAI

Extensive research using the M&G-AAI suggests that it yields a statistically significant difference between the classifications of normative and clinical AAIs, but that there remains substantial overlap between the two groups and that there is little evidence that anxious or disorganized attachment causes psychopathology (Bakermans-Kranenburg & van IJzendoorn, 2009; Dozier et al., 2008). However, as noted previously, some of the statistically significant findings are counter to theory.

One impetus to developing the DMM method was the inexplicable classifications of the transcripts of troubled individuals; the meta-analytical findings of Bakermans-Kranenburg and van IJzendoorn suggest that this finding is quite general. Further, having only one category (unresolved/disorganized/Cannot Classify) for all cases of severe problems limits greatly the power of the M&G method to address the array of individual differences that typify psychopathology. Both Dignam and his colleagues (2010) and Thompson and Raikes (2003) point to the DMM as having the possibility of realizing the potential of attachment theory to inform mental health treatment.

THE DYNAMIC-MATURATIONAL METHOD

Early research using the DMM classificatory system and discourse analysis method suggest that the DMM-AAI may include crucial detail relevant to individual differences in adaptation. Moreover, DMM theory provides a construct framework based on information processing that can assist therapists to organize treatment planning. For example, in work cited in Chapter 15, the fine-grained classifications using the DMM method indicate both matching and meshing of mother and child strategies across generations. Because the meshing occurs within anxious attachment, this finding has important implications for treatment. Understanding the reversal of strategy from mother to child may not only increase the effectiveness of intervention, but it may also reduce harmful effects of counter-indicated treatment.

Similarly, studies on clinical samples (reviewed in Chapter 15) suggest that the DMM-AAI may have the potential to refine treatment approaches to both individuals and diagnostic groups. Our data suggest four general conclusions. First, the AAIs of adults in treatment and in the normative population are distributed quite differently. Adults in treatment were essentially never assigned to the Ainsworth categories (i.e., B, A1–2, and C1–2) whereas adults in the normative population usually are, with smaller proportions assigned to midrange categories (i.e., A3–4, C3–4, and A1–4/C1–4), and about a fifth to categories associated with psychological disorder (i.e., A5–8, C5–8, and A5–8/C5–8); this fits with epidemiological predictions (Kessler, 1994).

Second, different diagnostic groups appear to have "signature" aspects to their classification. For example, eating disorders are typified by triangulated parent-child relationships that adults with eating disorders do not yet understand even in adulthood. Borderline personality disorder is associated with A/C classifications with unresolved trauma, depression, triangulation, and intrusions of forbidden negative affect. Familial sexual offending is associated with dismissed unresolved trauma and A4 (compulsive compliance) and A7 (delusional idealizing) strategies. Finally, PTSD is typified by complex lack of resolution of childhood trauma.

Third, the studies using the DMM-AAI suggest that individuals with the same diagnoses may use different self-protective strategies and different patterns of information processing. That is, people with the same diagnoses may have different psychological organizations that derive different meanings from the same information. This was observed for people who had eating disorders, PTSD, and patterns of sexual offending. Having a model of such processes could change the way we cluster people who suffer psychological distress. Knowing about those processes could change treatment dramatically, potentially improving treatment outcomes. Although we have only published findings on a few diagnostic groups, the principle of treatment-relevant differences within diagnostic categories has been established. We await studies of treatment to confirm the relevance of this finding and to indicate which treatments are most efficacious with which groups of people and in which order of presentation.

Fourth, the DMM-AAI identifies some distortions that are associated with psychological disorder in self or progeny, but not with psychiatric diagnoses. "Disorientation" is a particularly relevant example. Adults with a DO marker in their AAI almost always face interpersonal difficulties or their children display severe psychological disorders. Nevertheless, these adults are seen as normal and drawn from the normative population. Exploring the meaning of the functioning identified by the DMM-AAI constructs may be helpful to the adults or their children.

In sum, we believe that the DMM-AAI permits detailed functional distinctions among individuals needing psychological treatment, leading to the formulation of testable hypotheses about disorders and the effectiveness of alternative treatment choices. Efficacious treatment in this new framework would not target symptoms, but rather the psychological process by which people attempt to protect themselves, find safe reproductive partners, and protect their children. Safety, comfort, and healthy children—who could ask for anything more?

LIMITATIONS OF THE AAI

The Quality of Coders

This flexibility and complexity has a downside as well; the AAI has limitations. The quality of the coder's contribution is the greatest drawback. The high level of abstraction and the comprehensiveness of constructs require coders to engage in reflective integration to fully understand speakers' psychological organization. Coders, in other words, must both learn the content of the discourse analysis and also be able to apply it to a wide range of speakers without the coder's personal biases and limitations distorting the output. This is a severe limitation, one that means that there are not enough competent coders, especially for complex transcripts. Simply taking the AAI course is insufficient to achieve reliability and, for some would-be coders, only a process of personal integration can yield coder reliability. Given the rates of troubled histories and psychological distress among mental health practitioners (e.g., Johnson, 1991), finding competent coders who do not introduce personal distortions into assessments of other people is a major challenge. This limitation affects not only coding of AAIs but also treatment itself. The AAIs of therapists may assist the field to disentangle this effect from the effect of treatment techniques.

Assessing versus Measuring

On the other hand, if the key words in assessment are "empirical information" and "evidence-based procedures," a quantitative approach to the extraction of information from an AAI would be expected. Although this may be possible, currently the most useful way of drawing meaning from an AAI depends on an active psychological process of discovering discrepancies in the discourse and, following written guidelines, interpretation of the psychological and interpersonal meaning of the discrepancies. In other words, the AAI, in common with all other assessments of attachment, is not a psychological *measure* (and surely not a "test"). It might yield a measure, if significant connections were found between quantitative aspects of the linguistic analysis of discourse and the patterning of construct-related discourse markers, but until that time, it is an *assessment*. As such, it depends on the skill, coherence, and personal psychological integration of coders.

Lack of Nonverbal Information

In spite of the sophistication of the discourse analysis, the AAI procedure is still based on transcribing audio recordings and, therefore, the coder cannot observe nonverbal behavior. This is an artifact of the development of the tool when an inexpensive and expedient means of archiving the interviews was needed; cost, in other words, precluded the use of video in the development of the AAI. Because human communication is highly redundant, in most cases missing a few words or some nonverbal signals does not change communication appreciably. In other cases, however, the crucial representations do not exist in verbal form and, instead, can only be expressed somatically. To understand the speaker's strategic functioning in these cases, a videotaped interview may be very helpful and possibly crucial. It might be worth noting that the Strange Situation was developed prior to the availability of video technology. Once videos became commonplace, it was standard to use videos in this assessment, and there has been a proliferation of new observations and patterns, including both the DMM patterns and "disorganization." It may be time for a similar technology-based transformation for the AAI.

Generalizability

Generalizability is another problem. Even though considerable information can be obtained from an AAI, it remains just speech from one individual, indicative of his or her state of mind at one moment in time in front of a particular interviewer. The sample of verbal behavior might not be representative of the overall functioning of the individual, and it is not clear how far into the past or future the AAI results are relevant.

Lack of a Factual History

Differentiating fact from the process of recall is another limitation. Given all the reference to past experience in the AAI, it is tempting to think one is extracting a history. Nevertheless, the historical information provided by the speaker is unverified and incomplete. Its value lies in *how* it is told and the juxtaposition of different representations of the same experience. If, instead, the reader treats it as a reliable history, inaccurate conclusions may be drawn. Without external information about the individual's family, history, and current circumstances, the understandings taken from the AAI can be biased, contain misperceptions, and be vulnerable to all the inaccuracies (or even deceptions) of self-reported information. In other words, the AAI focuses on how adults tell their stories, that is, on psychological processes. When content is needed, the AAI cannot substitute for concrete evidence about historical facts.

A final limitation of the AAI is that it is costly to learn and to apply. This is quite understandable because the assessment focuses on human functioning applied to the crucial tasks of self-protection, reproduction, and protection of progeny. These conditions mean that behavioral organization will be at its maximum sophistication and complexity. Still, practical considerations are relevant for any assessment that could be applied clinically.

USING THE AAI

One might wonder whether obtaining an AAI classification warrants so much effort. To answer this question, it is important to keep in mind what can be learned from a DMM-AAI. With a detailed and accurate classification, considerable information is preserved in a concise manner about:

- The speaker's self-protective attachment strategy (i.e., the way the speaker uses information to organize behavior when he or she feels endangered, feels reproductive opportunity to be threatened, or believes progeny to be endangered).
- Representations of specific attachment relationships.
- A possible set of unresolved traumatic experiences that distort the person's behavior without his or her awareness of it.
- An overriding distortion of the strategy such as depression, disorientation, or reorganization.
- An interpreted developmental history of the speaker. This history combines information provided directly by the speaker with information derived from the pattern of errors (i.e., dysfluence) in the discourse. The interview cannot directly establish what actually happened to the speaker, but its interpretation can assist in understanding why the speaker thinks and behaves as he or she does.
- Level of parental reasoning (LPR, Crittenden, Lang, Claussen, & Partridge, 2000), that is, how the parent thinks about making caregiving decisions for children. The levels range from inarticulate to simplistic to complex interpersonal decision making. The LPR suggests the flexibility and sensitivity with which the parent will be able to interpret and respond to the child's behavior.

Clinical Uses of the AAI

DEVELOPING A TREATMENT PLAN

The most obvious use of this information is to guide treatment. At intake, as part of an individual or family assessment, the AAI can yield information relevant to (a) formulating the speaker's problem, (b) focusing the treatment, (c) selecting a mode of treatment (e.g., individual, family, or group treatment), (d) selecting specific treatment techniques (e.g., biofeedback, problem solving, dyadic enactment, reconstruction of past episodes, life narratives, psychoanalytically oriented approaches), and (e) evaluating whether the individual has the requisite skills to benefit from specific proposed treatments or whether other treatment approaches should be considered.

Given the amount of information that is potentially available to the therapist and the fact that responding to the AAI questions itself instigates psychological processing (thus promoting reorganization and change), the time needed to yield this information from an AAI is actually quite brief. For example, developing similar understanding during ongoing treatment can take weeks, or even months, with some trial and error in the selection of foci and techniques. In addition, the attitude required of the interviewer renders the AAI a useful procedure for establishing rapport when the chosen approach to treatment is nonjudgmental, encourages active cooperation of the individual, and values the speaker's knowledge about himself or herself.

WORKING WITH ONE'S OWN CLIENTS OR PATIENTS

On the other hand, coding reliably occurs only when no other information about the case is known. This presents problems for most clinicians who cannot be blind to their own clients' or patients' problems and histories. Clinicians may find it useful to collaborate with other clinician coders who can be completely blind to a case and, therefore, able to evaluate the AAI information without bias. Nevertheless, if clinicians who code their own patients' transcripts keep their biases in mind explicitly, the hypotheses drawn from the AAI can be tested and revised during the course of treatment.

Treatment presents repeated opportunities for discovery of discrepancy between expected effects and actual outcomes. These discrepancies can promote review of hypotheses about the client or patient as well as an opportunity to test other ideas and possibly redirect the treatment. Thus, the clinical use of the AAI is quite different from research or forensic applications, where the classification is the final step of the assessment process. For these applications, blind coders are essential.

Forensic Uses of the AAI

Forensic applications of the AAI are not yet as well established as clinical applications. Nevertheless, evaluation of attachment is considered relevant to court decisions regarding (a) progeny protection and parenting and (b) criminal dangerousness. Transcribed verbal behavior that others can evaluate independently strengthens expert opinions when compared to expert opinion based on unavailable evidence. Transparency and validity are crucial when consequent judgments can significantly and permanently change lives. To justify the use of the DMM-AAI in judicial proceedings, the general validity of the AAI must be further established empirically; its relevance to court decisions must be tested in studies with the strongest possible controls, given the ethical constraints of the forensic context; and coders with the highest level of reliability must be employed.

A working group within the International Association for the Study of Attachment (www.iasa-dmm.org) is currently developing a protocol for family forensic attachment reports. The goal is a standardized, evidence-based protocol that includes all family members, uses specified and developmentally attuned assessments that have validating studies, and generates attachment-related information that can be supported empirically. The protocol aims to produce tangible evidence that can be presented to the court for examination by other experts.

Expanded Applications of the AAI

Because attachment, as assessed by the DMM-AAI, involves information processing and self-protection, it is relevant to adaptation and psychological assessment in a very broad sense. In this closing section, we consider some of the "burning issues" of today, both in terms of how to use the AAI and also how to avoid misusing it. We then speculate on areas of future growth.

THE BEAUTY OF EMERGENT KNOWLEDGE

The AAI was developed to define mothers' attachment in ways that would match their children's attachment. Successful as that endeavor was, it only scratched the surface of what this sophisticated, carefully constructed tool can yield. Even its ability to statistically differentiate normative and clinical populations does not tap its full potential. The AAI stands out and holds our attention 25 years after its introduction because it serves as a lens through which to view complex psychological processes with ever-increasing scope and precision. By providing an accurate, behavioral record of responses to pertinent questions and, separately, by analyzing the observations with defined methods, it captures the best of both empirical precision and also emerging knowledge.

Because its three crucial components of theory, interview protocol, and discourse analysis can each be developed and modified separately, the DMM-AAI has had the benefit of continuing expansion and modification. Sometimes new transcripts reveal organizations that had not been seen before. Other times new theoretical insights illuminate unnoticed aspects of old texts. The back-and-forth play between theory and observation has repeatedly extended our understanding of self-protective organization.

THE BEAUTY OF OLD TEXTS

The AAI offers researchers, clinicians, and theoreticians the opportunity to build on past learning without having to throw out old tools. In fact, it invites us to return to previously analyzed transcripts with new ideas and methods to consider whether our new discoveries lie latent in these materials. That is, sometimes the best test of a new idea is to gather new observations, selected specifically to shed light on the topic. At other times, the most convincing evidence is demonstration that the idea was always present even if unnoticed. Theory, the AAI, and the DMM method of discourse analysis, both separately and together, have been shown to weather change robustly even as scientific knowledge has changed.

A Few Hot Questions

There are so many questions one could ask! We queried users of the DMM-AAI to ask what they would most like to know from the application of this tool. Here is what they said.

TREATMENT EFFECTS

One of the most exciting potential uses of the DMM-AAI is as a test of the effectiveness of psychological treatment, both in pre- and post-comparisons and intermittently across the course of therapy. The latter holds the potential to reveal something about how psychotherapy works and how the mind changes. But how can one surprise the mind with a familiar interview?

This is where the structure and process of the AAI become crucial. A different set of questions that retain the structure and process of the AAI, but change the content of the queries, may solve the problem. We are experimenting with Form B of the AAI (Crittenden, 2006). Although some of the original questions are retained, new questions surprise the speaker into accessing different recalled experiences and using these to understand current functioning. The use of the interviewer to create a dialogue that both protects and challenges the speaker remains constant.

Beyond the question of what treatments work, many of us would like to know how various treatments work. *How* do they modify psychological processing? And is that good for everyone or, like medication, does the treatment need to be matched to ... to what? The diagnosis? The personality domain? The self-protective strategy? The processing of information?

NEUROLOGY

That leads to questions about the physiological correlates of the strategies and processes that comprise the strategies. We assume there is a neural substrate that reflects the differences we see in verbal discourse and behavior, but where is the evidence? For example, we have Strathearn and his colleagues' fMRI data (2009) showing that Types A and B differ neurologically, but what about Type C? How are unresolved trauma and depression represented neurologically? What about reorganization? Are our assumptions about arousal measurable in physiological ways? Could brain-scan studies of respondents with A and C strategies help us to discover what is going on in the brain when people are coded as inhibiting or exaggerating affective states?

A great deal of attention has been directed toward anger and fear. The DMM, however, suggests that desire for comfort is also important and, in the context of danger without protection or comfort, it may lead to dispositions to action that seem far removed from comfort. Could that hypothesis be tested by observing how individuals with severe pathology respond physiologically and neurologically to images of comfort and love? We have a theory about these questions, but we lack empirical tests of our ideas and these are needed to refine the ideas.

DEVELOPMENT

Some questions are developmental: Do diagnostic groups have DMM-AAI "signatures" that connect developmental experience with later disorder? How does the absence of comfort during childhood affect violent and sexual behavior in adolescence and adulthood? How will parents' disorientation or unresolved loss or trauma, as identified by the AAI, affect their children's development? What is the interpersonal process that accounts for this? More generally, what developmental pathways contribute to various adult self-protective organizations and at which points in development are they most responsive to new input?

STRATEGIES AND DIAGNOSES

Then come the questions about disorders: What is the strategy (or strategies) used by severely violent offenders, and do they reflect an etiological route toward their current functioning? Does deliberate self-harm relate to intrusions of forbidden negative affect or to a coercive strategy? How can we understand the symptoms of obsessive-compulsive disorder and can that help us to find treatments that address the underlying issues, rather than simply applying cognitive behavioral treatment to the symptoms? Does an A5 (compulsively promiscuous) classification coincide with a diagnosis of sexual compulsivity? What about C5–6 (punitive and seductive) and sexual addiction or A6 (compulsive self-reliance) and lack of sexual arousal? Is C8 (paranoid) associated with a diagnosis of paranoia? How do the disorders regarded as "neuropsychiatric" present in an AAI—will there be a marker of an expressed somatic symptom ([ess])?

The gratifying aspect of these questions about very severe disorders is that the DMM-AAI users who proposed them felt confident that they "actually have a theoretical sense of how DMM theory applies to these kinds of behavior" (Gordon Sommerville, personal communication, May 8, 2010). Now we need data from properly controlled studies. Good theory and good assessments can assist us to extract answers. But just as biotechnical means of deriving data are complex, so must our behavioral methods be complex. The questions that need answering will not yield to simple theory or simple methods. Nevertheless, answering these and similar questions is important because the answers have implications for how we will transform danger and suffering into safety, comfort, and adaptation.

CHANGING DIRECTION

Attachment researchers, both in general and with regard to the AAI, have spent 25 years focused on disorganization, with little change in theory, assessment, or applications. As Bakermans-Kranenburg and van IJzendoorn put it, "It's time to take stock" (2009, p. 246).

The results are disappointing. ABC+D attachment in infancy and the preschool years explains approximately 2% of variance in adaptation and developmental outcomes (Friedman & Boyle, 2008). The DMM bumps that figure up to 12–19% (Spieker & Crittenden, 2010). A similar figure could not be obtained from Bakermans-Kranenburg and van IJzendoorn's review of published AAI studies, but there remained a familiar and inexplicably large overlap of classifications drawn from normative and maladaptive samples. Moreover, there were no effects found for gender or culture, but effects were found for adolescents as compared to adults. Failing to discriminate groups adequately on three variables (risk status, gender, and culture) that typically show difference and finding differences where one should not (age) nullifies the M&G-AAI for practical use. Further, no major new ideas or recommendations for differential treatment approaches have come from this model in more than two decades. Instead, the advice is to analyze the rating scales underlying the nondifferentiating classifications and seek data on reflective integration and security (Bakermans-Kranenburg & van IJzendoorn, 2009).

Others, however, have suggested that attachment theory itself is on the wrong track (Rutter et al., 2009; Thompson & Raikes, 2003). We note the following problems as they relate to application of the ABC+D model and Main and Goldwyn classificatory method to the AAI.

- There is little difference in the categories applied to infants and adults (whereas infant and adult behavior are dramatically different).
- There is confusion in the coding of subject and object whereby dismissing the self and dismissing others are both coded as "dismissing" (and similarly for preoccupied).
- The types of representations are limited to those identified by Bowlby in 1980 whereas procedural, imaged, connotative, and somatic representations all provide crucial differentiating information that is relevant to adaptation.
- Transformations of information are not formally considered, and

falsified, erroneous, denied, and delusional information are not identified at all.

- The array of responses to psychological trauma is constrained to preoccupying trauma whereas other forms, especially those with a dismissing, depressed, or mixed component, may be more characteristic of psychological disorder.
- A gradient of functioning from balanced to mildly maladaptive under some conditions to substantially maladaptive under many conditions to dangerously maladaptive under all but the most dangerous conditions is absent with, instead, only a secure/insecure dichotomy available to define adaptation.
- It may be important to attend to the safety or dangerousness of the context to understand differences in the distribution of strategies among groups of individuals and the adaptiveness of individuals' attachment organization.

In sum, we think the M&G method is insensitive to crucial aspects of adult functioning while, nevertheless, the AAI itself is a powerful and valuable tool for both assessment and initiating the process of psychological change. Moreover, we respect the contribution of both George and her colleagues (in having constructed the interview in a profoundly new and productive manner following the notions of information processing developed by Bowlby) and also of Main and Goldwyn (in having adapted ideas about discourse analysis to the framework of individual differences in attachment delineated by Ainsworth.) Nevertheless, we think it is time to move on, bypassing the diversion into disorganization and getting back on track.

What characterizes the main pathway? It is an open developmental model that integrates findings from all the human sciences to yield an ever-changing and complex representation of human adaptation. At the risk of seeming to rely on authority, we wish to refer to conclusions drawn by Crittenden and Ainsworth in a little-cited chapter written shortly after the AAI was introduced and Main and Solomon's paper on disorganization had been published. The chapter is focused on maltreatment, but the comments are easily applied to mental health issues.

Crittenden and Ainsworth emphasized the changing quality of attachment organization as a function of development (in all quotations of Crittenden and Ainsworth's sources in this section, all italics have been added):

Different types of maltreatment will be associated with different organizations of child behavior relative to the parent. Moreover, *such organizations can be expected to change as a function of ontogeny* and to reflect the competing desires of maltreated children. These changes reflect changes in the direction of development rather than arresting development at an infantile stage. (1989, p. 450)

We think that the ABC+D model has failed to capture the nature of development change in either children or theory, leaving researchers and clinicians mired in a four-category model of A, B, C, and disorganization/unresolved/Cannot Classify categories across the life-span—and through 25 years of research.

With regard to disorganization, Crittenden and Ainsworth wrote:

The suggestion is that young children organize their behavior most easily if the mother's behavior has been predictable, regardless of how sensitive or appropriate it is, but that *older children who have had to cope with major inconsistencies eventually integrate that information into their set of expectations and develop an organized pattern of responding.* The nature of that pattern awaits further research. (pp. 442–443)

Crittenden and Ainsworth did, however, speculate on some of the organized patterns that might be found:

Other indications that are less likely to be observed in infancy are: *compulsive compliance* to the wishes of the attachment figure, *compulsive caregiving*, or an excessive sense of *self-reliance* and emphasis on independence from any need for an attachment figure. (p. 443)

That is, based on Crittenden's work with maltreatment and Bowlby's ideas about the long-term effects of loss of an attachment figure in childhood (Bowlby, 1980; Crittenden, 1985a), Crittenden and Ainsworth proposed what are now labeled A4, A3, and A6 (respectively) in the DMM. Moreover, they noted the importance of information processing to the organization and application of these strategies: "The processes by which such patterns of behavior would generalize to include nonattachment relationships include the *perception and interpretation of experience* through internal models of reality" (p. 452).

Crittenden and Ainsworth emphasized that attaining protection and comfort were the central functions of attachment behavior: "When

there are signals of *danger*, the attachment system is activated" (p. 451).
When the child is securely attached, "he tends to be easily *comforted*."
They referred repeatedly to the "*need for comfort*" (p. 438).

With regard to treatment implications (the raison d'être of attachment
theory for Bowlby), Crittenden and Ainsworth wrote: "It is impossible
to develop appropriate diagnostic and treatment procedures without
an awareness of *developmentally salient issues*" (p. 434). In addition, they
thought that the breadth of causal factors needed a parsimonious
organization and proposed the concept of critical causes:

> There is a need to focus on the *critical causes* of maltreatment—that is,
> those causes which, if changed, would lead to improvements in the other
> detrimental conditions and, thus, to improved family functioning. Be-
> cause simply undoing the situation that caused maltreatment might not
> be the most effective or feasible way to correct it, such causes might
> imply one thing for the prevention of maltreatment and another for the
> amelioration of existing maltreatment. (p. 434)

When that was written, they proposed attachment as the critical
cause; today information processing seems more crucial.

Finally, Crittenden and Ainsworth considered the potential contribution of attachment theory to the field of psychology at large:

> Attachment theory also permits the integration of "external," i.e., en-
> vironmental, conditions with interpersonal conditions as interlocking
> influences upon the development of attachment. The advantage of com-
> bining these perspectives in the context of a focus on attachment is that
> risk status can be considered to vary across both families and time de-
> pending upon individuals' *past experiences, current contextual factors, and
> developmental processes as well as random (or unexpectable) events* without
> collapsing the model into an overly simplistic everything is intercon-
> nected approach. (p. 434)

At the same time, they were explicitly aware that attachment had a
place within a nested hierarchy of systems theories:

> The argument offered here is *not intended to focus on dyadic attachment-re-
> lated influences on maltreatment to the exclusion of organismic or societal influ-
> ences*. Rather it is intended to provide a means of (1) identifying a critical
> variable that can explain the impact of many associated conditions and

suggest why the impact of maltreatment affects so many areas of individual or family functioning and (2) identifying those individuals and families who are most vulnerable to other sources of influence. (pp. 457–458)

Crittenden and Ainsworth sought in the DMM to balance the simplicity of order based on information processing with the complexity of an infinity of individual differences and to do so in a way that had meaningful implications for both theory and treatment. The DMM offers greater variation than the ABC+D model, while still being more succinct and better organized conceptually than psychiatric diagnoses.

In sum, the seeds of current DMM theory were present in the work of Ainsworth and Crittenden, but awaited empirical validation. We think that the last 25 years have generated enough data to indicate that the ABC+D model is not sufficiently fruitful to justify continuing on that pathway. The data available on the DMM include numerous studies of children in infancy and in the preschool years, with emerging data in the school years and adolescence, and the findings cited in the previous chapter for adulthood. Further, we think that the Dynamic-Maturational Model of attachment and adaptation both continues the integrative process of theory and methodological development begun by Bowlby and Ainsworth and also more nearly meets Bowlby's motivating goal of improving the psychological well-being of threatened and endangered people.

BEYOND THE AAI

We think theory should inform practice, which in turn should modify theory, in a recursive process of elaboration, correction, and change. Attachment theory and the assessments generated by it are grounded in phenomenological observation that is interpreted to yield psychological understanding that, in turn, can guide therapeutic action in cases of maladaptation and distress.

DMM discourse analysis and the array of DMM strategies are not exclusively tied to the format of the AAI. Other interviews, focused on other topics, could use both the discourse analysis and also the array of strategies. That notion formed the basis for Form B of the AAI (Crittenden, 2006), the Transition to Adulthood Attachment Interview (TAAI, Crittenden, 2005), the School-age Assessment of Attachment (SAA, Crittenden, 1997–2005), and Parents Interview (Crittenden, 1981).

Moreover, the DMM strategies and discourse analysis need not be limited to formal assessments. We are particularly interested in the application of the AAI process of juxtaposing different representations of the same experience, when used within therapy sessions. Such flexibility in the use of the components of the AAI opens possibilities for the extension of these concepts to other assessments than the AAI and to other contexts, for example, counseling or therapy sessions.

On the other hand, pulling questions from the AAI and inserting them into other interviews may miss the point entirely. It is not the questions that are powerful and it is not the content of the answers that is important. Such uses are a bit like the hocus pocus of magic: Ask the magic questions and you'll get magical effects. Instead, it is the process that yields the effect. The questions are less important than the *intra*personal process of managing threat and the *inter*personal process of communicating about it.

CHANGING THE FOCUS FROM DISORDER TO FUNCTION

The uses of the DMM-AAI described in this chapter suggest alternate applications, expansions, and variations of the components of the DMM-AAI that highlight the exciting potential of this tool. Its functional emphasis, coupled with detailed examination of alternate DRs, fits thinking in all the major theories of psychological and behavioral disorder. Further, when functioning is understood as attempts to protect rather than to damage or harm, alliances between mental health professionals and people in need of care become more likely.

Many say that DMM theory and methods are complex, too complex for working clinicians. After a century of trying to understand and ameliorate mental illness, it seems unlikely that simple theory, simple assessment, and quick manualized treatment will be more successful than our past efforts. It is more likely that theory needs to be sufficiently complex to represent the crucial aspects of the life experiences of people with mental illnesses. The assessments need to be sensitively attuned to the encrypted communications of very distressed adults, and to be coded by skilled professionals trained to a high level of reliability. The treatments, of course, must be focused correctly, individualized for each person, and delivered with sufficient understanding to yield credible compassion.

Possibly, the greatest potential of the DMM-AAI is its capacity to focus observation precisely while retaining the openness to expand and change understanding of observations. We hope this book will be used to promote accuracy of observation, clarity of interpretation, and—most important—discovery of new ideas about human adaptation. Psychological tools that yield useful data without restricting thinking are very valuable. The DMM-AAI does more: It opens the door to groundbreaking basic and applied research of as much relevance for the social sciences as for the healing professions.

Appendix A

Glossary of Abbreviations

A+	Compulsive Type A strategies (A3 to A8)
A1	Idealizing
A2	Distancing
A3	Compulsive caregiving
A4	Compulsive compliance
A4-	Compulsive performance
A5	Compulsively promiscuous, sexual
A5-	Compulsively promiscuous, social
A6	Compulsively self-reliant, isolated
A6-	Compulsively self-reliant, social
A7	Delusional idealization
A8	Externally assembled self
AC	Blended Type AC strategy
A/C	Alternating Type A/C strategy
B1	Distanced from past
B2	Accepting
B3	Comfortably balanced
B4	Sentimental
B5	Complaining acceptance
BO	Balanced other
C+	Obsessive Type C strategies (C3 to C8)
C1	Threateningly angry
C2	Disarmingly desirous of comfort
C3	Aggressively angry
C4	Feigned helpless
C5	Punitively angry and obsessed with revenge

C6	Seductive and obsessed with rescue
C5–6+	Failing/stuck form of the C5–6 strategies
C7	Menacing
C8	Paranoid
[A]	False A: verbal description of Type A behavior presented with Type C discourse
Δ	Triangulated
DO	Disoriented strategy (modifier)
Dp	Depressed strategy (modifier)
DR	Dispositional representation
[ess]	Expression of somatic symptom (modifier)
[ina]	Intrusion of forbidden negative affect (modifier)
[ina]$_h$	Historical possible intrusion of forbidden negative affect (modifier)
IO	Insecure other
R	Reorganizing strategy (modifier)
Ul	Unresolved loss
Ul(a)	Anticipated form of unresolved loss
Ul(dlr)	Delusionally repaired form of unresolved loss
Ul(dlv)	Delusional revenge form of unresolved loss
Ul(dn)	Denied form of unresolved loss
Ul(dp)	Depressed form of unresolved loss
Ul(dpl)	Displaced form of unresolved loss
Ul(ds)	Dismissing form of unresolved loss
Ul(dx)	Disorganized form of unresolved loss
Ul(h)	Hinted form of unresolved loss
Ul(i)	Imagined form of unresolved loss
Ul(p)	Preoccupied form of unresolved loss
Ul(v)	Vicarious form of unresolved loss
Utr	Unresolved trauma
Utr(a)	Anticipated form of unresolved trauma
Utr(b)	Blocked form of unresolved trauma
Utr(dlr)	Delusionally repaired form of unresolved trauma
Utr(dlv)	Delusional revenge form of unresolved trauma
Utr(dn)	Denied form of unresolved trauma
Utr(dp)	Depressed form of unresolved trauma
Utr(dpl)	Displaced form of unresolved trauma
Utr(ds)	Dismissed form of unresolved trauma
Utr(dx)	Disorganized form of unresolved trauma
Utr(h)	Hinted form of unresolved trauma

Utr(i)   Imagined form of unresolved trauma
Utr(p)   Preoccupied form of unresolved trauma
Utr(s)   Suggested form of unresolved trauma
Utr(v)   Vicarious form of unresolved trauma

Appendix B

Correspondence Between DMM and M&G Classificatory Systems

DMM	M&G
B3	F3
B1	F1
B2	F2
B4	F4
B5	F5
A1	Ds1
A2	Ds3
A3	
A4	
A5	
A6	
A7	
A8	
C1	E2
C2	E1
C3	
C4	
C5	Ds2
C6	
C7	
C8	
A/C and AC	

Ul(a)	Ds4
Ul(dlr)	
Ul(dlv)	
Ul(dp)	
Ul(dpl)	
Ul(ds)	
Ul(dx)	
Ul(h)	
Ul(i)	
Ul(p)	Ul
Ul(v)	
Utr(a)	
Utr(b)	
Utr(dlr)	
Utr(dlv)	
Utr(dp)	
Utr(dpl)	
Utr(ds)	
Utr(dx)	
Utr(h)	
Utr(i)	
Utr(p)	Utr
Utr(s)	
Utr(v)	
Dp	
DO	
[ina]	
[ess]	
R	

E3 (often C3–8, but includes some A+)
CC (often A/C, but including some A+ and C+)

References

Ainsworth, M. D. S. (1967). *Infancy in Uganda: Infant care and the growth of love*. Baltimore, MD: Johns Hopkins University Press.

Ainsworth, M. D. S. (1973). The development of infant-mother attachment. In B. M. Caldwell & H. N. Ricciutti (Eds.), *Review of child development research* (Vol. 3, pp. 1–94). Chicago, IL: University of Chicago Press.

Ainsworth, M. D. S. (1979). Infant-mother attachment. *American Psychologist, 34*, 932–937.

Ainsworth, M. D. S. (1989). Attachment beyond infancy. *American Psychologist, 44*, 709–716.

Ainsworth, M. D. S., Blehar, M., Waters, E., & Wall, S. (1978). *Patterns of attachment: A psychological study of the strange situation*. Hillsdale, NJ: Erlbaum.

Angold, A., & Costello, E. J. (2009). Nosology and measurement in child and adolescent psychiatry. *Journal of Child Psychology and Psychiatry, 50*, 9–15.

Baddeley, A. (2009). The functional approach to autobiographical memory. *Applied Cognitive Psychology, 23*(8), 1045–1049. doi: 10.1002/acp.1608

Bakermans-Kranenburg, M. J., & van IJzendoorn, M. H. (2009). The first 10,000 adult attachment interviews: Distributions of adult attachment representations in clinical and non-clinical groups. *Attachment & Human Development, 11*(3), 223–263. doi: 10.1080/14616730902814762

Bandler, R., & Grinder, J. (1975). *The structure of magic: A book about language and therapy*. Palo Alto, CA: Science and Behavior Books.

Bateson, G. (1972). *Steps to an ecology of mind*. New York, NY: Ballantine.

Bell, S. M. (1970). Development of the concept of the object as related to infant-mother attachment. *Child Development, 41*, 291–311.

Black, K., Jaeger, L., McCartney, K., & Crittenden, P. M. (2000). Attachment modes, peer interaction behavior, and feelings about the self: Indications of maladjustment in dismissing/preoccupied (Ds/E) adolescents. In P. M. Crittenden & A. H. Claussen (Eds.), *The organization of attachment relationships: Maturation, culture, and context* (pp. 300–324). New York, NY: Cambridge University Press.

Bowlby, J. (1944). Forty-four juvenile thieves: Their characters and home life. *International Journal of Psychoanalysis, 25*, 1–57.

Bowlby, J. (1951). Maternal care and mental health. *Monograph Series, 2*. Geneva, Switzerland: World Health Organization.

Bowlby, J. (1958). The nature of the child's tie to its mother. *International Journal of Psychoanalysis, XXXIX*, 1–23.

Bowlby, J. (1969/1982). *Attachment and loss. Vol. I: Attachment*. New York, NY: Basic Books.

Bowlby, J. (1973). *Attachment and loss. Vol. II: Separation*. New York, NY: Basic Books.

Bowlby, J. (1979). *The making and breaking of affectional bonds*. London, UK: Tavistock

Bowlby, J. (1980). *Attachment and loss. Vol. III: Loss*. New York, NY: Basic Books.

Brown, G. W., & Harris, T. (1978). *Social origins of depression*. London, UK: Tavistock.

Brown, L. (1993). *The new shorter Oxford English dictionary on historical principles*. Oxford, UK: Clarendon.

Bruner, J. (1972). Nature and uses of immaturity. *American Psychologist, 27*, 687–708.

Cassidy, J. P. (2002). The Stockholm syndrome, battered woman syndrome and the cult personality: An integrative approach. *Dissertation Abstracts International, 62*(11-B), 5366.

Cicchetti, D., & Barnett, D. (1991). Attachment organization in maltreated preschoolers. *Development and Psychopathology, 3*, 397–411.

Cowan, N. (2010). The magical mystery four: How is working memory limited and why? *Current Directions in Psychological Science, 19*, 51–57. doi: 10.1177/0963721409359277

Crittenden, P. M. (1981). *Parents' interview*. Unpublished manuscript, University of Virginia, Charlottesville, VA.

Crittenden, P. M. (1985a). Maltreated infants: Vulnerability and resilience. *Journal of Child Psychology and Psychiatry, 26*, 85–96.

Crittenden, P. M. (1985b). Mother and infant patterns of interaction: Developmental relationships. *Dissertation Abstracts International: Section B, 45*(8), 2710.

Crittenden, P. M. (1985c). Social networks, quality of parenting, and child development. *Child Development, 56*, 1299–1313.

Crittenden, P. M. (1990). Internal representational models of attachment relationships. *Infant Mental Health Journal, 11*, 259–277.

Crittenden, P. M. (1992). Quality of attachment in the preschool years. *Development and Psychopathology, 4*, 209–241.

Crittenden, P. M. (1994). *Nuove prospettive sull'attaccamento: Teoria e pratica in famiglie ad alto rischio* [New perspectives on attachment: Theory and practice in high risk families]. (Trans. Andrea Landini). Milano, Italy: Guerini Studio.

Crittenden, P. M. (1995). Attachment and psychopathology. In S. Goldberg, R. Muir, & J. Kerr, (Eds.), *John Bowlby's attachment theory: Historical, clinical, and social significance* (pp. 367–406). New York, NY: The Analytic Press.

Crittenden, P. M. (1996). Language, attachment, and behavior disorders. In N. J. Cohen, J.H. Beitchman, R. Tannock, & M. Konstantareous (Eds.), *Language, learning, and behavior disorders: Emerging perspectives* (pp. 119–160). New York, NY: Cambridge University Press.

Crittenden, P. M. (1997a). A dynamic-maturational perspective on anxiety disorders. *Giornale Italiano di Psicopatologia, 3,* 28–37.

Crittenden, P. M. (1997b). Patterns of attachment and sexuality: Risk of dysfunction versus opportunity for creative integration. In L. Atkinson & K. J. Zuckerman (Eds.), *Attachment and psychopathology* (pp. 47–93). New York, NY: Guilford.

Crittenden, P. M. (1997c). Toward an integrative theory of trauma: A dynamic-maturational approach. In D. Cicchetti & S. Toth (Eds.), *The Rochester symposium on developmental psychopathology: Risk, trauma, and mental processes* (Vol. 10, pp. 34–84). Rochester, NY: University of Rochester.

Crittenden, P. M. (1997d). Truth, error, omission, distortion, and deception: The application of attachment theory to the assessment and treatment of psychological disorder. In S. M. C. Dollinger & L. F. DiLalla (Eds.), *Assessment and intervention across the lifespan* (pp. 35–76). Hillsdale, NJ: Erlbaum.

Crittenden, P. M. (1997–2005). *School-age assessment of attachment coding manual.* Unpublished manuscript, Miami, FL.

Crittenden, P. M. (1999a). *Attaccamento in età adulta. L'approccio dinamico-maturativo alla Adult Attachment Interview* [Attachment in adulthood: The dynamic-maturational approach to the Adult Attachment Interview]. (Edizione Italiana a cura di Graziella Fava Vizziello e Andrea Landini). Milano, Italy: Cortina.

Crittenden, P. M. (1999b). Danger and development: The organization of self-protective strategies. In J. I. Vondra & D. Barnett (Eds.), Atypical attachment in infancy and early childhood among children at developmental risk. *Monographs of the Society for Research on Child Development* (Vol. 64, 258, pp. 145–171). Malden, MA: Wiley-Blackwell.

Crittenden, P. M. (2000a). A dynamic-maturational approach to continuity and change in pattern of attachment. In P. M. Crittenden & A. H. Claussen (Eds.), *The organization of attachment relationships: Maturation, culture, and context* (pp. 343–357). New York, NY: Cambridge University Press.

Crittenden, P. M. (2000b). A dynamic-maturational exploration of the meaning of security and adaptation: Empirical, cultural, and theoretical considerations. In P. M. Crittenden & A. H. Claussen (Eds.), *The organization of attachment relationships: Maturation, culture, and context* (pp. 358–384). New York, NY: Cambridge University Press.

Crittenden, P. M. (2000c). Introduction. In P. M. Crittenden & A. H. Claussen (Eds.), *The organization of attachment relationships: Maturation, culture, and context* (pp. 1–12). New York, NY: Cambridge University Press.

Crittenden, P. M. (2002). Attachment theory, information processing, and psychiatric disorder. *World Journal of Psychiatry, 1,* 72–75.

Crittenden, P. M. (2005). *Transition to Adulthood Attachment Interview.* Unpublished manuscript, Miami, FL.

Crittenden, P. M. (2006). *Modified Adult Attachment Interview: Form B.* Unpublished manuscript, Miami, FL.

Crittenden, P. M. (2007). *Modified Adult Attachment Interview.* Unpublished manuscript, Miami, FL.

Crittenden, P. M. (2008). *Raising parents: Attachment, parenting, and child safety.* Collumpton, UK: Willan Publishing.

Crittenden, P. M., & Ainsworth M. D. S. (1989). Child maltreatment and attachment theory. In D. Cicchetti & V. Carlson (Eds.), *Handbook of child maltreatment* (pp. 432–463). New York, NY: Cambridge University Press.

Crittenden, P. M., Claussen, A. H., & Kozlowska, K. (2007). Choosing a valid assessment of attachment for clinical use: A comparative study. *Australian & New Zealand Journal of Family Therapy, 28,* 78–87.

Crittenden, P. M., & DiLalla, D. (1988). Compulsive compliance: The development of an inhibitory coping strategy in infancy. *Journal of Abnormal Child Psychology, 16,* 585–599.

Crittenden, P. M., & Heller, M. B. (Under review). Chronic PTSD and attachment: A comparison study of self-protective strategies and unresolved childhood trauma. Manuscript in preparation.

Crittenden, P. M., & Kulbotton, G. R. (2007). Familial contributions to ADHD: An attachment perspective. *Tidsskrift for Norsk Psykologorening, 10,* 1220–1229.

Crittenden, P. M., & Landini, A. (2009, March). Are parents of child patients normal? Comparing parents of child patients with adult patients and normative parents. Poster presented at the biennial meeting of the Society for Research in Child Development, Denver, CO.

Crittenden, P. M., Lang, C., Claussen, A. H., & Partridge, M. F. (2000). Relations among mothers' procedural, semantic, and episodic internal representational models of parenting. In P. M. Crittenden & A. H. Claussen (Eds.), *The organization of attachment relationships: Maturation, culture, and context* (pp. 214–233). New York, NY: Cambridge University Press.

Crittenden, P. M., & Newman, L. (2010). Comparing models of borderline personality disorder: Mothers' experience, self-protective strategies, and dispositional representations. *Clinical Child Psychology and Psychiatry, 15*(3), 433–452.

Crittenden, P. M., Partridge, M. F., & Claussen, A. H. (1991). Family patterns of relationship in normative and dysfunctional families. *Development and Psychopathology, 3*, 491–512.

Crittenden, P. M., & Poggioli, D. (2008). Il DPTS nell'infanzia e nell'adolescenza: Approcci teorici e implicazioni terapeutiche.

Damasio, A. R. (1994). *Descartes' error: Emotion, reason, and the human brain.* New York, NY: Avon.

Denton, W. H. (2007). Issues for DSM-V: Relational diagnosis: An essential component of biopsychosocial assessment [Editorial]. *American Journal of Psychiatry, 164*, 1146–1147. doi: 10.1176/appi.ajp.2007.07010181

Dignam, P., Parry, P., & Berk, M. (2010). Detached from attachment: Neurobiology and phenomenology have a human face. *Acta Neuropsychiatrica, 22*(4), 202–206. doi: 10.1111/j.1601-5215.2010.00478.x

Dozier, M., & Lee, S. W. (1995). Discrepancies between self- and other-report of psychiatric symptomatology: Effects of dismissing attachment strategies. *Development and Psychopathology, 7*(1), 217–226. doi: 10.1017/S095457940000643X

Dozier, M., Stovall-McClough, K. C., & Albus, K. E. (2008). Attachment and psychopathology in adulthood. In J. Cassidy & P. R. Shaver (Eds.), *Handbook of attachment: Theory, research, and clinical applications* (2nd ed., pp. 718–744). New York, NY: Guilford.

Edelman, G. (1987). *Neural Darwinism: The theory of neuronal group selection.* New York, NY: Basic Books.

Egeland, B., & Sroufe, A. (1981). Attachment and early maltreatment. *Child Development, 52*, 44–52.

Ellis, A. (1973). *Humanistic psychotherapy: The rational-emotive approach.* New York, NY: Julian Press.

First, M. B. (2009). Harmonisation of ICD-11 and DSM-V: Opportunities and challenges. *British Journal of Psychiatry, 195*, 382–390. doi: 10.1192/bjp.bp.108.060822

Fonagy, P., Leigh, T., Steele, M., Steele, H., Kennedy, R., Mattoon, G., Target, M., & Gerber, A. (1996). The relation of attachment status, psychiatric classification, and response to psychotherapy. *Journal of Consulting and Clinical Psychology, 64*, 22–31.

Fonagy, P., Steele, M., & Steele, H. (1991). Maternal representations of attachment during pregnancy predict the organization of infant-mother attachment at one year of age. *Child Development, 62*, 880–893.

Fonagy, P., Steele, M., Steele, H., Leigh, T., Kennedy, R., Mattoon, G., & Target, M. (1995). Attachment, the reflective self, and borderline states: The predictive specificity of the Adult Attachment Interview and pathological emotional development. In S. Goldberg, R. Muir, & J. Kerr (Eds.), *John Bowlby's attachment theory: Historical, clinical, and social significance* (pp. 233–278). New York, NY: Analytic Press.

Fonagy, P., Steele, M., Steele, H., & Target, M. (1997). *Reflective-functioning manual*. Version 4.1. Unpublished manuscript, Psychoanalysis Unit, University College London.

Fonagy, P., Target, M., Steele, M., Steele, H., Leigh, T., Levinson, A., & Kennedy, R. (1997). Morality, disruptive behavior, borderline personality disorder, crime and their relationship to security of attachment. In L. Atkinson & K. J. Zucker (Eds.), *Attachment and psychopathology* (pp. 223–276). New York, NY: Guilford.

Frances, A. (2010). The first draft of DSM-V: If accepted will fan the flames of false positive diagnoses [Editorial]. *British Medical Journal, 340* (c1168), 492. doi: 10.1136/bmj.c1168

Freud, S. (1927). The ego and the id. In E. Jones (Series Ed.), *International Psychoanalytic Library: No. 12* (pp. 1–88). Honolulu, HI: Hogarth Press and Institute of Psychoanalysis.

Friedman, S. L., & Boyle, D. E. (2008). Attachment in U.S. children experiencing nonmaternal care in the early 1990s. *Attachment & Human Development, 10,* 225–261. doi: 10.1080/14616730802113570

George, C., Kaplan, N., & Main, M. (1985). *Adult Attachment Interview*. Unpublished manuscript, Department of Psychology, University of California, Berkeley.

George, C., Kaplan, N., & Main, M. (1996). *The Attachment Interview for adults*. Unpublished manuscript, Department of Psychology, University of California, Berkeley.

Giles, J. W., Gopnik, A., & Heyman, G. D. (2002). Source monitoring reduces the suggestibility of preschool children. *Psychological Science, 13*(3), 288–291.

Goddard, C. R., & Stanley, J. R. (1994). Viewing the abusive parent and the abused child as captor and hostage: The application of hostage theory to the effects of child abuse. *Journal of Interpersonal Violence, 9*(2), 258–269.

Gogarty, H. (2002). *Attachment relationships in the triad of foster-care: A retrospective analysis*. (Doctoral thesis) University of Ulster, Coleraine, Ireland.

Goldberg, D. (2010). Should our major classifications of mental disorders be revised? *British Journal of Psychiatry, 196,* 255–256. doi: 10.1192/bjp.bp.109.072405

Green, J. T., Ivry, R. B., & Woodruff-Pak, D. S. (1999). Timing in eyeblink classical conditioning and timed-interval tapping. *Psychological Science, 10,* 19–23.

Grice, H. P. (1975). Logic and conversation. In P. Cole & J. L. Moran (Eds.), *Syntax and semantics III: Speech acts* (pp. 41–58). New York, NY: Academic Press.

Grinder, J., & Bandler, R. (1975). *The structure of magic II: A book about communication and change*. Palo Alto, CA: Science and Behavior Books.

Grossmann, K., Fremmer-Bombik, E., Rudolph, J., & Grossmann, K. E. (1988). Maternal attachment representations as related to patterns of infant-mother attachment and maternal care during the first year. In R. A. Hinde & J. Stevenson-Hinde (Eds.), *Relationships within families* (pp. 241–260). Oxford, UK: Oxford Science Publications.

Grove, A. (1996). *Only the paranoid survive: How to exploit the crisis points that can challenge every company and career.* New York, NY: Currency Doubleday.

Gullestad, S. E. (2003). The Adult Attachment Interview and psychoanalytic outcome studies. *International Journal of Psychoanalysis, 84,* 651–668.

Gustavson, C., Garcia, J., Hankins, W., & Rusiniak, K. (1974). Coyote predation control by aversive stimulus. *Science, 184,* 581–583.

Gut, E. (1989). *Productive and unproductive depression: Success or failure of a vital process.* New York, NY: Basic Books.

Haapasalo, J., Puupponen, M., & Crittenden, P. M. (1999). Victim to victimizer: The psychology of isomorphism in a case of a recidivist pedophile. *Journal of Child Sexual Abuse, 7,* 97–115.

Hautamäki, A., Hautamäki, L., Neuvonen, L., & Maliniemi-Piispanen, S. (2009). Transmission of attachment across three generations. *European Journal of Developmental Psychology,* doi: 10.1080/17405620902983519

Hautamäki, A., Hautamäki, L., Neuvonen, L., & Maliniemi-Piispanen, S. (2010). Transmission of attachment across three generations: Continuity and reversal. *Clinical Child Psychology and Psychiatry, 15*(3), 347–354.

Heller, M. B. (2010). Attachment and its relationship to mind, brain, trauma and the therapeutic endeavour. In R. Woolfe, S. Strawbridge, B. Douglas, & W. Dryden (Eds.), *Handbook of counselling psychology* (pp. 653–670). London, UK: Sage.

Heller, M. B., & Pollet, S. (2010). "It was an accident waiting to happen!" An investigation into the dynamic relationship between early-life traumas and chronic posttraumatic stress disorder in adulthood (pp. 140–155). *The work of psychoanalysts in the public health sector.* New York, NY: Routledge/Taylor & Francis.

Hesse, E. (1996). Discourse, memory, and the Adult Attachment Interview: A note with emphasis on the emerging cannot classify category. *Infant Mental Health Journal, 17,* 4–11.

Hughes, J. (1997). *Assessing adult attachment styles with clinically orientated interviews.* (Thesis, Graduate Faculty of Clinical Psychology) University of Leeds, Leeds, England.

Hughes, J., Hardy, G., & Kendrick, D. (2000). Assessing adult attachment status with clinically-orientated interviews: A brief report. *British Journal of Medical Psychology, 73,* 279–283.

Johnson, W. D. K. (1991). Predisposition to emotional distress and psychiatric illness amongst doctors: The role of unconscious and experiential factors. *British Journal of Medical Psychology, 64,* 317–329.

Kenardy, J. (2000). The current status of psychological debriefing. *British Medical Journal, 321,* 1032–1033.

Kessler, R. C. (1994). The national comorbidity survey of the United States. *International Review of Psychiatry, 6*(4), 365–376.

Klingberg, T. (2009). *The overflowing brain: Information overload and the limits of working memory.* New York, NY: Oxford University Press.

Kozlowska, K. (2007). The developmental origins of conversion disorders. *Clinical Child Psychology and Psychiatry, 12*(4), 487–510. doi: 10.1177/13591045070 80977

Kozlowska, K. (2009). Attachment relationships shape pain-signaling behavior. The *Journal of Pain, 10*(10), 1020–1028. doi: 10.1016/j.jpain.2009.03.014

Kozlowska, K. (2010). Family-of-origin issues and the generation of childhood illness. *Australian and New Zealand Journal of Family Therapy, 31*(1), 73–91. doi: 10.1375/anft.31.1.73

Kozlowska, K., Foley, S., & Crittenden, P. M. (2006). Factitious illness by proxy: Understanding underlying psychological processes and motivations. *Australian and New Zealand Journal of Family Therapy, 27*, 92–104.

Kozlowska, K., Rose, D., Khan, R., Kram, S., Lane, L., & Collins, J. (2008). A conceptual model and practice framework for managing chronic pain in children and adolescents. *Harvard Review of Psychiatry, 16*(2), 136–150. doi: 10.1080/10673220802069723

Kozlowska, K., & Williams, L. M. (2009). Self-protective organization in children with conversion and somatoform disorders. *Journal of Psychosomatic Research, 67*(3), 223–233. doi: 10.1016/j.jpsychores.2009.03.016

Kuleshnyk, I. (1984). The Stockholm syndrome: Toward an understanding. *Social Action and the Law, 10*(2), 37.

Lambruschi, F., Landini, A., & Crittenden, P. M. (October, 2008). *Minds that heal: Characteristics of therapists that promote successful psychotherapy.* Plenary presentation at the biennial meeting of the International Association for the Study of Attachment, Bertinoro, Italy.

Le Doux, J. E. (1995). In search of an emotional system in the brain: Leaping from fear to emotion and consciousness (pp. 1049–1061). In M. Gazzaniga (Ed.), *The cognitive neurosciences.* Boston, MA: MIT Press.

Lichtenberg, J., Lachmann, F. M., & Fosshage, J. L. (1996). *The clinical exchange: Techniques derived from self and motivational systems.* Hillsdale, NJ: Analytic Press.

MacLean, P. D. (1990). *The triune brain in evolution: Role in paleocerebral functions.* New York, NY: Plenum.

Main, M., & Cassidy, J. (1988). Categories of response to reunion with the parent at age 6: Predictable from infant attachment classifications and stable over a 1-month period. *Developmental Psychology, 24*, 415–442.

Main, M., & Goldwyn, R. (1984). *Adult attachment scoring and classification system.* Unpublished manuscript, University of California, Berkeley.

Main, M., & Goldwyn, R. (1994). *Adult attachment rating and classification systems,* version 6.0. Unpublished manuscript, University of California, Berkeley.

Main, M., Goldwyn, R., & Hesse, E. (2003). *Adult attachment scoring and classification system.* Unpublished manuscript, University of California, Berkeley.

Main, M., & Hesse, E. (1990). Lack of resolution of mourning in adulthood and its relationship to infant disorganization: Some speculations regarding causal mechanisms. In M. Greenberg, D. Cicchetti, & E. M. Cummings (Eds.), *Attachment in the preschool years* (pp. 161–182). Chicago, IL: University of Chicago Press.

Main, M., Hesse, E., & Goldwyn, R. (2008). Studying differences in language usage in recounting attachment history: An introduction to the AAI. In H. Steele & M. Steele (Eds.), *Clinical applications of the Adult Attachment Interview* (pp. 31–68). New York, NY: Guilford.

Main, M., Kaplan, N., & Cassidy, J. (1985). Security in infancy, childhood and adulthood: A move to the level of representation. In I. Bretherton & E. Waters (Eds.), *Growing points of attachment theory and research: Monographs of the society for research in child development* (Vol. 50, 209, pp. 66–104). Chicago, IL: University of Chicago Press.

Main, M., & Solomon, J. (1986). Discovery of an insecure disorganized/disoriented attachment pattern: Procedures, findings, and implications for the classification of behavior. In M. Yogman & T.B. Brazelton (Eds.), *Affective development in infancy* (pp. 121–160). Norwood, NJ: Ablex.

Main, M., & Solomon, J. (1990). Procedures for identifying infants as disorganized/disoriented during the Ainsworth strange situation. In M. Greenberg, D. Cicchetti, & E. M. Cummings (Eds.), *Attachment in the preschool years* (pp. 161–182). Chicago, IL: University of Chicago Press.

Main, M., & Weston, D. R. (1981). The quality of toddlers' relationship to mother and father: Related to conflict behavior and readiness to establish new relationships. *Child Development, 52,* 932–940.

O'Reilly, G. (2010, August). *Attachment and sexual offending: Theory, intervention & outcome.* Invited presentation at the biennial meeting of the International Association for the Study of Attachment, Cambridge, UK.

Perry, B. D. (1994). Neurobiological sequelae of childhood trauma: Posttraumatic stress disorders in children. In M. Murberg (Ed.), *Catecholamine function in post traumatic stress disorder: Emerging concepts* (pp. 233–255). Washington, DC: American Psychiatric Press.

Piaget, J. (1952). *The origins of intelligence.* New York, NY: International Universities Press.

Pleshkova, N. L., & Muhamedrahimov, R. J. (2010). Quality of attachment in St. Petersburg (Russian Federation): A sample of family-reared infants. *Clinical Child Psychology and Psychiatry, 15*(3), 355–362.

Pynoos, R. S., & Nader, K. (1989). Children's memory and proximity to violence. *Journal of the American Academy of Child and Adolescent Psychiatry, 28,* 236–241.

Radke-Yarrow, M., Cummings, E. M., Kuczynski, L., & Chapman, M. (1985).

Patterns of attachment in two- and three-year-olds in normal families and families with parental depression. *Child Development, 56,* 884–893.

Rindal, G. (2000). *Attachment patterns in patients diagnosed with avoidant personality disorder* [Maskespill, tilknytningsmxxnster hos pasienter med unnvikende personlighetsforstyrrelse]. (Unpublished dissertation) Institute of Psychology, University of Oslo.

Ringer, F., & Crittenden, P. (2007). Eating disorders and attachment: The effects of hidden processes on eating disorders. *European Eating Disorders Review, 15,* 119–130.

Robertson, J., & Bowlby, J. (1952). Responses of young children to separation from their mothers. *Courrier du Centre International de L'Enfance, 2,* 131–142.

Robertson, J., & Robertson, J. (1971). Young children in brief separation: A fresh look. *Psychoanalytic Study of the Child, 26,* 264–315.

Rozin, P., & Fallon, A. E. (1987). A perspective on disgust. *Psychological Review, 94,* 23–41.

Rutter, M., Kreppner, J., & Sonuga-Barke, E. (2009). Emanuel Miller lecture: Attachment insecurity, disinhibited attachment, and attachment disorders: Where do research findings leave the concepts? *Journal of Child Psychology and Psychiatry, 50*(5), 529–543. doi: 10.1111/j.1469–7610.2009.02042.x

Schacter, D. L. (1996). *Searching for memory: The brain, the mind, and the past.* New York, NY: Basic Books.

Schacter, D. L., & Tulving, E. (Eds.). (1994). What are the memory systems of 1994? In D. L. Schacter & E. Tulving (Eds.), *Memory systems 1994* (pp. 1–38). Cambridge, MA: MIT Press.

Schedlowski, M., & Pacheco-López, G. (2010). The learned immune response: Pavlov and beyond. *Brain, Behavior, and Immunity, 24*(2), 176–185. doi: 10.1016/j.bbi.2009.08.007

Scheier, M. F., & Carver, C. S. (1982). Cognition, affect, and self-regulation. In M. S. Clark & S. T. Fiske (Eds.), *Affect and cognition* (pp. 157–184). Hillsdale, NJ: Erlbaum.

Seefeldt, L. J. (1997). *Models of parenting in maltreating and non-maltreating mothers.* Unpublished dissertation, Graduate School of Nursing, University of Wisconsin, Milwaukee, WI.

Selye, H. (1976). *The stress of life.* New York, NY: McGraw-Hill.

Shah, P. E., Fonagy, P., & Strathearn, L. (2010). Is attachment transmitted across generations? The plot thickens. *Clinical Child Psychology and Psychiatry, 15*(3), 329–346.

Slade, A. (2007). Disorganized mother, disorganized child. In D. Oppenheim & D. F. Goldsmith (Eds.), *Attachment theory in clinical work with children: Bridging the gap between research and practice* (pp. 226–250). New York, NY: Guilford.

Spieker, S., & Crittenden, P. M. (2010). Comparing two attachment classification methods applied to preschool strange situations. *Clinical Child Psychology and Psychiatry, 15*(1), 97–120. doi: 10.1177/1359104509345878

Steinmetz, J. E. (1998). The localization of a simple type of learning and memory: The cerebellum and classical eyeblink conditioning. *Current Directions in Psychological Science, 7*, 72–77.

Strathearn, L., Fonagy, P., Amico, J. A., & Montague, P. R. (2009). Adult attachment predicts mother's brain and peripheral oxytocin response to infant cues. *Neuropsychopharmacology, 34,* 2655–2666. doi: 10.1038/npp.2009.103

Szajnberg, N., & Crittenden, P.M. (1997). The transference refracted through the lens of attachment. *Journal of the American Academy of Psychoanalysis, 25*(3), 409–438.

Taylor, S., & Brown, J. (1988). Illusion and well-being: A social psychological perspective on mental health. *Psychological Bulletin, 103,* 193–210.

Thompson, R. A., & Raikes, H. A. (2003). Toward the next quarter-century: Conceptual and methodological challenges for attachment theory. *Development and Psychopathology, 15*(3), 691–719.

Thompson, R. F., Bao, S., Chen, L., Cipriano, B. D., Grethe, J. S., Kim, J. J., Thompson, J. K., Tracy, J. A., Weninger, M. S., & Krupa, D. J. (1997). Associative learning. In R. J. Bradley, R. A. Harris, & P. Jenner (Series Eds.) & J. D. Schmahmann (Vol. Ed.), *International review of neurobiology: The cerebellum and cognition* (Vol. 41, pp. 152–189). San Diego, CA: Academic Press.

Tone Flo, S. (2009). Good guy – bad guy, which is it? Unpublished paper. Institutt for psykoterapi, Oslo, Norway.

Tracy, J. A., Ghose, S. S., Strecher, T., McFall, R. M., & Steinmetz, J. E. (1999). Classical conditioning in a non-clinical obsessive-compulsive population. *Psychological Science, 10,* 9–13.

Tulving, E. (1979). Memory research: What kind of progress? In L. G. Nilsson (Ed.), *Perspectives on memory research: Essays in honor of Uppsala University's 500th anniversary* (pp. 19–34). Hillsdale, NJ: Erlbaum.

Tulving, E. (1995). Organization of memory: Quo vadis? In M. S. Gazzaniga (Ed.), *The cognitive Neurosciences* (pp. 839–847). Cambridge, MA: MIT Press.

van IJzendoorn, M. (1995). Adult attachment representations, parental responsiveness, and infant attachment: A meta-analysis on the predictive validity of the Adult Attachment Interview. *Psychological Bulletin, 117,* 387–403.

van IJzendoorn, M. H., Goldberg, S., Kroonenberg, P. M., & Frenkel, O. J. (1992). The relative effects of maternal and child problems on the quality of attachment: A meta-analysis of attachment in clinical samples. *Child Development, 63,* 840–858.

Watzlawick, P., Beavin, J., & Jackson, D. (1967). *Pragmatics of human communication.* New York, NY: Norton.

Wiesel, E. (1960). *Night.* New York, NY: Hill &Wang.

Wilkinson, S. R. (2010). Another day older and deeper in therapy: Can the dynamic-maturational model offer a way out? *Clinical Child Psychology and Psychiatry, 15*(3), 423–432.

Zachrisson, H. D., & Kulbotton, G. (2006). Attachment in anorexia nervosa:

An exploration of associations with eating disorder psychopathology and psychiatric symptoms. *Eating & Weight Disorders, 11,* 163–170.

Zhong, C., Bohns, V. K., & Gino, F. (2010). Good lamps are the best police: Darkness increases dishonesty and self-interested behavior. *Psychological Science, 21,* 311–314. doi: 10.1177/0956797609360754

Zimbardo, P. (1969). The human choice: Individuation, reason, and order vs. deindividuation, impulse, and chaos. In W. J. Arnold & D. Levine (Eds.), *Nebraska symposium on motivation* (Vol. 17, pp. 237–307). Lincoln, NE: University of Nebraska Press.

Index